DODGE & PLYMOUTH VANS

1971-1983
SHOP MANUAL

ERIC JORGENSEN
Editor

JEFF ROBINSON
Publisher

CLYMER PUBLICATIONS

*World's largest publisher of books
devoted exclusively to automobiles and motorcycles*

12860 MUSCATINE STREET · P.O. BOX 20 · ARLETA, CALIFORNIA 91331

FIRST EDITION
First Printing June, 1980

SECOND EDITION
First Printing February, 1981

THIRD EDITION
Revised by Alan Ahlstrand to include 1981 models
First Printing December, 1981
Second Printing September, 1982

FOURTH EDITION
Revised by Kalton C. Lahue to include 1982 models
First Printing May, 1983

FIFTH EDITION
Revised by Kalton C. Lahue to include 1983 models
First Printing November, 1983
Second Printing February, 1985

Printed in U.S.A.

ISBN: 0-89287-314-0

Production Coordinator, Victor Williams

COVER: Photographed by Michael Brown Photographic Productions, Los Angeles, California. Assisted by Ray Wittbrod. Van courtesy of Dodge Division, Chrysler Motor Corporation.

CONTENTS

QUICK REFERENCE DATA

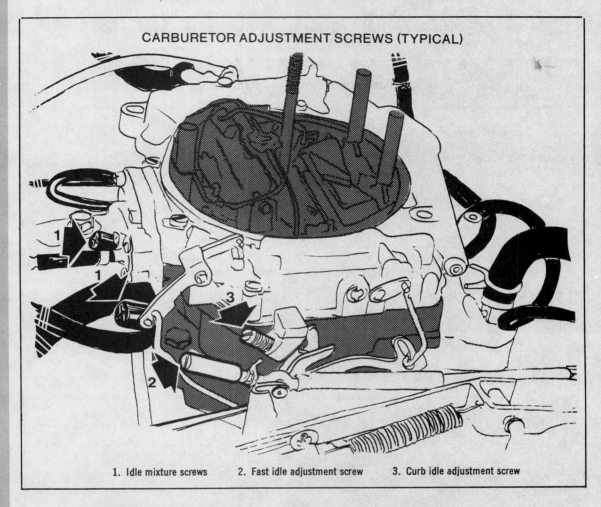

CARBURETOR ADJUSTMENT SCREWS (TYPICAL)

1. Idle mixture screws   2. Fast idle adjustment screw   3. Curb idle adjustment screw

CYLINDER HEAD BOLT TORQUE

Engine	(ft.-lb.)
225 cid 6	
1971-1975	65
1976-on	70
243 diesel	90
318 cid V8	
1971	85
1972-1977	95
1978-1980	105
1981	95
1982-on	105
360 cid V8	
1971	70
1972-1977	95
1978-1980	105
1981	95
1982-on	105
383 cid V8	70
400/440 cid V8	70

BATTERY CHARGE (SPECIFIC GRAVITY)

Specific Gravity	State of Charge (at 80 °F)*
1.110-1.130	Discharged
1.140-1.160	Almost discharged
1.170-1.190	One-quarter charged
1.210-1.220	One-half charged
1.230-1.250	Three-quarters charged
1.260-1.280	Fully charged

*For each 10 degrees battery temperature exceeds 80 °F, add 0.004 to the indicated reading; for each 10 degrees battery temperature is less than 80 °F, subtract 0.004 from the indicated reading.

TUNE-UP SPECIFICATIONS

See Table 9, Chapter Three for tune-up specifications. See **Ignition Timing**, Chapter Three, for basic ignition timing procedure. See Chapter Five for curb idle/mixture adjustment procedure. Spark plug types are given in Table 9, Chapter Three.

CYLINDER IDENTIFICATION/FIRING ORDER

6 Cylinder (including diesel)
    Firing order   1-5-3-6-2-4
    Identification (from front)   1-2-3-4-5-6
8 Cylinder
    Firing order   1-8-4-3-6-5-7-2
    Identification (from front)
        Left bank   1-3-5-7
        Right bank   2-4-6-8

VALVE CLEARANCES (6 CYLINDER GASOLINE)

Exhaust valves   0.020 in. (hot)
Intake valves   0.010 in. (hot)

VALVE CLEARANCES (DIESEL)

Exhaust and intake valves   0.3mm (0.012 in.) — engine cold

TIRE PRESSURES

See tire inflation decal on door pillar on driver's side. If decal is missing, see Table 1, Chapter Three.

BELT TENSION TORQUE VALUES

		Torque Values (Ft.-Lb.)*	
	225 cid engine	318 and 360 cid engines	383, 400, 440 cid engines
Power steering			
w/air pump	35-20	100-65	100-65
w/o air pump	90-50	50-35	45-30
Alternator			
w/AC	15-10	55-45	120-80
w/o AC	15-10	35-25	70-40
Air pump			
w/AC	35-20	75-50	55-35
w/o AC	40-25	100-65	55-35

*First number is for new belts, second number is for used belts.

APPROXIMATE REFILL CAPACITIES

Engine oil (less filter)

Engine	U.S. quarts	Liters	Imperial quarts
All gasoline	5	4.7	4 1/4
243 diesel	7	6.6	5 3/4

Cooling system

Engine size	U.S. quarts	Liters	Imperial quarts
225 (1)			
1971-1978	13	12.3	10 3/4
1979-on	12	11.4	10
243 diesel	13	12.3	10 3/4
318 (1)			
1971-1978	17	16	14 1/4
1979-on	16	15.2	13 1/4
360 (2)			
1971-1978	16	15.2	13 1/4
1979-on	14 1/2	13.8	12
400	15 1/2	14.7	13
440 (2)			
1971-1978	15 1/2	14.7	13
1979	14 1/2	13.8	12

Rear axle

Size	U.S. pints	Liters	Imperial pints
8 3/8 in. (Chrysler)	4 1/2	2.12	3 3/4
9 1/4 in. (Chrysler)	4 1/2	2.12	3 3/4
9 3/4 in. (Spicer 60)	6	2.84	5
10 1/2 in. (Spicer 70)	6 1/2	3.07	5 1/2

Transmission

Type	U.S. pints	Liters	Imperial pints
Manual			
745	3 1/4	1.5	2 3/4
A-230	4 1/4	2	3 1/2
A250	4 1/2	2.1	3 3/4
435	7	3.3	5 3/4
A-390	3 1/2	1.7	3
445D	7 1/2	3.5	6 1/4
Overdrive-4	7 1/2	3/5	6 1/4
Automatic	See text		

(1) Add one quart for air conditioning or increased cooling.
(2) On 1971-1978 models, add one quart for air conditioning or increased cooling. On 1979 and later models with optional heavy-duty cooling systems, add one quart on 360-3 or 440-3 engines. Add 2 quarts on 360-1 and 440-1 engines.

RECOMMENDED ENGINE OIL GRADES (SAE)

Engine	API service SE or SF
Gasoline engines	
Above 32° F (0° C)	30, 40
Above 10° F (-12° C)	20W-40, 20W-50
Above -10° F (-23° C)	10W-30, 10W-40, 10W-50
10-80° F (-12-+27° C)	20W-20
-10-+80° F (-23-+27° C)	10W
Below 80° F (27° C)	5W-20*, 5W-30, 5W-40
Diesel engines	
Above 32° F (0° C)	30, 40
Above 10° F (-12° C)	20W-40, 20W-50
10-60° F (-12-+16° C)	20W-20
All temperatures	10W-30, 10W-40, 10W-50

*5W-20 not recommended for sustained high speed driving.

LUBRICANTS & FLUIDS

Manual transmission	
A230 3-speed	DEXRON ATF[1]
745	SAE 50 engine oil[2]
435 4-speed	SAE 50 engine oil[2]
A390 3-speed	DEXRON ATF[1]
445-D 4-speed	SAE 50 engine oil[2]
Overdrive 4-speed	SAE 50 engine oil (see notes 2 & 3)
Automatic transmission	DEXRON ATF
Rear axle	
Type of lubricant	Multipurpose gear oil, API GL-5
Viscosity	
Above 90° F (32° C)	SAE 140, SAE 80W-140, SAE 85W-140
As low as -10° F (-23° C)	SAE 90, SAE 80W-90, SAE 80W-140, SAE 85W-140
Below -10° F (-23° C)	SAE 75W, SAE 75W-90, SAE 80W, SAE 80W-140
Antifreeze	Ethylene glycol base
Brake fluid	DOT 3
Power steering fluid	DEXRON II automatic transmission fluid

1. If gear rattle is heard during idle or acceleration, use one of the following oils: SAE 90, 75W, 75W-80, 80W-90 or 85W-90 gear oil.
2. If SAE 50 engine oil is not available, use one of the following oils:

Type	Multipurpose gear oil, API GL-5
Viscosity	
Above 90° F (32° C)	SAE 140
As low as -10° F (-23° C)	SAE 90
Below -10° F (-23° C)	SAE 80

3. DEXRON II is used in 1982 and later overdrive-4 transmissions.

DODGE & PLYMOUTH VANS

1971-1983
SHOP MANUAL

INTRODUCTION

This detailed, comprehensive manual covers the 1971-1983 Dodge and Plymouth vans. The expert text gives complete information on maintenance, repair and overhaul. Hundreds of photos and drawings guide you through every step. The book includes all you need to know to keep your van running right.

Chapters One through Eleven contain general information on all models and specific information on 1971-1981 models. The Supplement at the end of the book contains specific information on 1982 and later models that differs from earlier years.

Where repairs are practical for the owner/mechanic, complete procedures are given. Equally important, difficult jobs are pointed out. Such operations are usually more economically performed by a dealer or independent garage.

A shop manual is a reference. You want to be able to find information fast. As in all Clymer books, this one is designed with this in mind. All chapters are thumb tabbed. Important items are indexed at the rear of the book. Finally, all the most frequently used specifications and capacities are summarized on the *Quick Reference* pages at the front of the book.

Keep the book handy. Carry it in your glove box. It will help you to better understand your van, lower repair and maintenance costs, and generally improve your satisfaction with your vehicle.

CHAPTER ONE

GENERAL INFORMATION

The troubleshooting, tune-up, maintenance, and step-by-step repair procedures in this book are written for the owner and home mechanic. The text is accompanied by useful photos and diagrams to make the job as clear and correct as possible.

Troubleshooting, tune-up, maintenance, and repair are not difficult if you know what tools and equipment to use and what to do. Anyone not afraid to get their hands dirty, of average intelligence, and with some mechanical ability can perform most of the procedures in this book.

In some cases, a repair job may require tools or skills not reasonably expected of the home mechanic. These procedures are noted in each chapter and it is recommended that you take the job to your dealer, a competent mechanic, or machine shop.

MANUAL ORGANIZATION

This chapter provides general information and safety and service hints. Also included are lists of recommended shop and emergency tools as well as a brief description of troubleshooting and tune-up equipment.

Chapter Two provides methods and suggestions for quick and accurate diagnosis and repair of problems. Troubleshooting procedures discuss typical symptoms and logical methods to pinpoint the trouble.

Chapter Three explains all periodic lubrication and routine maintenance necessary to keep your vehicle running well. Chapter Three also includes recommended tune-up procedures, eliminating the need to constantly consult chapters on the various subassemblies.

Subsequent chapters cover specific systems such as the engine, transmission, and electrical systems. Each of these chapters provides disassembly, repair, and assembly procedures in a simple step-by-step format. If a repair requires special skills or tools, or is otherwise impractical for the home mechanic, it is so indicated. In these cases it is usually faster and less expensive to have the repairs made by a dealer or competent repair shop. Necessary specifications concerning a particular system are included at the end of the appropriate chapter.

When special tools are required to perform a procedure included in this manual, the tool is illustrated either in actual use or alone. It may be possible to rent or borrow these tools. The inventive mechanic may also be able to find a suitable substitute in his tool box, or to fabricate one.

The terms NOTE, CAUTION, and WARNING have specific meanings in this manual. A NOTE provides additional or explanatory information. A CAUTION is used to emphasize areas where equipment damage could result if proper precautions are not taken. A WARNING is used to stress those areas where personal injury or death could result from negligence, in addition to possible mechanical damage.

SERVICE HINTS

Observing the following practices will save time, effort, and frustration, as well as prevent possible injury.

Throughout this manual keep in mind two conventions. "Front" refers to the front of the vehicle. The front of any component, such as the transmission, is that end which faces toward the front of the vehicle. The "left" and "right" sides of the vehicle refer to the orientation of a person sitting in the vehicle facing forward. For example, the steering wheel is on the left side. These rules are simple, but even experienced mechanics occasionally become disoriented.

Most of the service procedures covered are straightforward and can be performed by anyone reasonably handy with tools. It is suggested, however, that you consider your own capabilities carefully before attempting any operation involving major disassembly of the engine.

Some operations, for example, require the use of a press. It would be wiser to have these performed by a shop equipped for such work, rather than to try to do the job yourself with makeshift equipment. Other procedures require precision measurements. Unless you have the skills and equipment required, it would be better to have a qualified repair shop make the measurements for you.

Repairs go much faster and easier if the parts that will be worked on are clean before you begin. There are special cleaners for washing the engine and related parts. Brush or spray on the cleaning solution, let it stand, then rinse it away with a garden hose. Clean all oily or greasy parts with cleaning solvent as you remove them.

WARNING
Never use gasoline as a cleaning agent. It presents an extreme fire hazard. Be sure to work in a well-ventilated area when using cleaning solvent. Keep a fire extinguisher, rated for gasoline fires, handy in any case.

Much of the labor charge for repairs made by dealers is for the removal and disassembly of other parts to reach the defective unit. It is frequently possible to perform the preliminary operations yourself and then take the defective unit in to the dealer for repair, at considerable savings.

Once you have decided to tackle the job yourself, make sure you locate the appropriate section in this manual, and read it entirely. Study the illustrations and text until you have a good idea of what is involved in completing the job satisfactorily. If special tools are required, make arrangements to get them before you start. Also, purchase any known defective parts prior to starting on the procedure. It is frustrating and time-consuming to get partially into a job and then be unable to complete it.

Simple wiring checks can be easily made at home, but knowledge of electronics is almost a necessity for performing tests with complicated electronic testing gear.

During disassembly of parts keep a few general cautions in mind. Force is rarely needed to get things apart. If parts are a tight fit, like a bearing in a case, there is usually a tool designed to separate them. Never use a screwdriver to pry apart parts with machined surfaces such as cylinder head and valve cover. You will mar the surfaces and end up with leaks.

Make diagrams wherever similar-appearing parts are found. You may think you can remember where everything came from — but mistakes are costly. There is also the possibility you may get sidetracked and not return to work for days or even weeks — in which interval, carefully laid out parts may have become disturbed.

Tag all similar internal parts for location, and mark all mating parts for position. Record number and thickness of any shims as they are removed. Small parts such as bolts can be identified by placing them in plastic sandwich bags that are sealed and labeled with masking tape.

Wiring should be tagged with masking tape and marked as each wire is removed. Again, do not rely on memory alone.

When working under the vehicle, do not trust a hydraulic or mechanical jack to hold the vehicle up by itself. Always use jackstands. See **Figure 1**.

Disconnect battery ground cable before working near electrical connections and before disconnecting wires. Never run the engine with the battery disconnected; the alternator could be seriously damaged.

Protect finished surfaces from physical damage or corrosion. Keep gasoline and brake fluid off painted surfaces.

Frozen or very tight bolts and screws can often be loosened by soaking with penetrating oil like Liquid Wrench or WD-40, then sharply striking the bolt head a few times with a hammer and punch (or screwdriver for screws). Avoid heat unless absolutely necessary, since it may melt, warp, or remove the temper from many parts.

Avoid flames or sparks when working near a charging battery or flammable liquids, such as brake fluid or gasoline.

No parts, except those assembled with a press fit, require unusual force during assembly. If a part is hard to remove or install, find out why before proceeding.

Cover all openings after removing parts to keep dirt, small tools, etc., from falling in.

When assembling two parts, start all fasteners, then tighten evenly.

The clutch plate, wiring connections, brake shoes, drums, pads, and discs should be kept clean and free of grease and oil.

When assembling parts, be sure all shims and washers are replaced exactly as they came out.

Whenever a rotating part butts against a stationary part, look for a shim or washer. Use new gaskets if there is any doubt about the condition of old ones. Generally, you should apply gasket cement to one mating surface only, so the parts may be easily disassembled in the future. A thin coat of oil on gaskets helps them seal effectively.

Heavy grease can be used to hold small parts in place if they tend to fall out during assembly. However, keep grease and oil away from electrical, clutch, and brake components.

High spots may be sanded off a piston with sandpaper, but emery cloth and oil do a much more professional job.

Carburetors are best cleaned by disassembling them and soaking the parts in a commercial carburetor cleaner. Never soak gaskets and rubber parts in these cleaners. Never use wire to clean out jets and air passages; they are easily damaged. Use compressed air to blow out the carburetor, but only if the float has been removed first.

Take your time and do the job right. Do not forget that a newly rebuilt engine must be broken in the same as a new one. Refer to your owner's manual for the proper break-in procedures.

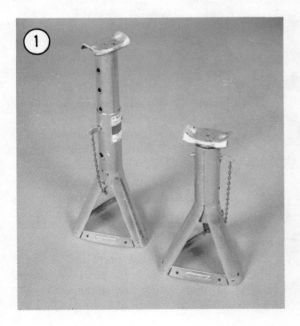

SAFETY FIRST

Professional mechanics can work for years and never sustain a serious injury. If you observe a few rules of common sense and safety, you can enjoy many safe hours servicing your vehicle. You could hurt yourself or damage the vehicle if you ignore these rules.

1. Never use gasoline as a cleaning solvent.

2. Never smoke or use a torch in the vicinity of flammable liquids such as cleaning solvent in open containers.

3. Never smoke or use a torch in an area where batteries are being charged. Highly explosive hydrogen gas is formed during the charging process.

4. Use the proper sized wrenches to avoid damage to nuts and injury to yourself.

5. When loosening a tight or stuck nut, be guided by what would happen if the wrench should slip. Protect yourself accordingly.

6. Keep your work area clean and uncluttered.

7. Wear safety goggles during all operations involving drilling, grinding, or use of a cold chisel.

8. Never use worn tools.

9. Keep a fire extinguisher handy and be sure it is rated for gasoline (Class B) and electrical (Class C) fires.

EXPENDABLE SUPPLIES

Certain expendable supplies are necessary. These include grease, oil, gasket cement, wiping rags, cleaning solvent, and distilled water.

Also, special locking compounds, silicone lubricants, and engine cleaners may be useful. Cleaning solvent is available at most service stations and distilled water for the battery is available at most supermarkets.

SHOP TOOLS

For proper servicing, you will need an assortment of ordinary hand tools (**Figure 2**).

As a minimum, these include:

a. Combination wrenches
b. Sockets
c. Plastic mallet
d. Small hammer
e. Snap ring pliers
f. Gas pliers
g. Phillips screwdrivers
h. Slot (common) screwdrivers
i. Feeler gauges
j. Spark plug gauge
k. Spark plug wrench

Special tools necessary are shown in the chapters covering the particular repair in which they are used.

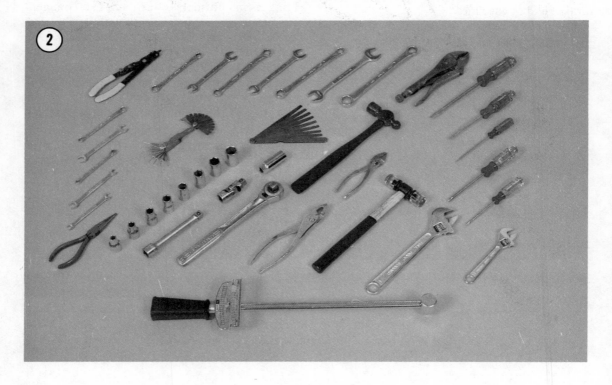

Engine tune-up and troubleshooting procedures require other special tools and equipment. These are described in detail in the following sections.

EMERGENCY TOOL KIT

A small emergency tool kit kept in the trunk is handy for road emergencies which otherwise could leave you stranded. The tools listed below and shown in **Figure 3** will let you handle most roadside repairs.

a. Combination wrenches

b. Crescent (adjustable) wrench

c. Screwdrivers — common and Phillips

d. Pliers — conventional (gas) and needle nose

e. Vise Grips

f. Hammer — plastic and metal

g. Small container of waterless hand cleaner

h. Rags for clean up

i. Silver waterproof sealing tape (duct tape)

j. Flashlight

k. Emergency road flares — at least four

l. Spare drive belts (water pump, alternator, etc.)

TROUBLESHOOTING AND TUNE-UP EQUIPMENT

Voltmeter, Ohmmeter, and Ammeter

For testing the ignition or electrical system, a good voltmeter is required. For automotive use, an instrument covering 0-20 volts is satisfac-

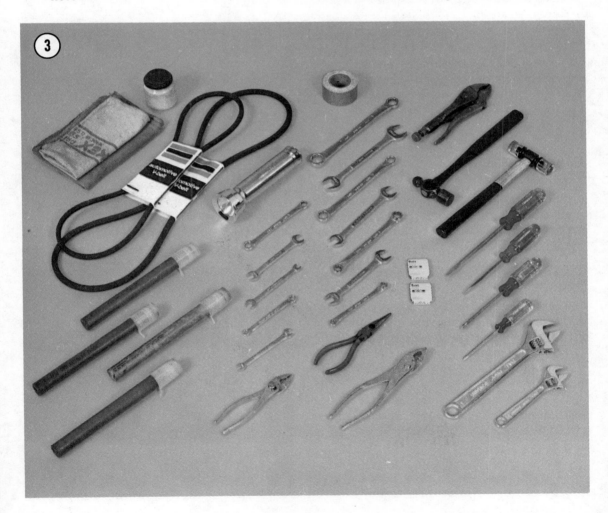

tory. One which also has a 0-2 volt scale is necessary for testing relays, points, or individual contacts where voltage drops are much smaller. Accuracy should be ± ½ volt.

An ohmmeter measures electrical resistance. This instrument is useful for checking continuity (open and short circuits), and testing fuses and lights.

The ammeter measures electrical current. Ammeters for automotive use should cover 0-50 amperes and 0-250 amperes. These are useful for checking battery charging and starting current.

Several inexpensive vom's (volt-ohm-milli-ammeter) combine all three instruments into one which fits easily in any tool box. See **Figure 4**. However, the ammeter ranges are usually too small for automotive work.

Hydrometer

The hydrometer gives a useful indication of battery condition and charge by measuring the specific gravity of the electrolyte in each cell. See **Figure 5**. Complete details on use and interpretation of readings are provided in the electrical chapter.

Compression Tester

The compression tester measures the compression pressure built up in each cylinder. The results, when properly interpreted, can indicate general cylinder and valve condition. See **Figure 6**.

Vacuum Gauge

The vacuum gauge (**Figure 7**) is one of the easiest instruments to use, but one of the most difficult for the inexperienced mechanic to interpret. The results, when interpreted with other findings, can provide valuable clues to possible trouble.

To use the vacuum gauge, connect it to a vacuum hose that goes to the intake manifold. Attach it either directly to the hose or to a T-fitting installed into the hose.

NOTE: *Subtract one inch from the reading for every 1,000 ft. elevation.*

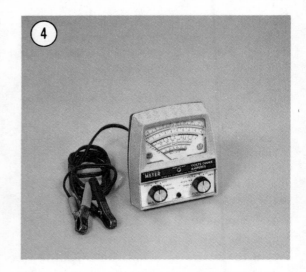

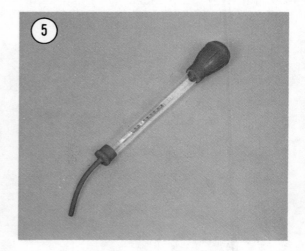

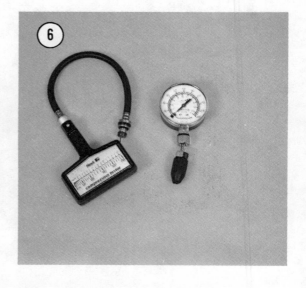

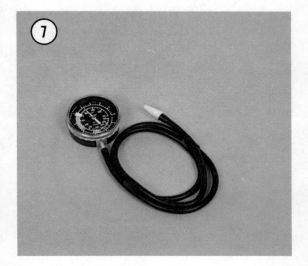

Fuel Pressure Gauge

This instrument is invaluable for evaluating fuel pump performance. Fuel system trouble-shooting procedures in this manual use a fuel pressure gauge. Usually a vacuum gauge and fuel pressure gauge are combined.

Dwell Meter (Contact Breaker Point Ignition Only)

A dwell meter measures the distance in degrees of cam rotation that the breaker points remain closed while the engine is running. Since this angle is determined by breaker point gap, dwell angle is an accurate indication of breaker point gap.

Many tachometers intended for tuning and testing incorporate a dwell meter as well. See **Figure 8**. Follow the manufacturer's instructions to measure dwell.

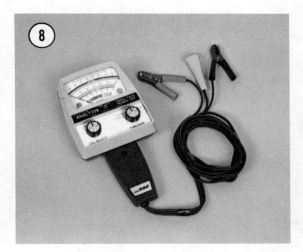

Tachometer

A tachometer is necessary for tuning. See **Figure 8**. Ignition timing and carburetor adjustments must be performed at the specified idle speed. The best instrument for this purpose is one with a low range of 0-1,000 or 0-2,000 rpm for setting idle, and a high range of 0-4,000 or more for setting ignition timing at 3,000 rpm. Extended range (0-6,000 or 0-8,000 rpm) instruments lack accuracy at lower speeds. The instrument should be capable of detecting changes of 25 rpm on the low range.

Strobe Timing Light

This instrument is necessary for tuning, as it permits very accurate ignition timing. The light flashes at precisely the same instant that No. 1 cylinder fires, at which time the timing marks on the engine should align. Refer to Chapter Three for exact location of the timing marks for your engine.

Suitable lights range from inexpensive neon bulb types ($2-3) to powerful xenon strobe lights ($20-40). See **Figure 9**. Neon timing lights are difficult to see and must be used in dimly lit areas. Xenon strobe timing lights can be used outside in bright sunlight. Both types work on this vehicle; use according to the manufacturer's instructions.

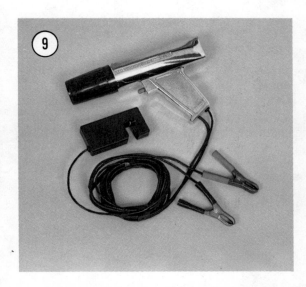

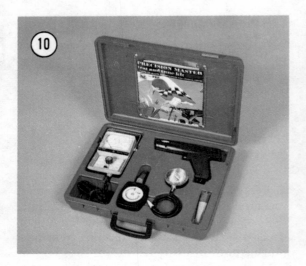

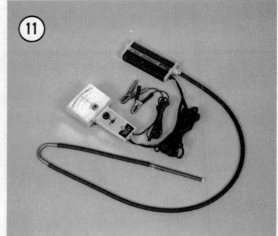

Tune-up Kits

Many manufacturers offer kits that combine several useful instruments. Some come in a convenient carry case and are usually less expensive than purchasing one instrument at a time. **Figure 10** shows one of the kits that is available. The prices vary with the number of instruments included in the kit.

Exhaust Gas Analyzer

Of all instruments described here, this is the least likely to be owned by a home mechanic. This instrument samples the exhaust gases from the tailpipe and measures the thermal conductivity of the exhaust gas. Since different gases conduct heat at varying rates, thermal conductivity of the exhaust is a good indication of gases present.

An exhaust gas analyzer is vital for accurately checking the effectiveness of exhaust emission control adjustments. They are relatively expensive to buy ($70 and up), but must be considered essential for the owner/mechanic to comply with today's emission laws. See **Figure 11**.

Fire Extinguisher

A fire extinguisher is a necessity when working on a vehicle. It should be rated for both *Class B* (flammable liquids — gasoline, oil, paint, etc.) and *Class C* (electrical — wiring, etc.) type fires. It should always be kept within reach. See **Figure 12**.

CHAPTER TWO

TROUBLESHOOTING

Troubleshooting can be a relatively simple matter if it is done logically. The first step in any troubleshooting procedure must be defining the symptoms as closely as possible. Subsequent steps involve testing and analyzing areas which could cause the symptoms. A haphazard approach may eventually find the trouble, but in terms of wasted time and unnecessary parts replacement, it can be very costly.

The troubleshooting procedures in this chapter analyze typical symptoms and show logical methods of isolation. These are not the only methods. There may be several approaches to a problem, but all methods must have one thing in common — a logical, systematic approach.

STARTING SYSTEM

The starting system consists of the starter motor and the starter solenoid. The ignition key controls the starter solenoid, which mechanically engages the starter with the engine flywheel, and supplies electrical current to turn the starter motor.

Starting system troubles are relatively easy to find. In most cases, the trouble is a loose or dirty electrical connection. **Figures 1 and 2** provide routines for finding the trouble.

CHARGING SYSTEM

The charging system consists of the alternator (or generator on older vehicles), voltage regulator, and battery. A drive belt driven by the engine crankshaft turns the alternator which produces electrical energy to charge the battery. As engine speed varies, the voltage from the alternator varies. A voltage regulator controls the charging current to the battery and maintains the voltage to the vehicle's electrical system at safe levels. A warning light or gauge on the instrument panel signals the driver when charging is not taking place. Refer to **Figure 3** for a typical charging system.

Complete troubleshooting of the charging system requires test equipment and skills which the average home mechanic does not possess. However, there are a few tests which can be done to pinpoint most troubles.

Charging system trouble may stem from a defective alternator (or generator), voltage regulator, battery, or drive belt. It may also be caused by something as simple as incorrect drive belt tension. The following are symptoms of typical problems you may encounter.

1. *Battery dies frequently, even though the warning lamp indicates no discharge* — This can be caused by a drive belt that is slightly too

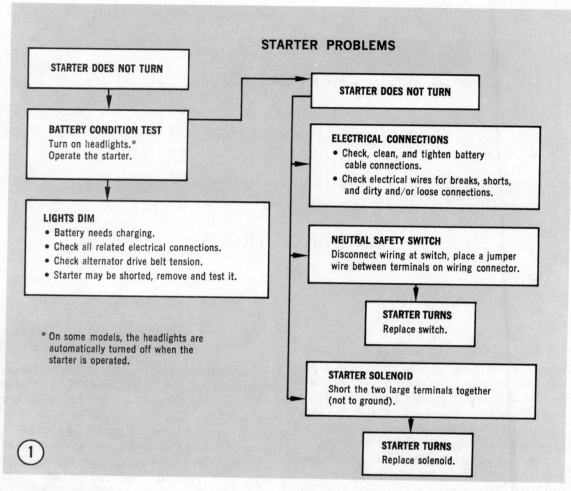

STARTER PROBLEMS

STARTER DOES NOT TURN

BATTERY CONDITION TEST
Turn on headlights.*
Operate the starter.

LIGHTS DIM
• Battery needs charging.
• Check all related electrical connections.
• Check alternator drive belt tension.
• Starter may be shorted, remove and test it.

* On some models, the headlights are
automatically turned off when the
starter is operated.

STARTER DOES NOT TURN

ELECTRICAL CONNECTIONS
• Check, clean, and tighten battery
  cable connections.
• Check electrical wires for breaks, shorts,
  and dirty and/or loose connections.

NEUTRAL SAFETY SWITCH
Disconnect wiring at switch, place a jumper
wire between terminals on wiring connector.

STARTER TURNS
Replace switch.

STARTER SOLENOID
Short the two large terminals together
(not to ground).

STARTER TURNS
Replace solenoid.

①

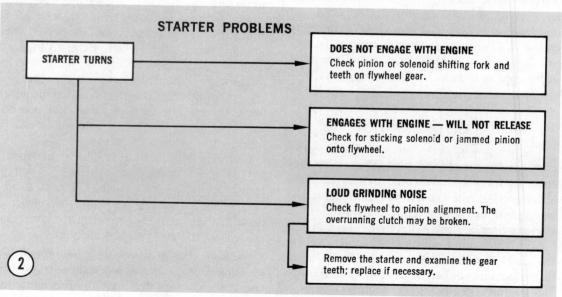

STARTER PROBLEMS

STARTER TURNS

DOES NOT ENGAGE WITH ENGINE
Check pinion or solenoid shifting fork and
teeth on flywheel gear.

ENGAGES WITH ENGINE — WILL NOT RELEASE
Check for sticking solenoid or jammed pinion
onto flywheel.

LOUD GRINDING NOISE
Check flywheel to pinion alignment. The
overrunning clutch may be broken.

Remove the starter and examine the gear
teeth; replace if necessary.

②

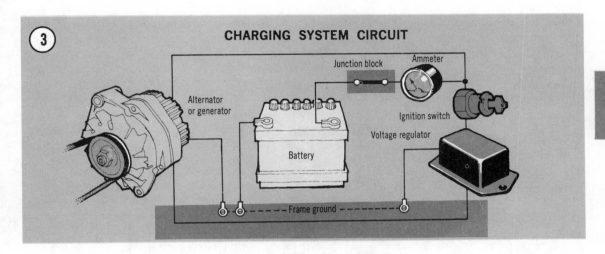

③   **CHARGING SYSTEM CIRCUIT**

Alternator or generator

Junction block

Ammeter

Ignition switch

Voltage regulator

Battery

- - - Frame ground - - - - -

2

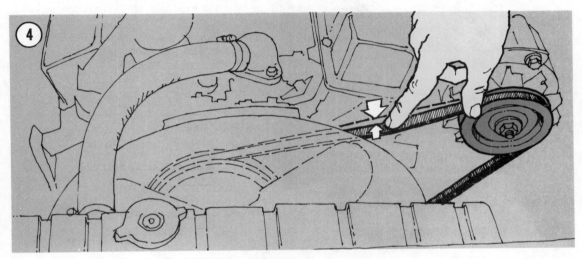

④

loose. Grasp the alternator (or generator) pulley and try to turn it. If the pulley can be turned without moving the belt, the drive belt is too loose. As a rule, keep the belt tight enough that it can be deflected about ½ in. under moderate thumb pressure between the pulleys (**Figure 4**). The battery may also be at fault; test the battery condition.

2. *Charging system warning lamp does not come on when ignition switch is turned on —* This may indicate a defective ignition switch, battery, voltage regulator, or lamp. First try to start the vehicle. If it doesn't start, check the ignition switch and battery. If the car starts, remove the warning lamp; test it for continuity with an ohmmeter or substitute a new lamp. If the lamp is good, locate the voltage regulator

and make sure it is properly grounded (try tightening the mounting screws). Also the alternator (or generator) brushes may not be making contact. Test the alternator (or generator) and voltage regulator.

3. *Alternator (or generator) warning lamp comes on and stays on —* This usually indicates that no charging is taking place. First check drive belt tension (**Figure 4**). Then check battery condition, and check all wiring connections in the charging system. If this does not locate the trouble, check the alternator (or generator) and voltage regulator.

4. *Charging system warning lamp flashes on and off intermittently —* This usually indicates the charging system is working intermittently.

Check the drive belt tension **(Figure 4)**, and check all electrical connections in the charging system. Check the alternator (or generator). *On generators only*, check the condition of the commutator.

5. *Battery requires frequent additions of water, or lamps require frequent replacement* — The alternator (or generator) is probably overcharging the battery. The voltage regulator is probably at fault.

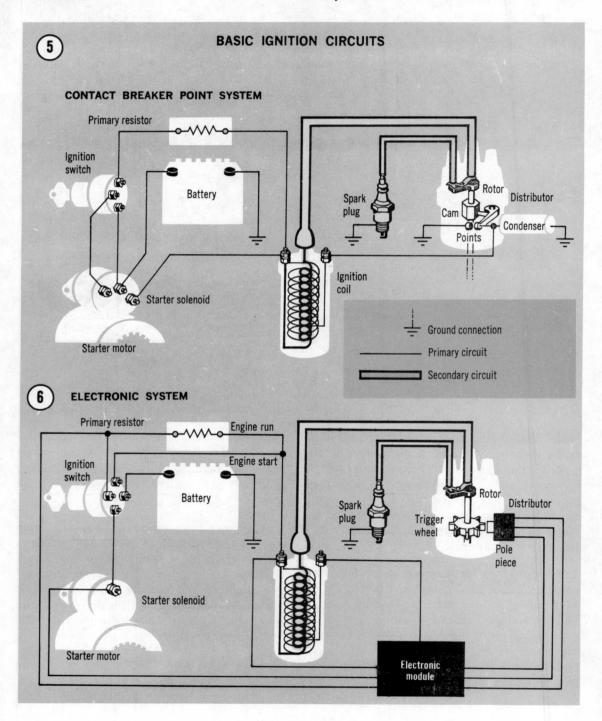

⑤ BASIC IGNITION CIRCUITS

CONTACT BREAKER POINT SYSTEM

Primary resistor

Ignition switch

Battery

Spark plug

Rotor

Distributor

Cam

Condenser

Points

Starter solenoid

Ignition coil

Starter motor

Ground connection

Primary circuit

Secondary circuit

⑥ **ELECTRONIC SYSTEM**

Primary resistor

Engine run

Ignition switch

Engine start

Battery

Spark plug

Rotor

Distributor

Trigger wheel

Pole piece

Starter solenoid

Starter motor

Electronic module

6. *Excessive noise from the alternator (or generator)* — Check for loose mounting brackets and bolts. The problem may also be worn bearings or the need of lubrication in some cases. If an alternator whines, a shorted diode may be indicated.

IGNITION SYSTEM

The ignition system may be either a conventional contact breaker type or an electronic ignition. See electrical chapter to determine which type you have. **Figures 5 and 6** show simplified diagrams of each type.

Most problems involving failure to start, poor performance, or rough running stem from trouble in the ignition system, particularly in contact breaker systems. Many novice trouble-shooters get into trouble when they assume that these symptoms point to the fuel system instead of the ignition system.

Ignition system troubles may be roughly divided between those affecting only one cylinder and those affecting all cylinders. If the trouble affects only one cylinder, it can only be in the spark plug, spark plug wire, or portion of the distributor associated with that cylinder. If the trouble affects all cylinders (weak spark or no spark), then the trouble is in the ignition coil, rotor, distributor, or associated wiring.

The troubleshooting procedures outlined in **Figure 7** (breaker point ignition) or **Figure 8**

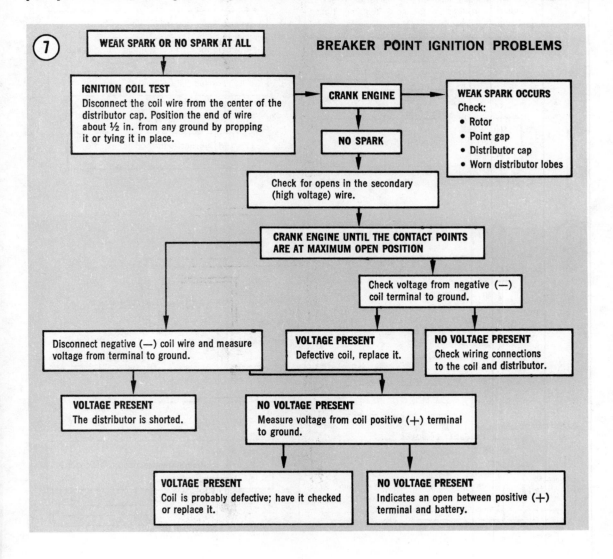

(electronic ignition) will help you isolate ignition problems fast. Of course, they assume that the battery is in good enough condition to crank the engine over at its normal rate.

ENGINE PERFORMANCE

A number of factors can make the engine difficult or impossible to start, or cause rough running, poor performance and so on. The majority of novice troubleshooters immediately suspect the carburetor or fuel injection system. In the majority of cases, though, the trouble exists in the ignition system.

The troubleshooting procedures outlined in **Figures 9 through 14** will help you solve the majority of engine starting troubles in a systematic manner.

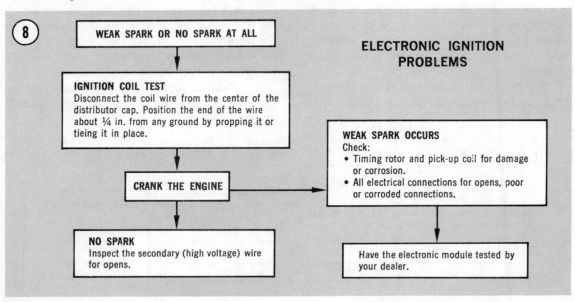

(8)

WEAK SPARK OR NO SPARK AT ALL

ELECTRONIC IGNITION PROBLEMS

IGNITION COIL TEST
Disconnect the coil wire from the center of the distributor cap. Position the end of the wire about ¼ in. from any ground by propping it or tieing it in place.

CRANK THE ENGINE

WEAK SPARK OCCURS
Check:
• Timing rotor and pick-up coil for damage or corrosion.
• All electrical connections for opens, poor or corroded connections.

NO SPARK
Inspect the secondary (high voltage) wire for opens.

Have the electronic module tested by your dealer.

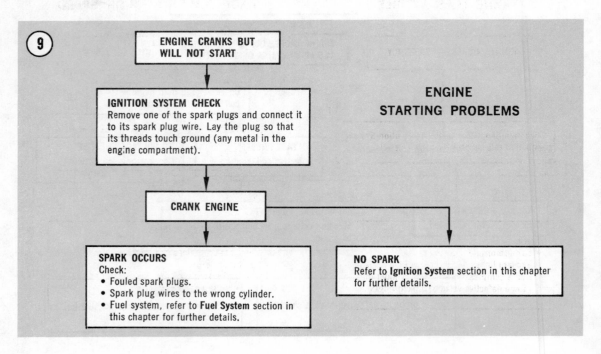

(9)

ENGINE CRANKS BUT WILL NOT START

ENGINE STARTING PROBLEMS

IGNITION SYSTEM CHECK
Remove one of the spark plugs and connect it to its spark plug wire. Lay the plug so that its threads touch ground (any metal in the engine compartment).

CRANK ENGINE

SPARK OCCURS
Check:
• Fouled spark plugs.
• Spark plug wires to the wrong cylinder.
• Fuel system, refer to **Fuel System** section in this chapter for further details.

NO SPARK
Refer to **Ignition System** section in this chapter for further details.

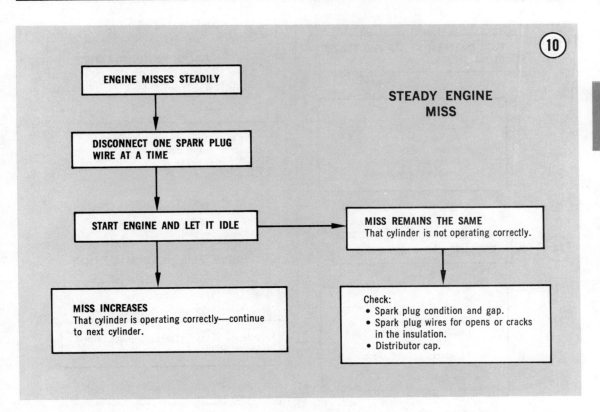

(10)

ENGINE MISSES STEADILY

STEADY ENGINE
MISS

DISCONNECT ONE SPARK PLUG
WIRE AT A TIME

START ENGINE AND LET IT IDLE → MISS REMAINS THE SAME
That cylinder is not operating correctly.

MISS INCREASES
That cylinder is operating correctly—continue
to next cylinder.

Check:
• Spark plug condition and gap.
• Spark plug wires for opens or cracks
  in the insulation.
• Distributor cap.

2

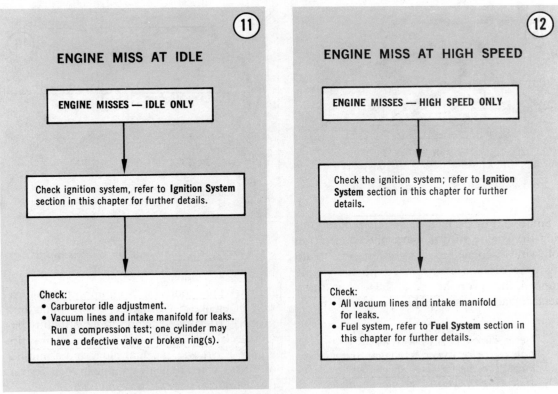

(11)

ENGINE MISS AT IDLE

ENGINE MISSES — IDLE ONLY

Check ignition system, refer to **Ignition System**
section in this chapter for further details.

Check:
• Carburetor idle adjustment.
• Vacuum lines and intake manifold for leaks.
  Run a compression test; one cylinder may
  have a defective valve or broken ring(s).

(12)

ENGINE MISS AT HIGH SPEED

ENGINE MISSES — HIGH SPEED ONLY

Check the ignition system; refer to **Ignition
System** section in this chapter for further
details.

Check:
• All vacuum lines and intake manifold
  for leaks.
• Fuel system, refer to **Fuel System** section in
  this chapter for further details.

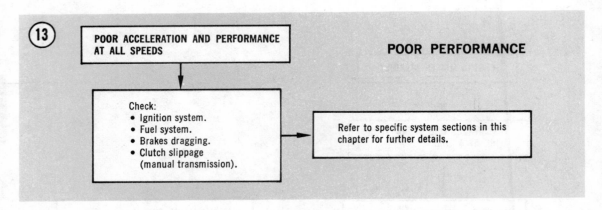

⑬ POOR ACCELERATION AND PERFORMANCE AT ALL SPEEDS

POOR PERFORMANCE

Check:
- Ignition system.
- Fuel system.
- Brakes dragging.
- Clutch slippage (manual transmission).

Refer to specific system sections in this chapter for further details.

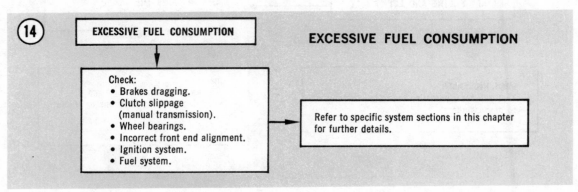

⑭ EXCESSIVE FUEL CONSUMPTION

EXCESSIVE FUEL CONSUMPTION

Check:
- Brakes dragging.
- Clutch slippage (manual transmission).
- Wheel bearings.
- Incorrect front end alignment.
- Ignition system.
- Fuel system.

Refer to specific system sections in this chapter for further details.

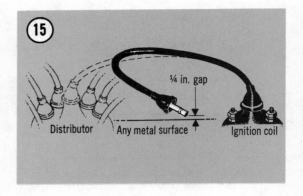

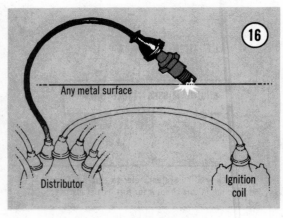

Some tests of the ignition system require running the engine with a spark plug or ignition coil wire disconnected. The safest way to do this is to disconnect the wire with the engine stopped, then prop the end of the wire next to a metal surface as shown in **Figures 15 and 16**.

WARNING
Never disconnect a spark plug or ignition coil wire while the engine is running. The high voltage in an ignition system, particularly the newer high-energy electronic ignition systems could cause serious injury or even death.

Spark plug condition is an important indication of engine performance. Spark plugs in a properly operating engine will have slightly pitted electrodes, and a light tan insulator tip. **Figure 17** shows a normal plug, and a number of others which indicate trouble in their respective cylinders.

NORMAL
- Appearance—Firing tip has deposits of light gray to light tan.
- Can be cleaned, regapped and reused.

CARBON FOULED
- Appearance—Dull, dry black with fluffy carbon deposits on the insulator tip, electrode and exposed shell.
- Caused by—Fuel/air mixture too rich, plug heat range too cold, weak ignition system, dirty air cleaner, faulty automatic choke or excessive idling.
- Can be cleaned, regapped and reused.

OIL FOULED
- Appearance—Wet black deposits on insulator and exposed shell.
- Caused by—Excessive oil entering the combustion chamber through worn rings, pistons, valve guides or bearings.
- Replace with new plugs (use a hotter plug if engine is not repaired).

LEAD FOULED
- Appearance — Yellow insulator deposits (may sometimes be dark gray, black or tan in color) on the insulator tip.
- Caused by—Highly leaded gasoline.
- Replace with new plugs.

LEAD FOULED
- Appearance—Yellow glazed deposits indicating melted lead deposits due to hard acceleration.
- Caused by—Highly leaded gasoline.
- Replace with new plugs.

OIL AND LEAD FOULED
- Appearance—Glazed yellow deposits with a slight brownish tint on the insulator tip and ground electrode.
- Replace with new plugs.

FUEL ADDITIVE RESIDUE
- Appearance — Brown colored hardened ash deposits on the insulator tip and ground electrode.
- Caused by—Fuel and/or oil additives.
- Replace with new plugs.

WORN
- Appearance — Severely worn or eroded electrodes.
- Caused by—Normal wear or unusual oil and/or fuel additives.
- Replace with new plugs.

PREIGNITION
- Appearance — Melted ground electrode.
- Caused by—Overadvanced ignition timing, inoperative ignition advance mechanism, too low of a fuel octane rating, lean fuel/air mixture or carbon deposits in combustion chamber.

PREIGNITION
- Appearance—Melted center electrode.
- Caused by—Abnormal combustion due to overadvanced ignition timing or incorrect advance, too low of a fuel octane rating, lean fuel/air mixture, or carbon deposits in combustion chamber.
- Correct engine problem and replace with new plugs.

INCORRECT HEAT RANGE
- Appearance—Melted center electrode and white blistered insulator tip.
- Caused by—Incorrect plug heat range selection.
- Replace with new plugs.

2

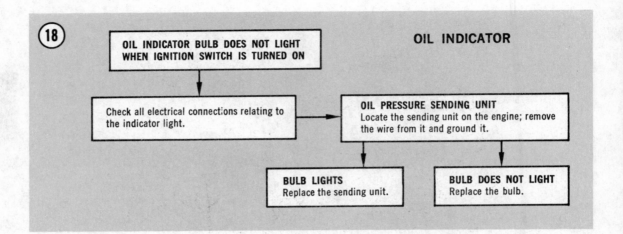

ENGINE OIL PRESSURE LIGHT

Proper oil pressure to the engine is vital. If oil pressure is insufficient, the engine can destroy itself in a comparatively short time.

The oil pressure warning circuit monitors oil pressure constantly. If pressure drops below a predetermined level, the light comes on.

Obviously, it is vital for the warning circuit to be working to signal low oil pressure. Each time you turn on the ignition, but before you start the car, the warning light should come on. If it doesn't, there is trouble in the warning circuit, not the oil pressure system. See **Figure 18** to troubleshoot the warning circuit.

Once the engine is running, the warning light should stay off. If the warning light comes on or acts erratically while the engine is running there is trouble with the engine oil pressure system. *Stop the engine immediately*. Refer to **Figure 19** for possible causes of the problem.

FUEL SYSTEM (CARBURETTED)

Fuel system problems must be isolated to the fuel pump (mechanical or electric), fuel lines, fuel filter, or carburetor. These procedures assume the ignition system is working properly and is correctly adjusted.

1. *Engine will not start* — First make sure that fuel is being delivered to the carburetor. Remove the air cleaner, look into the carburetor throat, and operate the accelerator

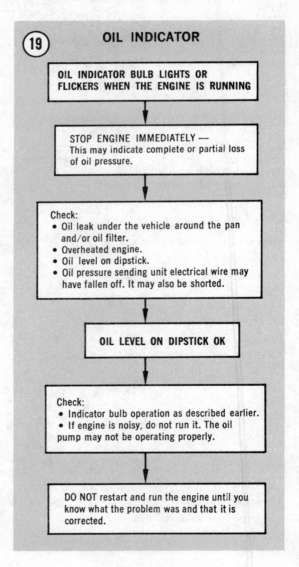

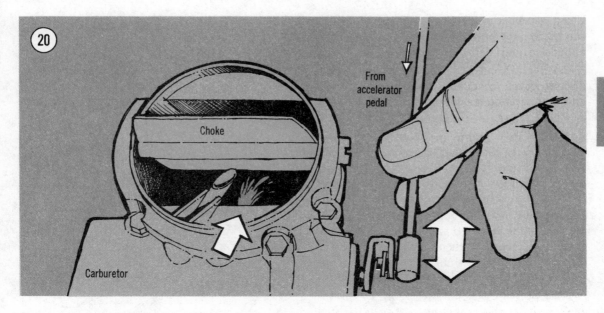

From accelerator pedal

Choke

Carburetor

linkage several times. There should be a stream of fuel from the accelerator pump discharge tube each time the accelerator linkage is depressed (**Figure 20**). If not, check fuel pump delivery (described later), float valve, and float adjustment. If the engine will not start, check the automatic choke parts for sticking or damage. If necessary, rebuild or replace the carburetor.

2. *Engine runs at fast idle* — Check the choke setting. Check the idle speed, idle mixture, and decel valve (if equipped) adjustment.

3. *Rough idle or engine miss with frequent stalling* — Check idle mixture and idle speed adjustments.

4. *Engine "diesels" (continues to run) when ignition is switched off* — Check idle mixture (probably too rich), ignition timing, and idle speed (probably too fast). Check the throttle solenoid (if equipped) for proper operation. Check for overheated engine.

5. *Stumbling when accelerating from idle* — Check the idle speed and mixture adjustments. Check the accelerator pump.

6. *Engine misses at high speed or lacks power* — This indicates possible fuel starvation. Check fuel pump pressure and capacity as described in this chapter. Check float needle valves. Check for a clogged fuel filter or air cleaner.

7. *Black exhaust smoke* — This indicates a badly overrich mixture. Check idle mixture and idle speed adjustment. Check choke setting. Check for excessive fuel pump pressure, leaky floats, or worn needle valves.

8. *Excessive fuel consumption* — Check for overrich mixture. Make sure choke mechanism works properly. Check idle mixture and idle speed. Check for excessive fuel pump pressure, leaky floats, or worn float needle valves.

FUEL SYSTEM
(FUEL INJECTED)

Troubleshooting a fuel injection system requires more thought, experience, and know-how than any other part of the vehicle. A logical approach and proper test equipment are essential in order to successfully find and fix these troubles.

It is best to leave fuel injection troubles to your dealer. In order to isolate a problem to the injection system make sure that the fuel pump is operating properly. Check its performance as described later in this section. Also make sure that fuel filter and air cleaner are not clogged.

FUEL PUMP TEST
(MECHANICAL AND ELECTRIC)

1. Disconnect the fuel inlet line where it enters the carburetor or fuel injection system.

2. Fit a rubber hose over the fuel line so fuel can be directed into a graduated container with about one quart capacity. See **Figure 21**.

3. To avoid accidental starting of the engine, disconnect the secondary coil wire from the coil or disconnect and insulate the coil primary wire.

4. Crank the engine for about 30 seconds.

5. If the fuel pump supplies the specified amount (refer to the fuel chapter later in this book), the trouble may be in the carburetor or fuel injection system. The fuel injection system should be tested by your dealer.

6. If there is no fuel present or the pump cannot supply the specified amount, either the fuel pump is defective or there is an obstruction in the fuel line. Replace the fuel pump and/or inspect the fuel lines for air leaks or obstructions.

7. Also pressure test the fuel pump by installing a T-fitting in the fuel line between the fuel pump and the carburetor. Connect a fuel pressure gauge to the fitting with a short tube **(Figure 22)**.

8. Reconnect the coil wire, start the engine, and record the pressure. Refer to the fuel chapter later in this book for the correct pressure. If the pressure varies from that specified, the pump should be replaced.

9. Stop the engine. The pressure should drop off very slowly. If it drops off rapidly, the outlet valve in the pump is leaking and the pump should be replaced.

EMISSION CONTROL SYSTEMS

Major emission control systems used on nearly all U.S. models include the following:

a. Positive crankcase ventilation (PCV)
b. Thermostatic air cleaner
c. Air injection reaction (AIR)
d. Fuel evaporation control
e. Exhaust gas recirculation (EGR)

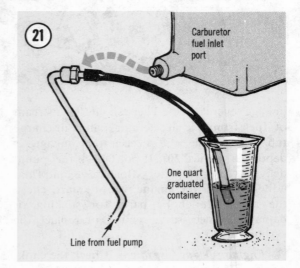

21

Carburetor fuel inlet port

One quart graduated container

Line from fuel pump

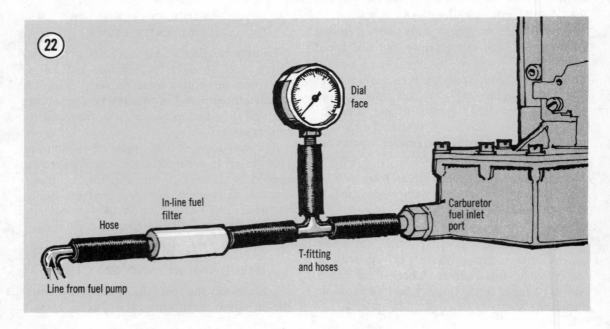

22

Dial face

In-line fuel filter

Hose

Carburetor fuel inlet port

T-fitting and hoses

Line from fuel pump

Emission control systems vary considerably from model to model. Individual models contain variations of the four systems described here. In addition, they may include other special systems. Use the index to find specific emission control components in other chapters.

Many of the systems and components are factory set and sealed. Without special expensive test equipment, it is impossible to adjust the systems to meet state and federal requirements.

Troubleshooting can also be difficult without special equipment. The procedures described below will help you find emission control parts which have failed, but repairs may have to be entrusted to a dealer or other properly equipped repair shop.

With the proper equipment, you can test the carbon monoxide and hydrocarbon levels.

Figure 23 provides some sources of trouble if the readings are not correct.

Positive Crankcase Ventilation

Fresh air drawn from the air cleaner housing scavenges emissions (e.g., piston blow-by) from the crankcase, then the intake manifold vacuum draws emissions into the intake manifold. They can then be reburned in the normal combustion process. **Figure 24** shows a typical system. **Figure 25** provides a testing procedure.

Thermostatic Air Cleaner

The thermostatically controlled air cleaner maintains incoming air to the engine at a predetermined level, usually about 100°F or higher. It mixes cold air with heated air from the exhaust manifold region. The air cleaner in-

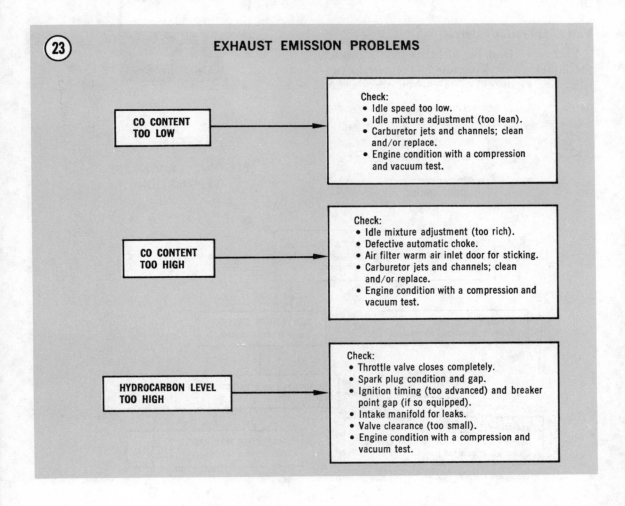

(23) **EXHAUST EMISSION PROBLEMS**

CO CONTENT TOO LOW

Check:
• Idle speed too low.
• Idle mixture adjustment (too lean).
• Carburetor jets and channels; clean and/or replace.
• Engine condition with a compression and vacuum test.

CO CONTENT TOO HIGH

Check:
• Idle mixture adjustment (too rich).
• Defective automatic choke.
• Air filter warm air inlet door for sticking.
• Carburetor jets and channels; clean and/or replace.
• Engine condition with a compression and vacuum test.

HYDROCARBON LEVEL TOO HIGH

Check:
• Throttle valve closes completely.
• Spark plug condition and gap.
• Ignition timing (too advanced) and breaker point gap (if so equipped).
• Intake manifold for leaks.
• Valve clearance (too small).
• Engine condition with a compression and vacuum test.

cludes a temperature sensor, vacuum motor, and a hinged door. See **Figure 26**.

The system is comparatively easy to test. See **Figure 27** for the procedure.

Air Injection Reaction System

The air injection reaction system reduces air pollution by oxidizing hydrocarbons and carbon monoxide as they leave the combustion chamber. See **Figure 28**.

The air injection pump, driven by the engine, compresses filtered air and injects it at the exhaust port of each cylinder. The fresh air mixes with the unburned gases in the exhaust and promotes further burning. A check valve prevents exhaust gases from entering and damaging the air pump if the pump becomes inoperative, e.g., from a fan belt failure.

Figure 29 explains the testing procedure for this system.

Fuel Evaporation Control

Fuel vapor from the fuel tank passes through the liquid/vapor separator to the carbon canister. See **Figure 30**. The carbon absorbs and

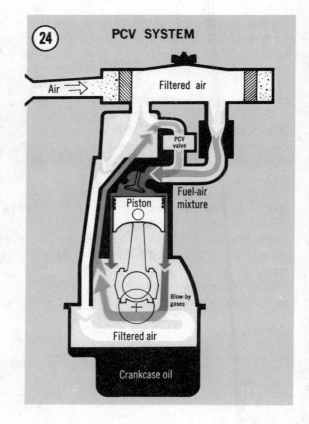

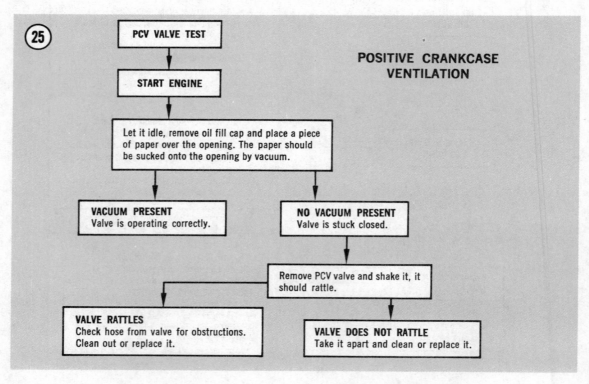

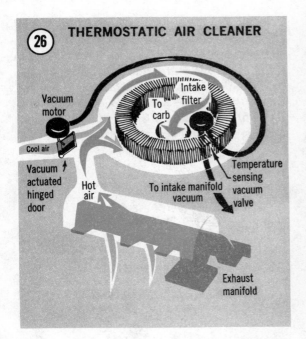

26 THERMOSTATIC AIR CLEANER

Vacuum motor

Cool air

Vacuum actuated hinged door

Hot air

To carb

Intake filter

To intake manifold vacuum

Temperature sensing vacuum valve

Exhaust manifold

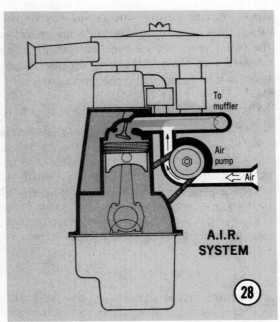

To muffler

Air pump

Air

A.I.R. SYSTEM

28

2

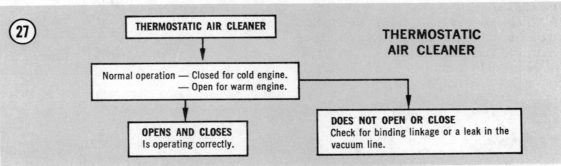

27

THERMOSTATIC AIR CLEANER

Normal operation — Closed for cold engine.
— Open for warm engine.

OPENS AND CLOSES
Is operating correctly.

DOES NOT OPEN OR CLOSE
Check for binding linkage or a leak in the vacuum line.

THERMOSTATIC AIR CLEANER

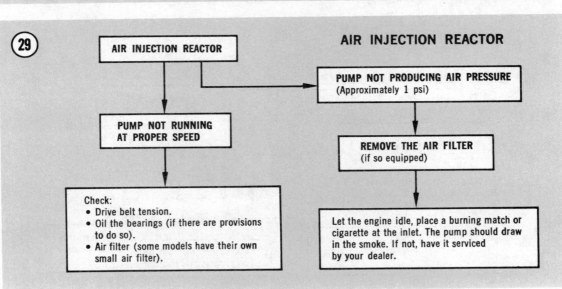

29

AIR INJECTION REACTOR

AIR INJECTION REACTOR

PUMP NOT PRODUCING AIR PRESSURE
(Approximately 1 psi)

PUMP NOT RUNNING AT PROPER SPEED

REMOVE THE AIR FILTER
(if so equipped)

Check:
• Drive belt tension.
• Oil the bearings (if there are provisions to do so).
• Air filter (some models have their own small air filter).

Let the engine idle, place a burning match or cigarette at the inlet. The pump should draw in the smoke. If not, have it serviced by your dealer.

stores the vapor when the engine is stopped. When the engine runs, manifold vacuum draws the vapor from the canister. Instead of being released into the atmosphere, the fuel vapor takes part in the normal combustion process.

Exhaust Gas Recirculation

The exhaust gas recirculation (EGR) system is used to reduce the emission of nitrogen oxides (NOx). Relatively inert exhaust gases are introduced into the combustion process to slightly reduce peak temperatures. This reduction in temperature reduces the formation of NOx.

Figure 31 provides a simple test of this system.

ENGINE NOISES

Often the first evidence of an internal engine trouble is a strange noise. That knocking, clicking, or tapping which you never heard before may be warning you of impending trouble.

While engine noises can indicate problems, they are sometimes difficult to interpret correctly; inexperienced mechanics can be seriously misled by them.

Professional mechanics often use a special stethoscope which looks similar to a doctor's stethoscope for isolating engine noises. You can do nearly as well with a "sounding stick" which can be an ordinary piece of doweling or a section of small hose. By placing one end in contact with the area to which you want to listen and the other end near your ear, you can hear

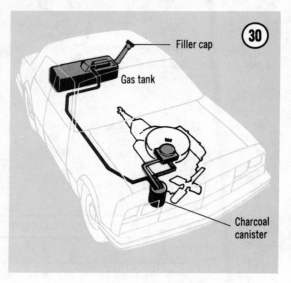

Filler cap

Gas tank

Charcoal canister

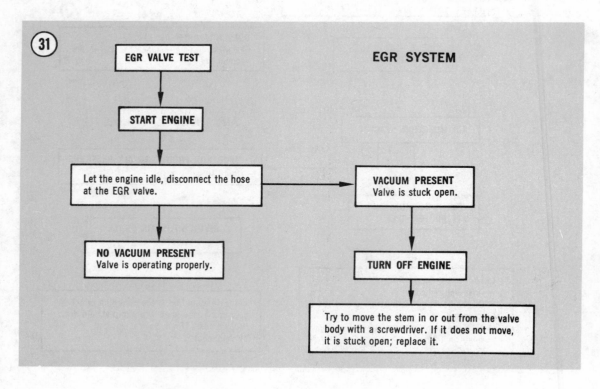

EGR SYSTEM

EGR VALVE TEST

START ENGINE

Let the engine idle, disconnect the hose at the EGR valve.

NO VACUUM PRESENT
Valve is operating properly.

VACUUM PRESENT
Valve is stuck open.

TURN OFF ENGINE

Try to move the stem in or out from the valve body with a screwdriver. If it does not move, it is stuck open; replace it.

sounds emanating from that area. The first time you do this, you may be horrified at the strange noises coming from even a normal engine. If you can, have an experienced friend or mechanic help you sort the noises out.

Clicking or Tapping Noises

Clicking or tapping noises usually come from the valve train, and indicate excessive valve clearance.

If your vehicle has adjustable valves, the procedure for adjusting the valve clearance is explained in Chapter Three. If your vehicle has hydraulic lifters, the clearance may not be adjustable. The noise may be coming from a collapsed lifter. These may be cleaned or replaced as described in the engine chapter.

A sticking valve may also sound like a valve with excessive clearance. In addition, excessive wear in valve train components can cause similar engine noises.

Knocking Noises

A heavy, dull knocking is usually caused by a worn main bearing. The noise is loudest when the engine is working hard, i.e., accelerating hard at low speed. You may be able to isolate the trouble to a single bearing by disconnecting

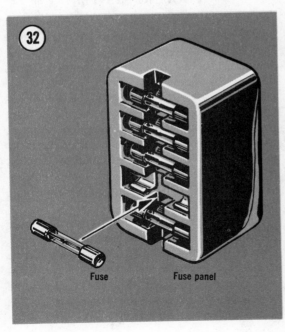

Fuse   Fuse panel

the spark plugs one at a time. When you reach the spark plug nearest the bearing, the knock will be reduced or disappear.

Worn connecting rod bearings may also produce a knock, but the sound is usually more "metallic." As with a main bearing, the noise is worse when accelerating. It may even increase further just as you go from accelerating to coasting. Disconnecting spark plugs will help isolate this knock as well.

A double knock or clicking usually indicates a worn piston pin. Disconnecting spark plugs will isolate this to a particular piston, however, the noise will *increase* when you reach the affected piston.

A loose flywheel and excessive crankshaft end play also produce knocking noises. While similar to main bearing noises, these are usually intermittent, not constant, and they do not change when spark plugs are disconnected.

Some mechanics confuse piston pin noise with piston slap. The double knock will distinguish the piston pin noise. Piston slap is identified by the fact that it is always louder when the engine is cold.

ELECTRICAL ACCESSORIES

Lights and Switches (Interior and Exterior)

1. *Bulb does not light* — Remove the bulb and check for a broken element. Also check the inside of the socket; make sure the contacts are clean and free of corrosion. If the bulb and socket are OK, check to see if a fuse has blown or a circuit breaker has tripped. The fuse panel (**Figure 32**) is usually located under the instrument panel. Replace the blown fuse or reset the circuit breaker. If the fuse blows or the breaker trips again, there is a short in that circuit. Check that circuit all the way to the battery. Look for worn wire insulation or burned wires.

If all the above are all right, check the switch controlling the bulb for continuity with an ohmmeter at the switch terminals. Check the switch contact terminals for loose or dirty electrical connections.

2. *Headlights work but will not switch from either high or low beam* — Check the beam selector switch for continuity with an ohmmeter

at the switch terminals. Check the switch contact terminals for loose or dirty electrical connections.

3. *Brake light switch inoperative* — On mechanically operated switches, usually mounted near the brake pedal arm, adjust the switch to achieve correct mechanical operation. Check the switch for continuity with an ohmmeter at the switch terminals. Check the switch contact terminals for loose or dirty electrical connections.

4. *Back-up lights do not operate* — Check light bulb as described earlier. Locate the switch, normally located near the shift lever. Adjust switch to achieve correct mechanical operation. Check the switch for continuity with an ohmmeter at the switch terminals. Bypass the switch with a jumper wire; if the lights work, replace the switch.

Directional Signals

1. *Directional signals do not operate* — If the indicator light on the instrument panel burns steadily instead of flashing, this usually indicates that one of the exterior lights is burned out. Check all lamps that normally flash. If all are all right, the flasher unit may be defective. Replace it with a good one.

2. *Directional signal indicator light on instrument panel does not light up* — Check the light bulbs as described earlier. Check all electrical connections and check the flasher unit.

3. *Directional signals will not self-cancel* — Check the self-cancelling mechanism located inside the steering column.

4. *Directional signals flash slowly* — Check the condition of the battery and the alternator (or generator) drive belt tension (**Figure 4**). Check the flasher unit and all related electrical connections.

Windshield Wipers

1. *Wipers do not operate* — Check for a blown fuse or circuit breaker that has tripped; replace or reset. Check all related terminals for loose or dirty electrical connections. Check continuity of the control switch with an ohmmeter at the switch terminals. Check the linkage and arms

for loose, broken, or binding parts. Straighten out or replace where necessary.

2. *Wiper motor hums but will not operate* — The motor may be shorted out internally; check and/or replace the motor. Also check for broken or binding linkage and arms.

3. *Wiper arms will not return to the stowed position when turned off* — The motor has a special internal switch for this purpose. Have it inspected by your dealer. Do not attempt this yourself.

Interior Heater

1. *Heater fan does not operate* — Check for a blown fuse or circuit breaker that has tripped. Check the switch for continuity with an ohmmeter at the switch terminals. Check the switch contact terminals for loose or dirty electrical connections.

2. *Heat output is insufficient* — Check the heater hose/engine coolant control valve usually located in the engine compartment; make sure it is in the open position. Ensure that the heater door(s) and cable(s) are operating correctly and are in the open position. Inspect the heat ducts; make sure that they are not crimped or blocked.

COOLING SYSTEM

The temperature gauge or warning light usually signals cooling system troubles before there is any damage. As long as you stop the vehicle at the first indication of trouble, serious damage is unlikely.

In most cases, the trouble will be obvious as soon as you open the hood. If there is coolant or steam leaking, look for a defective radiator, radiator hose, or heater hose. If there is no evidence of leakage, make sure that the fan belt is in good condition. If the trouble is not obvious, refer to **Figures 33 and 34** to help isolate the trouble.

Automotive cooling systems operate under pressure to permit higher operating temperatures without boil-over. The system should be checked periodically to make sure it can withstand normal pressure. **Figure 35** shows the equipment which nearly any service station has for testing the system pressure.

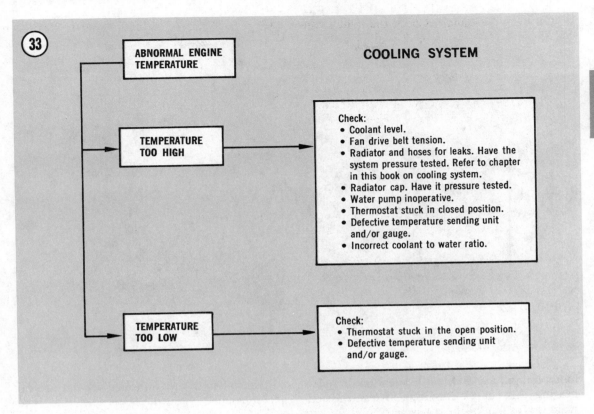

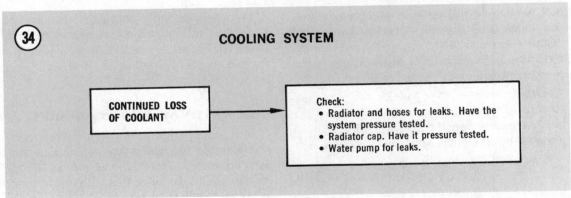

CLUTCH

All clutch troubles except adjustments require transmission removal to identify and cure the problem.

1. *Slippage* — This is most noticeable when accelerating in a high gear at relatively low speed. To check slippage, park the vehicle on a level surface with the handbrake set. Shift to 2nd gear and release the clutch as if driving off. If the clutch is good, the engine will slow and stall. If the clutch slips, continued engine speed will give it away.

Slippage results from insufficient clutch pedal free play, oil or grease on the clutch disc, worn pressure plate, or weak springs.

2. *Drag or failure to release* — This trouble usually causes difficult shifting and gear clash, especially when downshifting. The cause may be excessive clutch pedal free play, warped or bent pressure plate or clutch disc, broken or

loose linings, or lack of lubrication in pilot bearing. Also check condition of transmission main shaft splines.

3. *Chatter or grabbing* — A number of things can cause this trouble. Check tightness of engine mounts and engine-to-transmission mounting bolts. Check for worn or misaligned pressure plate and misaligned release plate.

4. *Other noises* — Noise usually indicates a dry or defective release or pilot bearing. Check the bearings and replace if necessary. Also check all parts for misalignment and uneven wear.

MANUAL TRANSMISSION/TRANSAXLE

Transmission and transaxle troubles are evident when one or more of the following symptoms appear:

   a. Difficulty changing gears

   b. Gears clash when downshifting

   c. Slipping out of gear

   d. Excessive noise in NEUTRAL

   e. Excessive noise in gear

   f. Oil leaks

Transmission and transaxle repairs are not recommended unless the many special tools required are available.

Transmission and transaxle troubles are sometimes difficult to distinguish from clutch troubles. Eliminate the clutch as a source of trouble before installing a new or rebuilt transmission or transaxle.

AUTOMATIC TRANSMISSION

Most automatic transmission repairs require considerable specialized knowledge and tools. It is impractical for the home mechanic to invest in the tools, since they cost more than a properly rebuilt transmission.

Check fluid level and condition frequently to help prevent future problems. If the fluid is orange or black in color or smells like varnish, it is an indication of some type of damage or failure within the transmission. Have the transmission serviced by your dealer or competent automatic transmission service facility.

BRAKES

Good brakes are vital to the safe operation of the vehicle. Performing the maintenance speci-

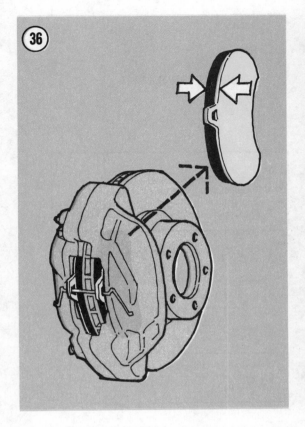

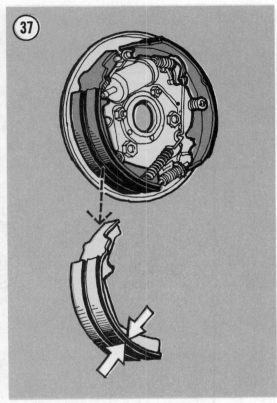

fied in Chapter Three will minimize problems with the brakes. Most importantly, check and maintain the level of fluid in the master cylinder, and check the thickness of the linings on the disc brake pads (**Figure 36**) or drum brake shoes (**Figure 37**).

If trouble develops, **Figures 38 through 40** will help you locate the problem. Refer to the brake chapter for actual repair procedures.

STEERING AND SUSPENSION

Trouble in the suspension or steering is evident when the following occur:

a. Steering is hard
b. Car pulls to one side
c. Car wanders or front wheels wobble
d. Steering has excessive play
e. Tire wear is abnormal

Unusual steering, pulling, or wandering is usually caused by bent or otherwise misaligned suspension parts. This is difficult to check without proper alignment equipment. Refer to the suspension chapter in this book for repairs that you can perform and those that must be left to a dealer or suspension specialist.

If your trouble seems to be excessive play, check wheel bearing adjustment first. This is the most frequent cause. Then check ball-joints (refer to Suspension chapter). Finally, check tie rod end ball-joints by shaking each tie rod. Also check steering gear, or rack-and-pinion assembly to see that it is securely bolted down.

TIRE WEAR ANALYSIS

Abnormal tire wear should be analyzed to determine its causes. The most common causes are the following:

a. Incorrect tire pressure
b. Improper driving
c. Overloading
d. Bad road surfaces
e. Incorrect wheel alignment

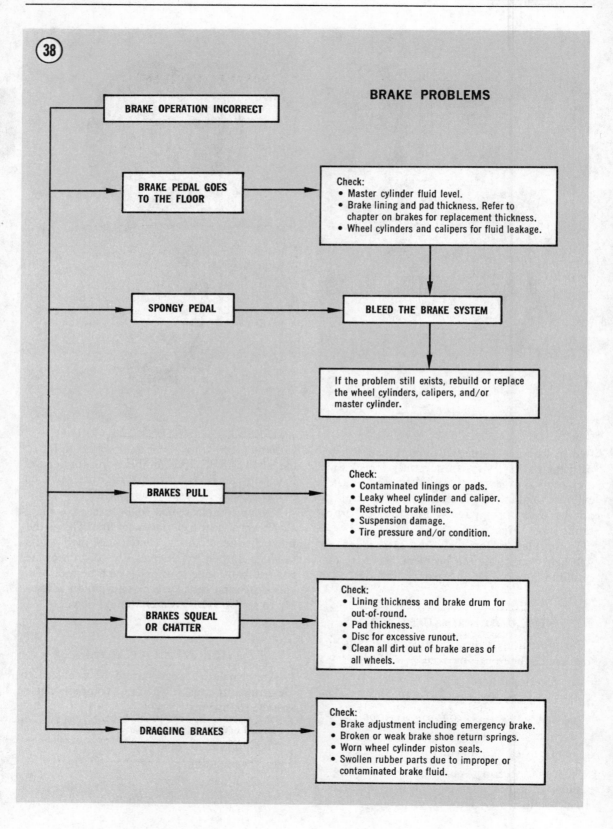

(38)

BRAKE PROBLEMS

BRAKE OPERATION INCORRECT

BRAKE PEDAL GOES TO THE FLOOR →

Check:
- Master cylinder fluid level.
- Brake lining and pad thickness. Refer to chapter on brakes for replacement thickness.
- Wheel cylinders and calipers for fluid leakage.

SPONGY PEDAL →

BLEED THE BRAKE SYSTEM

If the problem still exists, rebuild or replace the wheel cylinders, calipers, and/or master cylinder.

BRAKES PULL →

Check:
- Contaminated linings or pads.
- Leaky wheel cylinder and caliper.
- Restricted brake lines.
- Suspension damage.
- Tire pressure and/or condition.

BRAKES SQUEAL OR CHATTER →

Check:
- Lining thickness and brake drum for out-of-round.
- Pad thickness.
- Disc for excessive runout.
- Clean all dirt out of brake areas of all wheels.

DRAGGING BRAKES →

Check:
- Brake adjustment including emergency brake.
- Broken or weak brake shoe return springs.
- Worn wheel cylinder piston seals.
- Swollen rubber parts due to improper or contaminated brake fluid.

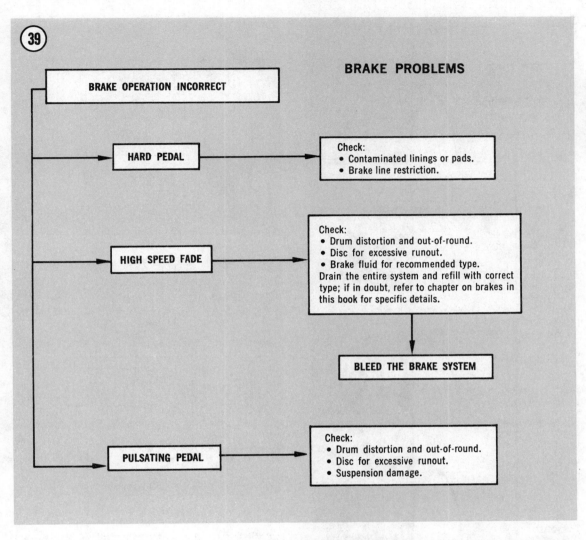

(39)

BRAKE PROBLEMS

BRAKE OPERATION INCORRECT

HARD PEDAL

Check:
• Contaminated linings or pads.
• Brake line restriction.

HIGH SPEED FADE

Check:
• Drum distortion and out-of-round.
• Disc for excessive runout.
• Brake fluid for recommended type.
Drain the entire system and refill with correct type; if in doubt, refer to chapter on brakes in this book for specific details.

BLEED THE BRAKE SYSTEM

PULSATING PEDAL

Check:
• Drum distortion and out-of-round.
• Disc for excessive runout.
• Suspension damage.

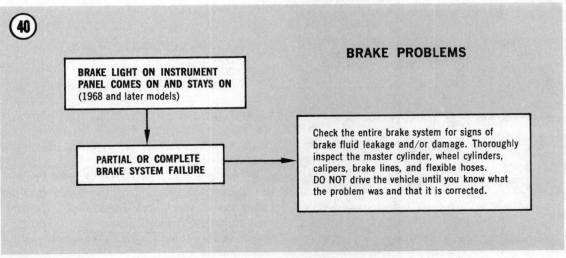

(40)

BRAKE PROBLEMS

BRAKE LIGHT ON INSTRUMENT PANEL COMES ON AND STAYS ON
(1968 and later models)

PARTIAL OR COMPLETE BRAKE SYSTEM FAILURE

Check the entire brake system for signs of brake fluid leakage and/or damage. Thoroughly inspect the master cylinder, wheel cylinders, calipers, brake lines, and flexible hoses.
DO NOT drive the vehicle until you know what the problem was and that it is corrected.

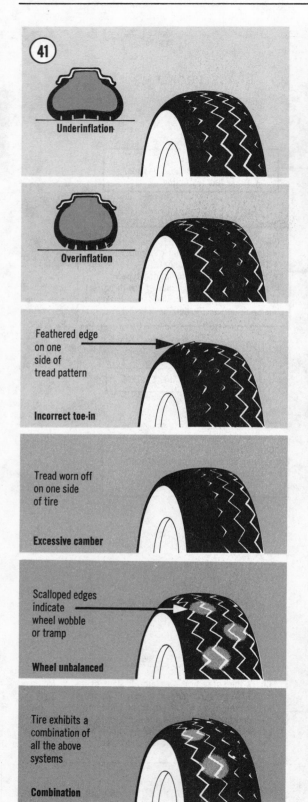

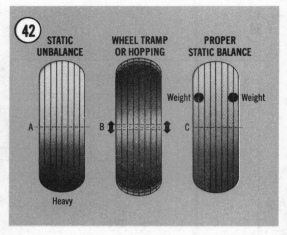

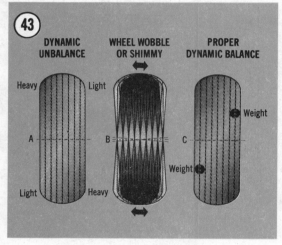

Figure 41 identifies wear patterns and indicates the most probable causes.

WHEEL BALANCING

All four wheels and tires must be in balance along two axes. To be in static balance (**Figure 42**), weight must be evenly distributed around the axis of rotation. (A) shows a statically unbalanced wheel; (B) shows the result — wheel tramp or hopping; (C) shows proper static balance.

To be in dynamic balance (**Figure 43**), the centerline of the weight must coincide with the centerline of the wheel. (A) shows a dynamically unbalanced wheel; (B) shows the result — wheel wobble or shimmy; (C) shows proper dynamic balance.

NOTE: If you own a 1982 or later model, first check the Supplement at the back of the book for any new service information.

CHAPTER THREE

3

LUBRICATION, MAINTENANCE AND TUNE-UP

To ensure good performance, dependability, and safety, regular preventive maintenance is essential. This chapter outlines periodic maintenance for a van subjected to average use (a combination of urban and highway driving and light-duty off-road use). A vehicle that is driven extensively off-road or used primarily in stop-and-go traffic may require more frequent attention; but even without use, rust, dirt, and corrosion cause unnecessary damage if the vehicle is neglected. Whether maintenance is performed by the owner or a dealer, regular routine attention helps avoid expensive repairs.

Tables 1-14 are at the end of the chapter.

ROUTINE CHECKS

The following simple checks should be performed at each fuel stop.

1. Check the engine oil level. The oil should be checked with the engine warm and the vehicle on level ground. The level should be between the 2 marks on the dipstick (see **Figure 1**)—never below and never above.

See **Figure 2** (6-cylinder gasoline engines), **Figure 3** (diesel engines) or **Figure 4** (V-8 engines).

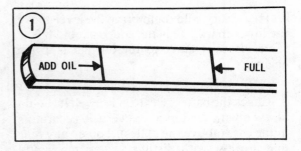

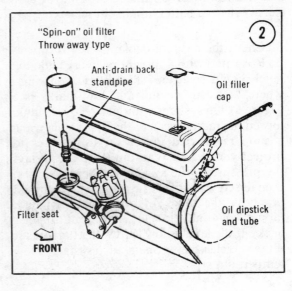

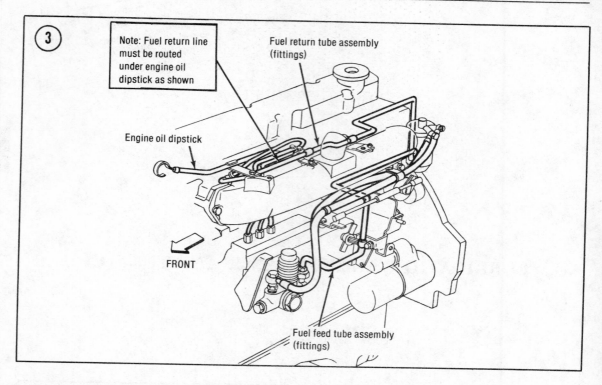

③ Note: Fuel return line must be routed under engine oil dipstick as shown

Fuel return tube assembly (fittings)

Engine oil dipstick

FRONT

Fuel feed tube assembly (fittings)

If necessary, add oil to bring the level above the lower mark. Oil being added should be the same viscosity grade as the oil that is in the engine.

2. Check the battery electrolyte level. It should be even with the top of the vertical separators in the case (above the plates). Top up any cells that are low with distilled water; never add electrolyte to a battery that is in service.

3. Check the radiator coolant level. If the vehicle is fitted with a coolant recovery tank, the level should be at the half-full mark or somewhere between the full and low marks (see **Figure 5**). On systems without a recovery tank, loosen the radiator cap to the first notch, using a shop rag folded in several thicknesses to protect your hand. Wait until you are certain the pressure in the system has been relieved, then unscrew the cap. The coolant level should be above the tubes in the top radiator tank (about 1 1/4 in. below the bottom of the filler neck). If the level is low, add water (or coolant if the vehicle is being operated in sustained low temperatures).

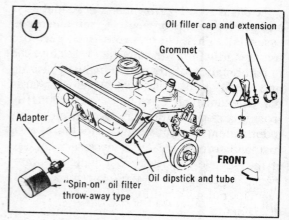

④ Oil filler cap and extension

Grommet

Adapter

FRONT

Oil dipstick and tube

"Spin-on" oil filter throw-away type

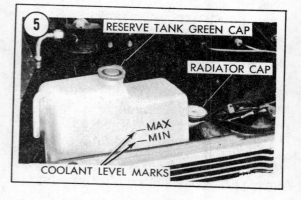

⑤ RESERVE TANK GREEN CAP

RADIATOR CAP

MAX
MIN

COOLANT LEVEL MARKS

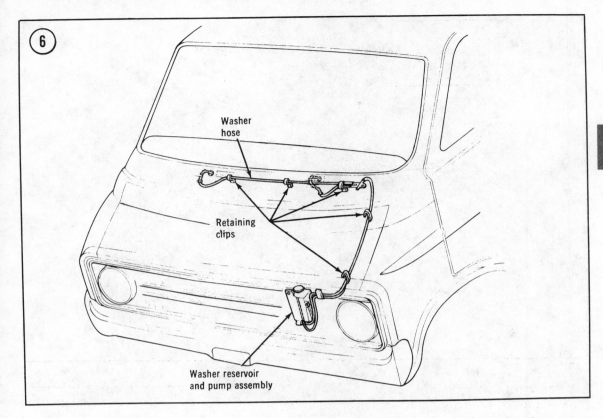

Washer hose

Retaining clips

Washer reservoir and pump assembly

4. Check the windshield washer fluid level and top it up if necessary (see **Figure 6**). If the vehicle is being operated in sustained low temperatures, add a windshield washer fluid compounded to resist freezing. Don't add cooling system antifreeze. It can damage painted surfaces.

5. Check tire pressures. Specified pressures are listed on the Safety Certification label located on the lock pillar on the driver's door. If tires other than those specified on the label are used, refer to **Table 1**.

> *NOTE*
> *Tire pressures should be checked when the tires are cold. If tire pressure is checked when tires are warm, it will be about 3 psi higher following a low-speed drive and about 7 psi higher following a high-speed drive.*

In addition to pressure, the condition of the tire tread and sidewalls should be checked for damage, cracking, and wear. Wear patterns are a good indicator of chassis and suspension alignment (see *Tire Wear Analysis*, Chapter Two).

Checking tire condition is particularly important following hard off-road usage. Pay particular attention to signs of severe rock damage usually evidenced by fractures and cuts in the tread and sidewalls. This type of damage presents an extreme driving hazard when the vehicle is operated at highway speeds. A damaged tire should be replaced as soon as it is detected.

When replacing a tire, the new tire should match the tread pattern of the other tires as closely as possible to ensure good performance. And, never mix radial ply with biased ply tires; the performance differences are sufficient to make the vehicle unsafe.

PERIODIC CHECKS
AND INSPECTIONS

The following checks and inspections should be made at least monthly, or at the intervals

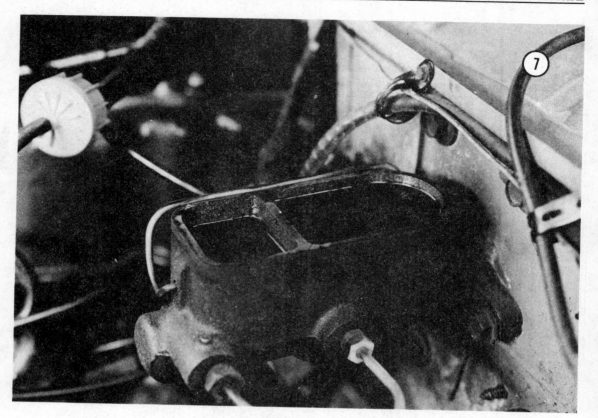

indicated. In addition, it is a good idea to perform these checks after the vehicle has been used off-road for an extended period of time.

Brake Fluid Level

Brake fluid level should be checked monthly as well as any time the pedal can be pushed within a couple of inches of the floor. The level should be 1/4-3/8 in. below the top of the reservoir (see **Figure 7**). If the level is lower than recommended, clean the area around the filler cap and remove it. Add brake fluid clearly marked DOT 3 only to bring it up to the recommended level.

Brake Pad and Lining Condition

Disc brake pads and drum brake shoe linings should be checked for oil or grease on the friction material and measured to determine their serviceability every 6,000-12,000 miles or when long pedal travel indicates the the likelihood of extreme wear.

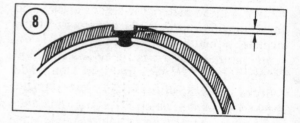

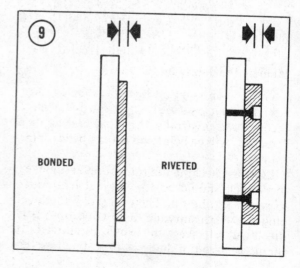

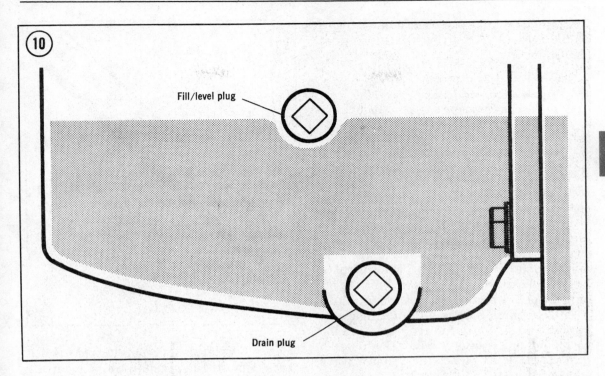

Fill/level plug

Drain plug

The shoes or pads should be replaced when they are worn beyond the service limits shown in **Table 2**. See **Figure 8** and **Figure 9**.

If the friction material is oily or greasy, the linings or pads must be replaced no matter how much material remains.

Brake Lines and Hoses

Brake lines and hoses should be routinely checked for signs of deterioration, chafing, and kinks. This is particularly important following rough, off-road use where likelihood of brush and rock damage is high. Any line that is less than perfect should be replaced immediately.

Manual Transmission Oil Level

The transmission oil level must be checked with the vehicle sitting level. If you do not have access to a hydraulic hoist, a mechanic's "creeper" will be helpful in getting beneath the vehicle.

Prior to checking the transmission oil level, the vehicle should be driven for several miles to warm up the oil. Then, unscrew the level plug on the transmission case (see **Figure 10**). If the level is correct, a small amount of oil should seep out of the level hole. If necessary,

carefully add fresh oil up to the bottom edge of the hole and install the fill/level plug and tighten it securely.

CAUTION
If the vehicle has been operated in deep water, pay particular attention to the condition of the oil. If water droplets are present, indicating that water has entered the transmission, change the oil immediately.

Automatic Transmission Oil Level

The transmission oil level must be checked with the vehicle sitting level and the engine and transmission warmed up to operating temperature. If the level is checked with the transmission cold, the level will appear to be low.

1. Set the handbrake, select PARK with the transmission control lever, start the engine, and allow it to run for a couple of minutes to ensure the fluid coupling is full of fluid. Shift the lever through all positions and return it to PARK.

2. Wipe the transmission dipstick handle and filler tube clean with a dry rag. Withdraw the dipstick and wipe it with a clean lint-free cloth.

The dipstick is located at the rear of the engine on the right side. Remove the engine cover to gain access.

3. Insert the clean dipstick all the way into the filler tube and then withdraw it again and check the level. See **Figure 11**. The level should be at or slightly below the FULL mark on the dipstick. If the level is below the ADD mark, fresh DEXRON automatic transmission fluid must be added. Keep in mind that the distance between the marks on the dipstick represents only about one pint. Use a clean funnel fitted with a fine-mesh filter to direct the fluid into the filler tube. Slowly add the fluid, with the engine running, a little at a time. Periodically recheck the level as described above while adding fluid.

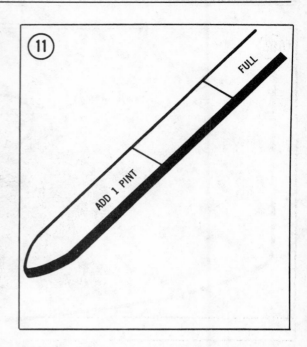

Intake/Exhaust Manifold Nuts and Bolts

The intake/exhaust manifold nuts and bolts should be checked for broken or missing lockwashers and for looseness. Nuts that are snug need to be tightened no further, but loose nuts should be tightened to specifications (see **Table 2**, Chapter Four). Overtightening of nuts can cause studs to break or castings to crack, requiring expensive repairs.

Drive Belts

Check the alternator, water pump, fan, air pump, air conditioning, and steering and brake pump belts for fraying, glazing, or cracking of the contact surfaces. Belts that are damaged or deteriorated should be replaced before they fail and cause serious problems from engine overheating, electrical system failure, or reduction of steering and brake control. Belt replacement is described in Chapter Seven.

In addition to being in good condition, it is important that the drive belts be correctly adjusted. See **Figure 12** (typical). A belt that is too loose will cause the driven components to operate at less than optimum efficiency. A belt that is adjusted too tightly will wear rapidly and place unnecessary side loads on the bearings of the driven components, possibly resulting in their premature wear or failure. See Chapter Seven for drive belt adjustment.

Vacuum Fittings and Hoses

Check the vacuum fittings and connections to make sure they are tight, and inspect the hoses for cracking, kinking, or deterioration. Any damaged or deteriorated lines should be replaced.

Coolant Condition

Remove the radiator cap and check the condition of the coolant. If it is dirty, drain and flush the radiator and cooling system and fill it with fresh coolant as described in Chapter Six. In any case, the coolant should be changed every 24 months regardless of condition or mileage.

Coolant Hoses

Inspect the heater and radiator hoses. Replace any that are cracked, deteriorated, extremely soft, or extremely hard. Make sure the hoses are correctly routed and installed and that all the clamps are tight.

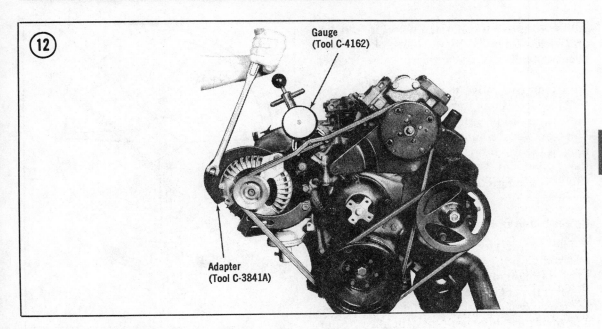

⑫

Gauge
(Tool C-4162)

Adapter
(Tool C-3841A)

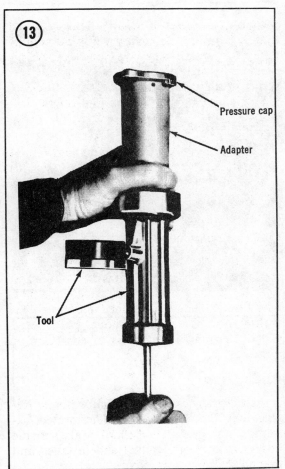

⑬

Pressure cap

Adapter

Tool

Radiator

Check the radiator for leaks and damage. Blow bugs and dirt out of the fins, from the rear of the radiator, with compressed air. *Carefully* straighten bent fins with a small screwdriver. Have a service station pressure test the radiator cap. See **Figure 13**. The cap should maintain pressure and the relief valve remain closed to 14-17 psi.

Wheel Alignment

Wheel alignment should be checked periodically by a dealer or an alignment specialist. Misalignment is usually indicated first by incorrect tire wear (see *Tire Wear Analysis*, Chapter Two). Wheel alignment specifications are provided as reference in Chapter Nine.

Steering

1. With the vehicle on level ground, and with the front wheels lined up straight ahead, grasp the steering wheel and check for rotational free play. The free play should not be greater than about one inch (see **Figure 14**). If it is, the front wheel bearings should be checked for condition and adjustment (see Chapter Nine), and the kingpins, steering linkage, and steering arm should be checked as possible causes of excessive play. These checks should be referred to a dealer.

2. Try to move the steering wheel in and out and check for axial play. If any play is felt, check the tightness of the steering wheel center nut.

3. Attempt to move the steering wheel from side to side without turning it. Movement is an indication of loose steering column mounting bolts or worn column bushings. Check and tighten the mounting bolts if necessary, and if the movement is still present, the vehicle should be referred to a dealer for corrective service.

Power Steering Fluid Level

The power steering fluid level must be checked with the engine and fluid warmed up to operating temperature.

1. Start the engine and turn the steering wheel as far as it will go to right and left several times and then turn the wheels straight ahead. Shut off the engine.

2. Wipe the outside of the case and cap to remove dirt that might fall into the reservoir. Remove the dipstick from the pump reservoir, wipe it clean with a lint-free cloth, reinsert it all the way into the tube, and withdraw it. The fluid level should be between the crosshatching at the bottom of the stick and the FULL mark. See **Figure 15**. If it is not, carefully add power steering fluid (Mopar part No. 2084329 or equivalent) and recheck the level. Do not overfill the reservoir. If the level after filling is above the FULL mark, fluid must be siphoned off until level is correct.

Fuel Filters (Gasoline Engines)

Gasoline engines are equipped with a fuel filter between the fuel tank and pump. **Figure 16** shows a typical fuel filter.

To replace the filter, disconnect the hoses from the old filter and connect them to a new filter.

Fuel Filters (Diesel Engine)

Diesel engines are equipped with a wire gauze filter (**Figure 17** and **Figure 18**) and a replaceable element filter (**Figure 19**).

To service the wire gauze filter, remove it from the fuel feed pump. Clean the filter in solvent, then reinstall it.

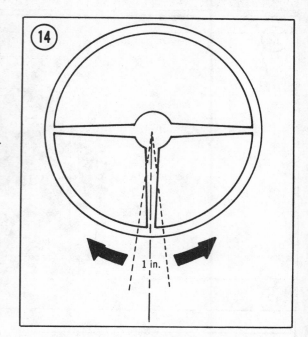

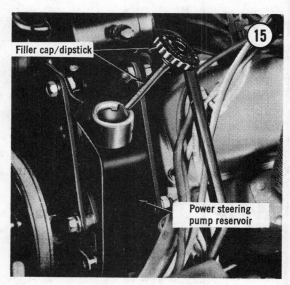

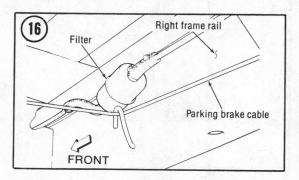

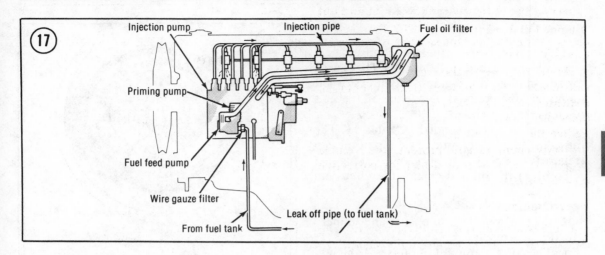

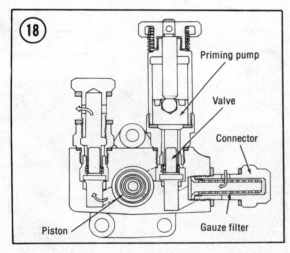

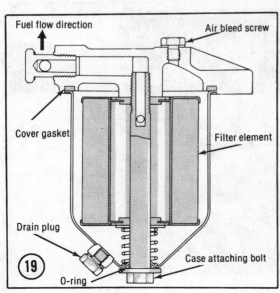

Replace the filter element as follows:

1. Place a pan beneath the drain plug (**Figure 19**). Remove the plug and let the fuel drain.

2. Remove the case attaching bolt and take the case off.

3. Clean the inside of the case with solvent.

4. Install the case and new filter element.

5. Loosen the fuel filter petcock or valve. Push the priming pump button on the fuel feed pump. See **Figure 17**. Keep pumping until fuel emerging from the petcock or valve is free of air bubbles.

6. Remove the air bleeder screw at the top of the injection pump.

7. Operate the priming pump until fuel emerging from the bleeder screw hole is free of air bubbles. Tighten the petcock or valve.

8. Install the bleeder screw.

LUBRICATION

Strict adherence to a detailed lubrication schedule is at least as important as timely preventive maintenance. The recommended lubrication schedules (see **Tables 3-8**) are based on average vehicle use — a combination of highway and urban driving with some light-duty off-road use, in moderate weather and climate. Abnormal use, such as mostly off-road use, in dusty and dirty conditions, or in extremely hot or cold climate, requires that the lubrication schedule be modified so that the lubricants are checked and changed more frequently. Capacities of the various systems are given in **Table 9**.

Engine Oil and Filter

If the van is given normal use, change the oil when recommended in **Tables 3-8**. If it is used for stop-and-go driving, in dusty areas or left idling for long periods, change the oil twice as often as recommended.

Use an oil recommended in **Table 11**. The rating (SE) is usually printed on top of the can (**Figure 20**).

To drain the oil and change the filter, you will need:

a. Drain pan

b. Oil can spout or can opener and funnel

c. Filter wrench

d. The correct amount of oil (see **Table 9**)

e. Oil filter (2 filters on diesels)

f. Adjustable wrench for drain plug

There are several ways to discard the old oil safely. The easiest is to pour it from the drain pan into a gallon bleach bottle. The oil can be taken to a service station for recycling or, where permitted, thrown in your household trash.

1. Warm the engine to operating temperature, then shut it off.

2. Put the drain pan under the drain plug (**Figure 21**). Remove the plug and let the oil drain for at least 10 minutes.

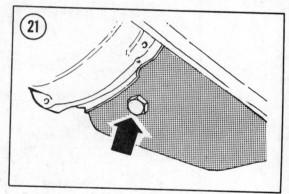

3. If equipped with an engine oil cooler, drain it. If the oil cooler has a drain plug, place the

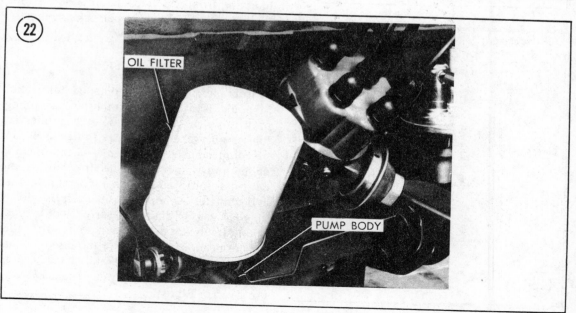

OIL FILTER

PUMP BODY

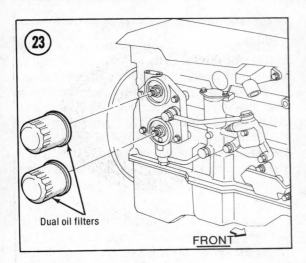

Dual oil filters

FRONT

drain pan beneath it and remove the plug. If the oil cooler doesn't have a drain plug, disconnect the lower cooler hose and place the end of the hose in the drain pan. Let the oil cooler drain for about 5 minutes.

4. Unscrew the oil filter(s) counterclockwise. Use a filter wrench if the filter is too tight to remove by hand. See **Figure 22** (6-cylinder gasoline engines), **Figure 23** (6-cylinder diesel), **Figure 24** (318 and 360 cid V-8) or **Figure 25** (400 and 440 cid V-8).

5. Wipe the gasket surface on the engine block clean with a lint-free cloth.

3

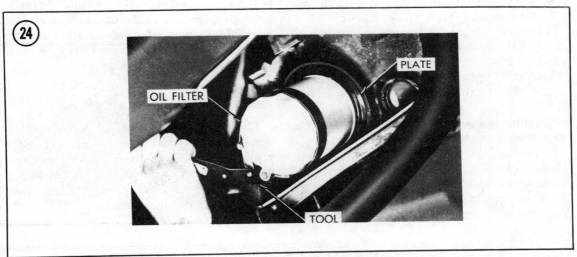

OIL FILTER

PLATE

TOOL

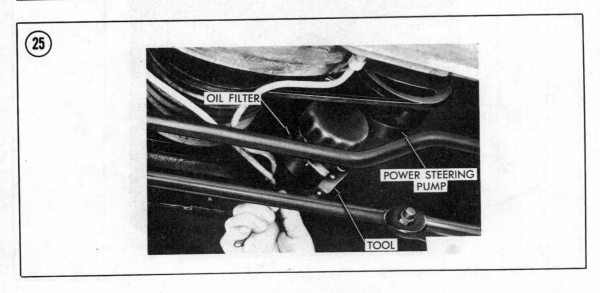

OIL FILTER

POWER STEERING PUMP

TOOL

6. Coat the neoprene gasket on the new filter with clean engine oil.

7. Screw the filter onto the engine *by hand* until the gasket just touches the engine block. At this point, there will be a very slight resistance when turning the filter.

8. Tighten the filter 1/2 turn more *by hand*. If the filter wrench is used, the filter will probably be overtightened. This will cause an oil leak.

9. Install the oil pan drain plug. Tighten it securely. Reinstall the oil cooler drain plug or hose if removed.

10. Remove the oil filler cap.

11. Pour oil into the engine. Capacity is listed in **Table 9**.

12. Start the engine and let it idle. The instrument panel oil pressure light will remain on for 15-30 seconds, then go out.

> *CAUTION*
> *Do not rev the engine to make the oil pressure light go out. It takes time for the oil to reach all areas of the engine and revving it could damage dry parts.*

13. While the engine is running, check the drain plug and oil filter for leaks.

14. Turn the engine off. Let the oil settle for several minutes, then check level on the dipstick (**Figures 2-4**). Add oil if necessary to bring the level up to the "H" mark, but *do not* overfill.

Manual Transmission Oil Change

Prior to draining the transmission, drive the vehicle for several miles to warm the oil so that it will flow freely. Remove the fill/level plug.

Place a drip pan beneath the transmission and unscrew the drain plug (see **Figure 26**). Allow the oil to drain for 10-15 minutes. Clean the drain plug and install it. Tighten the plug firmly but be careful not to overtighten it and risk stripping the threads on the transmission housing.

Refer to **Table 9** and fill the transmission with the correct amount and grade of oil. The transmission oil level is correct when oil just begins to seep out of the fill/level hole. Screw in and tighten the fill/level plug taking care not to overtighten, and wipe excess oil from the outside of the transmission. Check to make sure the drain plug does not leak.

Automatic Transmission Fluid Change

The fluid change interval for automatic transmissions is based on normal use. If the vehicle is operated for more than 50 percent of the time in heavy traffic and in hot weather, if it used to tow a trailer, or if it is used extensively off-road, it is recommended that the fluid be changed more often.

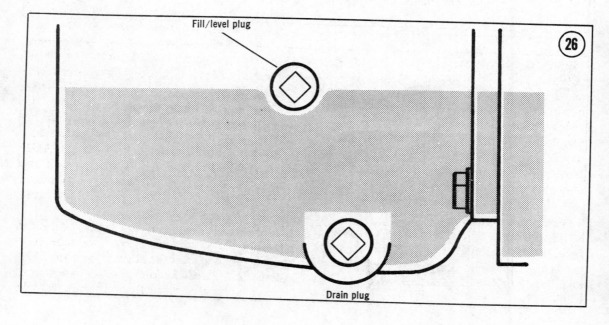

Fill/level plug

26

Drain plug

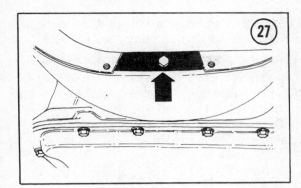

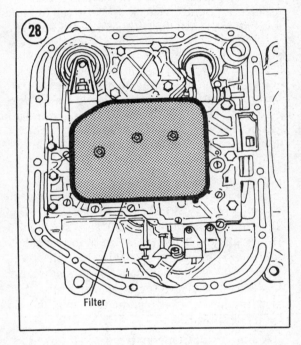

Filter

1. Place a drip pan beneath the transmission and unscrew the drain plug (if fitted), or loosen the oil pan bolts and tap the pan to break it loose. Allow the oil to drain and then unscrew the bolts and remove the pan.

2. Remove the access plate from the bell housing, in front of the torque converter, and unscrew the converter drain bolt (see **Figure 27**). After the converter has finished draining, install the drain bolt and tighten it to 90 in.-lb.

3. Unscrew the screws from the filter (see **Figure 28**), remove the filter, install a new filter and tighten the screws to 35 in.-lb.

4. Thoroughly clean and dry the oil pan and reinstall it using a *new gasket*. Tighten the pan bolts in a crisscross pattern to 150 in.-lb.

5. Using a clean funnel with a fine-mesh filter, pour DEXRON automatic transmission fluid into the transmission through the filler pipe.

On A727 transmissions through 1978, add 6 quarts of DEXRON type automatic transmission fluid. On A435 transmissions through 1978, add 10 quarts of DEXRON type ATF. On all 1979 and later models, add 4 quarts of DEXRON type ATF.

NOTE
Transmission type can be identified by the plate on the side of the transmission.

Start the engine and allow it to idle for several minutes. With the parking brake set and the service brake pedal depressed, move the selector through each of the gear positions, allowing time for engagement. Move the lever back to NEUTRAL.

6. Continue to add fluid, periodically checking the level, until the level is at the ADD ONE PINT mark on the dipstick. Then, allow the engine and transmission to reach operating temperature and recheck the level once again. The level should now be between the ADD ONE PINT and FULL marks. Install the dipstick and make sure it is completely seated and will not permit the entry of dirt and moisture.

7. When the fluid level is correct, check for and correct any leaks at the filler tube connection and around the edge of the pan. Then road test the vehicle to ensure that the transmission operates correctly. After the vehicle

In addition to the fluid change, it is recommended that the filter be changed and the bands adjusted. The filter change is simple; however, adjustment of the bands requires special tools and experience. Therefore, it is recommended that the entire job be entrusted to a dealer or a specialist. In the event that this is not possible or practical, the oil and filter changing procedure is presented.

Prior to draining the transmission, drive the vehicle for several miles to warm up the fluid so it will drain freely. The vehicle must sit level during draining and filling. If a hoist or a pit is not available, a mechanic's "creeper" will be helpful for working beneath the vehicle.

has been driven about 125 miles, check the level once again and correct it if necessary.

Rear Axle Oil Level Check

The oil level in the axle differential should be checked and corrected if necessary every 2,000-4,000 miles of road use, every 1,000 miles of off-road use, and daily if the vehicle is operated in deep water. (In this instance, the check is essential to determine if water has entered the axle, in which case, the contaminated oil must be drained and the axle filled with fresh oil.)

The vehicle must be sitting level when the axle oil level is checked. Wipe the area around the fill/level plug clean. Unscrew the fill/level plug from the differential case (see **Figure 29** or **Figure 30**). If the level is correct, a small amount of oil will begin to seep out of the hole. If it does not, slowly add oil to correct the level.

When delivered from the factory, all conventional differentials are filled with SAE 90 multipurpose gear lubricant. This lubricant is recommended for a temperature range from -10° F to 90° F (see **Table 11**). If this lubricant is not satisfactory for the prevailing temperature in which the vehicle is operated, the differentials must be drained and the correct lubricant used (see *Rear Axle Oil Change* below).

NOTE
In addition to the level, also check the condition of the oil for signs of water. If water is present, the differentials must be drained, the covers removed, the differentials cleaned, and the covers reinstalled using new gaskets.

When the level is correct, screw in and tighten the fill/level plug and wipe any excess oil from the outside of the differential case.

Rear Axle Oil Change

Prior to draining the oil from the differential, drive the vehicle for several miles to warm up the oil so it will flow freely. With the vehicle sitting level, wipe the area around the fill/level

plug clean and unscrew the plug. Remove the old oil with a suction pump. See **Figure 31**.

Refer to **Table 11** and fill the differential with the appropriate type of hypoid gear lubricant until the oil level reaches the bottom of the fill/level hole and just begins to seep out. Then install the fill/level plug and tighten it securely. Wipe any spilled oil from the differential housing.

After the vehicle has been driven for about 100 miles, check for and correct any leaks. If leakage is found, recheck and correct the oil level after the leak has been corrected.

Chassis Lubrication

Complete chassis lubrication should be performed at the intervals shown in **Tables 3-8**. For extensive off-road use, the interval should be every 1,000 miles, and if the vehicle is operated in deep water, chassis lubrication should be attended to daily.

Lubrication points and fittings for all models are covered in **Figure 32A**, **Figure 32B**, **Figure 33A** and **Figure 33B**. Recommended lubricants are also shown. If Mopar marketed lubricants are not available, equivalent lubricants available through most major oil companies can be substituted. However, make sure the oil dealer knows the specific application so that he can recommend a suitable substitute.

A simple hand-operated grease gun like the one shown in **Figure 34** is a worthwhile investment, particularly if the vehicle is used extensively off-road and in mud, snow, and water.

Do not overlook items such as gear selector linkage, clutch linkage (see **Figure 35**), parking brake linkage, speedometer cable, and the steering gearbox. Lack of lubrication on these items will make control operation difficult in addition to causing premature wear. However, lubricants should be used sparingly and excess oil should be wiped away to prevent it from attracting dirt which will also accelerate wear. Recommended lubricants for the points mentioned are shown in **Figure 32** and **Figure 33**.

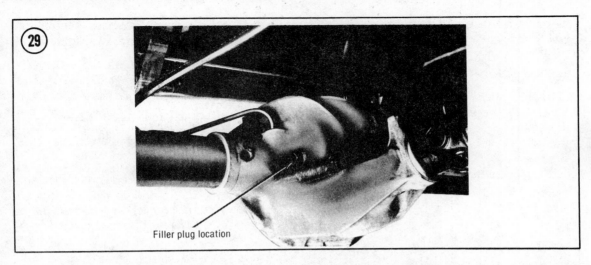

Filler plug location

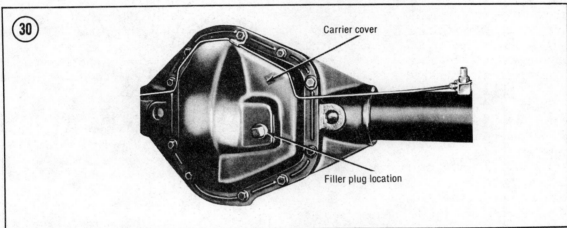

Carrier cover

Filler plug location

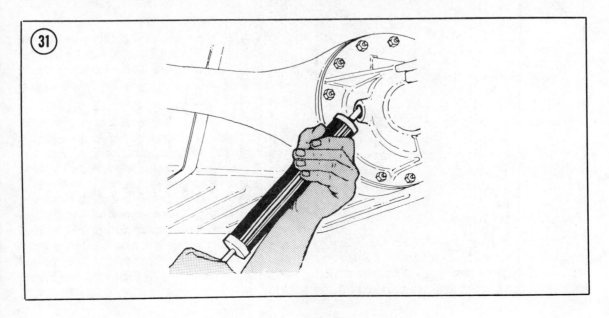

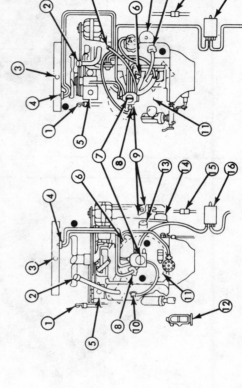

32 A

LUBRICATION CHART — B/PB SERIES VANS
1971-1974

FREQUENCY SYMBOLS

(2)—2,000 miles or 2 months
(4)—4,000 miles or 3 months
(6)—Every 6 months
(12)—12,000 miles or 12 months
(20)—Every 20,000 miles
(24)—24,000 miles or 24 months
(32)—Every 32,000 miles
(R)—Refer to procedure (this group)

ENGINE

Engine Coolant—Check level when refueling.
● Drain Locations
1. Crankcase Dipstick—Check oil level when refueling.
2. Oil Filler Cap
3. Radiator Cap (16 psi)
4. Temperature Control Valve✳
5. Power Steering Pump PSF—(4) Check fluid level.
6. Orifice Spark Advance Control (OSAC) Valve✳
7. Carburetor Choke Shaft CC (4) Apply solvent.
8. EGR Control Valve✳
9. Manifold Heat Valve—S (6) Apply solvent.
10. PCV Valve—(R) Check function.
11. Carburetor Air Cleaner (R) Clean every other oil change.
12. Master Cylinder—BF (4) Check fluid level.
13. Crankcase Inlet Air Cleaner—(R) Check function.
14. Oil Filter—Replace every second oil change.
15. Fuel Filter—(24) Replace.
16. Fuel Vapor Storage Canister✳

✳ Emission Control System Maintenance

3

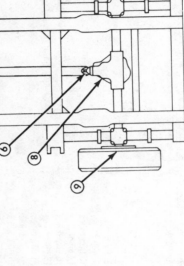

LUBRICATION CHART—B/PB SERIES VANS 1971-1974

CHASSIS

1. **Steering Linkage Ball-joints—MG (4)** Lubricate.

2. **Front Suspension Ball-joints—MG (4)** Inspect; **(24)** Relubricate (Off-highway operation)—**MG (4)** Relubricate.

3. **Front Wheel Bearings and Brakes MG (12)** Lubricate bearings during brake inspection.

4. **Clutch Torque Shafts and Bellcrank MG (4)** Lubricate.

5. **Transmission (Manual)—ATF or MPO (4)** Check fluid level; **(32)** Drain and refill.

5. **Transmission (Automatic) ATF (4)** Check fluid level; **ATF (20 or 32) (R)** Drain and refill.

6. **Universal Joints (4)** Inspect seals for leakage.

7. **Slip Spline (145 in. Wheelbase) MG (4)** Lubricate.

8. **Rear Axle/Sure-Grip—HL or SGL (4)** Check fluid level: 8⅜ in.—Maintain level ⅛-¼ in. below filler plug; 8¾ in. and Spicer 60—Maintain level to bottom of filler plug.

9. **Rear Wheel Bearings—MG (R)**
   Semi-floating: Lubricate when axle shafts are removed.
   Full-floating: Inspect lubricant every 12 months or 50,000 miles.

TIRE PRESSURES—Shown on decal of body pillar, left side.

KEY TO LUBRICANTS

PSF = Power steering fluid
CC = Carburetor cleaner
S = Manifold heat valve solvent
EO = Engine oil
BF = Brake fluid conforming to DOT 3
MG = Multipurpose grease NLGI Grade 2 E.P.
MPG = Mopar multipurpose grease (or equivalent)
MPO = Multipurpose gear oil (API-GL5)
ATF = Dexron type automatic transmission fluid
HL = Hypoid lubricant (except Sure-Grip)
SGL = Sure-Grip lubricant

FREQUENCY SYMBOLS

EOC—Engine oil change periods (all)—Every 6,000 miles or 6 months GVW

LDC—Light duty emission cycle (vehicles 6,000 GVW or less or 8,500 or less for California)

HDC—Heavy duty emission cycle (vehicles over 6,000 GVW or over 8,500 for California)

6—Every 6 months

6/12—6 months or 12,000 miles

12—12,000 miles

12/12—12 months or 12,000 miles

15—15,000 miles

18—18,000 miles

24—24,000 miles

30—30,000 miles

36—36,000 miles

48—48,000 miles

TIRE PRESSURES

Shown on decal on body pillar, left side

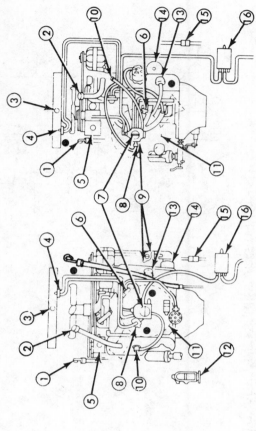

VAN LUBRICATION AND MAINTENANCE 1975 AND LATER

ENGINE

Engine Coolant (12/12) Inspect service

● **Drain Locations**

1. Crankcase Dipstick—Check oil level when refueling.
2. Oil Filler Cap EO
3. Radiator Cap (16 psi)
4. Temperature Control Valve (CCEGR)*
5. Power Steering Pump PSF (EOC) Check fluid level.
6. Orifice Spark Advance Control (OSAC) Valve*
7. Carburetor Choke Shaft CC (6/12) Apply solvent.
8. EGR Control Valve*
9. Manifold Heat Valve—S (30 LDC or 18 HDC)
10. PCV Valve (12 HDC—Check—24 Replace)
    (15 LDC—Check—30 Replace)
11. Carburetor Air Cleaner (12 HDC—Clean—24 Replace)
    (30 LDC Replace)
12. Master Cylinder—BF (EOC) Check fluid level.
13. Crankcase Inlet Air Cleaner—Check function*
    (clean 30 LDC or 12/12 HDC)
14. Oil Filter—Replace (first oil change) then every second oil change.
15. Fuel Filter—(30 LDC or 18 HDC) Replace
16. Fuel Vapor Storage Canister* (15 LDC or 18 HDC)

* See Emisssion Control Systems

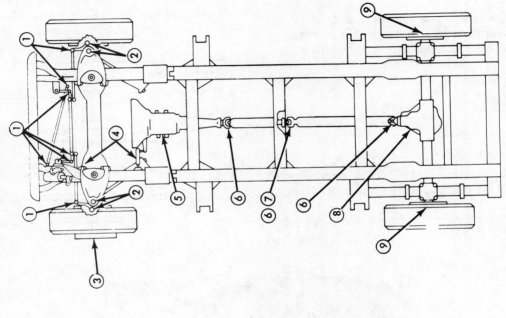

33 B

VAN LUBRICATION AND MAINTENANCE 1975 AND LATER

CHASSIS

1. **Steering Linkage Ball-joints—MG (EOC)** Lubricate.
2. **Front Suspension Ball-joints—MG (6)** Inspect; (24) Re-lubricate.
   (Off-highway Operation)—MG (EOC) Re-lubricate.
3. **Front Wheel Bearings and Brakes MG (All 24-minimum)** Lubricate bearings, also during brake inspection or service.
4. **Clutch Torque Shaft and Bellcrank MG (EOC)** Lubricate.
5. **Transmission (Manual)—ATF or MPO (EOC)** Check fluid level; (36) Drain and refill.
5. **Transmission (Automatic) ATF (EOC)** Check fluid level. ATF (24) Drain and refill—(12) for MB models.
6. **Universal Joints MPG (6)** Inspect seals for leakage.
7. **Slip Spline (145 in. Wheelbase) MG (6/6)** Lubricate.
8. **Rear Axle—HL (EOC)** Check for leakage— All maintain fluid level to bottom of filler plug opening.
   (36) Replace fluid—for anti-spin also add 4 oz. FM.
9. **Rear Wheel Bearings—MG**
   Semi-floating: Lubricate when axle shafts are removed.
   Full-floating: Inspect lubricant every 12 months or 48,000 miles.

KEY TO LUBRICANTS

CC = Carburetor cleaner
PSF = Power steering fluid
S = Manifold heat valve solvent
EO = Engine oil
FM = Friction modifier (P/N) 4057100 or equivalent
BF = Brake fluid conforming to DOT 3
MG = Multipurpose grease NLGI Grade 2 E.P.
MPG = MOPAR multipurpose grease (or equivalent)
MPO = Multipurpose gear oil
ATF = DEXRON type automatic transmission fluid
HL = Hypoid lubricant (API-GL5)

Body Lubrication

Door, hood, and tailgate hinges and latches, and front seat tracks should be lubricated every six months to ensure smooth operation and to reduce wear. Recommended lubricants are shown in **Table 12**.

Apply lubricant sparingly, operating the mechanism several times to aid penetration. Then, wipe off the excess lubricant with a clean, dry cloth to prevent it from attracting dirt and from soiling clothing, carpeting, and upholstery.

Steering Gear Oil

The oil level in 1971-1973 steering gears should be checked at the intervals shown in **Table 3** and corrected if necessary. Lubrication is not required on later models.

1. Unscrew the fill plug from the sector shaft cover (see **Figure 36**). The lubricant should be visible in the fill plug opening.

2. If lubricant must be added, use SAE 90 multipurpose gear oil. In extremely cold climates SAE 80 may be used. Add sufficient lubricant to raise the level to the top of the fill plug opening and install the fill plug.

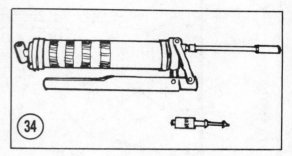

(34)

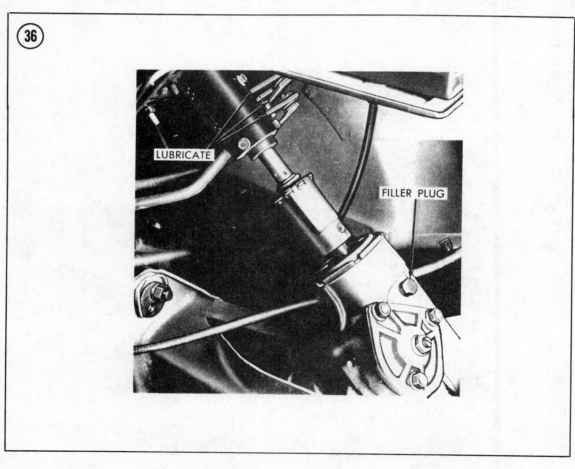

(36)

LUBRICATE

FILLER PLUG

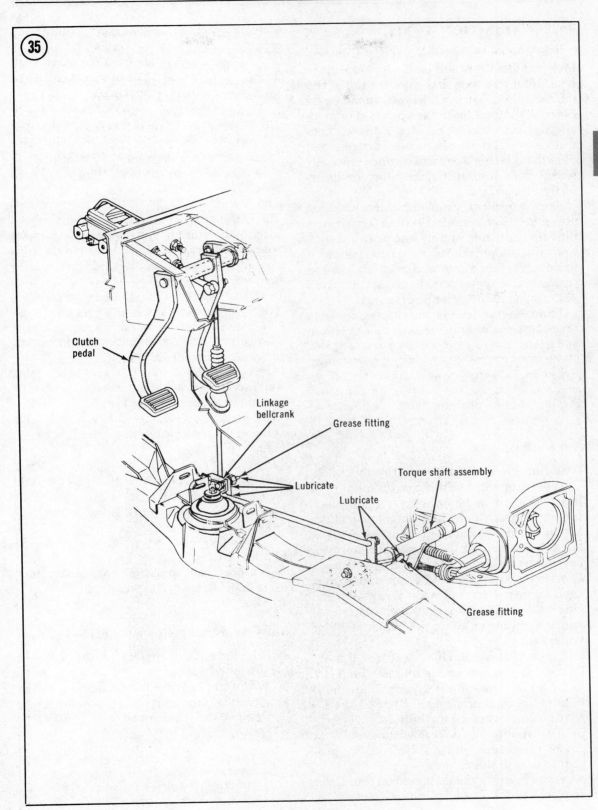

35

3

Clutch
pedal

Linkage
bellcrank

Grease fitting

Torque shaft assembly

Lubricate

Lubricate

Grease fitting

IGNITION TUNE-UP

The tune-up consists of a series of inspections, adjustments, and parts replacements to compensate for wear and deterioration of certain engine components. Regular tune-ups are especially important to the operation of modern high performance engines. Emission control systems, improved electrical systems, and other advances make these engines especially sensitive to improperly operating or incorrectly adjusted parts.

Since proper engine operation depends upon a number of interrelated system functions, a tune-up consisting of only one or two corrections will seldom get lasting results. Instead, a thorough, systematic procedure of analysis and correction will pay dividends in improved performance and operating economy.

Table 9, at the end of the chapter, contains tune-up specifications. Before using these specifications, check your engine compartment to determine if a Vehicle Emission Control Information sticker is present. If so, use the information contained on the sticker, as it pertains specifically to your engine.

Tune-up Sequence

During the periods covered by this book, Chrysler Corporation produced a number of different size 6- and 8- cylinder engines, which use both breaker point and electronic ignition systems. The sequence of tune-up steps given below may be used for all models; however, exceptions are noted wherever they occur.

1. Clean battery top and clean and tighten cable connections. Add water if required, and check the specific gravity of each battery cell with a hydrometer. Refer to Chapter Eight for battery tests.
2. Tighten intake manifold bolts to 20 ft.-lb. (2.8 mkg) for 6-cylinder and 40-50 ft.-lb. (5.5-6.9 mkg) for V-8's. Tighten cylinder head bolts in the appropriate pattern (see **Figure 37**) to the torque specified in **Table 14**.
3. If 6-cylinder valve mechanism is noisy or engine runs rough, adjust valve lash. See procedure later in this chapter.
4. Perform a cylinder compression test. Refer to *Compression Test* later in this chapter.

5. Clean or replace spark plugs, depending on service interval. Refer to *Spark Plug Replacement* in this chapter.
6. Check spark plug and coil secondary cables for resistance. Refer to *Cable Resistance Check* procedure in this chapter.
7A. On engines with breaker point ignition systems, inspect points, primary wire, and vacuum advance operation. Replace parts as required. Refer to *Breaker Point Adjustment* procedure in this chapter for necessary adjustments.
7B. On engines equipped with the Chrysler Electronic Ignition system, inspect primary wire and vacuum advance operation. Distributor adjustments are not required for a routine tune-up.
8. Reset ignition timing. Refer to *Ignition Timing* procedure later in this chapter.
9. Clean the carburetor air cleaner element with compressed air. Replace the filter at intervals specified in **Tables 3-8**.
10. Set carburetor idle mixture adjustment. Refer to *Idle Mixture Adjustment* procedure for your carburetor in Chapter Five.
11. Check fuel pump for pressure and volume. Refer to *Fuel Pump Checks* in Chapter Five.
12. Verify that manifold heat control valve is operating freely. Lubricate bushing and shaft with penetrating lubricant such as manifold heat control valve solvent, Chrysler part No. 3419129 or equivalent.
13. Inspect crankcase ventilation system. See Chapter Six.
14. Inspect and adjust all engine accessory drive belts. Refer to Chapter Seven.
15. Road-test the van.

Valve Adjustment (Gasoline Engines)

This procedure applies to the 225 cid 6-cylinder engine only.
1. Warm the engine to normal operating temperature, then let it idle for 5 minutes.
2. Remove the valve cover.

NOTE
To reduce oil splatter during the next step, cut the top off an old valve cover and install it on the engine. Be sure to remove all sharp edges.

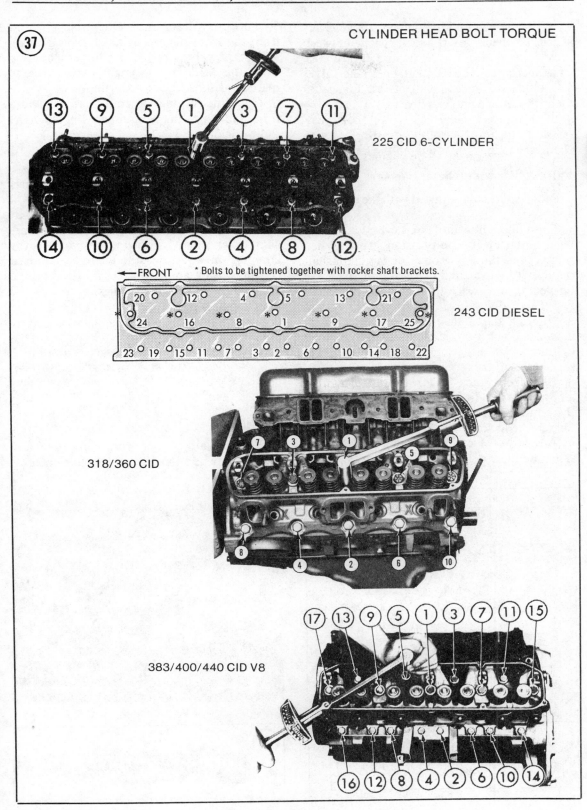

37

CYLINDER HEAD BOLT TORQUE

225 CID 6-CYLINDER

← FRONT   * Bolts to be tightened together with rocker shaft brackets.

243 CID DIESEL

318/360 CID

383/400/440 CID V8

3

3. With the engine idling, check valve clearances. To check, insert a feeler gauge between valve stem and rocker arm (**Figure 38**). Clearance should be 0.010 in. on intake valves and 0.020 in. on exhaust valves. **Figure 39** identifies intake and exhaust valves.

4. If clearance is incorrect, loosen the adjusting screw locknut. Turn the adjusting screw to change clearance, then tighten the locknut.

Valve Adjustment (Diesel Engine)

Diesel valves are adjusted with the engine off and cold.

1. Turn the engine until No. 1 cylinder is at top dead center on its compression stroke. When this occurs, the key groove in the crankshaft pulley will be straight up. In addition, there will be clearance between both No. 1 rocker arms and their valve stems.

2. Insert a 0.012 in. (0.3 mm) feeler gauge between a rocker arm and valve stem on No. 1 cylinder. See **Figure 40**. The feeler gauge should fit with a very slight drag.

3. If the feeler gauge fits loosely or doesn't fit at all, loosen the adjusting screw's locknut. Turn the adjusting screw to change clearance, then tighten the locknut.

4. Adjust No. 1 cylinder's other valve in the same manner.

5. Turn the crankshaft clockwise (viewed from the front of the engine) 120° (1/3 turn). Adjust the valves for No. 5 cylinder (counting from the front of the engine) in the same manner as those for No. 1 cylinder.

6. Continue turning the crankshaft, 120° at a time, and adjust the remaining cylinders in the following order: 3-6-2-4.

Compression Test

This procedure applies to gasoline engines only. Testing diesel compression requires a special adapter for the glow plug holes (part No. 31391-11101, **Figure 41**). The compression tester must be able to screw onto the adapter. In addition, the diesel's standard compression reading of 426 psi is beyond the range of most compression testers.

1. Remove all spark plugs.

NOTE
Use compressed air, if available, to remove all foreign matter from spark plug wells prior to removal. If compressed air is not available, use a tire pump or a vacuum cleaner. A small paintbrush will also serve.

2. Remove air cleaner from carburetor and block choke and throttle valves wide open.

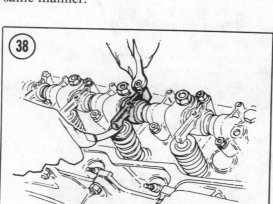

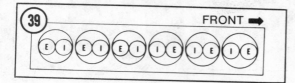

FRONT ➡

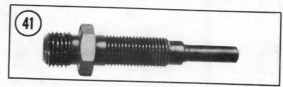

3. Remove the distributor primary lead wire from the negative post of the ignition coil.

4. Connect a remote starter button, using the manufacturer's instructions. If a remote starter is not available, have an assistant crank the engine, when required, from the driver's seat.

4. Install a compression gauge in the No. 1 cylinder (see **Figure 42**) and crank the engine through at least 4 compression strokes to obtain the hightest possible reading. Record the reading and repeat the step for each cylinder in turn.

> *NOTE*
> *The No. 1 cylinder is the one nearest the front of the vehicle. On V-8 engines observe that one bank of cylinders is offset closer to the front than the other. The No. 1 cylinder is in the closer bank.*

6. Check the readings against the specifications (100 psi minimum, with no more than 25 psi variation between highest and lowest cylinder reading on 6-cylinder engines, or 40 psi variations on V-8's). If one or more cylinders is below the minimum limit, the engine needs repairs. If there is more than the allowable variation between the lowest and highest readings, the engine cannot be properly tuned.

> *NOTE*
> *If all readings were above the specified minimum, and the variations between cylinders were within the specified tolerance, the remaining step may be omitted.*

7. Inject about a tablespoon of engine oil through the spark plug hole of each low-reading cylinder. Crank the engine through several compression strokes and then take another compression reading. If compression increases, the problem usually is worn rings. If no improvement is noted, valves are probably burned, sticking, or not seating properly.

> *NOTE*
> *If 2 adjacent cylinders read low and oil injection does not increase compression, the problem may be a defective head gasket.*

Spark Plug Replacement

1. Remove spark plugs and compare them to the illustrations in Chapter Two. Spark plug condition is an indication of engine condition.

2. Make sure all plugs to be installed are of the proper heat range (see **Table 13**, end of the chapter).

3. Measure spark plug gap with a wire gauge (**Figure 43** or **Figure 44**). The gauge should fit through with a very light drag. Adjust if necessary by bending the side electrode with the gapping tool. See **Figure 45**.

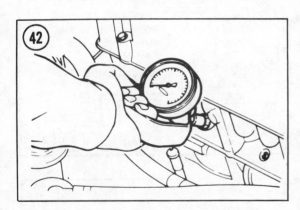

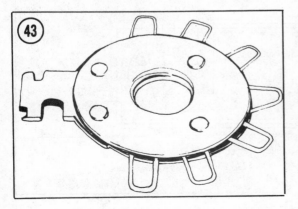

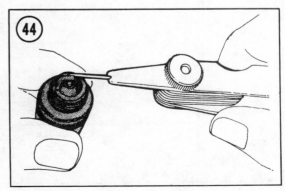

NOTE
Always adjust gap by bending the negative or side (never the center) electrode. Never adjust by tapping the electrode on a hard surface; this can damage the porcelain insulator.

4. Inspect the threads in the spark plug hole and clean if necessary.

NOTE
A 14 mm thread chaser can be used to remove corrosion, carbon buildup or minor flaws from the threads. Coat chaser with grease to catch chips or foreign matter. Use care to avoid cross threading.

5. Crank engine several times to blow out any dislodged material.

6. Coat spark plug threads lightly with engine oil—a drop from the dipstick will do—and install them in the cylinder head. Tighten

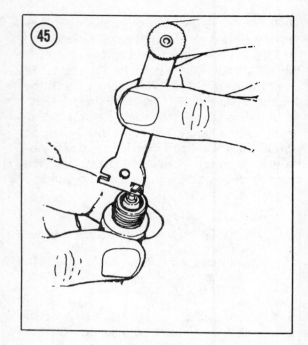

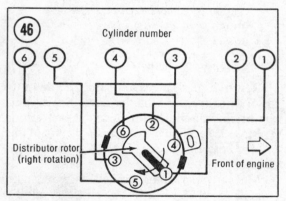

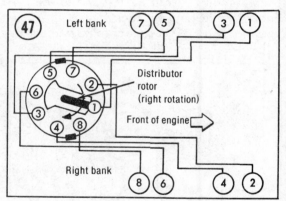

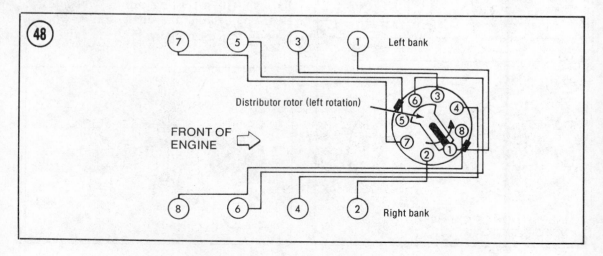

plugs to 30 ft.-lb. (4.15 mkg) on all V-8 engines and on 1971-1974 6-cylinder engines. Tighten plugs to 10 ft.-lb. (1.4 mkg) on 1975 and later 6-cylinder engines.

7. Reconnect the plug wires. To identify terminals, see **Figure 46** (6-cylinder), **Figure 47** (318-360 V-8) or **Figure 48** (400-440 V-8).

Distributor Cap, Wires and Rotor

1. Remove the distributor cap and wires as an assembly.

2. Check the cap and wires for visible defects. See **Figure 49**. Replace as needed.

3

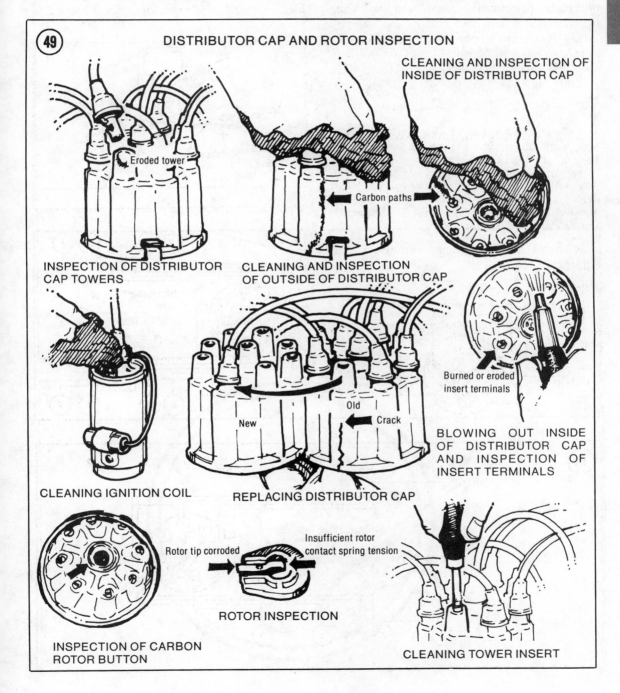

(49) DISTRIBUTOR CAP AND ROTOR INSPECTION

CLEANING AND INSPECTION OF INSIDE OF DISTRIBUTOR CAP

Eroded tower

Carbon paths

INSPECTION OF DISTRIBUTOR CAP TOWERS

CLEANING AND INSPECTION OF OUTSIDE OF DISTRIBUTOR CAP

Burned or eroded insert terminals

Old

New   Crack

CLEANING IGNITION COIL

REPLACING DISTRIBUTOR CAP

BLOWING OUT INSIDE OF DISTRIBUTOR CAP AND INSPECTION OF INSERT TERMINALS

Rotor tip corroded   Insufficient rotor contact spring tension

ROTOR INSPECTION

INSPECTION OF CARBON ROTOR BUTTON

CLEANING TOWER INSERT

3. If an ohmmeter is available, measure plug wire resistance (**Figure 50**). If more than 50,000 ohms, remove the wire from the cap and test it again. If still more than 50,000 ohms, replace the wire. If less than 50,000 ohms, replace the distributor cap.

4. To test coil wire resistance, connect the ohmmeter between the center terminal inside the distributor cap and one of the primary (thin wire) terminals on the coil. If resistance is more than 25,000 ohms, remove the wire and test again. If resistance is more than 15,000 ohms, replace the wire. If it is less, check for a loose connection or defective ignition coil.

5. Connect the wires to the distributor cap and spark plugs. See **Figure 46** (6-cylinder), **Figure 47** (318-360 V-8) or **Figure 48** (400-440 V-8).

Breaker Point Replacement and Adjustment
Single Point Distributor

1. Remove distributor cap and rotor. See **Figure 51**.

> *NOTE*
> *Do not remove wires from cap.*

2. Loosen point plate lockscrew and remove point set and condenser.

3. Remove all old grease from cam with a clean cloth and apply a small amount of fresh lubricant.

4. Install new point set and condenser. Verify that points are properly aligned (see **Figure 52**). Bend fixed contact to align. Turn engine over until point rubbing block is resting on the highest point of a cam lobe. See **Figure 53**.

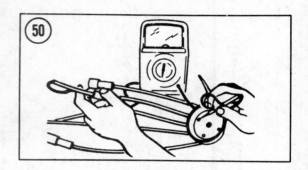

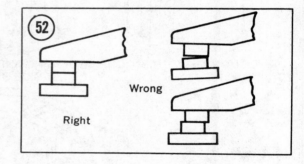

Right   Wrong

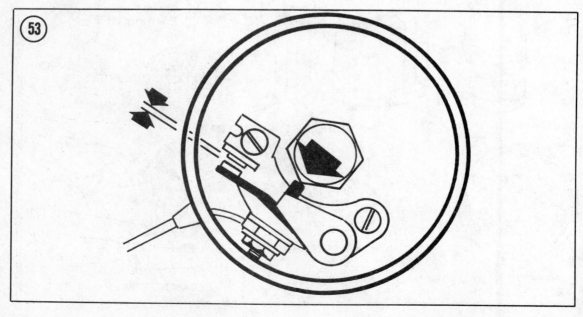

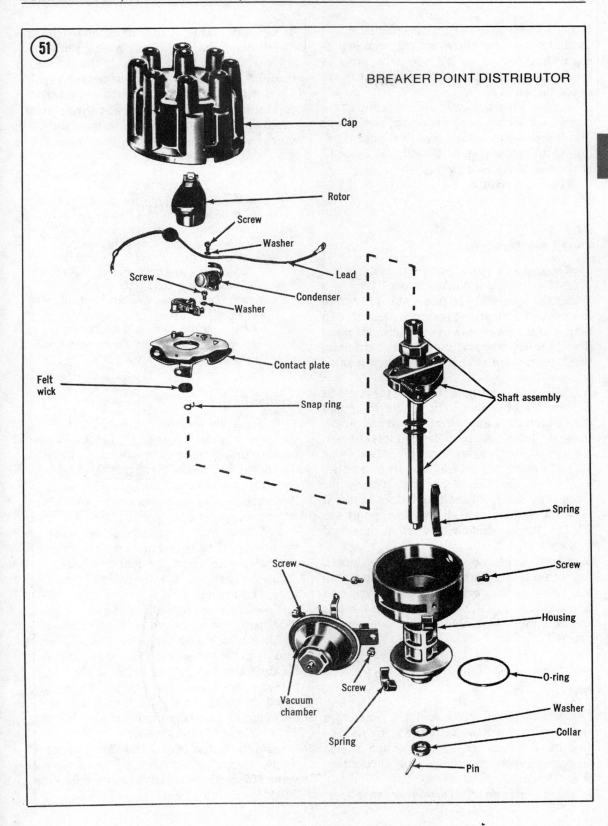

51

BREAKER POINT DISTRIBUTOR

3

Cap

Rotor

Screw

Washer

Lead

Screw

Condenser

Washer

Contact plate

Felt wick

Snap ring

Shaft assembly

Spring

Screw

Screw

Housing

O-ring

Vacuum chamber

Screw

Spring

Washer

Collar

Pin

Using a feeler gauge of the specified size (see **Table 13**, end of chapter), set the point gap. A slight drag should be felt when the gauge is removed. Tighten the locking screws and recheck the gap.

5. Replace distributor cap and rotor and check dwell angle with a dwell meter. See *Distributor Dwell* procedure below. Readjust gap, if required, to obtain specified dwell. See **Table 13** at the end of the chapter.

6. Road-test vehicle.

Dual Point Distributor

1. Remove and install point sets as described above for single point distributors.

2. Set the specified gap (see **Table 13**, end of chapter) on both sets of points, as described in Step 4 of the procedure above for single point distributors. Make sure the rubbing block is on the highest point of a cam lobe when making adjustments.

3. Place a clean insulator between the contacts on one set of points, replace the rotor and distributor cap, and check the dwell angle, using the procedure given later in this chapter. Verify that dwell angle is as specified (see **Table 13**, end of the chapter) for "one set of points."

4. Remove distributor cap and remove the clean insulator from the contacts and place it between the contacts of the other point set. Replace the cap and check dwell as described in Step 3.

5. After dwell has been individually adjusted for both sets of points, remove distributor cap and remove clean insulator. Replace cap and check dwell angle. Verify that angle meets specifications. See **Table 13** for "both sets of points."

Distributor Dwell

1. Connect dwell meter and tachometer to engine using the manufacturer's instructions.

2. Turn dwell meter selector switch to the proper setting for the engine being checked (6- or 8-cylinder).

3. Disconnect and plug vacuum advance hose.

4. Operate engine at idle speed and observe dwell meter reading. If not within specifications (see **Table 13**, at the end of the chapter), readjust point gap to obtain proper reading.

5. Slowly increase engine speed to 1,500 rpm and observe dwell meter. If reading varies more than 2° from first reading, have distributor checked for wear.

NOTE
Dwell variations of more than 2° at speeds above 1,500 rpm do not necessarily indicate distributor wear. Dwell and point gap must be within their respective specified limits at the same time. If this cannot be accomplished, verify that the correct points were installed. If points are correct, the distributor should be checked by your dealer or a competent mechanic having access to the specialized equipment needed for checking out the distributor.

Ignition Timing

1. Remove the engine cover and locate the timing marks on your engine. They are located on the timing chain cover and the vibration damper at the front of the engine. See **Figure 54** (typical).

2. Obtain timing specification from sticker in engine compartment, or from **Table 13** at the end of the chapter. Locate the proper mark on the timing indicator and mark with white paint or chalk. Also paint the mark on vibration damper. This will greatly assist in making timing adjustments.

3. Connect a timing light to the No. 1 spark plug, using the manufacturer's instructions.

4. Disconnect and plug the vacuum hose leading to the vacuum advance mechanism on the distributor. A golf tee makes a good plug.

5. Start the engine and operate at the idle speed shown in the Vehicle Emission Control Sticker in the engine compartment, or in **Table 13** at the end of the chapter.

6. Aim the timing light at the timing marks. If the ignition is properly timed, the marks will appear to stand still exactly opposite each other under the flashing light.

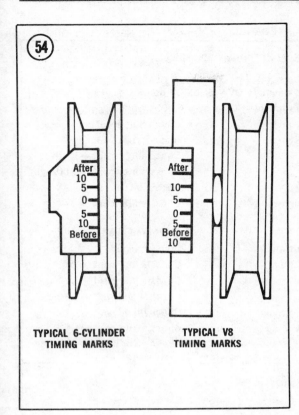

TYPICAL 6-CYLINDER
TIMING MARKS

TYPICAL V8
TIMING MARKS

7. If the timing requires adjustment, loosen the distributor hold-down bolt and turn the distributor body as required to align the timing marks under the flashing timing light. When the timing marks are aligned, tighten the hold-down bolt, recheck the alignment, and stop the engine.

8. Reconnect the vacuum hose to the distributor and remove the timing light.

Carburetor Adjustments

Refer to Chapter Five for carburetor adjustments.

Table 2   BRAKE MATERIAL SERVICE LIMIT

	Service Limit
Disc Brake Lining	1/32 in. above the shoe table or rivet head
Drum Brake Lining Bonded Riveted	1/16 in. 1/32 in. above rivet head

Table 1   TIRE INFLATION CHART

Tire Size Designation	Tire Load Limits at Various Cold Inflation Pressures							
	26	28	30	32	34	36	38	40
BIAS PLY								
E78-15	1130	1180	1230	1270(B)				
F78-15	1220	1270	1320	1370(B)				
G78-15	1310	1370	1420	1470(B)	1530	1570	1620	1670(D)
H78-15	1440	1500	1560	1610(B)				
L78-15	1590	1670	1730	1790(B)	1860	1910	1970	2030(D)
RADIAL PLY								
HR78-15	1590	1500	1560	1610(B)				
LR78-15	1590	1670	1730	1790(B)				

Table 3   SCHEDULED MAINTENANCE (1971-1975)

EVERY ENGINE OIL CHANGE (100 Through 300 Models)

Engine Oil Change Periods

5,000 miles or 6 months—"light duty cycle," trucks having a GVW of 6,000 pounds or less.

4,000 miles or 6 months—"heavy duty cycle," trucks having a GVW over 6,000 pounds.

Brake master cylinder	Check fluid level
Carburetor air cleaner (oil bath)	Inspect ③
Clutch torque shaft	Chassis lubricant—1 fitting
Drag link ball-joint	Chassis lubricant—2 fittings
Engine oil change	Engine oil ②
Front suspension ball-joints (all models used for off-highway type operation)	Chassis lubricant
Parking brake control leveler pivots	Light engine oil
Drive shaft universal joint (not equipped with grease fittings)	Inspect seals
Drive shaft universal joints (if equipped with grease fittings)	Chassis lubricant ① ②
Drive shaft splines (if equipped with grease fittings)	Chassis lubricant ① ②
Rear axles	Check fluid level
Transmission—manual or automatic	Check fluid level
Tie rod ball-joints	Chassis lubricant—4 fittings
	Chassis lubricant—2 fittings

EVERY 6 MONTHS

Carburetor choke shaft and linkage	Clean—solvent

EVERY 8 MONTHS OR 8,000 MILES

Carburetor air cleaner (oil bath)	Inspect

EVERY SECOND OIL CHANGE

Engine oil filter (100 through 300 models—begin filter changes with first oil change)	Replace

EVERY 6 MONTHS OR 10,000 MILES

Air brake camshafts	Chassis lubricant Front—2 fittings Rear—2 fittings

EVERY 12 MONTHS OR 12,000 MILES

Brake booster breather air cleaner (time only)	Replace
Carburetor air cleaner (dry-heavy duty cycle)	Clean element
Crankcase inlet air cleaner, PCV valve and hoses (heavy duty cycle)	Clean, lubricate (see text)
Front wheel bearings (heavy duty cycle)	Clean, lubricate
Rear wheel bearings (full floating—time or during brake service or 50,000 miles)	Inspect—repack

(continued)

Table 3   SCHEDULED MAINTENANCE (1971-1975) (continued)

EVERY 15 MONTHS OR 12,000 MILES	
Crankcase inlet air cleaner	Clean, lubricate

EVERY 15,000 MILES	
Carburetor air cleaner (dry-type—light duty cycle)	Clean element
Front wheel bearings (light duty cycle)	Clean, relubricate ②
Fuel filter (throwaway type—light duty cycle)	Replace
Manifold heat control valve (service cold)	Apply solvent

EVERY 16,000 MILES	
Fuel filter (heavy duty cycle)	Replace

EVERY 20,000 MILES	
Axle differential (100 through 300—severe service)	Drain—refill ②

EVERY 24,000 MILES	
Carburetor air cleaner (dry type—heavy duty cycle)	Replace element
PCV valve (heavy duty cycle)	Replace

EVERY 30,000 MILES	
Axle differential (100 through 300—normal service)	Drain—refill
Carburetor air cleaner (dry type—light duty cycle)	Replace element
Transmission (manual)	Drain—refill ②
(automatic)	Replace fluid, ② filter—adjust bands

① Lubricate every 1,000 miles or every month for severe service and off-highway type operation. Daily if vehicle is operated in water.

② See text for proper lubricant selection.

③ See text for procedure.

Note: Whenever chassis lubricant is specified, multipurpose grease, NLGI grade 2 E.P., should be used.

Table 4   SCHEDULED MAINTENANCE (1976-1978)

EVERY ENGINE OIL CHANGE   (Light Duty Cycle and Heavy Duty Cycle)

* Engine oil change periods (all—normal service) every 6,000 miles (9,600 kilometers) or 6 months, whichever occurs first	Change—also see "Engine Oil Filter"
Brake pedal linkage	Clean—light engine oil
Master cylinder	Check fluid level
Tie rod ball-joints	Chassis lubricant—4 fittings
Center link	Chassis lubricant—1 fitting
Clutch torque shaft	Multipurpose lubricant—1 fitting
Clutch bellcrank	Multipurpose lubricant—1 fitting
Parking brake control lever	Light engine oil, Lubriplate or equivalent
Transmission (manual and automatic)	Check fluid level
Rear axle	Check for leakage
Suspension ball-joints (models used for off-highway operation only)	Chassis lubricant—4 fittings
Power steering pump	Check fluid level
Wheel stops	Mopar Door-Ease (wax) lubricant, Part No. 3744990 or equivalent
Drive shaft slip spline (145 in. wheelbase)	Multipurpose lubricant NLGI grade 2 E.P.—1 fitting

EVERY OTHER ENGINE OIL CHANGE (Light Duty Cycle and Heavy Duty Cycle)

* Engine oil filter (normal service) (begin filter changes with first oil change)	Change
Rubber and plastic components	Inspect
Throttle control linkage	Clean and lubricate

EVERY 6 MONTHS OR 12,000 MILES (19,200 KILOMETERS)

* Carburetor choke valve shaft, fast idle cam, and pivot pin (light duty cycle and heavy duty cycle)	Clean, apply solvent
4-speed overdrive (control mechanism)	Lubricate

EVERY 12 MONTHS OR 12,000 MILES (19,200 KILOMETERS)

* Cooling system (light duty cycle and heavy duty cycle)	Service
* Crankcase inlet air cleaner (heavy duty cycle)	Clean and lubricate

EVERY 12,000 MILES (19,200 KILOMETERS)

* Exhaust gas recirculation (EGR) system (heavy duty cycle—California only)	Check
* Crankcase PCV valve (heavy duty cycle)	Check, clean hoses and passages
	Replace PCV valve if necessary
* Carburetor air cleaner—dry type (heavy duty cycle)	Clean

(continued)

Table 4   SCHEDULED MAINTENANCE (1976-1978) (continued)

Automatic transmission (MB300 and MB400)—normal service	Change fluid and filter, adjust bands
Automatic transmission (models as noted below)	Change fluid and filter, adjust bands
1. Prolonged operation with heavy loading, especially in hot weather (all models)	
2. Vehicle used for off-the-highway operation (all models)	
3. Vehicles used for towing trailers (all models)	
4. Vehicles used for taxi, limousine, bus, and other types of commercial service (Sportsman and Voyager models only)	

EVERY 15,000 MILES (24,000 KILOMETERS)

✱ Rubber and plastic components—emission hoses (light duty cycle)	Inspect
✱ Idle adjustment (light duty cycle)	Check and adjust
✱ Tappet adjustment (light duty cycle)—6-cylinder engines	Check and adjust
✱ Fuel vapor storage canister—carbon filled (light duty cycle)	Replace element
✱ Crankcase PCV valve (light duty cycle)	Check, clean hoses and passages
	Replace PCV valve if necessary

EVERY 18,000 MILES (29,000 KILOMETERS)

✱ Manifold heat control valve (heavy duty cycle—225, 318-1, 360, and 440 CID engines	Check, apply solvent
✱ Idle adjustment (heavy duty cycle)	Check and adjust
✱ Ignition timing (heavy duty cycle)	Check and adjust
✱ Spark plugs (heavy duty cycle)	Check and replace if required
✱ Ignition system (heavy duty cycle)	Check and replace parts as necessary
✱ Tappet adjustment (heavy duty cycle)—6-cylinder engines	Check and adjust
✱ Automatic choke system (heavy duty cycle)—all 6-cylinder and 318-1, 360, and 440 CID engines	Check, clean, and adjust
✱ Fuel filter—paper element throwaway type (heavy duty cycle)	Replace
✱ Drive belts (heavy duty cycle)	Check and adjust, replace if necessary
✱ Rubber and plastic components—emission hoses (heavy duty cycle)	Check and replace if necessary
✱ Fuel vapor storage canister—carbon filled (heavy duty cycle)—California only	Replace element
Manual transmission—severe service	Drain and refill
Rear axle (conventional and limited slip differential)—severe service	Drain and refill

EVERY 24,000 MILES (39,000 KILOMETERS)

✱ Crankcase PCV valve (heavy duty cycle)	Replace
✱ Carburetor air cleaner—dry type (heavy duty cycle)	Replace filter element and wrapper (if so equipped)
Automatic transmission—normal service	Change fluid and filter, adjust bands
Wheel bearings (front)	Inspect and lubricate

(continued)

Table 4   SCHEDULED MAINTENANCE (1976-1978) (continued)

EVERY 2 YEARS OR 24,000 MILES (39,000 KILOMETERS)

Front suspension ball-joints   Lubricate

EVERY 30,000 MILES (48,000 KILOMETERS)

*Crankcase PCV valve (light duty cycle)   Replace

*Crankcase inlet air cleaner (light duty cycle)   Clean and lubricate

*Carburetor air cleaner—dry type (light duty cycle)   Replace filter element and
                                             wrapper (if so equipped)

*Manifold heat control valve (light duty cycle)—225, 318-1, and   Check and apply solvent
    360 CID engines

*Ignition system (light duty cycle)   Check and replace parts
                                          as necessary

*Automatic choke system (light duty cycle)—all 6-cylinder   Check and adjust
    and 318-1 and 360 CID engines

*Fuel filter—paper element throwaway type (light duty cycle)   Replace

*Spark plugs (light duty cycle)   Check and replace if required

EVERY 36,000 MILES (58,000 KILOMETERS)

Manual transmission—normal service   Drain and refill

Rear axle (conventional and limited slip differential)—normal service   Drain and refill

EVERY 12 MONTHS OR 48,000 MILES (77,000 KILOMETERS)

Rear wheel bearings in full-floating rear axles—all except   Inspect, clean, and lubricate
    B100, B200, PB100, and PB200   as required

BODY COMPONENTS — EVERY 6 MONTHS

Lubricate:
- Cargo door hinges
- Hood latch release mechanism
  and safety catch
- Sliding door lower track

- Tailgate release handle (pivot and slide
  contact surfaces)
- Liftgate handle shaft

Lubricate as required:
- Remainder of body components

POINTS NOT LUBRICATED PERIODICALLY

Some points should not be lubricated; either because they are permanently
lubricated, because lubricants will be detrimental to their operating
characteristics, or because lubricants will cause component failure. Rubber
bushings, for example, should not be lubricated because lubrication will
destroy their necessary frictional characteristics. The following parts
should not be lubricated:

- Alternator bearings
- Brake booster cylinder
- Clutch release bearings
- Distributor
- Drive belts
- Fan belt idler pulley bearings
- Front spring shackle bolts and fixed eye bolts
- Drive shaft center bearings
- Rear spring shackle bolts and fixed eye bolts

- Rear wheel bearings (semi-floating axles)
  Models B100-200, PB100-200, D100,
  W100 AD100/AW100
- Rubber bushings
- Starter motor
- Throttle control cable
- Throttle linkage ball-joints
- Water pump—6-cylinder gasoline engines and
  318, 360, and 440 cu. in. V8 gasoline
  engines

*Required emission control maintenance services

Table 5 SCHEDULED MAINTENANCE, 1979
LIGHT DUTY (UNDER 8,500 LB. GVWR)

EVERY 7,500 MILES OR 12 MONTHS	
Engine oil	Change oil filter at first oil change, then at alternate oil changes.
Carburetor choke shaft	Apply solvent
Fast idle cam and pivot pin	Apply solvent

EVERY 15,000 MILES	
Cooling system (D schedule)	Inspect
PCV valve (D schedule)	Inspect, replace as needed
Valve clearances, 6-cylinder engines (D schedule)	Adjust
Curb idle (D schedule)	Adjust
Fuel and emission hoses (D schedule)	Inspect

EVERY 18,000 MILES OR 12 MONTHS	
Cooling system	Drain, flush, and refill

EVERY 22,500 MILES	
Automatic choke (G schedule)	Inspect
Air cleaner element (G schedule)	Replace
Cooling system (G schedule)	Inspect
PCV system air cleaner (G schedule)	Clean
PCV valve (G schedule)	Check, replace as needed
Fuel filter (G schedule)	Replace
Curb idle (G schedule)	Adjust
Ignition system (G schedule)	Inspect
Manifold heat control valve (G schedule)	Apply solvent
Spark plugs	Replace
Valve clearances, 6-cylinder engines (G schedule)	Adjust
Fuel and emission hoses (G schedule)	Inspect
Vapor storage canister filter element	Replace
Drive shaft universal joints	Lubricate
Automatic transmission fluid	Change
Wheel stops	Lubricate
Front wheel bearings	Inspect
Brake linings	Inspect

EVERY 22,500 MILES OR 2 YEARS	
Steering linkage	Lubricate
Front suspension ball-joints	Lubricate
Transmission shift control (4-speed overdrive)	Lubricate
Clutch torque shaft	Lubricate
Parking brake lever pivot	Lubricate

EVERY 30,000 MILES	
Automatic choke (D schedule)	Inspect
Air cleaner element (D schedule)	Replace
PCV system air cleaner (D schedule)	Clean
Fuel filter (D schedule)	Replace
Ignition system (D schedule)	Inspect
Manifold heat control valve (D schedule)	Apply solvent
PCV valve (D schedule)	Replace
Spark plugs (D schedule)	Replace
Vapor storage canister filter element	Replace

EVERY 37,500 MILES	
Manual transmission	Change oil

EVERY 48,000 MILES	
Rear wheel bearings (Spicer axles)	Clean and lubricate

3

Table 6 SCHEDULED MAINTENANCE, 1980
LIGHT DUTY (UNDER 8,500 LB. GVWR)

EVERY 7,500 MILES (12 MONTHS)

Engine oil	Change
Carburetor choke shaft (B schedule)	Apply solvent
Fast idle cam and pivot pin (B schedule)	Apply solvent

EVERY 15,000 MILES

Oil filter	Change (1)
Drive belts	Check and adjust
Curb idle (B schedule)	Adjust
PCV valve (B schedule)	Inspect, replace as needed
Spark plugs (without catalytic converter)	Replace
Valve clearances, 6-cylinder engines	Adjust
Fuel and emission hoses (B schedule)	Inspect
Cooling system	Drain, flush and refill (2)

EVERY 22,500 MILES

Drive shaft universal joints	Lubricate
Automatic transmission	Change fluid
Wheel stops	Lubricate
Brake linings	Inspect

EVERY 22,500 MILES OR 2 YEARS

Steering linkage	Lubricate
Front suspension ball-joints	Lubricate
Transmission shift control (4-speed overdrive)	Lubricate
Automatic transmission	Change fluid
Parking brake lever pivot	Lubricate
Clutch torque shaft	Lubricate

EVERY 30,000 MILES

Automatic choke (B schedule)	Check, adjust as needed
Carburetor choke shaft (A schedule)	Apply solvent
Carburetor air cleaner element	Replace
PCV air cleaner element (B schedule)	Clean
Fuel filter (B schedule)	Replace
Ignition cables (B schedule)	Inspect
Manifold heat control valve (B schedule)	Apply solvent
Spark plugs (with catalytic converter)	Replace
Vapor storage canister filter element	Replace

EVERY 37,500 MILES

Manual transmission	Change oil

EVERY 48,000 MILES

Rear wheel bearings (Spicer axles)	Clean and lubricate

(1) Change filter at first oil change, then at alternate oil changes.
(2) First drain, flush and refill at first 24,000 miles or 2 years, then every 15,000 miles or 12 months.

Table 7 SCHEDULED MAINTENANCE, 1981
LIGHT DUTY (UNDER 8,500 LB. GVWR)

EVERY 7,500 MILES (12 MONTHS)	
Engine oil	Change
Carburetor choke shaft (B schedule)	Apply solvent
Fast idle cam and pivot pin (B schedule)	Apply solvent
Brake hoses	Inspect

EVERY 12 MONTHS	
Cooling system	Inspect

EVERY 15,000 MILES	
Oil filter	Change (1)
Drive belts	Check and adjust
Idle speed (B schedule)	Adjust
PCV valve (B schedule)	Inspect, replace as needed
Spark plugs (without catalytic converter, A and B schedules)	Replace
Fuel and emission hoses (B schedule)	Inspect

EVERY 22,500 MILES	
Drive shaft universal joints	Lubricate
Wheel stops	Lubricate
Brake linings	Inspect

EVERY 22,500 MILES OR 2 YEARS	
Steering linkage	Lubricate
Front suspension balljoints	Lubricate
Transmission shift control (4-speed overdrive)	Lubricate
Parking brake lever pivot	Lubricate

EVERY 30,000 MILES	
Carburetor choke shaft (A, B, and C schedules)	Apply solvent
Carburetor air cleaner element (A and B schedules)	Replace
PCV air cleaner element (B schedule)	Clean
Fuel filter (B schedule)	Replace
Ignition system (B schedule)	Inspect
Manifold heat control valve (B schedule)	Apply solvent
Spark plugs (with catalytic converter)	Replace
Vapor storage canister filter element	Replace
Cooling system	Drain, flush and refill (2)

EVERY 37,500 MILES	
Manual transmission	Change oil
Automatic transmission	Change fluid

EVERY 48,000 MILES	
Rear wheel bearings (Spicer axles)	Clean and lubricate

(1) Change filter at every oil change if the van is driven less than 7,500 miles per year.
(2) First drain, flush and refill at 52,500 miles or 3 years. Then every 30,000 miles or 2 years.

3

Table 8 SCHEDULED MAINTENANCE, 1979-ON
HEAVY DUTY (MORE THAN 8,500 LB. GVWR)

EVERY 6,000 MILES OR 12 MONTHS	
Engine oil	Change
Brake hoses	Inspect

EVERY 12,000 MILES OR 12 MONTHS	
Oil filter	Change (1)
Carburetor choke shaft	Apply solvent
Fast idle cam and pivot pin	Apply solvent
Air cleaner element	Clean
PCV system air cleaner	Clean
PCV valve	Inspect, replace as needed

EVERY 12 MONTHS	
Cooling system	Inspect

EVERY 18,000 MILES	
Automatic choke	Inspect, adjust as needed
Spark plugs	Replace
Ignition timing	Adjust
Curb idle	Adjust
Manifold heat control valve	Apply solvent
Fuel and emission hoses	Inspect

EVERY 24,000 MILES	
Air cleaner element	Replace
PCV valve	Replace
Automatic transmission fluid	Change
Wheel stops	Lubricate
Front wheel bearings	Lubricate
Brake linings	Inspect

EVERY 24,000 MILES OR 2 YEARS	
Steering linkage	Lubricate
Drive shaft universal joints	Lubricate
Front suspension balljoints	Lubricate

EVERY 30,000 MILES OR 2 YEARS	
Cooling system	Drain, flush and refill (2)

EVERY 36,000 MILES	
Manual transmission oil	Change

EVERY 48,000 MILES	
Rear wheel bearings (Spicer axles)	Clean, lubricate

(1) Replace at first oil change, then at alternate oil changes.
(2) Drain, flush, and refill at first 48,000 or 3 years, then every 30,000 miles or 2 years.

Table 9 APPROXIMATE REFILL CAPACITIES

Engine oil (less filter)			
Engine	U.S. quarts	Liters	Imperial quarts
All gasoline	5	4.7	4 1/4
243 diesel	7	6.6	5 3/4
Cooling system			
Engine size	U.S. quarts	Liters	Imperial quarts
225 (1)			
1971-1978	13	12.3	10 3/4
1979-on	12	11.4	10
243 diesel	13	12.3	10 3/4
318 (1)			
1971-1978	17	16	14 1/4
1979-on	16	15.2	13 1/4
360 (2)			
1971-1978	16	15.2	13 1/4
1979-on	14 1/2	13.8	12
400	15 1/2	14.7	13
440 (2)			
1971-1978	15 1/2	14.7	13
1979	14 1/2	13.8	12
Rear axle			
Size	U.S. pints	Liters	Imperial pints
8 3/8 in. (Chrysler)	4 1/2	2.12	3 3/4
9 1/4 in. (Chrysler)	4 1/2	2.12	3 3/4
9 3/4 in. (Spicer 60)	6	2.84	5
10 1/2 in. (Spicer 70)	6 1/2	3.07	5 1/2
Transmission			
Type	U.S. pints	Liters	Imperial pints
Manual			
745	3 1/4	1.5	2 3/4
A-230	4 1/4	2	3 1/2
A250	4 1/2	2.1	3 3/4
435	7	3.3	5 3/4
A-390	3 1/2	1.7	3
445D	7 1/2	3.5	6 1/4
Overdrive-4	7 1/2	3/5	6 1/4
Automatic	See text		

(1) Add one quart for air conditioning or increased cooling.
(2) On 1971-1978 models, add one quart for air conditioning or increased cooling. On 1979 and later models with optional heavy-duty cooling systems, add one quart on 360-3 or 440-3 engines. Add 2 quarts on 360-1 and 440-1 engines.

3

Table 10 RECOMMENDED ENGINE OIL GRADES (SAE)

Engine	API service SE
Gasoline engines	
Above 32° F (0° C)	30, 40
Above 10° F (-12° C)	20W-40, 20W-50
Above -10° F (-23° C)	10W-30, 10W-40, 10W-50
10-80° F (-12-+27° C)	20W-20
-10-+80° F (-23-+27° C)	10W
Below 80° F (27° C)	5W-20*, 5W-30, 5W-40
Diesel engines	
Above 32° F (0° C)	30, 40
Above 10° F (-12° C)	20W-40, 20W-50
10-60° F (-12-+16° C)	20W-20
All temperatures	10W-30, 10W-40, 10W-50

*5W-20 not recommended for sustained high speed driving.

Table 11 LUBRICANTS AND FLUIDS

Manual transmissions	
A230 3-speed	DEXRON ATF (1)
745	SAE 50 engine oil (2)
435 4-speed	SAE 50 engine oil (2)
A390 3-speed	DEXRON ATF (1)
445-D 4-speed	SAE 50 engine oil (2)
Overdrive 4-speed	SAE 50 engine oil (2)
Automatic transmission	DEXRON ATF
Rear axle	
Type of lubricant	Multipurpose gear oil, API GL-5
Viscosity	
Above 90° F (32° C)	SAE 140, SAE 80W-140, SAE 85W-140
As low as -10° F (-23° C)	SAE 90, SAE 80W-90,
	SAE 80W-140, SAE 85W-140
Below -10° F (-23° C)	SAE 75W, SAE 75W-90,
	SAE 80W, SAE 80W-140
Antifreeze	Ethylene glycol base
Brake fluid	DOT 3
Power steering fluid	Dexron type

(1) If gear rattle is heard during idle or acceleration, use one of the following oils: SAE 90, 75W, 75W-80, 80W-90, or 85W-90 gear oil.
(2) If SAE 50 motor oil is not available, use one of the following oils:

Type	Multipurpose gear oil, API GL-5
Viscosity	
Above 90° F (32° C)	SAE 140
As low as -10° F (-23° C)	SAE 90
Below -10° F (-23° C)	SAE 80

Table 12 BODY LUBRICANTS

Component	Lubricant
All door hinges	Lubriplate ①
Door latches, rotors and strikers	Lubriplate ①
Fresh air vent pivots and links	Lubriplate ①
Hood hinges, fender locks and hinges	Grease ②
Remote control linkage	Lubriplate ①
Seat regulator and track adjuster	Lubriplate ①
Window regulators and door latch remote controls	Lubriplate ①
Windshield wipers—operating linkage	Bushings at pivots, and motor crank should be lubricated with light engine oil. Put a few drops of light oil on wiper arm hinges.

① MOPAR Lubriplate, part number 3744859, or equivalent, is a material of this type, and is recommended.

② MOPAR Multi-Mileage Lubricant, part number 2525035, or equivalent.

3

REFERENCES FOR TABLE 13

1. M = Manual; A = Automatic.
2. − 2½ °, set at curb idle.
3. S2 = Step 2 of fast idle cam.
4. ± 0.003 in.
5. TDC with distributor No. 3656275; 2.5 ° ATDC with distributor No. 3656272; 2.5 ° BTDC with distributor No. 3656287.
6. Set to 1900 rpm for carburetor No. R6368A.
7. Adjust California Heavy Duty Cycle engine to 2.5 ° ATDC.
8. LD = Light duty; HD = Heavy duty.
9. 1600 with carburetor No. 6613S.
10. 0.5 for Canadian vehicles.
11. P = In front of catalyst; T = At tailpipe.
12. 2 ° ATDC for Canada D-100. Set curb idle at 750 rpm and propane enriched idle at 840 rpm.
13. Classification for emission control purposes only. LD = light duty (to 6,000 lb. GVWR); M = medium duty (6,001-8,500 lb. GVWR, Calif. only); HD = heavy duty (over 6,000 lb. GVWR, Fed. and Canada, over 8,500 lb. GVWR, Calif.).

Table 13 TUNE-UP SPECIFICATIONS

1971

ENGINE (Cylinders/Carburetor or Model/ Displacement in cu. in.)	Transmission[1]	Basic Timing[2]	Curb Idle (rpm)	Fast Idle (rpm)	Spark Plugs (Champion)	Point Setting[4]	Dwell Angle	Air Fuel Ratio
6/1 bbl 4838S/225 (Fed.)	M	TDC	750	1800S2[3]	N11Y	0.020	41-46°	14.2:1
6/1 bbl 4839S/225 (Fed.)	A	TDC	700	1800S2[3]	N11Y	0.020	41-46°	14.2:1
6/2 bbl 4905S/225 (Fed.)	M	TDC	750	—	N11Y	0.020	41-46°	14.2:1
6/1 bbl 4906S/225 (Fed.)	A	TDC	750	1800S2[3]	N11Y	0.020	41-46°	14.2:1
6/1 bbl 4836S/225 (Calif.)	M	TDC	700	—	N11Y	0.020	41-46°	14.2:1
6/1 bbl 4837S/225 (Calif.)	A	TDC	750	1800S2[3]	N11Y	0.020	41-46°	14.2:1
6/1 bbl 6025S, 6027S, 6116S/225	M	TDC	750	1900S2[3]	N11Y	0.020	41-46°	14.2:1
6/1 bbl 6026S and 4906S/225	A	TDC	750	1800S2[3]	N11Y	0.020	41-46°	14.2:1
8/2 bbl all models except those equipped with #3438227 distributor/318	M	2½° ATDC	750	1600	N11Y	0.017	30-34°	14.2:1
8/2 bbl with #3438227 distributor/318	M	5° BTDC	750	1600	N11Y	0.017	30-34°	14.2:1
8/2 bbl all models except those equipped with #3438227 distributor/318	A	2½° ATDC	700	2000S2[3]	N11Y	0.017	30-34°	14.2:1
8/2 bbl with #3438227 distributor/318	A	5° BTDC	700	2000S2[3]	N11Y	0.017	30-34°	14.2:1
8/2 bbl/383	M	TDC	750	1700	JBY	0.018	28.5-32.5°	14.2:1
8/2 bbl/383	A	2½° BTDC	650	1700	JBY	0.018	28.5-32.5°	14.2:1

Table 13 TUNE-UP SPECIFICATIONS (continued)

1972

ENGINE (Cylinders/Carburetor/Displacement in Cu. In.)	Transmission[1]	Basic Timing[2]	Curb Idle (rpm)	Fast Idle (rpm)	Spark Plugs (Champion)	Point Setting[4]	Dwell Angle	Air Fuel Ratio	Remarks
6/1 bbl/225 (Fed.)	M	TDC	750	2000	N11Y	0.020	41-46°	14.2:1	Holley 1920
6/1 bbl/225 (Fed.)	A	TDC	750	1900	N11Y	0.020	41-46°	14.2:1	Holley 1920
6/1 bbl/225 (Calif.)	M	TDC	650	2200	N11Y	0.020	41-46°	14.2:1	Holley 1920
6/1 bbl/225 (Calif.)	A	TDC	650	2000	N11Y	0.020	41-46°	14.2:1	Holley 1920
6/1 bbl/225	M	TDC	700	2000	N11Y	0.020	41-46°	14.2:1	Carter BBS-6219S
6/1 bbl/225	A	TDC	700	1800	N11Y	0.020	41-46°	14.2:1	Carter BBS-6218S
6/1 bbl/225	M	TDC	700	2800	N11Y	0.020	41-46°	14.2:1	Carter BBS-6220S
8/2 bbl/318 (Fed.)	M	(5)	750	1700	N11Y	0.017	30-34°	14.2:1	
8/2 bbl/318 (Fed.)	A	(5)	750	1900	N11Y	0.017	30-34°	14.2:1	
8/2 bbl/318 (Calif.)	M	(5)	700	1800	N11Y	0.017	30-34°	14.2:1	
8/2 bbl/318 (Calif.)	A	(5)	750	2000	N11Y	0.017	30-34°	14.2:1	
8/2 bbl/360 (Fed.)	M&A	(5)	700	2000	JBY	0.018	30-34°	14.2:1	
8/2 bbl/360 (Fed.)	M&A	(5)	750	2000	JBY	0.018	30-34°	14.2:1	Holley 2210, Models R-6275A and R-6276A
8/2 bbl/360 (Calif.)	M&A	(5)	750	2000	JBY	0.018	30-34°	14.2:1	Holley 2210, Models R-6163A and R-6164A
8/2 bbl/400 (Fed. and Calif.)	M&A	5° BTDC	700	2000[6]	J11Y	0.017	30-34°	14.2:1	Holley 2210, Models R-6161A and R-6162A

3

Table 13 TUNE-UP SPECIFICATIONS (continued)

1973

ENGINE (Cylinders/Carburetor/ Displacement in Cu. In.)	Transmission[1]	Basic Timing[2]	Curb Idle (rpm)	Fast Idle (rpm)	Spark Plugs (Champion)	Air-Fuel Ratio	Carburetor
6/1 bbl/225 (Red. and Calif.)	M	TDC	750	2000	N14Y	14.2:1	Holley 1920
6/1 bbl/225 (Fed. and Calif.)	A	TDC	750	1700	N14Y	14.2:1	Holley 1920
6/1 bbl/225 (Calif.)	M	TDC[7]	800	2000	N14Y	14.2:1	Carter BBS
6/1 bbl/225 (Calif.)	A	TDC[7]	800	1800	N14Y	14.2:1	Carter BBS
6/1 bbl/225 (Fed.)	M	TDC	700	2000	N14Y	14.2:1	Carer BBS
6/1 bbl/225 (Fed.)	A	TDC	700	1800	N14Y	14.2:1	Carter BBS
8/2 bbl/318LD[8] (All)	M	2.5° BTDC	750	1700	N11Y	14.2:1	
8/2 bbl/318LD[8] (All)	A	TDC	700	1700	N11Y	14.2:1	
8/2 bbl/318HD[8] (Fed.)	M	5° BTDC	750	1600	N11Y	14.2:1	
8/2 bbl/318HD[8] (Fed.)	A	5° BTDC	750	1900	N11Y	14.2:1	
8/2 bbl/318HD[8] (Calif.)	M	TDC	750	1600	N11Y	14.2:1	
8/2 bbl/318HD[8] (Calif.)	A	TDC	750	1700	N11Y	14.2:1	
8/2 bbl/360 (Calif.)	M&A	TDC	750	1900	N13Y	14.2:1	
8/2 bbl/360 (Fed.)	M	TDC	750	1900	N13Y	14.2:1	
8/2 bbl/360 (Fed.)	A	TDC	700	1900	N13Y	14.2:1	
8/2 bbl/400LD[8] (All)	A	10° BTDC	700	1800	J11Y	14.2:1	
8/2 bbl/400HD[8] (All)	A&M	2.5° BTDC	700	1800	J11Y	14.2:1	
8/4 bbl/440 (All)	A&M	10° BTDC	700	1700	J11Y	14.2:1	

Table 13 TUNE-UP SPECIFICATIONS (continued)

1974

ENGINE (Cylinders/Carburetor/Displacement in Cu. In.)	Transmission[1]	Basic Timing[2]	Curb Idle (rpm)	Fast Idle (rpm)	Spark Plugs (Champion)	Air Fuel Ratio	Carburetor
6/1 bbl/225LD[8] (All)	M	TDC	800	1600	N11Y	14.2:1	Holley 1945
6/1 bbl/225LD[8] (All)	A	TDC	750	1800	N11Y	14.2:1	Holley 1945
6/1 bbl/225HD[8] (All)	M	2.5° ATDC	800	2000	N11Y	14.2:1	Carter BBS
6/1 bbl/225HD[8] (All)	A	2.5° ATDC	800	1800	N11Y	14.2:1	Carter BBS
8/2 bbl/318LD[8] (All)	M	TDC	750	1700	N11Y	14.2:1	
8/2 bbl/318LD[8] (All)	A	TDC	750	1500[9]	N11Y	14.2:1	
8/2 bbl/318HD[8] (All)	M	2.5° ATDC	750	1700	N11Y	14.2:1	
8/2 bbl/318HD[8] (All)	A	2.5° ATDC	750	1500	N11Y	14.2:1	
8/2 bbl/360LD[8] (Fed.)	M	2.5° BTDC	750	1700	N12Y	14.2:1	Holley 2245
8/2 bbl/360LD[8] (Fed.)	A	5° BTDC	750	1800	N12Y	14.2:1	Holley 2245
8/4 bbl/360LD[8] (Calif.)	A	2.5° BTDC	750	1800	N12Y	14.2:1	Carter Thermo-Quad
8/2 bbl/360HD[8] (All)	M	TDC	750	1700	Y12Y	14.2:1	
8/2 bbl/360HD[8] (All)	A	TDC	750	1800	Y12Y	14.2:1	
8/2 bbl/400LD[8] (All)	A	7.5° BTDC	750	1600	J13Y	14.2:1	
8/2 bbl/400HD[8] (All)	M&A	2.5° BTDC	750	1800	J11Y	14.2:1	
8/4 bbl/440LD[8] (Fed.)	A	10° BTDC	700	1700	J11Y	14.2:1	
8/4 bbl/440LD[8] (Calif.)	A	5° BTDC	700	1700	J11Y	14.2:1	
8/4 bbl/440HD[8] (All)	M&A	7.5° BTDC	700	1700	J11Y	14.2:1	

3

Table 13 TUNE-UP SPECIFICATIONS (continued)

1975

ENGINE (Cylinders/Carburetor/Displacement in Cu. In.)[8]	Transmission[1]	Basic Timing[2]	Curb Idle (rpm)	Fast Idle (rpm)	Spark Plugs (Champion)	Carbon Monoxide (Percent)
6/1 bbl/225LD (All)	M	TDC	800	1600	BL11Y	0.3[10]
6, bbl/225LD (All)	A	TDC	750	1700	BL11Y	0.3[10]
6/1 bbl/225HD (All)	M	TDC	700	1600	BL11Y	1.0
6/1 bbl/225HD (All)	A	TDC	700	1700	BL11Y	1.0
8/2 bbl/318LD (Fed.)	M	2° BTDC	750	1500	N11Y	0.3
8/2 bbl/318LD (Calif.)	M	TDC	750	1500	N11Y	0.3
8/2 bbl/318LD (Canada)	M	2° BTDC	800	1500	N11Y	0.5
8/2 bbl/318LD (Fed.)	A	2° BTDC	750	1500	N11Y	0.3
8/2 bbl/318LD (Calif.)	A	TDC	750	1500	N11Y	0.3
8/2 bbl/318LD (Canada)	A	2° BTDC	750	1500	N11Y	0.5
8/2 bbl/318HD (Fed./Canada)	M	2° ATDC	750	1700	N11Y	1.0
8/2 bbl/318HD (Calif.)	M&A	TDC	700	1500	N11Y	1.0
8/2 bbl/360HD (Fed./Canada)	M	TDC	750	1700	N12Y	1.0
8/2 bbl/360HD (Fed./Canada)	A	TDC	750	1800	N12Y	1.0
8/2 bbl/360HD (Calif.)	M&A	4° BTDC	700	1600	N12Y	1.0
8/4 bbl/440HD (All)	M&A	8° BTDC	700	1700	J11Y	1.0

Table 13 TUNE-UP SPECIFICATIONS (continued)

1976

ENGINE (Cylinders/Carburetor/Displacement in Cu. In.)[8]	Transmission[1]	Basic Timing[2]	Curb Idle (rpm)	Fast Idle (rpm)	Spark Plugs (Champion)	Carbon Monoxide (Percent)[11]
6/1 bbl/225LD (Fed./Canada)	M	2° BTDC	750	1600	BL11Y	0.3P
6/1 bbl/225LD (Fed./Canada)	A	2° BTDC	750	1700	BL11Y	0.3P
6/1 bbl/225LD (Calif.)	M	TDC	750	1600	BL11Y	0.3P
6/1 bbl/225LD (Calif.)	A	TDC	750	1700	BL11Y	0.3P
6/1 bbl/225HD (All)	M	TDC	700	1600	BL11Y	1.0T
6/1 bbl/225HD (All)	A	TDC	700	1700	BL11Y	1.0T
8/2 bbl/318LD (Fed./Canada)	M&A	2° BTDC	750	1500	N11Y	0.3P
8/2 bbl/318LD (Calif.)	M&A	TDC	750	1500	N11Y	0.3P
8/2 bbl/318HD (Fed./Canada)	M	2° ATDC	750	1700	N11Y	1.0T
8/2 bbl/318HD (Fed./Canada)	A	2° TDC	750	1500	N11Y	1.0T
8/2 bbl/318HD (Calif.)	M&A	TDC	750	1500	N11Y	1.0T
8/2 bbl/360LD (Fed./Canada)	A	6° BTDC	750	1600	N12Y	0.3P
8/2 bbl/360LD (Calif.)	A	4° BTDC	700	1600	N12Y	1.0T
8/2 bbl/360HD (Calif.)	M	TDC	750	1700	N12Y	1.0T
8/2 bbl/360HD (Fed./Canada)	A	TDC	750	1800	N12Y	1.0T
8/2 bbl/400HD (Fed./Canada)	A	2° BTDC	700	1400	J11Y	1.0T
8/4 bbl/440HD (All)	A	8° BTDC	700	1700	J11Y	1.0T

3

Table 13 TUNE-UP SPECIFICATIONS (continued)

1977

ENGINE (Cylinders/Carburetor/Displacement in Cu. In.)[10]	Transmission[1]	Basic Timing[2]	Curb Idle (rpm)	Propane Enriched Idle (rpm)	Fast Idle (rpm)	Spark Plugs (Champion)	Carbon Monoxide (Percent)
6/1 bbl/225LD (Fed./Canada)	M	2° BTDC[12]	750[12]	900[12]	1,600	RBL15Y	—
6/1 bbl/225LD (Fed./Canada)	A	2° BTDC[12]	750[12]	850[12]	1,700	RBL15Y	—
6/1 bbl/225LD (Calif.)	M	TDC	750	—	1,600	RBL15Y	0.3
6/1 bbl/225LD (Calif.)	A	2° ATDC	750	—	1,700	RBL15Y	0.3
6/2 bbl/225HD (Fed./Canada)	M	TDC	700	750	1,500	RBL15Y	—
6/2 bbl/225HD (Fed./Canada)	A	TDC	700	770	1,500	RBL15Y	—
8/2 bbl/318LD (Fed./Canada)	M	2° BTDC	750	850	1,500	RN11Y	—
8/2 bbl/318LD (Fed./Canada)	A	2° BTDC	750	920	1,500	RN11Y	0.3
8/2 bbl/318LD (Calif.)	M-A	2° BTDC	750	—	1,500	RN11Y	0.3
8/2 bbl/318HD (Fed./Canada)	M	2° ATDC	750	800	1,600	RN11Y	—
8/2 bbl/318HD (Fed./Canada)	A	2° ATDC	750	820	1,500	RN11Y	—
8/2 bbl/318HD (Calif.)	A	TDC	700	—	1,500	RN11Y	0.5
8/2 bbl/360HD (Fed./Canada)	M	TDC	750	790	1,700	RN12Y	—
8/2 bbl/360HD (Fed./Canada)	A	TDC	750	810	1,800	RN12Y	—
8/2 bbl/360HD (Calif.)	A	TDC	700	—	1,600	RN12Y	1.0 T[11]
8/2 bbl/400LD (Canada)	A	6° BTDC	700	760	1,600	RJ11Y	—
8/2 bbl/400HD (Fed./Canada)	M	2° BTDC	700	740	1,600	RJ11Y	—
8/2 bbl/400HD (Fed./Canada)	A	2° BTDC	700	760	1,600	RJ11Y	—
8/4 bbl/440HD (Fed./Canada)	M	8° BTDC	700	740	1,700	RJ11Y	—
8/4 bbl/440HD (Fed./Canada)	A	8° BTDC	700	760	1,700	RJ11Y	—
8/4 bbl/440HD (Calif.)	M-A	8° BTDC	700	—	1,700	RJ11Y	0.5

Table 13 TUNE-UP SPECIFICATIONS (continued)

1978

ENGINE (Cylinders/Carburetor/Displacement in Cu. In./Duty Cycle¹³)	Transmission¹	Basic Timing²	Curb Idle (rpm)	Propane Enriched Idle (rpm)	Fast Idle (rpm)	Spark Plugs (Champion)	Carbon Monoxide (Percent)
6/2 bbl/225LD (Fed./Canada)	M	12° BTDC	750	930	1,400	RBL16Y	—
6/2 bbl/225LD (Fed./Canada)	A	12° BTDC	750	900	1,600	RBL16Y	0.3
6/2 bbl/225LD/MD (Calif.)	M	8° BTDC	750	910	1,400	RBL16Y	0.3
6/2 bbl/225/LD/MD (Calif.)	A	8° BTDC	750	910	1,600	RBL16Y	0.3
6/2 bbl/225/225HD (Fed./Canada)	M	TDC	700	750	1,600	RBL16Y	—
6/2 bbl/225HD (Fed./Canada)	A	TDC	700	770	1,700	RBL16Y	0.3
6/2 bbl/225/HD (Fed./Canada)	M-A	12° BTDC	750	880	1,600	RN11Y	0.3
8/4 bbl/318/LD (Calif./Canada)	M	2° ATDC	750	800	1,700	RN11Y	—
8/2 bbl/318/HD (Fed./Canada)	A	2° ATDC	750	820	1,500	RN11Y	0.3
8/2 bbl/318/HD (Fed./Canada)	M-A	12° BTDC	750	880	1,600	RN11Y	—
8/4 bbl/318/MD (Calif.)	A	6° BTDC	750	890	1,600	RN12Y	—
8/2 bbl/360/LD (Fed./Canada)	A	TDC	750	830	1,600	RN12Y	—
8/2 bbl/360/LD (Canada)	M	4° BTDC	750	790	1,700	RN12Y	—
8/2 bbl/360/HD (Fed./Canada)	A	4° BTDC	750	810	1,700	RN12Y	0.3
8/2 bbl/360/HD (Fed./Canada)	M	6° BTDC	750	880	1,700	RN12Y	0.3
8/4 bbl/360/LD/MD (Calif.)	A	6° BTDC	750	880	1,600	RN12Y	0.3
8/4 bbl/360/LD/MD (Calif.)	M-A	TDC	700	800	1,600	RN12Y	—
8/2 bbl/360/HD (Calif.)	A	10° BTDC	700	750	1,600	OJ11Y	—
8/2 bbl/400/LD (Canada)	M	2° BTDC	700	740	1,600	OJ11Y	—
8/2 bbl/400/HD (Fed./Canada)	A	2° BTDC	700	760	1,600	OJ11Y	—
8/2 bbl/400/HD (Fed./Canada)	A	8° BTDC	700	760	1,400	OJ11Y	—
8/4 bbl/440/HD (Fed./Canada)	A	8° BTDC	750	840	1,400	OJ11Y	0.3
8/4 bbl/440/MD (Calif.)	A	8° BTDC	700	780	1,400	OJ11Y	1.0

3

Table 13 TUNE-UP SPECIFICATIONS (continued)

ENGINE (Cylinders/Carburetor/Displacement in Cu. In./Duty Cycle[13])	Transmission[1]	Basic Timing[2]	Curb Idle (rpm)	1979 Propane Enriched Idle (rpm)	Fast Idle (rpm)	Spark Plugs (Champion)	Carbon Monoxide (Percent)
6/1 bbl/225/LD (Fed./Canada)	M-A	12° BTDC	675	875	1,600	RBL16Y	—
6/1 bbl/225/HD (Canada)	M-A	12° BTDC	675	875	1,600	RBL16Y	—
6/2 bbl/225/MD (Calif.)	M	8° BTDC	800	975	1,400	RBL16Y	0.3
6/2 bbl/225/MD (Calif.)	A	8° BTDC	800	975	1,600	RBL16Y	0.3
8/2 bbl/318/LD (Fed./Canada)	M	12° BTDC	680	820	1,400	RN11Y	—
8/2 bbl/318/LD (Fed./Canada)	A	12° BTDC	680	820	1,500	RN11Y	—
8/4 bbl/318/LD-MD (Calif.)	M (and MD A)	6° BTDC	750	865	1,600	RN11Y	0.3
8/4 bbl/318/LD (Calif.)	A	8° BTDC	750	860	1,600	RN11Y	0.3
8/2 bbl/360/LD (Fed.)	M	10° BTDC	750	1,000	1,600	RN12Y	—
8/2 bbl/360/LD (Fed.)	A	10° BTDC	750	975	1,600	RN12Y	—
8/2 bbl/360/HD (Canada)	M	4° BTDC	750	790	1,600	RN12Y	—
8/2 bbl/360/HD (Canada)	A	4° BTDC	750	810	1,600	RN12Y	—
8/4 bbl/360/MD (Fed./Canada)	M-A	4° BTDC	700	750	1,600	RN12Y	—
8/4 bbl/360/MD (Calif.)	M	10° BTDC	750	980	1,600	RN12Y	0.5
8/4 bbl/360/MD (Calif.)	A	10° BTDC	750	960	1,600	RN12Y	0.5
8/4 bbl/360/HD (Calif.)	A	4° BTDC	700	750	1,600	RN12Y	0.5
8/4 bbl/440/HD (All)	A	8° BTDC	700	780	1,400	OJ11Y	—

Table 13 TUNE-UP SPECIFICATIONS (continued)

Engine Cyl./Carb.	CID/Duty/ Usage	Transmission	Basic Timing Degrees (BTDC)	Curb Idle	Propane Enriched Idle
		1980			
6/1bbl	225/LD/Fed	M-A	12	600	730
6/1bbl	225/LD-HD/Can	M-A	12	675	875
6/1bbl	225/MD/Cal	M-A	12	800	900
8/2bbl	318/LD/Fed-Can	M-A	12	600	740
8/2bbl	318/HD/Can	M-A	2 ATDC	750	800
8/4bbl	318/LD/Can	A	10	750	850
8/4bbl	318/MD/Cal	A	6	750	850
8/4bbl	318/HD/Fed/Cal	M-A	8	750	810
8/2bbl	360/HD/Can	M-A	4	750	810
8/4bbl	360/MD/Cal	M-A	10	750	875
8/4bbl	360/LD/Fed/Can	M-A	12	650	750
8/4bbl	360/HD/Cal	M-A	10	750	810
8/4bbl	360/HD/Fed/Can	M-A	4	700	800
8/4bbl	360/LD/Fed/Can	A	10	750	850

Spark plug type

225 CID 6	Mopar 560 PR, Champion RBL16Y
318 CID V-8	Mopar 64 PR, Champion RN11Y
360-1 CID V-8	Mopar 65 PR, Champion RN12Y
360-3 CID V-8	Mopar 65 PR tapered seat
Spark plug gap	0.035 in. (0.9mm)

Engine Cyl./Carb.	CID/Duty/ Usage	Transmission	Basic Timing Degrees (BTDC)	Curb Idle	Propane Enriched Idle
		1981			
6/1bbl	225/LD/Fed	M	12	600	675
6/1bbl	225/LD/Cal	M	12	800	900
6/1bbl	225/LD/Can	M	12	725	825

(continued)

Table 13 TUNE-UP SPECIFICATIONS (continued)

1981					
Engine Cyl./Carb.	CID/Duty/ Usage	Transmission	Basic Timing Degrees (BTDC)	Curb Idle	Propane Enriched Idle
6/1 bbl	225/LD/Fed	A	16	600	675
6/1 bbl	225/LD/Cal	A	16	800	900
6/1 bbl	225/LD/Can	A	16	725	850
6/1 bbl	225/HD/Can	M	12	725	825
6/1 bbl	225/HD/Can	A	16	750	850
8/2 bbl	318/LD/Fed	M	10	650	750
8/2 bbl	318/LD/Can	M	10	750	850
8/2 bbl	318/LD/Fed	A	16	650	790
8/2 bbl	318/HD/Can	M-A	2 ATDC	750	820
8/4 bbl	318/LD/Cal	M	2	750	830
8/4 bbl	318/LD/Fed/Cal	A	16	750	810
8/4 bbl	318/LD/Can	A	10	750	850
8/4 bbl	318/HD/Fed/Cal/Can	M-A	12	750	810
8/2 bbl	360/HD/Can	A	4	750	810
8/4 bbl	360/LD/Fed	M	12	600	680
8/4 bbl	360/LD/Cal	M	12	750	810
8/4 bbl	360/LD/Fed	A	16	625	700
8/4 bbl	360/LD/Cal	A	16	750	850
8/4 bbl	360-1/HD/Fed/ Cal/Can	A	4*	700	800
8/4 bbl	360-1/HD/Cal	A	4**	700	810
8/4 bbl	360-3/HD/Cal/Can		4*	700	800
8/4 bbl	360-3/HD/Cal		10**	750	810

*With catalytic converter

**Without catalytic converter

Table 14 CYLINDER HEAD BOLT TORQUE

Engine	Torque (ft.-lb.)
225 cid 6	
1971-1975	65
1976-on	70
243 diesel	90
318 cid V-8	
1971	85
1972-1977	95
1978-1980	105
1981	95
360 cid V-8	
1971	70
1972-1977	95
1978-1980	105
1981	95
383 cid V-8	70
400/440 cid V-8	70

3

CHAPTER FOUR

ENGINE

Standard equipment in all years since 1971 has been an in-line 6-cylinder, 225 cubic-inch displacement engine. Four V-8 engines, with 318, 360, 400, and 440 cubic-inch displacement, have been offered in various years as optional equipment. The basic designs of all engines have remained essentially unchanged, although some minor changes have been made. The 6-cylinder engine was given a new modular cast iron crankshaft in 1977, with narrower main and connecting rod bearing journals and wider counterweights. These and other related parts, such as bearings, are not interchangeable with those manufactured for the previous engines with forged crankshafts. The new crankshafts can be identified by the letter "E" stamped on the identification pad.

A 2-barrel carburetor version of the 6-cylinder also was introduced in 1977. While similar in design, the 2-barrel version has a different intake manifold and a larger bore exhaust pipe.

All 6-cylinder gasoline engines are slanted to the right 30° from vertical and have in-line overhead valves with mechanical valve lifters that require periodic adjustment. All have a maximum compression ratio of 8.4:1.

The V-8 engines are of the same basic design, with the main differences being in the bore, stroke, distributor drive and location, and oil pump location and configuration. All utilize overhead valves and hydraulic lifters that require no adjustment. Service procedures are identical for all engines, unless otherwise noted.

Overhaul of the 243 diesel engine by the home mechanic is not recommended at this time. Service should be limited to the maintenance procedures given in Chapter Three.

Engine specifications are given in **Table 1** and tightening torques in **Table 2**, both at the end of this chapter.

ENGINE REMOVAL

An engine lifting fixture is a necessity for removing the engine from a van. The fixture can be fabricated from 1 1/2 in. pipe (or larger) and fittings. Dimensions are shown in **Figure 1**. A special lifting bracket is helpful for removing 6-cylinder engines. Chrysler recommends tool C-4145, but a substitute can be fabricated locally. Dimensions are given in **Figure 2**.

①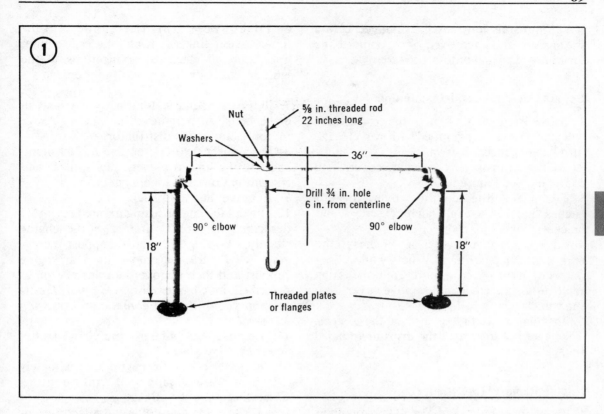

Nut

Washers

⅝ in. threaded rod
22 inches long

36″

Drill ¾ in. hole
6 in. from centerline

90° elbow

90° elbow

18″

18″

Threaded plates
or flanges

②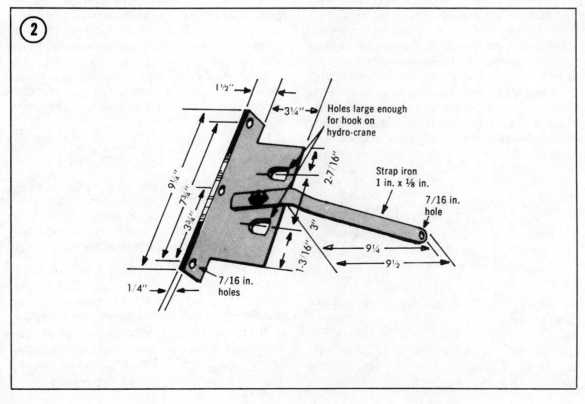

1½″

3¼″

Holes large enough
for hook on
hydro-crane

2-7/16″

Strap iron
1 in. x ⅛ in.

7/16 in.
hole

9¼″

7¾″

3¾″

3″

1-3/16″

9¼

9½

1/4″

7/16 in.
holes

4

The transmission must be removed before the engine can be removed. See Chapter Nine for removal/installation procedures.

Engine Cover Removal/Installation

1. Move front seats as far to the rear as they will go. If the van is equipped with swivel seats, turn passenger seat rearward.
2. Remove ash tray from engine cover, if so equipped. See **Figure 3**.
3. Disengage the engine cover forward latches and remove all latching screws and brackets at the floor level.
4. Slide the engine cover 3 or 4 inches to the rear (to clear instrument panel) while lifting the front of the cover upward. Continue lifting the front of the cover and remove cover from the vehicle.
5. Installation is the reverse of these steps. Take care not to scratch the instrument panel finish.

Engine Removal (6-Cylinder)

1. Disconnect battery, drain all coolant from radiator and engine, and drain engine oil.
2. Remove the engine cover as previously described. Remove the carburetor air cleaner. Remove starter and disconnect the exhaust pipe.
3. If equipped with air conditioning, have the system discharged by a dealer or air conditioning shop. Cap all openings immediately to prevent contamination of the system.

> *WARNING*
> *Do not disconnect air conditioner hoses until the system has been discharged. The hoses contain refrigerant under high pressure, which can cause frostbite if it touches skin and blindness if it touches the eyes. If discharged near an open flame, the refrigerant forms poisonous gas.*

4. Remove the front bumper, grille, and support brace. Disconnect radiator hoses and remove radiator and support as an assembly.
5. Remove the power steering pump and the air pump, if so equipped, with hoses attached and position them out of the way.

6. Disconnect throttle and clutch/transmission linkage, heater hoses, vacuum lines, and all electrical connections to the ignition coil, alternator, and other engine accessories.
7. Remove the alternator, fan, pulley, and all drive belts. Also remove the heater blower motor. Remove the distributor.
8. Disconnect flexible fuel line to fuel pump and cap the line to prevent fuel spillage and contamination of the fuel system.
9. Remove the oil dipstick.
10. Install the engine lifting fixture previously described (**Figure 1**) and raise the engine slightly, allowing the tool to support the engine. See **Figure 4**. Remove the rear engine support and then remove the transmission as described in Chapter Nine, *Manual Transmission Removal* and *Automatic Transmission Removal.*
11. Remove the clutch assembly and the flywheel or drive plate.
12. Raise the rear of the engine approximately 2 to 3 inches and support it with the lifting fixture. Remove the oil pan.
13. Remove the manifolds and attach the engine lifting bracket (**Figure 2**) to the 3rd, 4th, and 5th manifold lower studs on the cylinder head and to the engine bracket front bolt. See **Figure 5**.
14. Attach the hook of a portable engine lifting device to the lifting bracket (**Figure 5**) after inserting the boom of the lifting device into the opening in the front of the vehicle.
15. Raise the boom slightly to support the engine and remove the lifting and support fixture from the rear of the engine.
16. Remove the engine front mounts and insulators. Carefully withdraw the engine from the front of the vehicle. Raise the front of the vehicle slightly, if necessary, so the boom can remain horizontal. Place the engine on a suitable work stand or bench.

Engine Installation (6-Cylinder)

1. With the manifolds removed, attach the lifting bracket to the 3rd, 4th, and 5th lower studs on the cylinder head and to the engine bracket front bolt as shown in **Figure 5**.

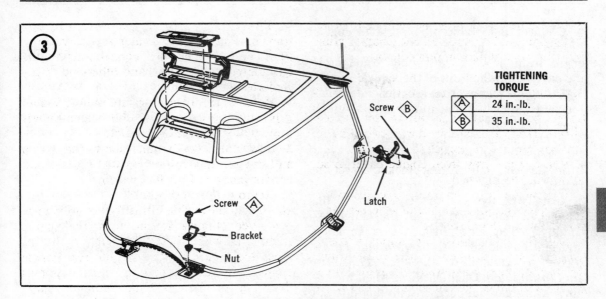

③

TIGHTENING TORQUE	
Ⓐ	24 in.-lb.
Ⓑ	35 in.-lb.

Screw Ⓑ

Latch

Screw Ⓐ

Bracket

Nut

4

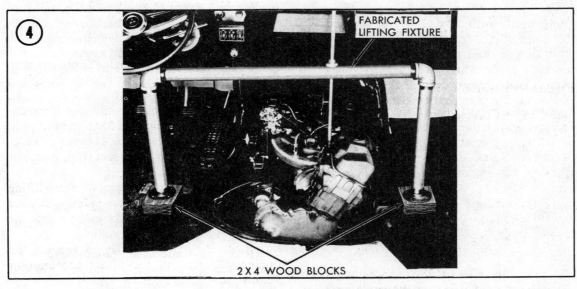

④

FABRICATED LIFTING FIXTURE

2 X 4 WOOD BLOCKS

⑤

2. Connect the boom of a portable engine lifting device to the lifting bracket, remove the engine from the work stand or bench and insert the engine into the front of the vehicle.

3. Install the engine front mounts and insulators and tighten bolts and nuts to specifications shown in **Figure 6**.

4. Install the engine lifting fixture to the rear of the engine (**Figure 4**) and remove the portable lifting device and the lifting bracket. Lower the rear of the engine about 2 inches.

5. Install the flywheel or drive plate to the crankshaft flange and install the clutch assembly, if so equipped. Install the transmission and rear engine support. See *Manual Transmission Installation* or *Automatic Transmission Installation*, Chapter Nine. Align the engine with rear support, install the through bolts, and tighten to specifications (**Figure 7**). Remove the lifting fixture.

6. Connect the clutch/transmission linkage and all lines and wires, including the speedometer cable, that were removed during transmission removal. Install the starter.

7. Install the manifolds and hook up the exhaust pipe. Connect the fuel line, and install the oil dipstick.

8. Install the alternator, fan assembly, and the power steering pump and air pump, if so equipped. Install drive belts and adjust tension. See *Accessory Drive Belts*, Chapter Seven.

9. Connect the throttle linkage, distributor, heater and vacuum hoses, and all electrical connections to the engine.

10. Install the radiator and support, grille, and front bumper. Reconnect the radiator hoses and connect the battery. Connect lines to air conditioner condenser and recharge the system. See Chapter Twelve.

11. Fill the transmission, engine crankcase, and cooling system. See Chapter Three for fluid types and capacities. Check all systems for leaks.

12. Check ignition timing, valve clearances (if disturbed), and dwell (if equipped with breaker point ignition).

13. Check and adjust, if required, accelerator and transmission linkages and then road test the vehicle.

Engine Removal (8-Cylinder)

1. Disconnect battery and drain cooling system and engine oil pan. Remove oil filter.

2. Remove the engine cover as previously described. Remove the carburetor air cleaner.

3. If equipped with air conditioning, have the system discharged by a dealer or air conditioning shop. Cap all openings immediately to prevent contamination of the system.

WARNING
Do not disconnect air conditioner hoses until the system has been discharged. The hoses contain refrigerant under high pressure, which can cause frostbite if it touches skin and blindness if it touches the eyes. If discharged near an open flame, the refrigerant forms poisonous gas.

4. Remove the front bumper, grille, and support brace. Disconnect radiator hoses and remove radiator, air conditioner condenser (if so equipped) and support as an assembly.

5. Remove the air conditioner compressor, if so equipped, and seal or cap all lines and openings to prevent contamination of the system.

6. Remove power steering pump and, if so equipped, the air pump. Leave hoses attached to power steering pump and position it to one side, out of the way.

7. Disconnect throttle linkage, heater and vacuum hoses, and electrical leads to the ignition coil, alternator, and other engine accessories.

8. Remove the alternator, fan, pulley, and all drive belts not previously removed. Remove the heater blower motor.

9. Disconnect flexible fuel line at the fuel pump and plug the line to prevent fuel spillage.

10. Remove the intake manifold and carburetor as an assembly. Disconnect the exhaust pipe and remove the left exhaust manifold (both manifolds on 400-440 engines). If the vehicle has air conditioning, remove the right cylinder head cover to provide clearance of the expansion valve and other air conditioner components during engine removal.

11. Remove the oil dipstick tube.

12. Raise the engine slightly with a jack and install engine lifting fixture (**Figure 1**) as shown in **Figure 8**.

⑥ FRONT ENGINE MOUNTS
(6-CYLINDER)

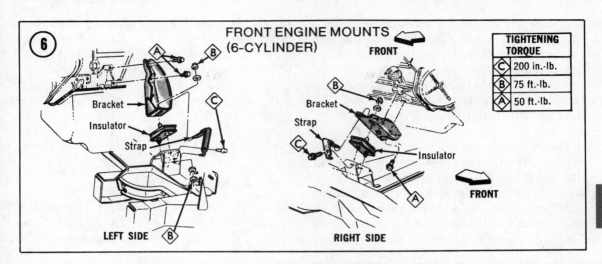

FRONT

TIGHTENING TORQUE	
C	200 in.-lb.
B	75 ft.-lb.
A	50 ft.-lb.

Bracket
Insulator
Strap

Bracket
Strap
Insulator

FRONT

LEFT SIDE

RIGHT SIDE

⑦ REAR ENGINE MOUNTS
(ALL)

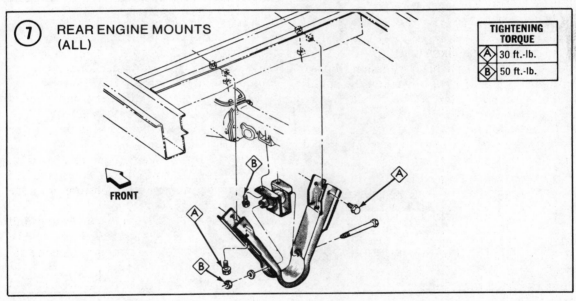

TIGHTENING TORQUE	
A	30 ft.-lb.
B	50 ft.-lb.

FRONT

⑧

TOOL C-3809

2 x 4 WOOD BLOCKS

4

13. Raise the vehicle and remove the starter.

14. Remove the propeller shaft and the rear engine support, then remove the transmission. See *Manual Transmission Removal* or *Automatic Transmission Removal*, Chapter Nine.

15. Remove the clutch assembly and the flywheel (manual transmission vehicles) or the drive plate (automatics). Raise the rear of the engine about 2 inches.

16. On 318-360 engines, turn crankshaft so that notch in flange is positioned in the 3 o'clock position (**Figure 9**). Remove oil pan attaching screws, then lower pan and reach in and reposition oil pick-up tube as shown in the figure. Remove the oil pan.

17. Install a short length of heavy chain between the centers of the cylinder heads, using the intake manifold attaching bolts. This chain will provide a lifting bridle for the engine.

18. Attach the hook of a portable engine lifting device to the lifting bridle after inserting the boom of the lifting device into the opening in the front of the vehicle. Raise the boom slightly to support the engine.

19. Remove the engine front mounts and the engine lifting fixture (**Figure 7**).

20. Carefully guide and remove the engine from the front of the vehicle. Raise the vehicle slightly, if necessary, so the boom can remain

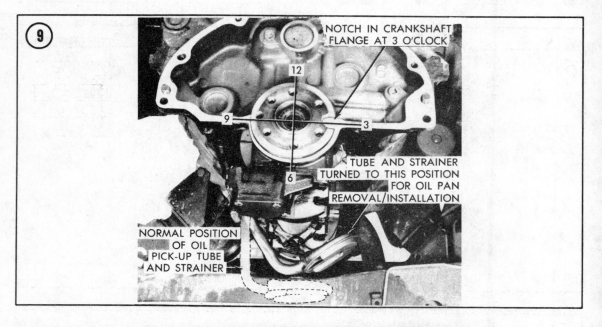

(9) NOTCH IN CRANKSHAFT FLANGE AT 3 O'CLOCK

12

9   3

TUBE AND STRAINER TURNED TO THIS POSITION FOR OIL PAN REMOVAL/INSTALLATION

6

NORMAL POSITION OF OIL PICK-UP TUBE AND STRAINER

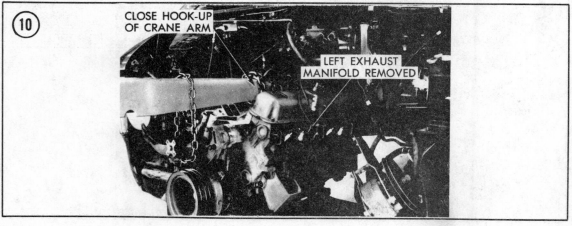

(10) CLOSE HOOK-UP OF CRANE ARM

LEFT EXHAUST MANIFOLD REMOVED

horizontal. Place the engine on a suitable work stand or bench.

Engine Installation (8-Cylinder)

1. Install lifting bridle on engine as described in *Engine Removal (8-Cylinder)*, Step 17. On 318-360 engines, intake manifold, left exhaust manifold, and oil pan should be removed. On 400-440 engine, intake manifold and both exhaust manifolds should be removed. Pick up engine with portable lifting device and carefully guide the engine into the front of the vehicle. See **Figure 10** (318-360 engines) or **Figure 11** (400-440 engines).

2. Install front engine mounts and tighten to specifications given in **Figure 12** (318-360 engines) or **Figure 13** (400-440 engines).

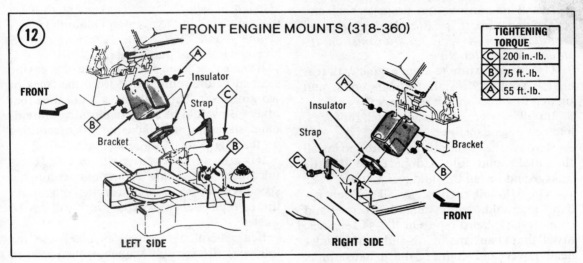

FRONT ENGINE MOUNTS (318-360)

TIGHTENING TORQUE	
C	200 in.-lb.
B	75 ft.-lb.
A	55 ft.-lb.

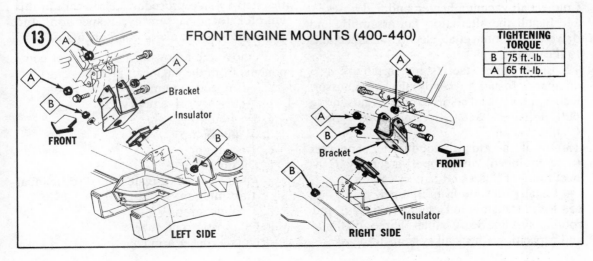

FRONT ENGINE MOUNTS (400-440)

TIGHTENING TORQUE	
B	75 ft.-lb.
A	65 ft.-lb.

3. Install the engine lifting fixture (**Figure 8**) to support the rear of the engine and remove the portable lifting device.

4. On 318-360 engines, turn the crankshaft so the crankshaft flange notch is at the 3 o'clock position (**Figure 9**) and position the oil pick-up tube as shown in the figure. Install the oil pan with new gaskets. Before installing attaching screws, reach into the rear of the oil pan and reposition the oil pick-up tube to its proper position (dashed lines, **Figure 9**). Install attaching screws and tighten to 200 in.-lb. See *Oil Pan Removal/Installation*, this chapter.

5. Lower the rear of the engine about 2 inches and install the flywheel and clutch assembly (manual transmission) or the drive plate (automatic transmission).

6. Install the transmission, propeller shaft and rear engine support. See *Manual Transmission Installation* or *Automatic Transmission Installation*, Chapter Nine.

7. Use lifting fixture to align engine with rear engine support, install through bolts, and tighten to values shown in **Figure 7**.

8. Install starter, shift and clutch linkages, and new engine oil filter.

9. Remove the engine lifting fixture and install the intake manifold. Connect the throttle linkage and install the oil dipstick tube.

10. On 318-360 engines, install the left exhaust manifold, right cylinder head cover and connect the exhaust pipe. On 400-440 engines, install the exhaust manifolds and right cylinder head cover and connect the exhaust pipe. Connect all vacuum, heater, and fuel hoses.

11. Install the alternator, fan assembly, and drive belts. Connect all electrical connections to the engine.

12. Install power steering and air pumps, if so equipped. Install air conditioner compressor, if so equipped, and all drive belts. Adjust drive belt tension. See *Accessory Drive Belts*, Chapter Seven.

13. Install radiator, air conditioner condenser (if so equipped), and support assembly. Connect radiator hoses and battery cables.

14. Install grille and front bumper.

15. Refill transmission, engine crankcase, and cooling system. See Chapter Three for fluids and capacities. Check all systems for leaks.

16. Check ignition timing and carburetor settings and adjust as required. See *Ignition Timing*, Chapter Three, and *Idle Speed Adjustment*, Chapter Five.

17. If equipped with air conditioner, connect condenser to system and recharge the system.

18. Adjust the accelerator and the transmission linkages as required and test drive the vehicle.

OVERHAUL SEQUENCE

All of the overhaul procedures, with the exception of crankshaft removal and installation, can be performed with the engine in the van. However, if a general overhaul, or even more than two or three tasks, are planned, it will be more convenient to have the engine out of the truck and mounted on an engine stand. These stands often can be obtained from an equipment rental business.

It also is a good idea to have the engine cleaned before removing it from the truck or working on it. This will save a lot of time that otherwise would be spent in cleaning individual parts, and it will make the task of working on the engine much more pleasant.

If bearings or other parts with specified close tolerances (see **Table 1**) are not within the specified limits, or are near the maximum limits, replace them so your work will not be wasted.

If a general overhaul is planned, use the following disassembly sequence, then refer to the step-by-step procedures elsewhere in this chapter for disassembly, inspection, and reassembly of the major components.

1. Remove the following accessories or components from the engine, if present.
   a. Air injection pump
   b. Accessory drive pulleys
   c. Fuel pump
   d. Water pump
   e. Distributor
   f. Oil filter
   g. Clutch pressure plate and disc (manual transmission)
   h. Ground strap
   i. Oil dipstick and tube
2. Remove rocker arm cover(s).

3. Remove intake and exhaust manifolds.

4. Remove rocker arms, pushrods, and valve lifters. Store these items in order of removal so they can be returned to their original positions if they are to be reused.

5. Remove cylinder head(s).

6. Remove vibration damper.

7. Remove oil pan.

8. Remove engine front cover.

9. Remove oil pump and pick-up.

10. Verify that connecting rods and bearing caps are marked with numbers identifying the cylinders in which they are installed. If not, permanently mark them.

11. Check the tops of the cylinder bores for ridges. If present, remove ridges with a ridge reamer.

12. Remove connecting rod bearing caps, then remove connecting rod-piston assemblies from the engine.

13. Remove timing sprockets and timing chain, then remove camshaft.

14. Remove flywheel or drive plate.

15. Remove main bearing caps and remove crankshaft from the engine.

16. Remove the rear main bearing seal.

17. Remove the front oil seal from the front engine cover.

18. Discard all seals and gaskets removed during the above steps.

REASSEMBLY SEQUENCE

NOTE

Use only new gaskets and seals on the engine during assembly. Overhaul gasket kits are available and should be used. In some cases, these kits are designed for several model years and may contain similar, but not identical, gaskets for use in the same location. Study the instructions accompanying the kit and the parts involved carefully to determine the proper gasket for your engine.

1. Install a new rear main bearing seal in the rear main bearing cap and the cylinder block. Install a new seal in the front of the engine cover.

2. Install bearings in the cylinder block and the main bearing caps. Install crankshaft and main bearing caps.

3. Install flywheel.

4. Install the piston and the connecting rod assemblies.

5. Install the camshaft, then install the timing sprockets and timing chain.

6. Install oil pump and pick-up.

7. Install the engine front cover.

8. Install oil pan.

9. Install cylinder head(s).

10. Install valve lifters, pushrods, and rocker arm assemblies.

11. Install vibration damper.

12. Install intake and exhaust manifolds.

13. Install rocker arm covers.

14. Install the accessories removed in Step 1 of *Overhaul Sequence.*

ENGINE SERVICE GROUPS

Procedures for servicing the engine have been separated into three groups:

a. Cylinder head/valve train

b. Cylinder block/pistons/connecting rods

c. Crankshaft/main bearings/seals/oil pump

Although the in-line 6-cylinder and V-8 engines are different in external configuration, they are remarkably alike in principle. The procedures for servicing them are identical in most cases. Where differences occur, they will be noted.

As previously stated, all procedures except crankshaft removal and installation can be performed with the engine in the vehicle. The procedures that follow in this chapter assume that the engine has not been removed, with the exception of those related to crankshaft removal/installation. If you have removed the engine from your vehicle, disregard the obviously preliminary steps such as "drain cooling system."

Pay particular attention to the inspection procedures. If in doubt about the condition of a part, take it to your dealer's service shop or to an experienced mechanic for an expert opinion. The same applies if you do not have precision measuring equipment (micrometers, bore gauges, etc.) to check parts with critical clearance requirements. Even if you have this equipment, get a second opinion or measurement from an expert unless you use the equipment regularly and have confidence in your ability to correctly use and read the instruments.

CYLINDER HEAD/VALVE TRAIN SERVICE

Rocker Arms/Shaft Assembly Removal (6-Cylinder)

1. Disconnect PCV hose, distributor advance hose, vapor canister hose, temperature gauge hose, electric choke wire, and alternator wiring harness.
2. Remove fender support bracket.
3. Remove valve cover mounting bolts and remove valve cover. If truck is equipped with an air conditioner, have an assistant hold the air conditioner hoses out of the way during valve cover removal. Remove and discard valve cover gasket.
4. Remove bolts and retainers and remove the rocker arms and shaft assembly.

Rocker Arms/Shaft Assembly Installation (6-Cylinder)

NOTE
Hydraulic lifters are used on 1981 engines. Omit steps 4-11, as adjustment is not required.

1. Position rocker arms on shaft as shown in **Figure 14**. Flat area on end of rocker shaft must be up and point to front of engine. This allows proper alignment of lubrication passages.
2. Install rocker shaft retainers on shaft. Make sure long retainer is in center position, and that all retainers are resting only on the shaft—and not on the rocker arm bushings.
3. Install rocker arms and shaft with rocker arm retaining bolts. Make sure the special shouldered bolt (see **Figure 14**) is in the rear position. Tighten all bolts to 25 ft.-lbs. Reconnect alternator wiring harness.

NOTE
Before tightening rocker arm shaft retaining bolts, make sure the rocker arm adjusting screws are properly seated in the pushrod cups.

4. Turn the engine until No. 1 piston is at top dead center on its compression stroke. When this occurs, the 0 degree mark on the timing scale will align with the notch in the crankshaft pulley. See **Figure 15**. In addition, the distrib-

utor rotor will point to No. 1 terminal in the distributor cap (**Figure 16**).

NOTE
Be sure to remove the distributor cap and check rotor position. The timing marks also line up when No. 6 piston is at top dead center on its compression stroke.

5. Measure clearance between No. 1 cylinder's rocker arms and valve stems with a feeler gauge. See **Figure 17A**. Exhaust valve clearance should be 0.028 in. Intake valve clearance should be 0.012 in. **Figure 17B** identifies intake and exhaust valves.
6. If clearance is incorrect, loosen the adjusting screw's locknut. Turn the adjusting screw to change clearance, then tighten the locknut.
7. Turn the crankshaft clockwise (viewed from the front of the engine) 120° (1/3 turn). Adjust the valves for No. 5 cylinder (counting from the front of the engine) in the same manner as those for No. 1 cylinder.
8. Keep turning the engine, 120° at a time, and adjust the remaining cylinders' valves in the following order: 3-6-2-4.
9. Temporarily install the valve cover. Warm the engine to normal operating temperature, then remove the valve cover.
10. With the engine idling, adjust intake valves to 0.010 in. and exhaust valves to 0.020 in.

NOTE
To cut down on oil splash, cut the top off an old valve cover and install it on the engine. Be sure to remove all sharp edges.

11. If the valves are difficult to adjust with the engine idling, turn the engine off. Adjust the valves as described in Steps 4-8. Set intake valves at 0.010 in. and exhaust valves at 0.020 in.

NOTE
Adjust the valves quickly so the engine doesn't cool off. If it does cool off, warm it to operating temperature again.

12. Check the valve cover gasket surface for distortion. Have the surface straightened if necessary. Make sure all old gasket material is removed.
13. Using a new gasket, install the valve cover and evenly tighten the retaining bolts to 40 in.-lb. Do not overtighten, as this will distort

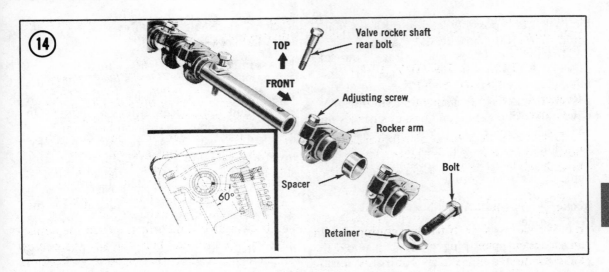

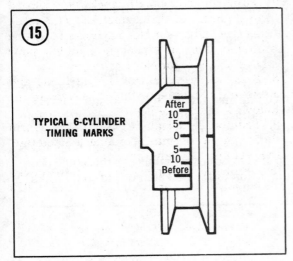

TYPICAL 6-CYLINDER
TIMING MARKS

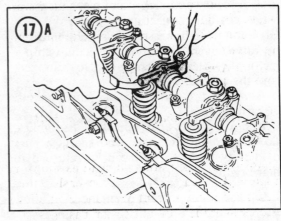

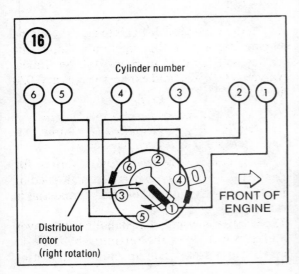

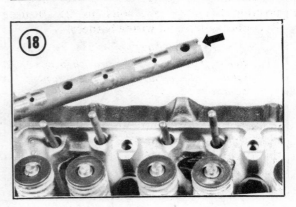

the gasket and possibly lead to oil leaks (and could snap off the bolt heads).

14. Install the hoses and wires removed during the removal procedure, start the engine, and check for oil leaks around the gasket. If leaks are present, remove the valve cover, clean the gasket and gasket surfaces on the head cover, and reinstall, using a reputable gasket cement on the gasket surfaces. Do not attempt to remedy leaks by applying additional torque.

Rocker Arms/Shaft Assembly Removal (V-8 Engines)

1. Disconnect spark plug wires.
2. Disconnect evaporative control system hoses from the carburetor and place them out of the way. Disconnect and remove the PCV valve and the crankcase inlet air cleaner from the valve covers. Remove the vacuum amplifier or the solenoid valve(s), if so equipped, from the left valve cover.
3. Remove the valve covers and gaskets. Discard gaskets.
4. Remove rocker arms and shaft assemblies. If rocker arms are removed from shafts, be sure to identify them so they can be returned to their original positions.

Rocker Arm/Shaft Assembly Installation (V-8 Engines)

1. Assemble rocker arms on shafts. On 318-360 cid engines, notches on end of shafts (see **Figure 18**) must point toward front of engine and toward centerline of engine. On other V-8 engines, 3/16 in. lubrication holes in shafts must point downward and 15° inward. See **Figure 19**. If reused, rocker arms should be returned to their original positions. If new arms are used, install a left and right rocker arm (see **Figure 20**) together on the shaft for each pair of valves, as shown in **Figure 21**. Make sure longer retainers are installed in the Nos. 2 and 4 positions (see **Figure 22**).
2. Install rocker arms/shaft assembly on cylinder head with bolts and retainers, making sure pushrods are properly seated in rocker arms. Tighten bolts to 15 ft.-lb. (318-360 engines) or 25 ft.-lb. (400-440 engines).
3. Thoroughly clean valve cover gasket surface and inspect surface for distortion. Have the surface straightened, if necessary. Clean head gasket surface.
4. Install valve cover and tighten bolts to 40 in.-lb. Do not over-tighten, as this could cause distortion of the gasket and lead to oil leaks.

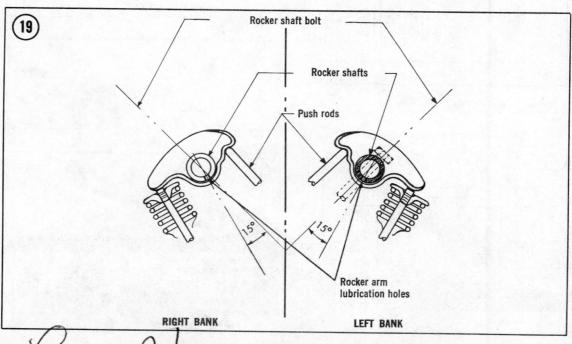

(19)

Rocker shaft bolt

Rocker shafts

Push rods

15°   15°

Rocker arm
lubrication holes

RIGHT BANK   **LEFT BANK**

5. Install wires and hoses removed during the removal procedure.

6. Start the engine and check for oil leaks. If leaks are present, remove the valve covers, apply gasket cement to all gasket surfaces, and reinstall the covers.

Cylinder Head Removal
(All Models)

1. Drain cooling system and disconnect battery ground cable.

2. Remove rocker arms/shaft assemblies as previously described.

3. Remove carburetor air cleaner and fuel line. On V-8 engines, disconnect and remove alternator and air pump (if so equipped).

4. Disconnect accelerator linkage and position out of the way.

5. Remove vacuum control tube at carburetor and distributor.

6. Remove distributor cap and spark plug wires. Identify wires for easy installation.

7. Disconnect heater hoses(s) and clamp holding bypass hose. On V-8 engines, disconnect coil wires and remove distributor.

8. Disconnect heat indicator sending unit wire.

9. On V-8 engines, remove intake manifold, carburetor, and coil as a unit. Then remove exhaust manifolds.

10. On 6-cylinder models, disconnect exhaust pipe for exhaust manifold and, if so equipped, disconnect diverter valve vacuum line from intake manifold and remove air tube assembly from cylinder head.

11. Remove pushrods and identify them positively so they can be returned to their original positions.

12. On V-8 engines, remove the 10 (318-360) or 17 (400-440) cylinder head bolts from each head and remove the heads. On 6-cylinder engines, remove the 14 bolts and remove the cylinder head, intake manifold, exhaust manifold, and carburetor as an assembly (some assistance may be required, as this assembly is very heavy).

13. Remove spark plugs.

14. If cylinder head service is required on 6-cylinder engines, remove the carburetor, intake manifold and exhaust manifold.

15. Remove the valve lifters. Use a pencil magnet on 6-cylinder engines.

Cylinder Head Disassembly

NOTE
If the need for cylinder head and valve service is evident or suspected it is strongly recommended that you take the assembled

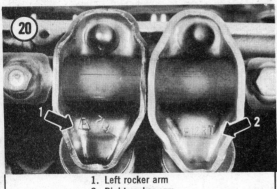

1. Left rocker arm
2. Right rocker arm

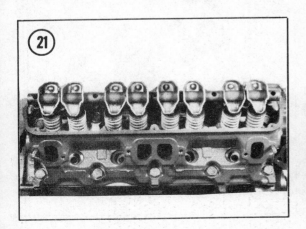

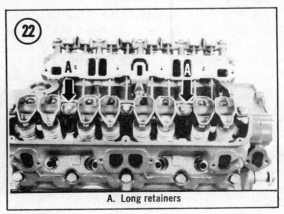

A. Long retainers

head to a reliable automotive machine shop. They can clean, disassemble, repair, and reassemble the head for a fraction of the cost of the tools and special equipment required to properly service the assembly.

1. Using a plastic scraper, or a soft wire brush, remove all carbon from the combustion chamber areas of the head and the valve heads.
2. Remove all gasket material from the gasket surfaces of the head.
3. Using a suitable tool (see **Figure 23**), compress valve springs and remove locks. Release the pressure on the valve springs and remove the retainers, springs, and oil shields or seals. Remove the valves. If valves are to be reused, be sure to identify them so they can be returned to their original positions.

NOTE
Check the valve stems for burrs and remove them, if present, before removing the valves. This will help prevent damage to the valve guides.

Valve Inspection (All Models)

1. Clean valves and check them for damage. Discard those that are burned, warped, or cracked.
2. Measure diameter of valve stem for wear. A new intake valve should measure between 0.372 and 0.373 in., and the exhaust valve should measure between 0.371 and 0.372 in. If wear exceeds 0.002 in., the valve should be replaced.
3. Remove carbon and varnish deposits from the inside of the valve guides. Using a dial indicator and tool C-3973 (or equivalent), measure the clearance between the valve guide bores and a valve known to be within the tolerances given in Step 2. Tool C-3973 is a sleeve into which the valve is inserted and which will hold the valve at the correct height for clearance measurement when the valve stem is inserted into the valve guide. See **Figure 24**. Attach the dial indicator to the cylinder head at right angle to the valve being measured. See **Figure 25**. Move the valve toward and away from the indicator. Total movement should not exceed 0.017 in. Have valve guides reamed for valves with oversize stems if movement exceeds this distance.

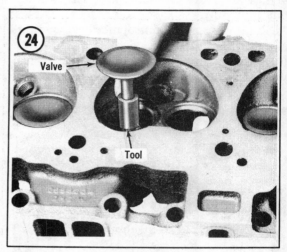

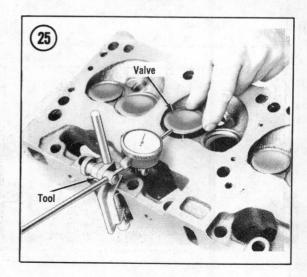

NOTE
Valves are available with 0.005, 0.015,
and 0.030 in. oversize stems.

Valve and Valve Seat Service

Refacing of valves and valve seats is a job for a competent machine shop. Although it is possible to "grind" valves by hand, this procedure is not recommended for modern engines. See **Table 1** for valve face and valve seat specifications.

Valve Spring Inspection
(All Models)

While the cylinder head is disassembled, the valve springs should be cleaned and checked as follows:

1. Have the spring load at compressed length checked on a test device as shown in **Figure 26**. See **Table 1** for specifications. Replace springs not within limits.
2. Check each spring for squareness, using a steel square and surface plate as shown in **Figure 27**. If the spring is more than 1/16 in. out of square, replace it.

Cylinder Head Assembly (All Models)

1. Lubricate valve stems and insert them in cylinder head.
2. If valves have been resurfaced, check stem lengths with tool C-3968, as shown in **Figure 28**. If stem is too long, grind off tip until it is within limits.

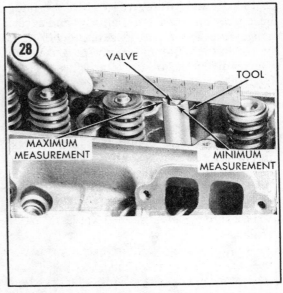

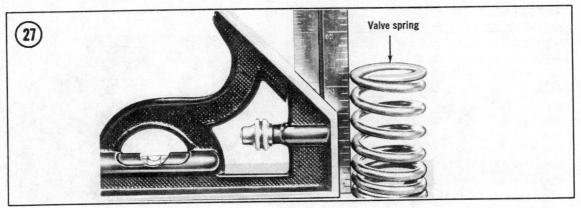

NOTE
If engine is equipped with valve rotators,
do not grind stems. Select another valve.

3. Install new oil seals on valve stems. On
6-cylinder engines, install long shields on
intake valves and short shields on exhaust
valves. Refer to **Figure 29** for installation
order of seals and other related parts.
4. Install valve springs and retainers. Use a
valve spring compressor (see **Figure 23**) to
compress the springs and install the locks.
Remove compressor.

Cylinder Head Installation
(All Models)

1. Make sure all gasket surfaces on the cylinder
head and cylinder block are cleaned.
2. Inspect all mating surfaces of the cylinder
head with an accurate straightedge and a feeler
gauge. See **Figure 30**. Maximum allowable
out-of-flat is 0.009 in. in any 12 inches. For
shorter distances, multiply the inches of length
by 0.00075 to determine the maximum allowable distortion.
3. Lubricate and install valve lifters. See **Figure 31** (318 engine shown).
4. For 6-cylinder engines, install the intake
and exhaust manifolds and the carburetor on

the cylinder head. Install spark plugs and
tighten to 10 ft.-lb.
5. Lightly coat new head gasket(s) with
Chrysler sealer, part No. 3419005, or equivalent, and install gasket(s) on cylinder block.
6. Install the cylinder head(s) on the cylinder
block and install the cylinder head bolts. On
6-cylinder engines, tighten all bolts to 35
ft.-lb. following the sequence shown in **Figure
32**, then retighten them in the same sequence
to 70 ft.-lb. On 318-360 engines, tighten head
bolts to 50 ft.-lb., following the sequence
shown in **Figure 33**, and then retighten them
in the same sequence to 95 ft.-lb. On 400-440
engines, tighten head bolts to 40 ft.-lb.,
following the sequence shown in **Figure 34**,
then retighten them in the same sequence to
70 ft.-lb.
7. Install pushrods and rocker arms/shaft
assembly(ies) as previously described.

NOTE
Steps 8 through 15 apply only to V8
engines.

8. Apply a glue-type gasket sealer such as
Gasgacinch or Permatex High-Tack (tube
type, not spray) to the rails at front and rear of
the block. Install the front and rear seal strips
over the dowels.

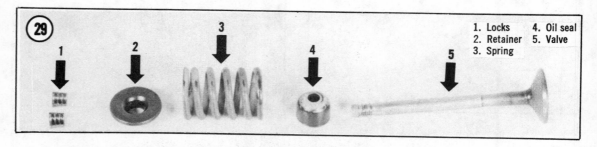

29
1. Locks 4. Oil seal
2. Retainer 5. Valve
3. Spring

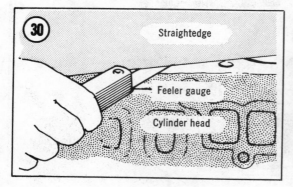

30 Straightedge / Feeler gauge / Cylinder head

31

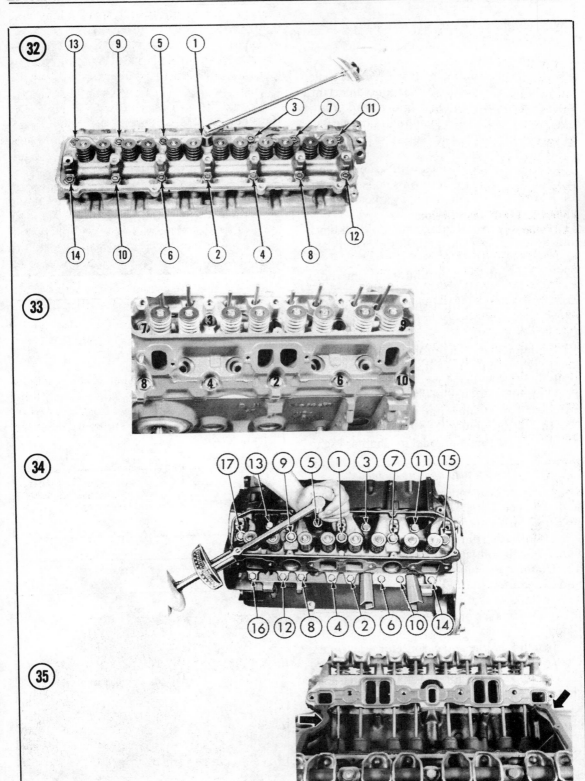

See **Figure 35**. Engage the end holes in the seals with the tabs on the cylinder head gaskets. See **Figure 36**.

9. Apply 1/4 in. diameter drop of rubber sealer (Chrysler part No. 4026070 or equivalent) into each corner between the cylinder head tabs.

10. Install the intake manifold side gaskets. On 318 cid engines and on 360 cid engines *without* composition side gaskets, lightly coat the gaskets on both sides with sealer. On 360 cid engines with composition side gaskets and on all other V-8's, do not use gasket sealer on the side gaskets.

11. Carefully install intake manifold on block and heads. Inspect to make sure gaskets and seals are in place.

12. Install intake manifold retaining bolts finger-tight. Tighten bolts to 25 ft.-lb., in a sequence similar to that shown in **Figure 37**. Then tighten all bolts to 40 ft.-lb., following the same sequence.

13. Install exhaust manifolds, using new gaskets. Tighten nuts to 15 ft.-lb. and bolts to 20 ft.-lb. on 318-360 engines. Tighten nuts to 30 ft.-lb. on other V8 engines.

14. Install spark plugs and tighten to 30 ft.-lb.

15. Install distributor. See *Distributor Installation* for your engine model in Chapter Eight.

NOTE
The following steps apply to all models.

16. Connect heat indicator sending unit wire and connect heater hose(s). Connect clamp holding bypass hose.

17. Install distributor cap and spark plug wires. Install coil wires on V8 engines.

18. Connect vacuum tube between carburetor and distributor.

19. Install and adjust accelerator linkage. Make sure linkage operates freely and does not bind.

20. Install fuel line and carburetor air cleaner. On V8 engines, install alternator and air pump, if so equipped, and adjust belts to proper tension. See *Accessory Drive Belts*, Chapter Seven.

21. Fill cooling system and connect battery ground cable.

Timing Chain Cover
Removal/Installation (All Models)

1. Drain cooling system and remove radiator and cooling fan.

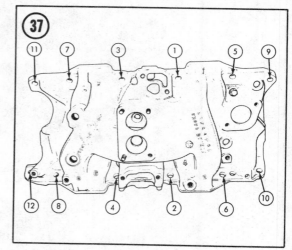

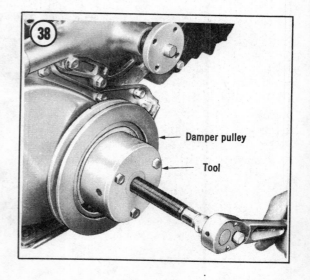

Damper pulley

Tool

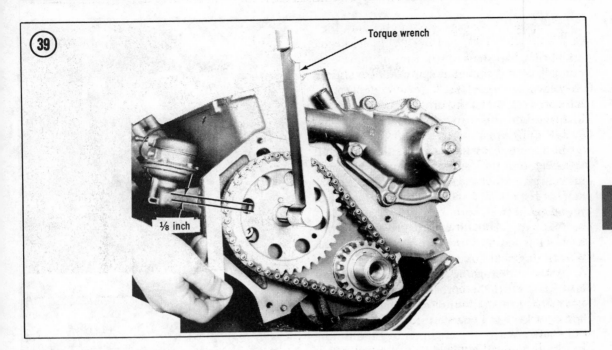

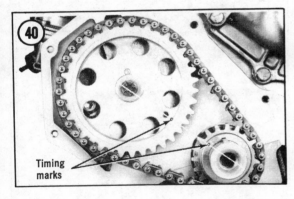

2. On V8 engines, remove fuel pump. Then remove retaining bolts and remove water pump.

3. Remove vibration damper, using a suitable puller. See **Figure 38** (6-cylinder).

4. On V8 engines, remove fuel lines and fuel pump.

5. Loosen oil pan bolts to allow clearance. On V8 engines, remove the front bolt on each side.

6. Remove timing chain cover, using care to avoid damage to oil pan gasket.

7. Installation is the reverse of these steps. Use a new gasket, and tighten cover attaching bolts to 30 ft.-lb. and oil pan bolts to 15 ft.-lb. Tighten vibration damper-to-crankcase bolts to 100 ft.-lb. (135 ft.-lb. on 400-440).

Timing Chain Inspection (All Models)

1. Remove timing chain cover as previously described.

2. Block crankshaft so it will not move.

3. Using a torque wrench and socket applied to the camshaft sprocket (see **Figure 39**), apply torque in one direction (30 ft.-lb. if cylinder head(s) is on, 15 ft.-lb. if off) to remove all slack from chain.

4. Place a scale by the chain so that a reading can be taken from the edge of any link (see **Figure 39**) and apply the same amount of torque in the opposite direction. If the edge of the link moves more than 1/8 in. (3/16 in. on 225 engine), the timing chain should be replaced.

Timing Chain
Removal/Installation (6-Cylinder)

1. Turn crankshaft until timing marks on crankshaft and camshaft sprockets are aligned as shown in **Figure 40**.

2. Remove camshaft sprocket lock bolt and washer and remove sprocket and timing chain.

3. Install new timing chain and sprocket. Make sure timing marks are still properly aligned (**Figure 40**).

4. Install washer and lock bolt. Tighten bolt to 35 ft.-lb.

Timing Chain
Removal/Installation (V-8 Engines)

1. Turn crankshaft until timing marks on crankshaft and camshaft sprockets are aligned as shown in **Figure 41**.

2. Remove camshaft sprocket attaching bolt and washer (also fuel pump eccentric on 318-360 engine).

3. Slide the camshaft sprocket, crankshaft sprocket, and timing chain from the camshaft and crankshaft at the same time. If necessary, start the sprockets with a suitable puller. Remove chain from sprockets.

4. Place sprockets on workbench with timing marks aligned as shown in **Figure 41**. Install new timing chain over sprockets.

5. Without disturbing the sprockets-chain relationships, lift the sprockets and slide them over the camshaft and crankshaft so that sprocket keyways engage the keys installed in the shafts. Verify the alignment of the timing marks with a straightedge.

NOTE
*With the camshaft sprocket removed, there will be a considerable amount of play in the camshaft. The cup washer and bolt can be temporarily installed (see **Figure 42**) to draw the camshaft out to engage the keyway with the key. After engagement is made, remove the washer and bolts.*

6. Install fuel pump eccentric (318-360 engines), washer, and bolt (see **Figure 43**).

7. On 318-360 engines, check end play of camshaft with dial indicator. If more than 0.010 in. (used thrust plate) or not between 0.002-0.006 in. (new thrust plate), install a new thrust plate.

Front Oil Seal Removal/ Installation
(6-Cylinder)

1. With vibration damper removed, but engine front cover installed, use a suitable tool to pry out the oil seal. Take care not to damage the seal surface of the front cover.

2. Insert a new seal into the opening with the seal spring toward the engine.

3. Press the seal into place, using a suitable tool (Chrysler C-4251 or equivalent). Tighten until tool is flush with front cover.

4. Install vibration damper pulley, using a suitable tool (Chrysler C3732A or equivalent). See **Figure 44**.

Front Oil Seal Removal/Installation (V-8 Engines)

1. With engine front cover removed, use a drift and a hammer to tap lightly at several places to deform the oil seal (seal must be removed and installed from inside the cover).

2. Remove seal by applying Vise-Grip pliers at several places and twisting and pulling the seal out of its seat.

3. Use a suitable tool to press the new seal into the seat. Seal must be fully seated. Check by trying to insert a 0.0015 in. feeler gauge between the seal and seat at several places.

Camshaft Removal/Installation (6-Cylinder)

1. Remove cylinder head and tappets as previously described in this section.

2. Remove timing sprocket and chain as previously described.

3. Remove distributor as described in Chapter Eight. See *Distributor Removal/Installation (6-Cylinder)*.

4. Remove oil pump, as described later in this chapter.

5. Remove fuel pump by disconnecting fuel lines and removing attaching bolts.

6. Install a long bolt (7/16 in.) in the lock bolt hole in the front of the camshaft as a removal aid. Withdraw the camshaft, taking care not to damage the camshaft bearings.

7. Installation is the reverse of these steps. Thoroughly lubricate the lobes and bearings before inserting the camshaft in the engine.

Camshaft Removal/Installation (318-360 Engines)

1. Remove cylinder heads and tappets as previously described in this section.

2. Remove the distributor and lift out the distributor/oil pump drive shaft (see arrow, **Figure 45**).

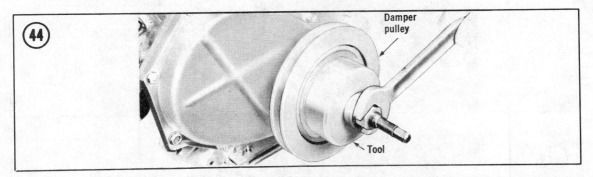

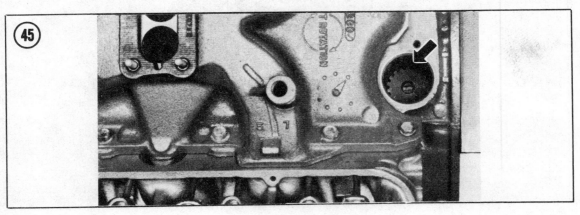

3. Remove the engine front cover and the timing chain and sprockets as previously described in this section.

4. Remove the camshaft thrust plate (see 1, **Figure 46**.) Some models have an oil tab attached to the thrust plate by the lower right bolt (see 2, **Figure 46**). If present, carefully note the position of the tab for installation. If tab is present, thrust plate will be installed with 3 bolts instead of 4. See 3, **Figure 46**, for bolt that will be missing.

5. Withdraw the camshaft from the engine, taking care not to damage the camshaft bearings. See **Figure 47**.

6. Installation is the reverse of these steps. Lubricate camshaft lobes and bearing journals before inserting the camshaft into the engine.

NOTE
Chrysler recommends the use of a restraining tool (C-3509) to keep the camshaft from being inserted too far and knocking out the plug in the rear of the cylinder block. If this tool is not available, use care so the plug will not be accidentally knocked out.

Camshaft Removal/Installation (400-440 Engines)

1. Remove cylinder heads and tappets as previously described in this section.

2. Remove timing chain and sprockets as previously described in this chapter.

3. Remove the distributor and lift out the oil pump/distributor drive shaft. See **Figure 48**.

4. Remove the fuel pump.

5. Carefully withdraw the camshaft, taking care not to damage camshaft bearings with camshaft lobes.

6. Installation is the reverse of these steps. Lubricate camshaft lobes and bearing journals before inserting the camshaft into the engine.

NOTE
Chrysler recommends the use of a restraining tool to keep the camshaft from being inserted too far and knocking out the welch plug in the rear of the engine. If this tool is not available, use care so the plug will not be accidentally knocked out.

Camshaft Bearings (All Models)

Removal and installation of camshaft bearings requires special tools and skills. This task should be performed by a properly-equipped automotive machine shop.

CYLINDER BLOCK PISTONS, AND CONNECTING RODS

Piston Removal (All Models)

1. Remove cylinder head(s) as described elsewhere in this chapter.

2. Raise vehicle and drain oil from crankcase.

3. Remove oil pan as described elsewhere in this chapter.

4. Cover tops of pistons with a cloth and, using a reliable ridge reamer, remove the ridges from the tops of the cylinder bores. Remove cloth from cylinder, making sure all metal shavings are removed at the same time.

5. Rotate crankshaft so the connecting rod of the piston to be removed is centered in the cylinder bore. Remove bearing cap and then remove the piston and connecting rod assembly by pushing it out through the top of the cylinder block.

6. If connecting rods and rod bearing caps are to be reused, check them as they are removed for cylinder identification. If no markings are present, permanently mark each rod and each cap with the number of the cylinder from which it was removed.

NOTE
Cylinders are numbered from the front of the engine. On 6-cylinder engines, cylinder numbers are, starting from the front, 1-2-3-4-5-6. On V-8 engines, note that the left bank of cylinders is closer to the front of the engine than the right bank. Cylinders in the left bank are 1-3-5-7, and those in the right bank are 2-4-6-8.

Cylinder Block Cleaning and Inspection

1. Clean the cylinder block thoroughly.

NOTE
Some mechanics recommend taking the block to an automotive machine shop

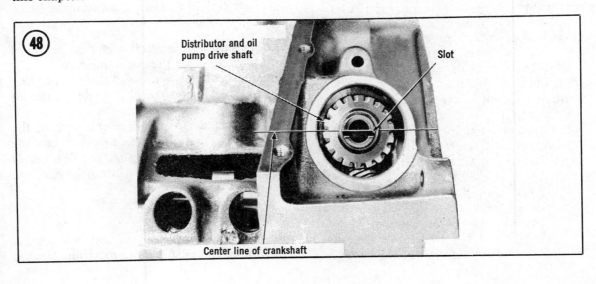

48 Distributor and oil pump drive shaft   Slot

Center line of crankshaft

and having it cleaned in a "hot tank" (a tank filled with a hot cleaning solution). This is a good way to ensure that all water and oil passages are thoroughly cleaned, but the cleaning solution removes much of the oil from all surfaces. This could lead to rust and corrosion if the block is not used immediately.

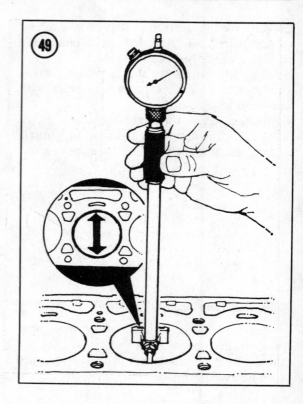

2. Check freeze plugs for signs of leakage and replace those that show damage. If the engine is being rebuilt, it is good practice to replace all freeze plugs regardless of appearance. Remove old plugs by deforming them and prying them out of the block. Coat new plug edges and the sides of the holes in the block with sealer (part No. 3837795 or equivalent) and use a wooden or soft metal drift and a hammer to tap the plugs into the block. Plugs are properly installed when their lips are 1/64 in. below the chamfered area.

3. Check all block surfaces for cracks and fractures. If any are found, take the block to an automotive machine shop to see if the damage can be repaired.

4. Using a bore gauge as shown in **Figure 49**, measure each cylinder bore at 3 places (top, center, and bottom) within the contact area of the piston rings. Record the measurements and compare them. This will give you the taper of each cylinder. If the difference in the readings (taper) is more than 0.010 in. in any cylinder, the cylinder block should be rebored and honed and oversize pistons and rings fitted.

5. Using the bore gauge, take 3 measurements in each cylinder at right angles (lengthwise instead of crosswise) to those taken in Step 4 and compare the 2 sets of measurements taken at each level for each cylinder. This will give you the "out-of-round" measurement for the cylinder. If any cylinder shows an out-of-round condition of more than 0.005 in., rebore and hone cylinder block and fit oversize pistons and rings.

NOTE
Pistons (including pins) are available in standard and 0.020 in. oversize for 6-cylinder engines and standard and 0.005, 0.020, and 0.040 in. oversize for V-8 engines. All pistons are machined to

the same weight (in grams), but Chrysler recommends that all cylinders be rebored if one or more require reboring to 0.020 oversize.

Fitting New Pistons

NOTE
Pistons and cylinder bores should be measured at normal room temperature (approx. 70° F). Piston and cylinder wall must be clean and dry.

1. Measure the piston diameter at the top of the skirt, 90° from the piston pin axis.
2. Measure the cylinder wall halfway between the top and the bottom, 90° from the crankshaft axis.
3. Subtract the first measurement from the second to determine clearance between the piston and the cylinder wall. If the clearance is not within these limits, try fitting the piston to another cylinder.

Fitting Piston Rings

1. Insert piston ring into cylinder in which it is to be used and push it down to within 2 inches

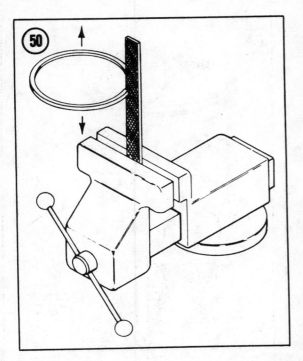

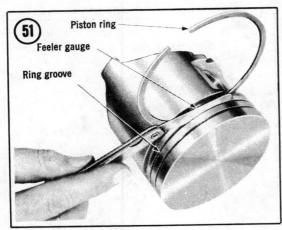

Piston ring

Feeler gauge

Ring groove

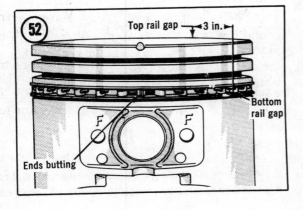

Top rail gap — 3 in.

Bottom rail gap

F   F

Ends butting

from the bottom of the cylinder bore, using an inverted piston. This will position the ring squarely in the bore.

2. Use a feeler gauge to measure the gap between the ends of the ring. See **Table 3** for specified gap tolerances.

NOTE

Table 3 clearances apply to standard cylinder bores. Maximum gaps for standard rings used in 0.005 oversize bores (all models) is 0.060 in. for compression rings and 0.070 in. for oil ring rails.

3. If a ring gap is smaller than specified, the gap can be enlarged by careful filling as shown in **Figure 50**. Before attempting this remedy, however, try fitting the ring in another cylinder.

4. Measure the side clearance between each piston ring and the piston grooves. See **Figure 51**. Clearance should be 0.0015 to 0.003 in. for compression rings, and should not exceed 0.005 in. for oil rings (all models). However, oil ring rails should be free to move in the ring. If a ring does not fit one piston, try fitting it to another. If a ring cannot be found to properly fit a given piston, the piston should be replaced.

5. Install the fitted rings on the pistons. Compression rings should be installed with the stamped marking TOP facing up.

NOTE

On 318-360 engines, keys on the oil ring expander must be inserted in the piston hole located in the ring groove over the piston pin front boss. On all V-8 engines, oil ring rails must be spaced as shown in **Figure 52** *on the inboard side of the piston. Stagger compression ring gaps so neither is in line with an oil ring rail gap. On 6-cylinder engines, compression ring gaps should be on the left side of the engine, staggered about 60° apart. The oil ring expander ends should meet on the right side of the engine and the oil ring rail gaps should be opposite each other and located above the piston pin holes. Make sure compression ring gaps do not line up with oil ring rail gaps.*

Piston Pin Removal/Installation

Special tools and an arbor press are required

for removing and installing piston pins. These jobs should be referred to your dealer's service shop or to a well-equipped automotive machine shop. On 6-cylinder engines, pistons, pins, and connecting rods should be assembled with the notch in the top of the cylinder and the oil hole in the connecting rod toward the front of the engine. See **Figure 53**.

When assembling pistons, pins, and connecting rods for V-8 engines, note that the large bore of the connecting rod has a larger chamfer (beveled edge) on one side. When assembling pistons and rods for the right bank (cylinders 2-4-6-8), this larger chamfer must go on the opposite side from the notch in the top surface of the piston. When assembling pistons and rods for the left bank (cylinders 1-3-5-7), the larger chamfer goes on the same side as the notch. See **Figure 54**. Keep the 2 groups of assemblies separated, and make sure they are installed in their proper banks. Otherwise early engine failure could result.

Piston/Connecting Rod Installation

1. Dip the piston head and rings in clean engine oil and install a ring compressor over the piston rings.
2. Install bearing half in connecting rod so that bearing tang fits into machined notch in rod.
3. Place protectors over connecting rod bolts. See **Figure 55**. Masking tape can be substituted if protectors are not available.
4. Make sure the crankshaft journal is centered with the bore of the cylinder in which the assembly will be installed.
5. Insert the piston into the cylinder bore with the notch on the top of the piston facing toward the front of the engine. Make sure the piston is the one fitted to the cylinder and, if working on a V-8 engine, that the connecting rod is properly assembled as described earlier for the right or left cylinder bank.
6. Use a hammer handle or other wooden tool to tap the piston into the cylinder (see **Figure 56**). If firm resistance is felt, the ring compressor probably needs adjustment. Withdraw the piston assembly, remove and reinstall the compressor, and reinsert the piston. Do not use excessive force, as this could cause damage.

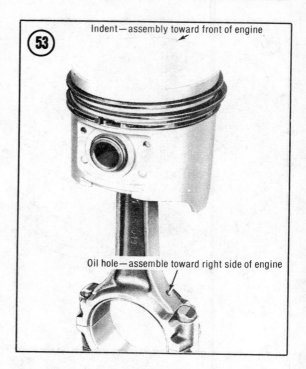

Indent—assembly toward front of engine

Oil hole—assemble toward right side of engine

53

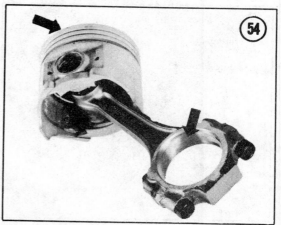

54

7. As the piston enters the cylinder, guide the connecting rod bearing onto the crankshaft journal. Take care to avoid damage to either the crankshaft or the bearing. Make sure both bearing and journal are free of oil.
8. Install a piece of Plastigage lengthwise across the journal (avoid oil holes in journal) and install the connecting rod bearing cap (with bearing installed). Tighten nuts to 45 ft.-lb.
9. Remove the bearing cap and measure the width of the flattened Plastigage with the scale

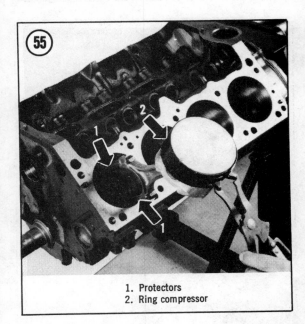

1. Protectors
2. Ring compressor

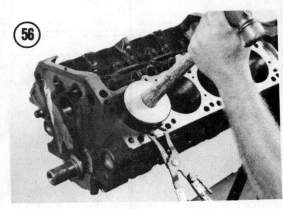

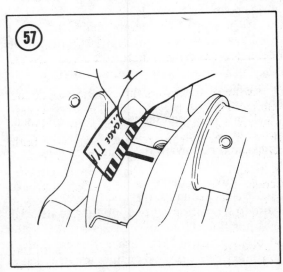

on the package (see **Figure 57**). Clearance should be between 0.0005 and 0.0025 in. for 225; 0.005 and 0.002 in. for 318 and 400 2 bbl; 0.001 and 0.0025 in. for 360; and 0.001 and 0.002 for 400 4 bbl and 440 engines.

> *NOTE*
> *Bearings are available in standard and 0.001, 0.002, 0.003, 0.010, and 0.012 in. undersize. The following bearing shell pairs can be used together to obtain the proper clearance; standard and 0.001; 0.001 and 0.001; 0.001 and 0.002. Do not use 2 shells that are more than 0.001 in. apart.*

10. Measure the maximum and minimum widths of the deformed Plastigage. If the difference is more than 0.001 in., the crankshaft journal probably has excessive taper and should be reground or replaced. However, make another measurement or take the crankshaft to an expert for another opinion before making a decision.

11. After connecting rod bearings have been fitted, remove all traces of the Plastigage and reinstall the bearing cap. Torque to 45 ft.-lb.

12. Repeat the above steps for all cylinders.

CRANKSHAFT, MAIN BEARINGS, SEALS, AND OIL PUMP

Oil Pan Removal/Installation (6-Cylinder)

1. Disconnect battery ground cable and remove engine oil dipstick and tube. Remove engine cover as described elsewhere in this chapter. Remove carburetor air cleaner.

2. Remove the front bumper, grille, and radiator and support.

3. Disconnect throttle linkage at rear of engine. Also disconnect the clutch and/or transmission linkage.

4. Raise the engine slightly and support it with an engine support fixture (**Figure 1** and **Figure 4**).

5. Drain the engine oil and remove the starter.

6. Remove the propeller shaft, rear engine support, and transmission. See *Manual Transmission Removal* or *Automatic Transmission Removal*, Chapter Nine. Remove the clutch assembly and flywheel (manual

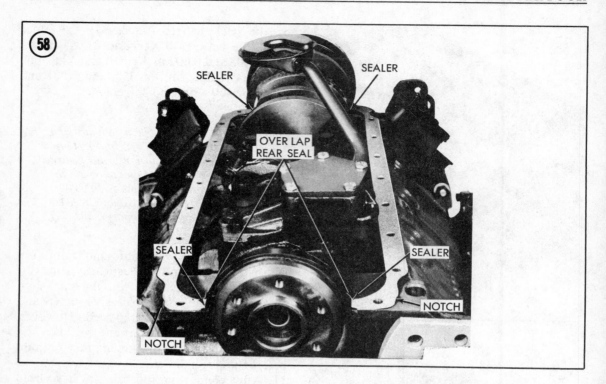

transmission) or the drive plate (automatic). Raise the rear of engine about 6 inches.

7. Remove oil pan attaching screws and then remove the oil pan. Position crankshaft as required to permit clearance of the counter-weights and crankpins. Lower pan and rotate slightly to left to clear oil pick-up tube and screen.

8. Installation is the reverse of these steps. Use a new gasket set on oil pan and add small drops (1/8 in. diameter) of gasket sealer to each corner. Tighten oil pan attaching screws to 75 in.-lb., and then retighten to 200 in.-lb. Do not overtighten. Tighten engine rear support bolts and nuts to values given in **Figure 7**.

Oil Pan Removal/Installation (318-360 Engines)

1. Disconnect battery ground cable and re-move engine oil dipstick. Remove engine cover as previously described and remove the carburetor air cleaner.

2. Disconnect the throttle linkage at the rear of the engine. Also disconnect clutch and/or transmission linkage.

3. Raise the engine slightly and support it with an engine support fixture (**Figure 1** and **Figure 8**).

4. Drain engine oil, and remove starter and oil filter.

5. Remove propeller shaft, rear engine mount, and transmission. See *Manual Transmission Removal* or *Automatic Transmission Removal*, Chapter Nine. Remove clutch and flywheel (manual transmission) or drive plate (automatic).

6. Raise rear of engine about 2 inches. Posi-tion fan so maximum clearance is available between it and the radiator.

7. Turn crankshaft so that notch on the crankshaft flange is in the 3 o'clock position. See **Figure 9**.

8. Remove oil pan screws and drop oil pan far enough to reach inside and reposition oil pick-up tube toward the right side as shown in **Figure 9**.

9. Remove oil pan.

10. Installation is the reverse of these steps. Be sure to reposition oil pick-up tube to its origi-nal position. Use a new gasket set and add a drop of sealer at each corner. Be sure notches on side gaskets on 360 engines are installed as

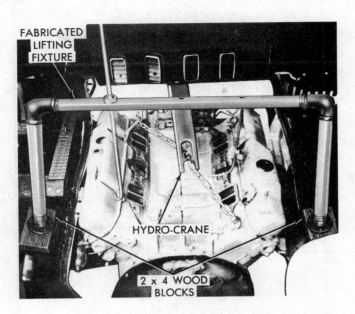

FABRICATED LIFTING FIXTURE

HYDRO-CRANE

2 x 4 WOOD BLOCKS

4

shown in **Figure 58**. Torque oil pan screw to 200 in.-lb. Do not overtighten. Tighten engine rear support bolts and nuts to values given in **Figure 7**.

Oil Pan Removal/Installation (400-440 Engines)

1. Disconnect battery ground cable and remove engine cover as previously described.
2. Remove carburetor and install lifting bridle. Install engine lifting fixture (**Figure 1**) and support the rear of the engine (**Figure 59**).
3. Remove idler arm brackets from frame and disconnect the strut bars from the lower control arms.
4. Remove shock absorbers and motor mount insulator upper nuts.
5. Mark the frame and crossmember on both sides for alignment during installation and remove the crossmember by removing outboard retaining bolts, and replacing them with 4 1/4 in. long bolts, placing floor stands under the crossmember, removing the inboard bolts, and lowering the crossmember and floor stands.
6. Drain engine oil and remove the oil dipstick and tube. Remove the oil pan retaining bolts and remove the pan.

7. Installation is the reverse of these steps. Use a new gasket set and tighten oil pan attaching screws to 200 in.-lb. Do not overtighten. Make sure that crossmember is properly aligned, and torque inboard and outboard bolts to 75 ft.-lb.

Oil Pump Removal/Installation (6-Cylinder)

1. Remove the oil pan as previously described in this section.
2. Remove the oil filter.
3. Remove the oil pump attaching bolts and remove the oil pump assembly.
4. Installation is the reverse of these steps. Prime pump by filling cavity with engine oil, and tighten attaching bolts to 200 in.-lb.

Oil Pump Removal/Installation (V-8 Engines)

1. Remove the oil pan as previously described in this section.
2. Remove the attaching bolts and remove the oil pump from the lower side of the engine.
3. Installation is the reverse of these steps. Prime pump by filling cavity with engine oil and tighten attaching bolts to 30 ft.-lb.

Oil Pump Disassembly/Assembly (All Models)

> *NOTE*
> *Although the external configurations are different, the internal parts of the oil pumps for 6-cylinder and V-8 engines are similar in appearance and function.* **Figure 60** *is an exploded view of the 6-cylinder pump,* **Figure 61** *shows the 318-360 version, and* **Figure 62** *shows the 400-440 version.*

1. Remove relief valve cotter pin (if so equipped) and retainer cap. On V-8 engine pumps, drill a 1/8 in. hole in the cap and install a self-tapping screw. Clamp the screw in a vise, support the pump body, and lightly tap the body with a soft hammer to remove the cap.

2. Remove retaining bolts and lift off the pump cover and O-ring seal. Discard the seal.

3. On 6-cylinder models, support the pump body and press the drive gear off the inner rotor shaft. A small gear puller tool can be used for this purpose.

4. Remove the inner rotor and shaft and then lift out the outer rotor.

5. Assembly is the reverse of these steps. Tighten cover bolts to 95 in.-lb. Use a new O-ring seal and new parts as required (see *Oil Pump Inspection*, this section). Use a new relief valve retainer cap and cotter pin.

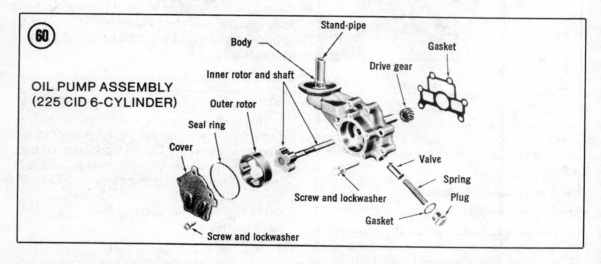

60 OIL PUMP ASSEMBLY (225 CID 6-CYLINDER)

Stand-pipe
Body
Drive gear
Gasket
Inner rotor and shaft
Outer rotor
Seal ring
Cover
Valve
Spring
Plug
Screw and lockwasher
Gasket
Screw and lockwasher

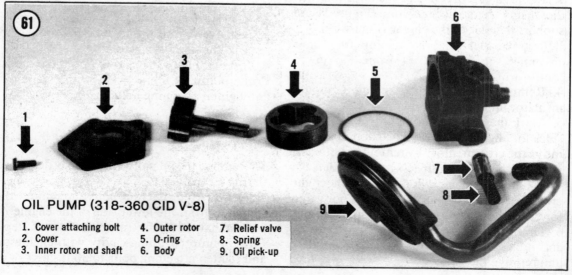

61 OIL PUMP (318-360 CID V-8)

1. Cover attaching bolt
2. Cover
3. Inner rotor and shaft
4. Outer rotor
5. O-ring
6. Body
7. Relief valve
8. Spring
9. Oil pick-up

Oil Pump Inspection
(All Models)

1. Clean all parts thoroughly in solvent.

2. Inspect the mating surfaces of the pump cover. If these surfaces are scratched or grooved, discard the pump assembly and install a new one.

3. Check the flatness of the pump cover with a straightedge and a feeler gauge. See **Figure 63**

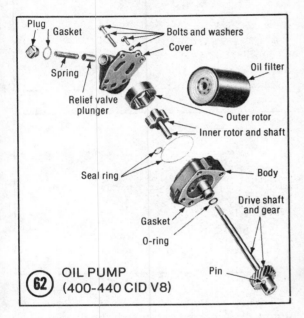

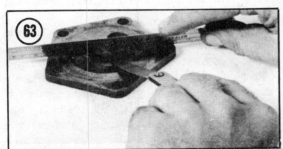

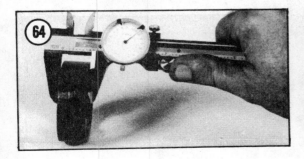

(typical). If a 0.0015 in. feeler gauge can be inserted between the straightedge and the cover, replace the pump assembly.

4. Check the thickness of the outer rotor (see **Figure 64**). If thickness is 0.649 in. or less on 6-cylinder engines, 0.825 in. or less on the 318 cid V-8, or 0.943 in. or less on other V-8 engines, replace the rotor.

5. Check the diameter of the outer rotor. If diameter is 2.469 or less, replace the rotor.

6. Check the thickness of the inner rotor (see **Figure 65**). If thickness is 0.649 in. or less for 6-cylinder, 0.825 in. or less for 318 cid V-8, or 0.943 in. or less for other V-8 engines, replace the inner rotor.

7. Install the rotors in the pump body and measure the clearance between the outer rotor and the pump body (see **Figure 66**). If clearance is greater than 0.014 in., replace the oil pump assembly.

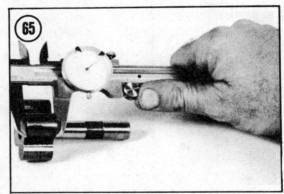

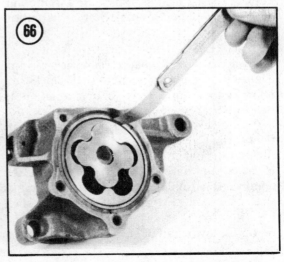

8. Check the clearance between the inner and outer rotors as shown in **Figure 67**. If clearance is greater than 0.010 in., replace both rotors and shaft.

9. Place a straightedge across the pump body and rotors as shown in **Figure 68**. If a feeler gauge of 0.004 in. can be inserted between the straightedge and the rotors, replace the pump assembly.

10. Check relief valve plunger for scoring and for free operation in its bore. Small marks can be removed with crocus cloth or 400 grit emery cloth.

11. Check the free length of the relief valve spring. It should be 2 1/4 in. for 6-cylinder and 400-440 V-8 engines, and 2 1/32 to 2 3/64 in. for 318-360 V-8 engines. Replace spring if it does not meet specifications.

Main Bearing Removal/Installation (All Models)

> *NOTE*
> *Upper bearing shell halves have oil holes and are not interchangeable with lower halves. No. 3 bearing is a thrust bearing and has shoulders. On V-8 engines, No. 5 bearing is wider than 1, 2, and 4.*

1. Remove oil pan as described elsewhere in this section.

2. Remove one bearing cap, leaving the others in place to support the crankshaft. If removing No. 1 cap, support crankshaft at vibration damper.

3. Install special tool (part No. C-3059 or equivalent) in crankshaft oil hole as shown in **Figure 69**. Slowly rotate crankshaft clockwise, allowing tool to force out the upper half of the bearing shell.

4. Remove lower half of the bearing shell from the bearing cap.

5. Start the upper half of the new bearing shell in place and insert the special tool in the crankshaft oil hole. Slowly rotate the crankshaft counterclockwise to seat the bearing shell half. Remove the tool.

6. Install lower half of bearing shell in bearing cap.

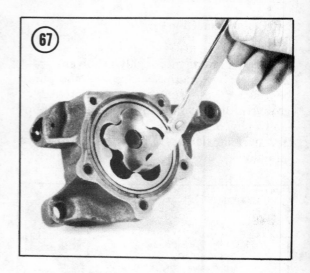

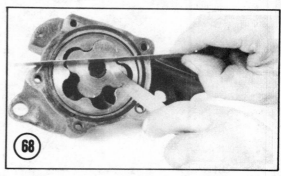

7. Place a piece of Plastigage across the crankshaft journal and install the bearing cap. Tighten bolts to 85 ft.-lb.

8. Remove the bearing cap and measure the width of the deformed Plastigage, using the scale provided on the Plastigage package. Clearance should be between 0.0005 and 0.005 in. (0.0005 and 0.002 on 400-440 engines). If clearance is larger than 0.0025, try fitting undersize bearing halves together to obtain the proper clearance.

> *NOTE*
> *Main bearings are available in standard and 0.001, 0.002, 0.003, 0.010, and 0.012 in. undersize. The following combination may be used to obtain specified clearance: standard and 0.001 in.; and 0.001 and 0.002 in. Do not use shells more than 0.001 in. apart.*

9. Measure the width of the Plastigage at the front and rear of the journal. If difference is

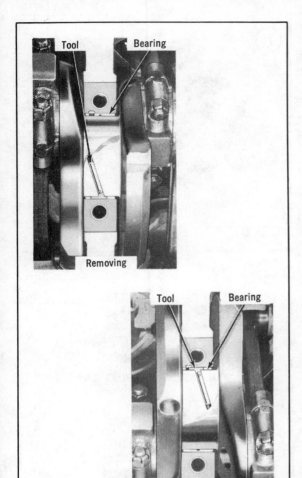

Tool   Bearing

Removing

Tool   Bearing

Installing

69

more than 0.001 in., the crankshaft journal has excessive taper and should be reground or replaced.

10. After bearings are fitted to obtain specified clearance, remove all traces of Plastigage and reinstall the bearing cap. Tighten to 85 ft.-lb.

11. Repeat the above steps for all main bearings.

12. Check the crankshaft end play with a dial indicator placed against a crankshaft counterweight. If end play is less than 0.002 in., loosen the bolts at the No. 3 (thrust) bearing cap, tighten the bolts finger-tight, and force the crankshaft forward and backward. Re-torque the bearing cap bolt and remeasure end play. If still less than 0.002 in., install a new thrust bearing. If end play exceeds 0.009 in., install a new thrust bearing.

Rear Main Oil Seal
Removal/ Installation (6-Cylinder)

1. Remove oil pan as described elsewhere in this section and remove rear main seal retainer and rear main bearing caps.

2. Remove old seal from retainer by prying it out with a small screwdriver.

3. Thread a special seal removal tool (part No. C-4148 or equivalent) into the upper seal half (see **Figure 70**), taking care to avoid damage to the crankshaft. Carefully rotate the crankshaft and pull out the seal with the tool.

4. Clean the crankshaft surface thoroughly and apply a light coat of oil to the area where the seal will be installed. Also lightly oil the lip of the seal.

5. Position seal with paint strip toward the rear of the engine and hold it firmly against the crankshaft with your thumb, and start the seal into the block groove. Make sure the seal does not catch on the sharp edge of the groove. Slide the seal into the block. If necessary, rotate the crankshaft while inserting the seal. Take care to avoid damage to the seal lip.

6. Install the other half of seal in seal retainer. Make sure paint strip is facing rear of engine.

7. Install bearing cap and tighten bolts to 85 ft.-lb.

8. Install side seals in grooves in seal retainer and apply a light coat of oil to the side seals for ease of installation. Apply a small amount of

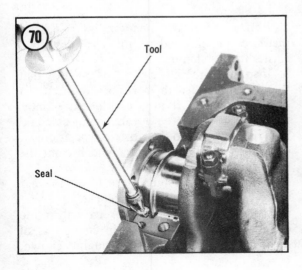

70

Tool

Seal

gasket cement to the bottom of the seal retainer (but not to the ends or lips of the crankshaft seal) and install the retainer. Tighten bolts to 30 ft.-lb.

Rear Main Oil Seal
Removal/Installation (V-8 Engines)

1. Remove oil pan and oil pump as described elsewhere in this section.
2. Remove the rear main bearing cap and use a small screwdriver to pry out the lower half of the oil seal.
3. Thread special seal removal tool (part No. C-4148 or equivalent) into the upper seal half and pull out the seal while rotating the crankshaft. See **Figure 70** (which shows tool being used on 6-cylinder engine). Take care when installing tool not to damage crankshaft.
4. Thoroughly clean crankshaft surface and apply a light coat of oil to the area where seal will be installed. Lightly oil lips of the new seal and install it in the cylinder block groove with paint strip toward the rear of the engine. Take care to prevent the end of the seal from hanging up on the sharp edges of the groove. Rotate the seal half into the groove. Turn the crankshaft, if necessary, and be careful not to cut or shave the seal.
5. Install the lower half of the seal in the bearing cap groove with paint strip to the rear (see **Figure 71**).
6. On 318 cid engine, insert cap seals into the slots in the bearing cap as shown in **Figure 72**. The seal with the yellow paint goes into the right side (installed-on-engine position), and both seals must be installed with narrow sealing edge up, and both must be exactly aligned with shoulders in the bearing cap to avert oil leakage.
7. On 360 cid engine, apply sealer (part No. 4026070 or equivalent) next to the seal as shown in **Figure 72**.
8. Install bearing cap and tighten bolts to 85 ft.-lb.

Crankshaft Removal/Installation
(All Models)

1. Remove engine from van and place on an engine stand as described earlier in this chapter.

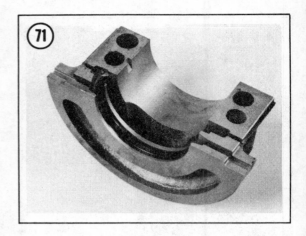

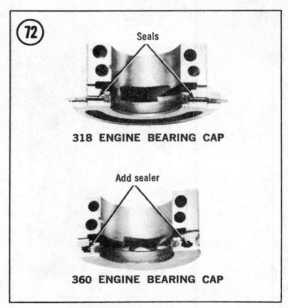

Seals

318 ENGINE BEARING CAP

Add sealer

360 ENGINE BEARING CAP

2. Remove cylinder head(s), oil pan, and piston/connecting rod assemblies as described earlier in this chapter.
3. Inspect the main bearing caps to verify that they are marked with their position numbers (see **Figure 73**). If not, permanently mark them, as the caps are not interchangeable and must be returned to their original positions.
4. Remove the bearing caps and lift out the crankshaft.
5. Remove the rear main oil seal from the rear bearing cap and the cylinder block.
6. Install a new rear main oil seal half in the cylinder block with paint strip facing rear of engine. See **Figure 74** (V-8 engine shown,

6-cylinder similar). End of seal should be flush with cylinder block. Install other seal half in rear main bearing cap as described in *Rear Main Oil Seal Removal/Installation*, this chapter.

7. Install main bearing shell halves in cylinder block and bearing caps.

8. Install crankshaft in cylinder block.

9. Fit bearings and install bearing caps as described in *Main Bearing Removal/Installation*, elsewhere in this chapter.

10. Install piston/connecting rod assemblies, oil pan, and cylinder heads as described earlier in this chapter.

11. Install engine in vehicle as described earlier in this chapter.

Tables are on the following pages.

Table 1   ENGINE SPECIFICATIONS

	225 cid 6-Cylinder	318 cid V-8	360 cid V-8	400 cid V-8	440 cid V-8
General					
Bore	3.40 in.	3.91 in.	4.000 in.	4.342 in.	4.320 in.
Stroke	4.125 in.	3.312 in.	3.580 in.	3.375 in.	3.750 in.
Displacement	225 cu. in.	318 cu. in.	360 cu. in.	400 cu. in.	440 cu. in.
Minimum compression	100 psi	100 psi	100 psi	100 psi	100 psi
Maximum variation					
between cylinders	35 psi	40 psi	40 psi	40 psi	40 psi
Firing order	1-5-3-6-2-4	1-8-4-3-6-5-7-2	1-8-4-3-6-5-7-2	1-8-4-3-6-5-7-2	1-8-4-3-6-5-7-2
Crankshaft					
Main bearing journal					
diameter	2.7495-2.7505 in.	2.4995-2.5005 in.	2.8095-2.8105 in.	2.6245-2.6255 in.	2.7495-2.7505 in.
Maximum out-of-round	0.001 in.	0.001 in.	0.001 in.	0.001 in.	0.001 in.
Maximum taper	0.001 in.	0.001 in.	0.001 in.	0.001 in.	0.001 in.
Connecting rod journal					
diameter	2.1865-2.1875 in.	2.124-2.125 in.	2.124-2.125 in.	2.375-2.376 in.	2.375-2.376 in.
Maximum out-of-round	0.001 in.	0.001 in.	0.001 in.	0.001 in.	0.001 in.
Maximum taper	0.001 in.	0.001 in.	0.001 in.	0.001 in.	0.001 in.
Maximum end play	0.002-0.009 in.	0.006-0.014 in.	0.006-0.014 in.	0.010 in.	0.010 in.
Main bearing clearance					
Desired	0.0005-0.0015 in.	0.0005-0.0015 in.	0.0005-0.0015 in.	0.0005-0.002 in.	0.0005-0.002 in.
Maximum allowable	0.0025 in.	0.0025 in.	0.0025 in.	0.0025 in.	0.0025 in.
Connecting rod bearing					
clearance					
Desired	0.0005-0.0025 in.	0.0005-0.0025 in.	0.0005-0.0025 in.	0.0005-0.003 in.*	0.0005-0.003 in.
Maximum allowable	0.0025 in.	0.003 in.	0.0025 in.	0.003 in.	0.003 in.
Piston pins					
Clearance in rod	Press fit	Press fit	Press fit	Press fit	Press fit
Clearance in piston					
(light thumb					
pressure @ 70 °F)	0.00035- 0.00085 in.	0.00045- 0.00075 in.	0.00025- 0.00075 in.	0.00045- 0.00075 in.	0.00045- 0.00075 in.
End play	None	None	None	None	None
Camshaft					
Desired clearance	0.001-0.003 in.	0.001-0.003 in.	0.001-0.003 in.	0.001-0.003 in.	0.001-0.003 in.
Maximum allowable					
clearance	0.005 in.	0.005 in.	0.005 in.	0.005 in.	0.005 in.
Valve lifters					
Type	Mechanical	Hydraulic	Hydraulic	Hydraulic	Hydraulic
Clearance (hot and idling)					
Intake	0.010 in.	N.A.	N.A.	N.A.	N.A.
Exhaust	0.020 in.	N.A.	N.A.	N.A.	N.A.
Pistons					
Clearance at top of skirt	0.0005-0.0015 in.	0.0005-0.0015 in.	0.0005-0.0015 in.	0.0003-0.0013 in.	0.0003-0.0013 in.

* 0.005-0.0025 in. for engines with 2-barrel carburetors.

(continued)

Table 1   ENGINE SPECIFICATIONS (continued)

	225 cid 6-Cylinder	318 cid V-8	360 cid V-8	400 cid V-8	440 cid V-8
Piston rings					
Gap					
Compression rings	0.010-0.020 in.	0.010-0.020 in.	0.010-0.020 in.	0.013-0.023 in.	0.013-0.023 in.
Oil ring rails	0.015-0.055 in.	0.015-0.055 in.	0.015-0.055 in.	0.015-0.055 in.	0.015-0.055 in.
Side clearance					
Compression rings	0.0015-0.0030 in.	0.0015-0.003 in.	0.0015-0.003 in.	0.0015-0.003 in.	0.0015-0.003 in.
Oil rings	0.0002-0.0050 in.	0.0005-0.005 in.	0.0005-0.005 in.	0.000-0.005 in.	0.000-0.005 in.
Valves					
Intake					
Head diameter	1.615-1.625 in.	1.780 in.	1.880 in.	2.08 in.	2.08 in.
Stem diameter	0.372-0.373 in.	0.372-0.373 in.	0.372-0.373 in.	0.372-0.373 in.	0.372-0.373 in.
Stem-to-guide clearance	0.001-0.003 in.	0.001-0.003 in.	0.001-0.003 in.	0.0011-0.0028 in.	0.0011-0.0028 in.
Face angle	43°	45°	45°	45°	45°
Exhaust					
Head diameter	1.355-1.365 in.	1.500 in.	1.600 in.	1.74 in.	1.74 in.
Stem diameter	0.371-0.372 in.	0.371-0.372 in.	0.371-0.372 in.	0.371-0.372 in.	0.371-0.372 in.
Stem-to-guide clearance	0.002-0.004 in.	0.002-0.004 in.	0.0020.004 in.	0.0021-0.0038 in.	0.0021-0.0038 in.
Face angle	43°	45°	45°	45°	45°
Valve springs					
Free length	1.92 in.	2.00 in.	2.00 in.	2.58 in.	2.58 in.
Installed height (spring seat to retainer)	$1\frac{5}{8}$-$1\frac{11}{16}$ in.	$1\frac{5}{8}$-$1\frac{11}{16}$ in.	$1\frac{5}{8}$-$1\frac{11}{16}$ in.	$1\frac{7}{16}$-$1\frac{55}{64}$ in.	$1\frac{7}{16}$-$1\frac{55}{64}$ in.

4

Table 2   TIGHTENING TORQUES

6 Cylinder Engines	
Location	**Torque Foot-Pounds**
Alternator adjusting strap bolt	200 in.-lb.
Alternator adjusting strap mounting bolt	30
Alternator bracket bolt	200 in.-lb.
Alternator mounting pivot nut	30
Camshaft lockbolt	50
Carburetor to manifold nut	200 in.-lb.
Chain case cover bolt	200 in.-lb.
Clutch housing bolt	30
Connecting rod nut	45
Crankshaft rear bearing seal retainer	30
Cylinder head bolt	70
Cylinder head cover	40 in.-lb.
Distributor clamp bolt	95 in.-lb.
Engine front mount insulator to engine bolt	65
Engine front mount insulator to bracket nut	75

(continued)

Table 2   TIGHTENING TORQUES (continued)

6 Cylinder Engines

Location	Torque Foot-Pounds
Engine rear mount insulator to crossmember nut	50
Engine rear mount insulator to extension	50
Engine rear mount crossmember to frame nut	30
Exhaust manifold nut	120 in.-lb.
Exhaust pipe flange nut	35
Exhaust pipe support bolt	50
Exhaust pipe support clamp nut	95 in.-lb.
Fan blade attaching bolts	200 in.-lb.
Flex plate to converter	270 in.-lb.
Flex plate to crankshaft	55
Fuel pump attaching bolt	30
Intake to exhaust manifold stud	240 in.-lb.
Intake to exhaust manifold bolt	200 in.-lb.
Main bearing cap bolt	85
Oil pan drain plug	20
Oil pan screw	200 in.-lb.
Oil pump cover bolt	95 in.-lb.
Oil pump attaching bolt	200 in.-lb.
Oil filter attaching stud	10
Oil pressure gauge sending unit	60 in.-lb.
Rocker shaft bracket bolt	24
Spark plug	10
Starter mounting bolt	50
Temperature gauge sending unit	60 in.-lb.
Water pump to housing bolt	30
A/C compressor bracket to water pump bolt	30
A/C compressor to bracket bolt	50
A/C compressor to support bolts	30

318-360 V-8 Engines

Location	Torque Foot-Pounds
Alternator adjusting strap bolt	200 in.-lb.
Alternator adjusting strap mounting bolt	30
Alternator bracket bolt	30
Alternator mounting pivot nut	30
Camshaft sprocket lockbolt	50
Camshaft thrust plate	210 in.-lb.
Chain case cover bolt	35
Clutch housing bolt	30
Connecting rod nut	45
Crankshaft bolt (vibration damper)	100
Cylinder head bolt	
1971 (318)	85
1971 (360)	70
1972-1977	95
1978-1980	105
1981	95

(continued)

Table 2   TIGHTENING TORQUES (continued)

318-360 V-8 Engines	
Location	**Torque Foot-Pounds**
Cylinder head cover	40 in.-lb.
Distributor clamp bolt	200 in.-lb.
Engine front mount insulator to frame nut	75
Engine front mount insulator to engine nut	65
Engine rear mount insulator to crossmember nut	50
Engine rear mount insulator to extension	50
Engine rear mount crossmember to frame nut	75
Exhaust manifold screw	20
Nut	15
Exhaust pipe flange nut	24
Fan blade attaching bolts	200 in.-lb.
Flex plate to converter	270 in.-lb.
Flex plate to crankshaft	55
Flywheel to crankshaft	55
Fuel pump attaching bolt	30
Intake manifold bolt	45
Main bearing cap bolt	85
Oil pan drain plug	20
Oil pan screw	200 in.-lb.
Oil pump cover bolt	95 in.-lb.
Oil pump attaching bolt	30
Oil filter attaching stud	45
Oil pressure gauge sending unit	60 in.-lb.
Rocker shaft bracket bolt	200 in.-lb.
Spark plug	30
Starter mounting bolt	50
Temperature gauge sending unit	60 in.-lb.
Vibration damper screw to crankshaft	100
Water pump to housing bolt	30
A/C compressor bracket to water pump bolt	30
A/C compressor to bracket nut	50
A/C compressor support bolts	30

400-440 V-8 Engines	
Location	**Torque Foot-Pounds**
Alternator bracket bolts	30
Alternator mounting pivot bolt or nut	30
Alternator adjusting strap bolt	200 in.-lb.
Camshaft sprocket bolt	50
Chain case cover bolt	200 in.-lb.
Connecting rod nut	45
Crankshaft bolt (vibration damper)	135
Crankshaft rear bearing seal retainer	25
Cylinder head bolt	70
Cylinder head cover	
Bolt	40 in.-lb.
Nut	40 in.-lb.

(continued)

4

Table 2   TIGHTENING TORQUES (continued)

400-440 V-8 Engines	
Location	Torque Foot-Pounds
Exhaust manifold	30
Exhaust manifold flange joint	40
Fan attaching bolt	200 in.-lb.
Fuel pump attaching bolt	30
Flywheel to crankshaft	55
Flywheel housing to cylinder block	50
Flex plate to crankshaft	55
Flex plate to converter	270 in.-lb.
Flywheel housing cover bolts	40 in.-lb.
Ignition distributor clamp bolt	200 in.-lb.
Intake manifold bolt	45
Main bearing cap bolt	85
Oil pan drain plug	20
Oil pan screw	200 in.-lb.
Oil pump cover bolt	10
Oil pump attaching bolt	30
Rocker shaft retainer bolt	25
Spark plugs	30
Starter mounting bolt	50
Thermostat housing bolt	35
Valve tappet cover end bolt	180 in.-lb.
Vibration damper pulley bolt	200 in.-lb.
Water pump to housing bolt	30
Water pump housing to cylinder block bolt	30

NOTE: If you own a 1982 or later model, first check the Supplement at the back of the book for any new service information.

CHAPTER FIVE

FUEL AND EXHAUST SYSTEMS

FUEL SYSTEMS

The only carburetor service required in normal tune-up work is the adjustment of curb idle speed. Curb idle speed is set by adjusting the air/fuel mixture to the proper ratio and then adjusting the idle speed adjusting screw to obtain the specified revolutions per minute (rpm).

A propane enrichment tool (Chrysler part No. C-4464) is required to set curb idle on 1977 and later non-California models. See **Figure 1**.

The 1977 and later California models, as well as all 1975-1976 pickups, require a Chrysler Huntsville exhaust analyzer (or equivalent). On 1974 and earlier models, a different type of exhaust analyzer is required to set air-fuel ratio to specifications. Procedures for using both types of analyzer are given in this chapter.

Curb idle adjustment on 1981 models is required only after major carburetor overhaul. Since the procedure requires drilling several precisely placed holes in the carburetor, it should be done by a dealer or a mechanic familiar with Dodge emission controls.

You may be able to obtain the propane tool through your Chrysler-Dodge dealer, or an equivalent tool may be available through an auto parts dealer. If you cannot find the tool (or other special tools) locally, try Miller Special Tools, Division of Utica Tool Company, Inc., 32615 Park Lane, Garden City,

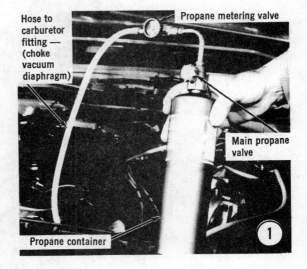

Hose to carburetor fitting — (choke vacuum diaphragm)

Propane metering valve

Main propane valve

Propane container

Michigan 48135. In Canada, try C&D Riley Enterprises, Ltd., P.O. Box 2483, Walkerville, Ontario N8Y 4Y2. The U.S. address should be used when inquiring from other nations.

The propane tool should not be excessively expensive, and you should consider purchasing one if you plan to do all of your own service work.

Exhaust analyzers of the type and quality required are fairly expensive. However, you may be able to rent one from an equipment rental company.

Carburetor adjustment is critical on late models. Correct adjustment is necessary on all models to ensure proper operation of other

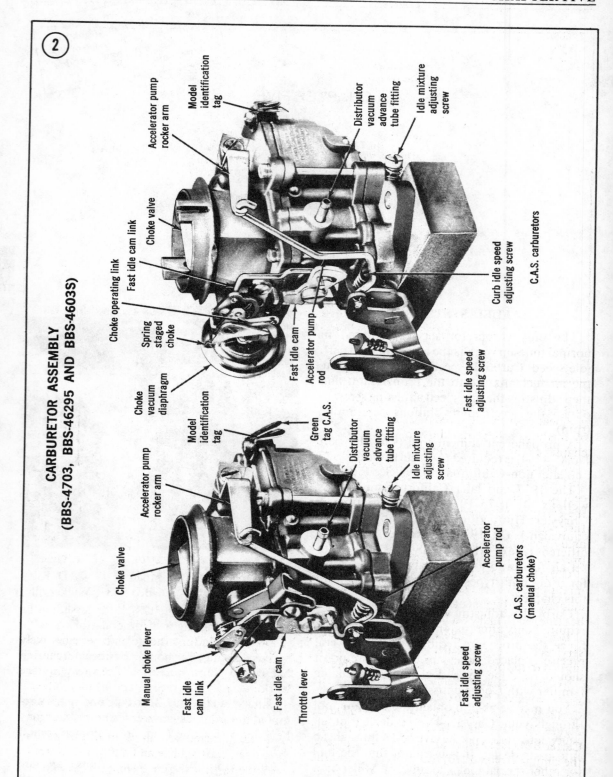

(2)

**CARBURETOR ASSEMBLY
(BBS-4703, BBS-46295 AND BBS-4603S)**

Accelerator pump rocker arm

Model identification tag

Distributor vacuum advance tube fitting

Idle mixture adjusting screw

Choke valve

Choke operating link

Fast idle cam link

Curb idle speed adjusting screw

C.A.S. carburetors

Spring staged choke

Choke vacuum diaphragm

Fast idle cam

Accelerator pump rod

Fast idle speed adjusting screw

Model identification tag

Green tag C.A.S.

Distributor vacuum advance tube fitting

Idle mixture adjusting screw

Accelerator pump rocker arm

Choke valve

Accelerator pump rod

C.A.S. carburetors (manual choke)

Manual choke lever

Fast idle cam link

Fast idle cam

Throttle lever

Fast idle speed adjusting screw

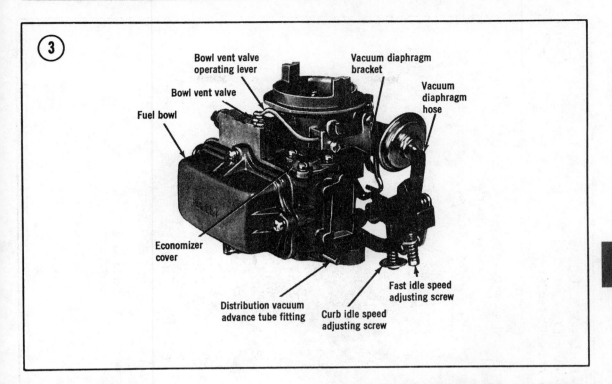

Bowl vent valve operating lever

Bowl vent valve

Fuel bowl

Vacuum diaphragm bracket

Vacuum diaphragm hose

Economizer cover

Distribution vacuum advance tube fitting

Curb idle speed adjusting screw

Fast idle speed adjusting screw

emission control systems. For this reason, adjustment of curb idle speed and air-fuel mixture by methods other than those described in this chapter are not recommended.

A procedure is also given for adjusting the air-fuel ratio without an analyzer. This procedure should be used only in emergencies. If the emergency procedure is used, have the air-fuel ratio set by your dealer or a competent, analyzer-equipped shop, as soon as possible, to prevent overheating of the catalytic converter.

Chrysler Corporation equips carburetor idle mixture screws with plastic caps which limit the amount of adjustment. These caps should not be removed to make adjustments.

Because of the complexity of the carburetors, service by the amateur mechanic should be limited to the procedures given in this chapter.

Six carburetors have been used during the years covered by this book. These are the Carter BBS (see **Figure 2**); the Holley 1920 (see **Figure 3**); the Holley 1945 (see **Figure 4**); the Carter BBD (see **Figure 5**); the Holley 2245 (and the similar Holley 2210) (see **Figure 6**); and the Carber Thermo-Quad (see **Figure 7**). The first is a single barrel, the last is a 4-barrel, and the others are 2-barrel carburetors.

a. Idle mixture adjusting screws

b. Fast idle adjustment screw

c. Fast idle cam

Curb Idle Speed Adjustment (1977-1978 Non-California Models)

Make all adjustments with engine fully warmed up, headlights and air conditioner off, and transmission in neutral. The vacuum hoses at the exhaust gas recirculation (EGR) valve, if so equipped, and the distributor or spark control unit must be disconnected and plugged.

1. With transmission in neutral and parking brake set, start vehicle and allow it to warm up with the fast idle screw resting on the 2nd step of the fast idle cam (see **Figure 8**, typical). Allow engine to reach normal operating tem-

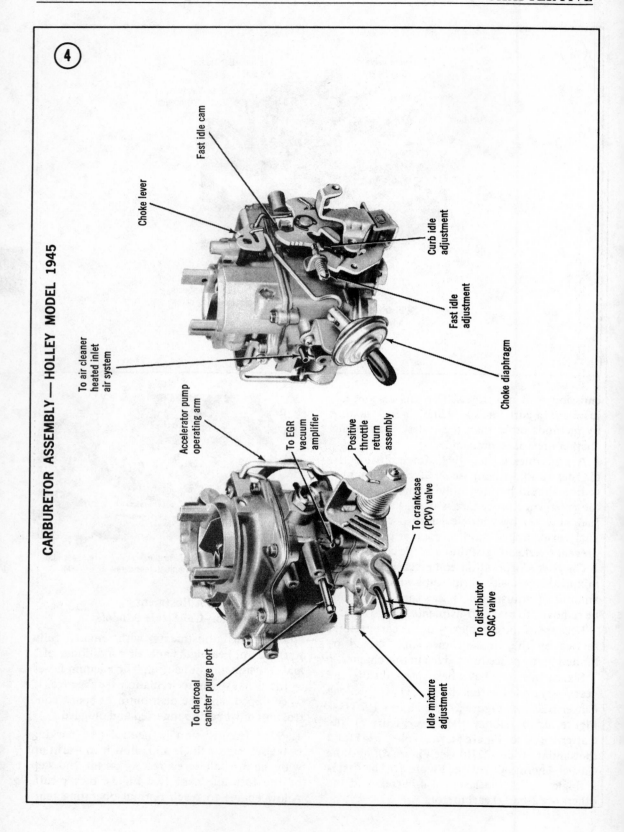

④

CARBURETOR ASSEMBLY—HOLLEY MODEL 1945

Fast idle cam

Choke lever

Curb idle adjustment

Fast idle adjustment

Choke diaphragm

To air cleaner heated inlet air system

Accelerator pump operating arm

To EGR vacuum amplifier

Positive throttle return assembly

To crankcase (PCV) valve

To distributor OSAC valve

To charcoal canister purge port

Idle mixture adjustment

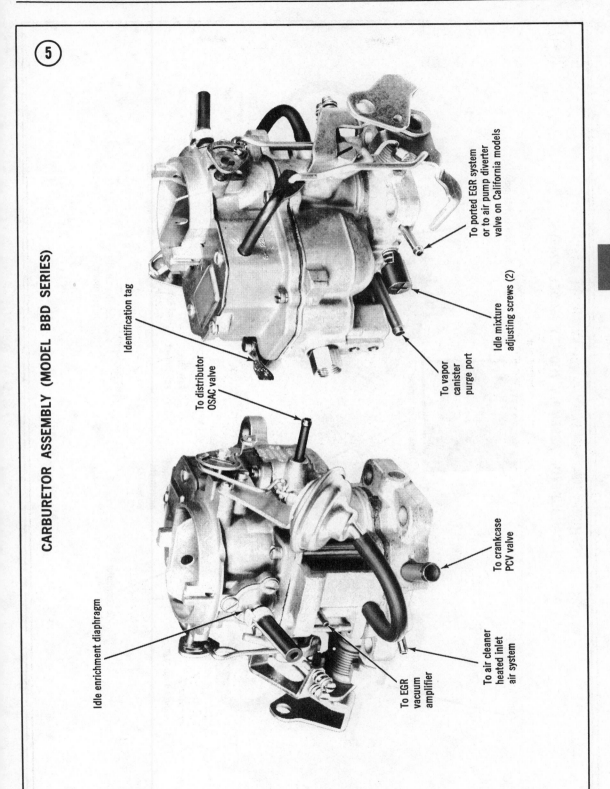

5

CARBURETOR ASSEMBLY (MODEL BBD SERIES)

Idle enrichment diaphragm

To EGR vacuum amplifier

To air cleaner heated inlet air system

To crankcase PCV valve

Identification tag

To distributor OSAC valve

To vapor canister purge port

Idle mixture adjusting screws (2)

To ported EGR system or to air pump diverter valve on California models

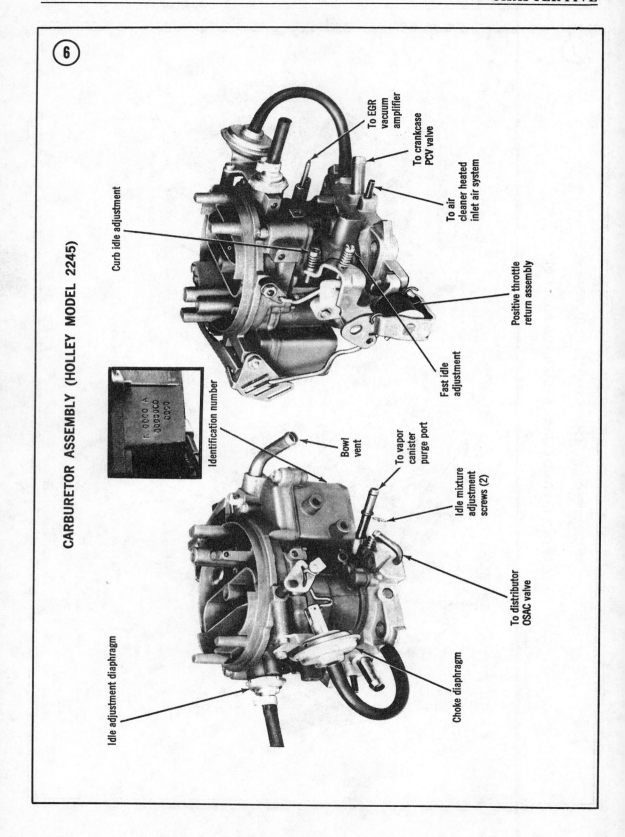

⑥

CARBURETOR ASSEMBLY (HOLLEY MODEL 2245)

Curb idle adjustment

To EGR vacuum amplifier

To crankcase PCV valve

To air cleaner heated inlet air system

Positive throttle return assembly

Fast idle adjustment

Identification number

Bowl vent

To vapor canister purge port

Idle mixture adjustment screws (2)

To distributor OSAC valve

Choke diaphragm

Idle adjustment diaphragm

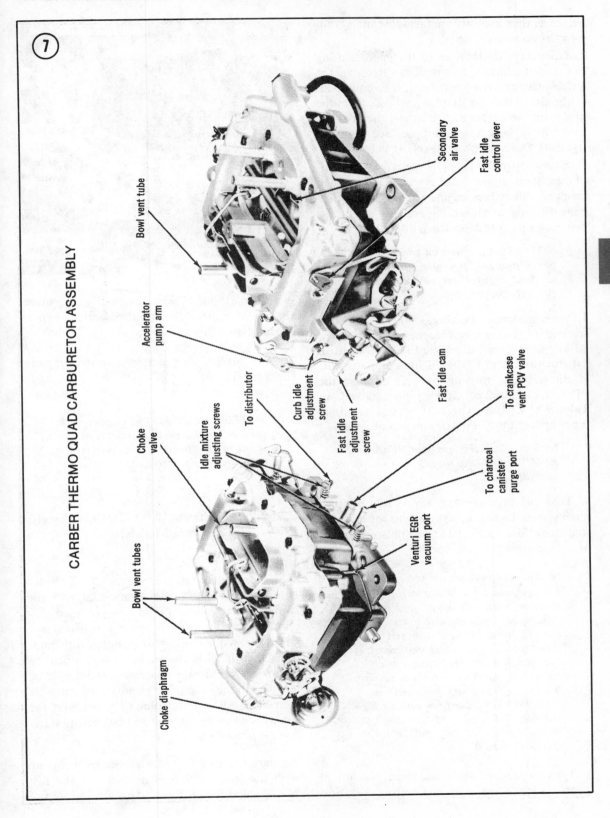

7

CARBER THERMO QUAD CARBURETOR ASSEMBLY

Bowl vent tube

Secondary air valve

Fast idle control lever

Accelerator pump arm

Fast idle cam

To crankcase vent PCV valve

To distributor

Curb idle adjustment screw

Fast idle adjustment screw

Choke valve

Idle mixture adjusting screws

To charcoal canister purge port

Venturi EGR vacuum port

Bowl vent tubes

Choke diaphragm

5

perature, then kick off the fast idle cam by tapping the accelerator pedal.

2. Connect a tachometer to the engine, using the manufacturer's instructions. Remove the air cleaner vacuum supply hose, if so equipped, or the choke vacuum diaphragm hose, from the nipple on the carburetor. Connect the propane tool supply hose to the nipple. See **Figure 9** (typical). Open the propane ON-OFF valve.

3. Slowly open the propane metering valve until maximum engine speed is reached (too much propane will reduce engine speed). Leave propane flowing at this rate, and do not touch metering valve until throttle is adjusted.

> NOTE: *Start test with an adequate supply of propane. If engine speed begins to drop off for no obvious reason, check the propane supply.*

4. With propane flowing, adjust curb idle screw until engine speed reaches the "Enriched RPM" shown on the Vehicle Emission Control Information label in the engine compartment. If this label is missing or defaced, use the "Propane Enriched Idle" speed given in **Table 9** of Chapter Three. If necessary, adjust the propane flow for maximum engine speed.

> NOTE: *When the specified "Enriched RPM" is obtained, do not readjust the curb idle speed.*

5. Turn off propane and adjust idle mixture screws (see **Figure 8**, typical) to obtain the smoothest idle within 100 rpm (plus or minus) of the specified curb idle speed.

> NOTE: *Idle mixture adjusting screws are equipped with limiter caps. If the specified curb idle speed and quality cannot be obtained within the range allowed by the limiter cap, verify the speed specification, check and adjust, if required, basic engine timing, and check for carburetor and manifold vacuum leaks before removing the limiter cap.*
>
> *On 1977 318 cid engines with the high altitude package, adjust for the smoothest idle at 100 rpm below the specified curb idle speed.*

6. Turn on propane again and check maximum speed to make sure the idle setting was not

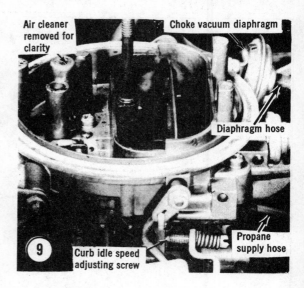

Air cleaner removed for clarity

Choke vacuum diaphragm

Diaphragm hose

⑨ Curb idle speed adjusting screw

Propane supply hose

disturbed. If the maximum speed varies more than 25 rpm from the specified enriched rpm, repeat steps 4 through 6.

7. Turn off propane and remove the propane enrichment tool.

> NOTE: *On 1977 318 cid engines with the high altitude package, reset curb idle speed to specification by adjusting the curb idle speed solenoid.*

Curb Idle Adjustment (All 1975-1976 Models; 1977-1980 California Models)

This procedure requires the use of a Chrysler Huntsville exhaust emission analyzer (or equivalent), which should be installed according to the manufacturer's instructions. Check the Vehicle Emission Control Information (VECI) label in the engine compartment to determine whether the analyzer probe should be installed in the tailpipe or ahead of the catalytic converter. Allow the engine to sit without the engine running for at least an hour before starting this procedure.

1. Start the engine and allow it to warm up with the transmission in neutral and the fast idle speed adjustment screw on the 2nd step of

the fast idle cam. Allow the engine to reach normal operating temperature (5-10 minutes).

2. Disconnect the plug distributor vacuum hose.

3. Disconnect and plug the air supply hose from the air pump.

4. Use the idle mixture screw (see **Figure 8**) to adjust the air-fuel mixture to obtain the specified percentage of carbon monoxide (CO). Then use the idle speed adjusting screw to obtain the smoothest idle with 100 rpm (plus or minus) of the specified curb idle speed. See the VECI label for specifications. If this label is missing or defaced, refer to **Table 9** of Chapter Three.

> NOTE: *Before making each idle speed or mixture adjustment, "blow out" the engine by accelerating to 2,000 rpm for at least 10 seconds and then returning to curb idle speed. Allow at least 30 seconds, but no longer than one minute, for the meter to stabilize before taking the reading. Take the reading with the engine operating at idle, with transmission in neutral and air conditioner and headlights off.*

5. Recheck the CO content of the exhaust. Repeat Step 3 if necessary to bring CO content and idle speed within specifications.

6. Disconnect and plug the exhaust gas recirculation (EGR) vacuum line at the EGR valve. Position the fast idle adjustment screw on the 2nd step of the fast idle cam (see **Figure 8**) and, if necessary, adjust the fast idle speed to the specified rpm (see VECI label).

7. Reconnect the distributor and the EGR vacuum hoses. If exhaust sample was taken ahead of catalytic converter, remove probe and install plug. Torque plug to 100-140 in.-lb. If sample was taken from tailpipe, remove probe.

Curb Idle Adjustment (1974 and Earlier)

This procedure requires the use of an accurate ignition tachometer and a Sun Electric Combustion-Vacuum Unit, Model 80, Exhaust Condenser, Model EC, and Hose 669-14, or equivalent.

1. Operate engine until normal operating temperature is reached. Verify that ignition timing meets specifications. See Vehicle Emission Control Information sticker or **Table 9**, Chapter Three. Do not remove air cleaner.

2. Place automatic transmission (if so equipped) in NEUTRAL position — not PARK.

3. Turn on air conditioning, if so equipped.

4. Connect tachometer to engine, using the manufacturer's instructions.

5. Insert analyzer probe into tailpipe as far as possible (at least 2 ft.). Use left tailpipe on dual exhaust cars.

> NOTE: *Probe and connecting tube must be free of leaks to obtain correct readings.*

6. Connect analyzer, allow it to warm up, and calibrate it, using manufacturer's instructions.

7. Set idle speed to the specified value (see **Table 9**, Chapter Three) as follows:

> NOTE: *The analyzer is very sensitive. To obtain true reading, make adjustments to idle mixture screws in steps of no more than 1/16 turn.*

a. Turn each idle mixture screw (see **Figures 2 through 7**) $\frac{1}{16}$ turn counterclockwise. Wait at least 10 seconds and note analyzer reading.

b. Repeat Step A until meter indicates a definitely lower (richer) reading.

c. Adjust carburetor to give a 14.2 air/fuel ratio reading on the analyzer. Turn idle mixture screws counterclockwise to lower and clockwise to increase meter reading.

> NOTE: *Do not remove limiter caps from idle mixture screws.*

d. When the air/fuel ratio has been set, use the curb idle adjustment screw to obtain the specified engine idle speed.

Curb Idle Adjustment (Emergency)

CAUTION
Use this procedure only in an emergency. If the idle mixture setting is altered

on 1975 or later models, have the setting adjusted by your dealer as soon as possible to avoid damage and overheating.

1. Warm up engine to normal operating temperature. Do not remove air cleaner. Turn air conditioner (if so equipped) on.

2. Connect a tachometer to the engine, using the manufacturer's instructions.

3. Disconnect vacuum hose from the distributor and plug hose.

4. Verify that timing is properly set, using the procedure given in *Ignition Timing*, Chapter Three. Reconnect vacuum hose to distributor.

5. Turn idle speed adjustment screw to obtain specified rpm. See VECI sticker or **Table 9**, Chapter Three.

6. Turn idle mixture screw (either screw on 2- and 4-barrel carburetors) in to obtain a drop of 20 rpm.

7. Turn idle mixture screw out 1/4 turn.

8. On 2- and 4-barrel carburetors, repeat Steps 6 and 7 for second idle mixture screw.

9. Readjust idle speed adjustment screw to specified rpm, if necessary.

IDLE SPEED ADJUSTMENT (DIESEL)

Diesel idle speed adjustment requires a mechanical tachometer like the one shown in **Figure 10**. Start the procedure with the engine cold.

1. Remove the cover and gasket from the tachometer take-off (**Figure 10**). This is located just forward of the oil filters.

2. Floor the accelerator and start the engine. Hold the accelerator down until the engine reaches a speed of 1,250-1,500 rpm.

3. Slowly release the accelerator until the engine runs smoothly. As the engine warms up, reduce engine speed to idle.

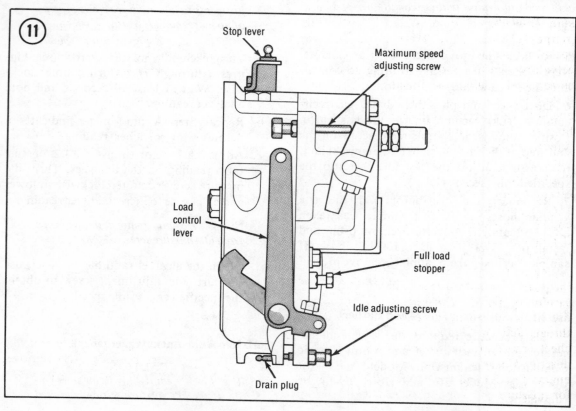

4. Be sure the load control lever is in the position shown in **Figure 11**.

5. Check idle speed on the tachometer. It should be 600-700 rpm.

6. If idle speed is incorrect, loosen the idle adjusting screw locknut (**Figure 11**). Turn the idle adjusting screw in to raise idle speed or out to lower it.

7. Tighten the locknut and recheck idle speed.

8. If idle speed has changed, adjust it again. If not, remove the tachometer, then install the gasket and cover.

CARBURETOR OVERHAUL

Special skills are required to successfully rebuild a carburetor. As the carburetor is considered a part of the emission control system on modern engines, overhaul by the amateur mechanic is not recommended and is beyond the scope of this book.

Before suspecting the carburetor as the cause of engine performance problems, make sure that the ignition system is working properly and that timing is set to specifications. Check all vacuum hoses and actuators for leaks and repair or replace parts as required. Tighten all intake manifold and carburetor mounting bolts. On 6-cylinder engines, tighten intake-to-exhaust manifold bolts to 17 ft.-lb., intake-to-exhaust manifold nuts to 20 ft.-lb., and carburetor-to-manifold nuts to 17 ft.-lb. On V8 engines, tighten intake manifold bolts to 45 ft.-lb. and carburetor-to-manifold nuts to 20 ft.-lb.

Also perform a compression test on the engine. See *Compression Test*, Chapter Three. If compression is okay, clean the exterior of the carburetor with a carburetor spray cleaner, paying particular attention to the areas where the choke and throttle shafts penetrate the carburetor body. With the engine running, use the same cleaner to clean the carburetor throats and choke and throttle plates. Then check and adjust the idle mixture and speed as described earlier in this chapter. Allow the engine to cool and then check the fuel pump for pressure and volume as described later in this chapter. Make sure the manifold heat control valve and the crankcase ventilation system are working properly, and that the carburetor air filter element is clean.

If the engine still does not operate properly after all other systems have been checked and found to be working, remove the carburetor and take it to your dealer or a reputable shop and have it overhauled.

NOTE
Although some labor charges can be avoided by removing and installing the carburetor yourself, the mechanic who does the job probably will want to check the operation of the carburetor on your car after overhaul. Be sure to check with whomever is going to do the job before removing the carburetor.

If you are sure of your mechanical skills and plan to overhaul the carburetor yourself, buy an overhaul kit and follow the instructions that come with the kit.

NOTE
*When buying an overhaul kit, take in the identifying number of your carburetor. See **Figure 2** and **Figure 6** for typical number locations. Be sure to get the correct kit for your carburetor.*

If possible, check the instructions before you purchase the kit to make sure that you understand what is required, and make sure that the instructions include an exploded view of the carburetor or step-by-step illustrations of the procedure. Start work only when you understand everything that is required.

Carburetor Removal/Installation

CAUTION
Carburetor removal should be attempted only on a cold engine. Fuel spilled on a hot engine could be accidentally ignited.

1. Remove the battery ground cable and the carburetor air cleaner housing. Also remove the fuel tank filler cap to relieve any pressure that might be present.

2. Place a suitable container under the carburetor fuel inlet fitting to catch fuel spillage and disconnect the fuel line from the carburetor. Use two wrenches to avoid twisting the line.

3. Disconnect the throttle linkage, choke linkage, and all vacuum lines from the carburetor.

NOTE
Mark hoses and their connections with identifiers so they can be reconnected to their original positions.

4. Remove the carburetor-to-manifold attaching nuts and remove the carburetor from the vehicle, holding it upright to avoid fuel spillage.

5. Installation is the reverse of these steps. Use a new flange gasket, and make sure it is properly oriented. Draw the attaching nuts up evenly to prevent air leaks. Tighten attaching nuts to 17 ft.-lb. (6-cylinder) or 20 ft.-lb. (V-8). Replace all worn or loose vacuum hoses and reinstall them in their original positions. When installation is correct, check linkage to make sure it is operating properly and then set idle mixture and speed to specifications. Procedures are given earlier in this chapter.

FUEL PUMP CHECKS

Fuel pumps used on models covered in this book cannot be repaired. A faulty fuel pump must be replaced with a new one. If replacement becomes necessary, be sure to obtain a pump with the proper part number. Pumps that look alike may have different pumping pressures.

A fuel pump suspected of being defective should be tested, using the procedures below, before it is removed from the vehicle.

Pressure Test

1. Install a T-fitting between the fuel pump and the carburetor (see **Figure 12**).

2. Install a pressure gauge as shown in **Figure 12**. Make sure the connecting hose is not longer than 6 in. A longer hose could affect the pressure reading.

3. Vent fuel pump to relieve air trapped in fuel chamber.

4. Connect a tachometer, start engine, and operate at specified idle speed. Reading should be 3 1/2-5 psi for 6-cylinder or 5-7 psi for V-8 engines, and remain constant or return slowly to zero when engine is stopped. An instant drop to zero indicates a leaky outlet valve. If this occurs, or pressure is too high or too low, replace pump.

Volume Test

1. Disconnect fuel line at carburetor. Attach a hose to fuel line to deliver gasoline to a one quart (32 ounce) container.

2. Start engine and measure time it takes to fill container. Container should fill in approximately one minute.

WARNING
Use care when conducting this test as gasoline is highly flammable.

EXHAUST SYSTEM

The exhaust system consists of exhaust pipe(s), catalytic converters (if so equipped), muffler, and a tail pipe. A resonator is used on some models and, when used, is located in the tail pipe behind the muffler. Repair is by replacement of defective components. See **Figure 13** (typical).

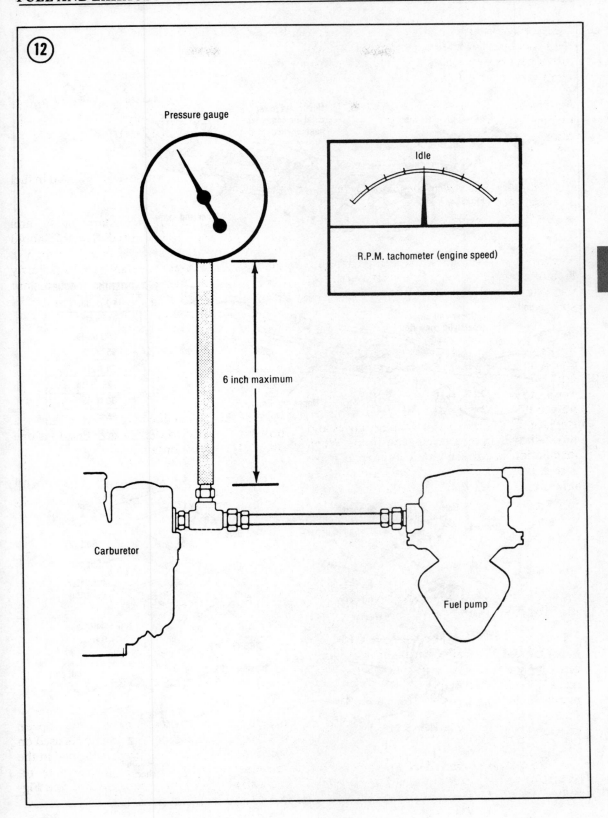

Pressure gauge

Idle

R.P.M. tachometer (engine speed)

6 inch maximum

Carburetor

Fuel pump

5

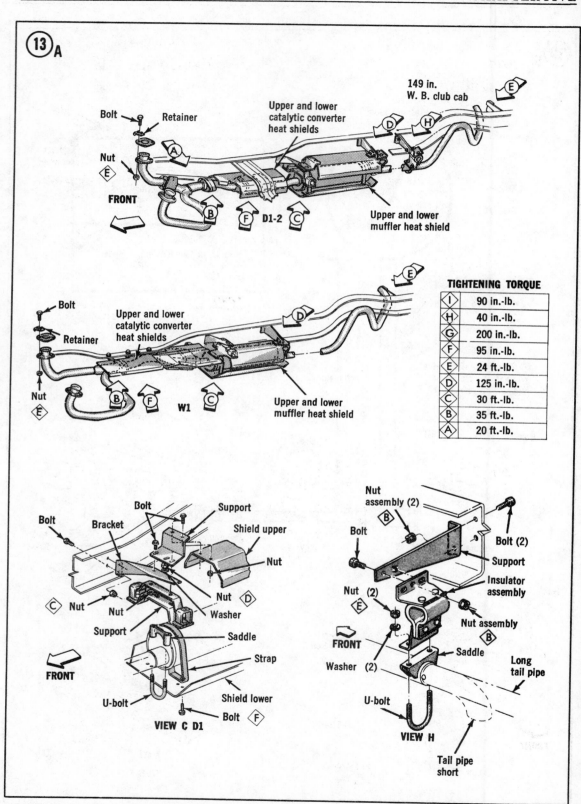

13 A

Bolt — Retainer

Nut

E

FRONT

Upper and lower
catalytic converter
heat shields

A

149 in.
W. B. club cab

D H E

B F D1-2 C

Upper and lower
muffler heat shield

Bolt

Retainer

Nut

E

Upper and lower
catalytic converter
heat shields

B F W1 C

D

E

Upper and lower
muffler heat shield

TIGHTENING TORQUE

I	90 in.-lb.
H	40 in.-lb.
G	200 in.-lb.
F	95 in.-lb.
E	24 ft.-lb.
D	125 in.-lb.
C	30 ft.-lb.
B	35 ft.-lb.
A	20 ft.-lb.

Bolt

Bolt

Bracket

Support

Shield upper

Nut

Bolt

Support

Support

C Nut Nut Nut

Washer

Saddle

Strap

D

FRONT

U-bolt

Shield lower

Bolt F

VIEW C D1

Nut
assembly (2)

B

Bolt

Bolt (2)

Support

Insulator
assembly

Nut (2)

E

FRONT

Washer (2)

U-bolt

Nut assembly

B

Saddle

Long
tail pipe

VIEW H

Tail pipe
short

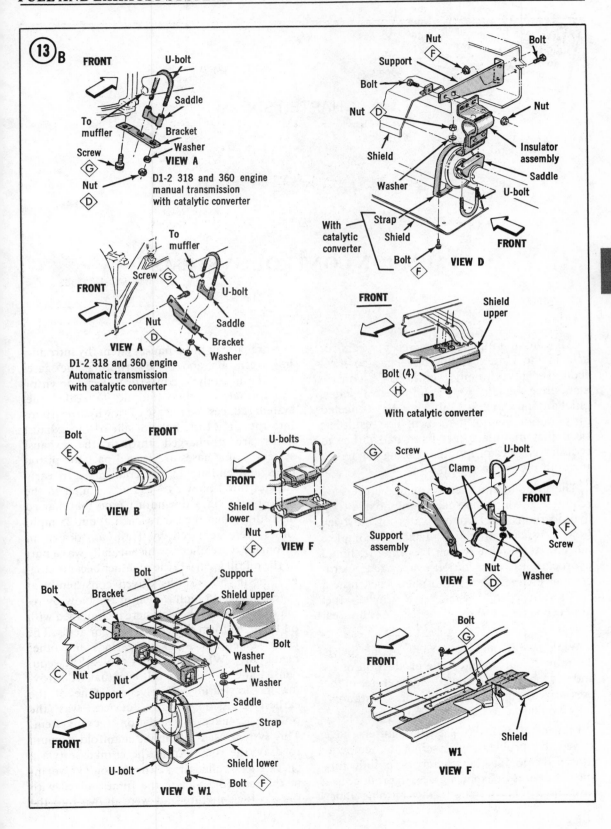

(13)B

FRONT

U-bolt
Saddle
To muffler
Bracket
Washer
Screw
G
VIEW A
Nut
D

D1-2 318 and 360 engine manual transmission with catalytic converter

To muffler
FRONT
Screw
G
U-bolt
Nut
Saddle
Bracket
D
Washer
VIEW A

D1-2 318 and 360 engine Automatic transmission with catalytic converter

Bolt
E
FRONT
VIEW B

U-bolts
FRONT
Shield lower
Nut
F
VIEW F

Nut
Support
Bolt
F
Bolt
Nut
D
Shield
Nut
Insulator assembly
Saddle
U-bolt
Washer
With catalytic converter
Strap
Shield
Bolt
F
VIEW D
FRONT

FRONT
Shield upper
Bolt (4)
H
D1
With catalytic converter

G
Screw
Clamp
U-bolt
FRONT
F
Support assembly
Nut
Washer
Screw
VIEW E
D

Bolt
Support
Bolt
Bracket
Shield upper
Bolt
Washer
Nut
C
Nut
Nut
Washer
Support
Saddle
Strap
FRONT
U-bolt
Shield lower
Bolt
F
VIEW C W1

Bolt
G
FRONT
Shield
W1
VIEW F

5

NOTE: If you own a 1982 or later model, first check the Supplement at the back of the book for any new service information.

CHAPTER SIX

EMISSION CONTROL SYSTEMS

All vans manufactured in recent years for sale in the United States have had to meet federal government emission control standards. In addition, a number of states, chief among which is California, have enacted air pollution laws of their own. The result has been that manufacturers have had either to redesign engines or modify existing engines to meet all the requirements.

The air pollutants that the manufacturers are required to control are carbon monoxide (CO), hydrocarbons (HC), and oxides of nitrogen (NOx). CO and HC are the products of incomplete burning of gasoline (which is a volatile, liquid hydrocarbon). In addition, vaporized hydrocarbons escape to the atmosphere each time a car is refueled and whenever a vehicle's fuel tank cap is removed (or if the cap does not seal the tank).

While more complete burning of the fuel is desirable to cut down on the production of CO and HC, the resulting higher temperatures in the pressurized combustion chambers paradoxically would lead to the formation of more NOx.

In general terms, the manufacturers have solved this problem by lowering the temperature in the combustion chambers (by injecting small amounts of exhaust gases) to produce less NOx, and by encouraging further burning under

less pressure in the exhaust system (by introducing fresh air and/or by routing the gases through a catalytic converter) to cut down on the formation of CO and HC. A sealed fuel system reduces the release of raw hydrocarbons into the air. Most, but not all, of the exhaust gases are discharged through the exhaust system. Some gases are forced past the piston rings and end up in the crankcase. In early engines this "blow-by" gas was vented to the atmosphere via a downdraft pipe that started operating when the car reached about 25 mph. Gases were replaced by fresh air drawn in through a "breather," which usually was a part of the oil filler cap. If the breather became clogged, or if the car was driven consistently at speeds under 25 mph, much of the blow-by remained in the crankcase where it combined with oil fumes to form sludge, varnish, or acids. The latter sometimes attacked bearings and other metal parts. When the fumes cooled, they condensed and diluted the oil, eventually destroying its lubricating effectiveness. One of the earliest emission control devices was the positive crankcase ventilation (PCV) system. This system used the intake manifold vacuum to draw the fumes from the crankcase (via a check valve, called the PCV or "smog" valve) into the manifold. There the fumes mixed with the air/fuel mixture and were drawn into the

combustion chambers and reburned. Fumes were replaced in the crankcase by fresh air, usually drawn in through a filter.

SYSTEM DESCRIPTION AND SERVICE

Chrysler uses a number of interrelated systems to control harmful emission. These include:

a. Heated inlet air

b. Positive crankcase ventilation (PCV) system

c. Carburetor calibration

d. Manifold heat control valve

e. Distributor calibration

f. Air injection system

g. Initial ignition timing

h. Vapor saver system

i. Exhaust gas recirculation (EGR) system

j. Electric assist choke system

k. Orifice spark advance control (OSAC) system

l. Coolant controlled idle enrichment system

m. Catalytic converter

n. Aspirator air system

The carburetor and the ignition system are interrelated with the other systems to form the overall emission control system. Required maintenance services are discussed in Chapter Three. The heated inlet air system reduces hydrocarbons by promoting more efficient burning of fuel while the engine is warming up.

NOTE: *Not all emission control systems are used on all trucks.*

POSITIVE CRANKCASE VENTILATION SYSTEM

This system (see **Figure 1**) consists of a crankcase ventilation valve (PCV valve), mounted on a cylinder head cover, connected by a hose to the base of the carburetor. Another hose connects the carburetor air cleaner to the closed crankcase inlet filter (or filler cap in earlier models). The system is operated by manifold vacuum. Air is drawn into the crankcase via the carburetor air filter-to-crankcase inlet air cleaner hose. The air circulates through the cylinder head covers and crankcase and collects fumes. The fume-laden air exits through the PCV valve and the passage in to the carburetor body and is mixed with the air/fuel mixture being drawn into the cylinders. Thus the fumes are burned and expelled through the exhaust system.

Service to the system consists of inspection and replacement of the PCV valve at the intervals given in Chapter Three. The filter located in the inlet hose (see **Figure 2**) should be cleaned in solvent and dried at specified intervals.

MANIFOLD HEAT CONTROL VALVE

This thermostatically controlled valve, located in the exhaust manifold system, channels exhaust gases through a ''heat chamber'' adjacent to the fuel intake system (carburetor or intake manifold) during engine warm-up. this heat helps in the vaporization of the fuel mixture when the engine is cold. As the engine becomes warm, the valve directs the exhaust gases directly into the exhaust pipe.

Service to the manifold heat control valve consists of cleaning and lubrication of the valve

6

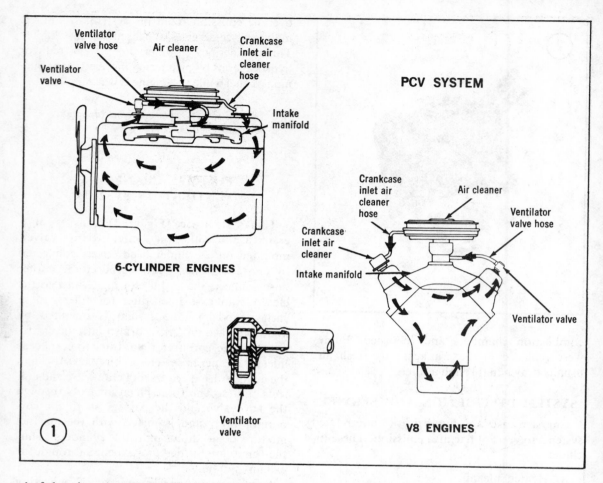

Ventilator valve hose — Air cleaner — Crankcase inlet air cleaner hose

Ventilator valve

Intake manifold

PCV SYSTEM

6-CYLINDER ENGINES

Ventilator valve

Crankcase inlet air cleaner hose — Air cleaner

Ventilator valve hose

Crankcase inlet air cleaner

Intake manifold

Ventilator valve

V8 ENGINES

①

shaft bearings (see **Figure 3**, typical) with a solvent (not oil) at the intervals given in **Table 3 or 4**, Chapter Three.

AIR INJECTION SYSTEM (AIR PUMP)

This system injects a controlled amount of air into the exhaust system, causing the gases to oxidize. This reduces the amount of carbon monoxide in the exhaust. The system consists of an air pump, a diverter valve, a check valve, injection tubes, and connecting hoses (see **Figure 4**). The diverter valve also serves as a pressure relief valve.

Service is limited to checking the drive belt annually for proper tension (see *Accessory Drive Belts*, Chapter Seven) and adjusting as required and replacing damaged centrifugal filter fans. The pump is non-repairable, and must be replaced if damaged.

Air Pump Replacement

1. Disconnect air and vacuum hoses from diverter valve.

2. Loosen attachment bolts and remove belt. Remove bolts.

3. Remove pump from vehicle and remove diverter valve, brackets, and pulley from pump.

4. Reverse the above steps to install pump.

5. Adjust belt tension (refer to *Accessory Drive Belts*, Chapter Seven).

Filter Fan Replacement

NOTE: *It is almost impossible to remove a filter fan without destroying it. The fan should not be removed unless it requires replacement.*

1. Remove damaged fan by inserting needle nosed pliers between fins and breaking fan

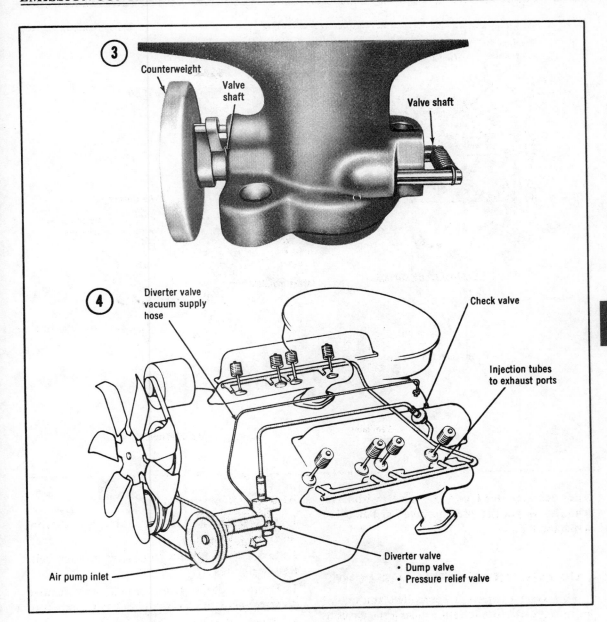

from hub. Do not pry off with screwdriver. Take care to prevent fragments from entering pump (see **Figure 5**).

2. Place new fan on shaft, then use pulley and bolts as tool to press fan into place (see **Figure 6**). Apply torque evenly and make certain that outer edge of fan enters housing.

CAUTION
Do not install fan by hammering or pressing on it, as damage to fan will result.

NOTE: *Slight interference between fan and pump housing bore is normal and some squealing may occur during the first 20-30 miles of operation.*

VAPOR SAVER SYSTEM

This system controls the emission of gasoline vapors from the carburetor and fuel tank into the atmosphere. It consists of a charcoal canister, a pressure/vacuum fuel tank cap, and

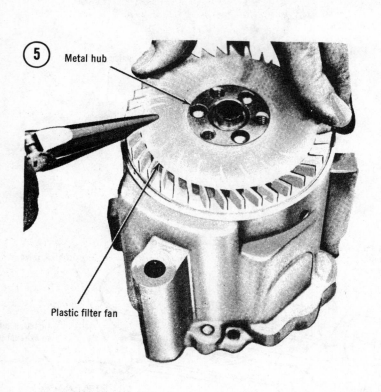

(5) Metal hub

Plastic filter fan

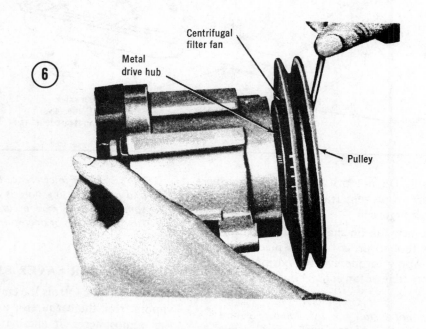

(6)

Centrifugal
filter fan

Metal
drive hub

Pulley

connecting lines between the fuel tank, the carburetor, and canister (see **Figure 7**). When fuel evaporates in the carburetor float chamber or the fuel tank, the vapors are collected in the charcoal canister. Vapors are held until they can be drawn into the intake manifold when the engine is running.

The only service required for this system is replacement of the canister filter element (see **Figure 8**) at the intervals given in Table 4, Chapter Three.

EXHAUST GAS RECIRCULATION (EGR) SYSTEM

This system controls the amount of oxides of nitrogen (NOx) in engine exhaust gases by allowing a predetermined amount of hot exhaust gas to recirculate and dilute the incoming air/fuel mixture (see **Figure 9**, typical).

Service consists of inspecting the system and replacing hardened or cracked hoses and faulty connectors, and checking the operation of the EGR valve, as follows.

1. Warm engine to normal operating temperature. Allow engine to idle with throttle closed, then accelerate abruptly to about 2,000 rpm (not over 3,000 rpm).

2. Observe EGR valve stem during acceleration or visible movement (change in the relative position of the groove on the valve stem). See **Figure 10**.

3. Repeat test several times, if required, to confirm movement.

NOTE: *Valve stem movement indicates correct system functioning. If the valve stem does not move during repeated testing, have system checked to isolate problem area.*

ELECTRIC ASSIST CHOKE SYSTEM

This system consists essentially of an electric heating element which supplements engine heat during engine warming to reduce the duration of choke operation (see **Figure 11**, typical).

The electric assist choke system does not require periodic servicing or adjustment.

6

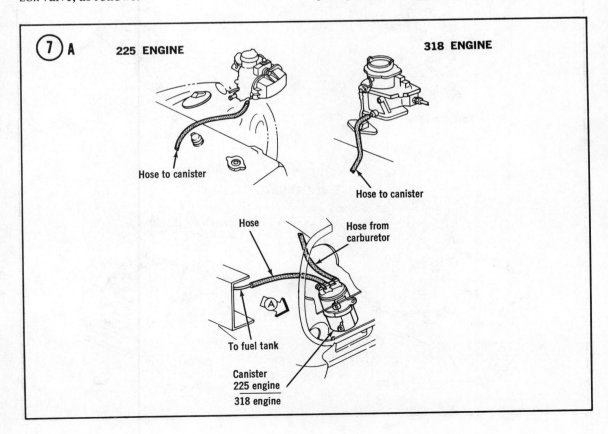

(7) A   225 ENGINE   318 ENGINE

Hose to canister

Hose to canister

Hose

Hose from carburetor

A

To fuel tank

Canister
225 engine
318 engine

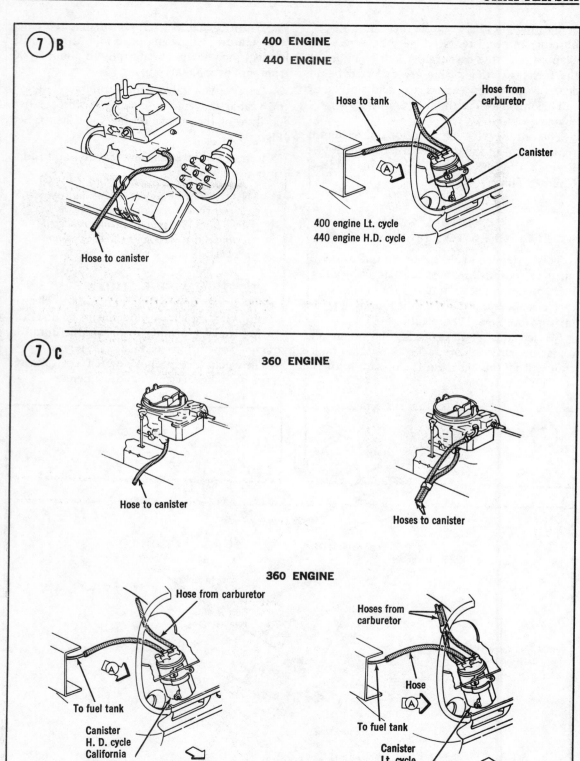

(7) B

400 ENGINE
440 ENGINE

Hose to tank

Hose from carburetor

Canister

400 engine Lt. cycle
440 engine H.D. cycle

Hose to canister

(7) C

360 ENGINE

Hose to canister

Hoses to canister

360 ENGINE

Hose from carburetor

To fuel tank

Canister
H. D. cycle
California
36 engine

FRONT

Hoses from carburetor

Hose

To fuel tank

Canister
Lt. cycle
360 engine

FRONT

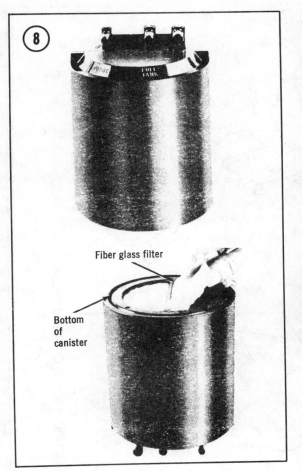

8

Fiber glass filter

Bottom
of
canister

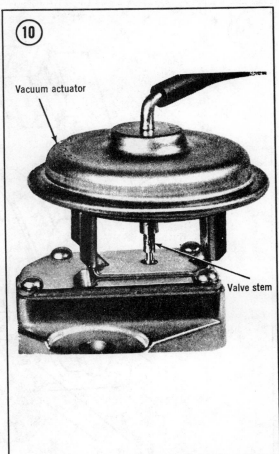

10

Vacuum actuator

Valve stem

6

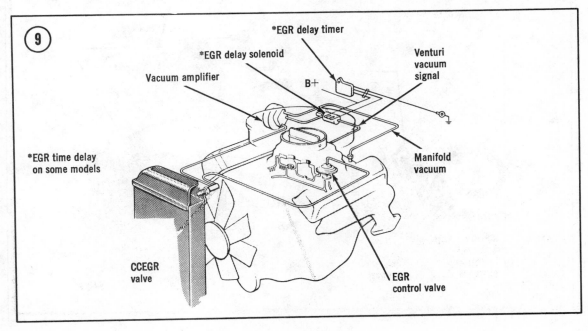

9

*EGR delay timer

*EGR delay solenoid

Vacuum amplifier

Venturi
vacuum
signal

B+

Manifold
vacuum

*EGR time delay
on some models

CCEGR
valve

EGR
control valve

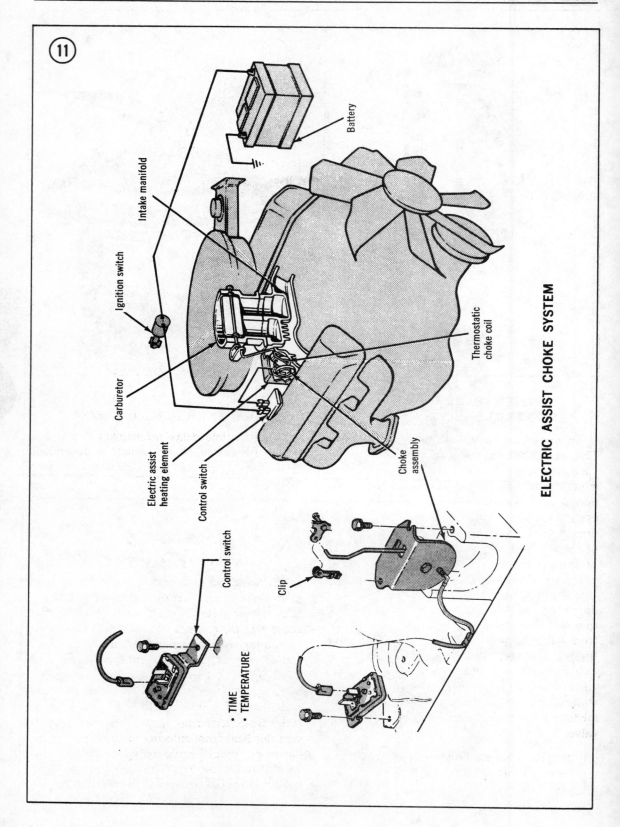

⑪

Battery

Intake manifold

Ignition switch

Carburetor

Electric assist
heating element

Control switch

Thermostatic
choke coil

Choke
assembly

Control switch

Clip

• TIME
• TEMPERATURE

ELECTRIC ASSIST CHOKE SYSTEM

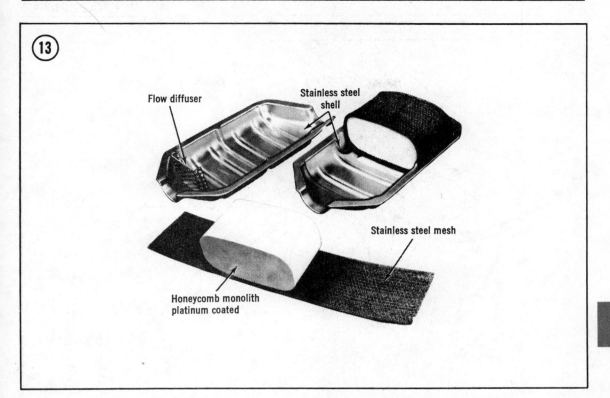

⑬

Flow diffuser

Stainless steel
shell

Stainless steel mesh

Honeycomb monolith
platinum coated

6

ORIFICE SPARK ADVANCE CONTROL SYSTEM (OSAC)

An orifice in the OSAC valve (see **Figure 12A and 12B**) causes a delay in the ported vacuum to the distributor when accelerating from idle to port throttle when ambient temperature is above 60°F (15°C). During deceleration the valve allows instantaneous application of vacuum to the distributor. This control of spark advance aids in the control of oxides of nitrogen in the exhaust.

The OSAC valve does not require periodic service, and is non-repairable. To check valve operation, operate engine in NEUTRAL at 2,000 rpm and disconnect hose leading to distributor from valve. Connect a vacuum gauge to valve fitting. If a very gradual increase in vacuum over a period of about 15 seconds is noted, the valve is operating properly (the time will vary with different engines). If vacuum pops up immediately, or no vacuum is observed, replace valve.

NOTE: *This test should be conducted when outside temperature is about 68°F (20°C).*

COOLANT CONTROLLED IDLE ENRICHMENT SYSTEM

This is a time delay mechanism in the EGR system (discussed above) which is dependent upon a thermostatic valve in the engine cooling system.

CATALYTIC CONVERTER

The catalytic converter is used to oxidize hydrocarbons and carbon monoxide engine exhaust. The converter, which is located in the exhaust system, consists of a stainless steel shell containing two ceramic monolithic elements coated with a catalytic agent (palladium and platinum). See **Figure 13**. Combustion results when exhaust gases pass over the catalyst, resulting in temperatures up to 1,600°F (880°C). Special heat shields are used to prevent this heat from entering the passenger compartment. Trucks equipped with catalytic converters must use lead-free gasoline, as lead destroys the effectiveness of the catalyst.

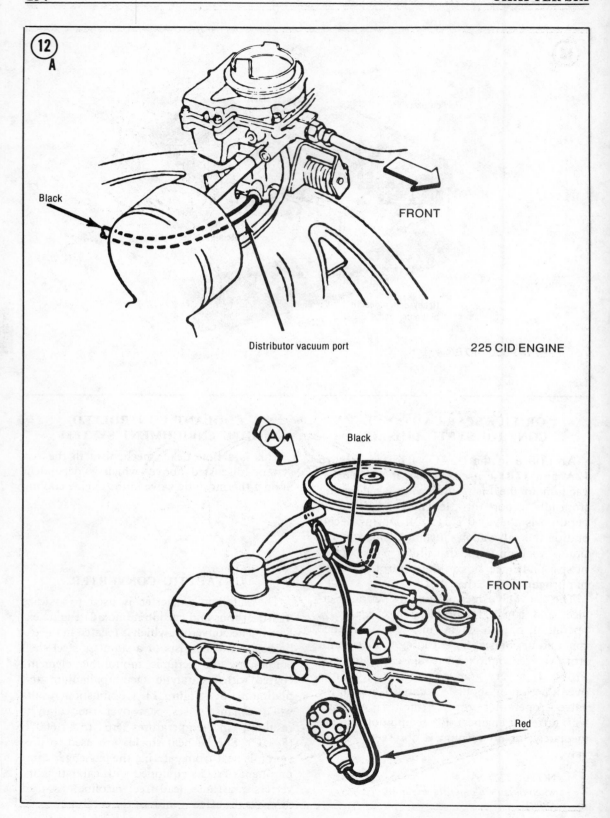

(12) A

Black

FRONT

Distributor vacuum port

225 CID ENGINE

Black

A

FRONT

A

Red

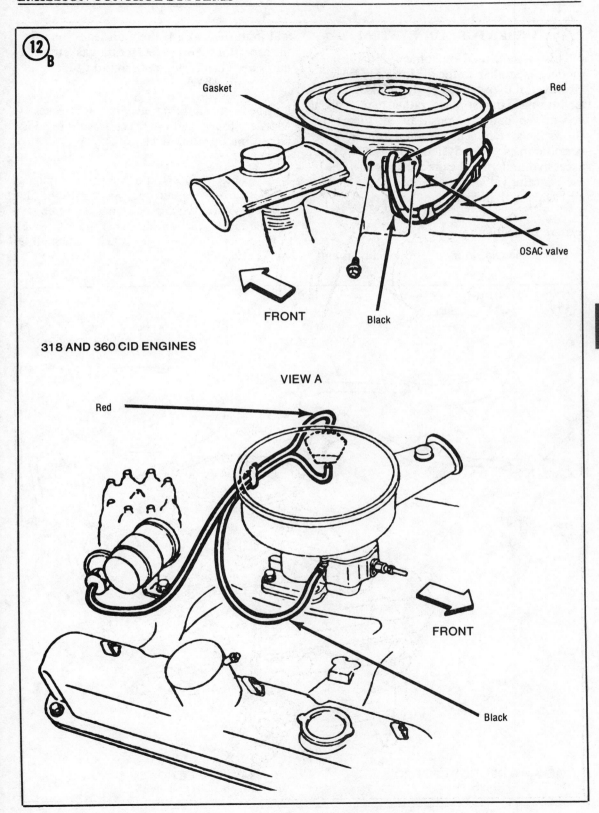

Gasket

Red

OSAC valve

FRONT

Black

318 AND 360 CID ENGINES

VIEW A

Red

FRONT

Black

ASPIRATOR AIR SYSTEM

This system, used on some 1980 and later models, is similar to the air injection system. However, it uses exhaust system pulses to pull air into the exhaust ports, rather than using a belt-driven pump to push air in. **Figure 14** shows the system. The system doesn't require periodic inspection. System failure will cause excessive underhood exhaust noise at idle. If the aspirator valve fails, the hose from valve to air cleaner will harden.

System Inspection

1. Check the aspirator tube-to-exhaust manifold joint for leaks. If the joint leaks, remove the aspirator tube and replace the gasket with a new one. Then install the aspirator tube.

2. Check the hose connections for leaks. If leaks are found and the hoses are still in good condition, install hose clamps.

3. To check the aspirator valve, disconnect the hose from its inlet side (nearest to the air cleaner). With the engine idling, you should be able to feel vacuum pulses at the inlet side of the valve. If exhaust gas is leaking from the valve, replace it.

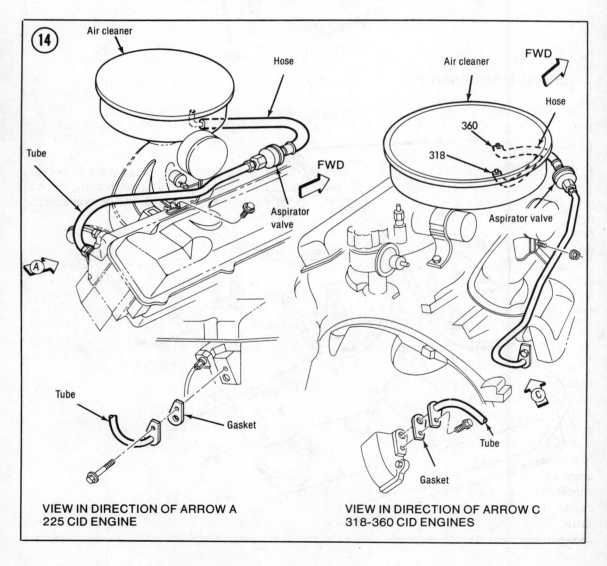

VIEW IN DIRECTION OF ARROW A
225 CID ENGINE

VIEW IN DIRECTION OF ARROW C
318-360 CID ENGINES

CHAPTER SEVEN

COOLING, AIR CONDITIONING AND HEATING SYSTEMS

All Chrysler-built vehicles are equipped with one of the following types of cooling systems:

1. Standard system without air conditioning.
2. Standard system with air conditioning.

Both systems include a radiator, a 16 psi pressure radiator cap, a centrifugal-type water pump, a thermostat, a fan, a coolant reserve system (some models), a transmission oil cooler (automatic transmission models), and a shroud.

Air conditioned models (factory equipped) generally have a larger radiator, a larger fan and shroud, and, on some models, a thermostatically-controlled fluid fan drive.

ACCESSORY BELT DRIVERS

Satisfactory operation of accessories such as the alternator, power steering pump, air conditioning compressor, air pump, and water pump and fan, depends to a large extent on proper drive belt tension.

All drive belts should be inspected periodically and replaced when they show signs of wear, cracking, or fraying. Belt tension should be checked at the same time, or whenever the engine is tuned or a belt is replaced, and adjusted if required. These three methods may be used for checking belt tension. These are:

a. Gauge method
b. Torque method (1971-1978 only)
c. Deflection method

Procedures are given below for all three methods. However, the gauge method is preferred because it gives a direct reading of belt tension. If a tension gauge is not available, a torque wrench may be used to adjust the belt tension on those accessories having a 1/2 in. square hole in their mounting brackets (1971-1978 only). Adjustment of the alternator by the torque method requires the use of a special tool to engage the alternator fins. If neither a torque wrench and/or the special tool (Chrysler No. C-3841A), nor a tension gauge are available, the belt deflection method may be used.

Gauge Method

1. Loosen accessory mounting bolts and attach a tension gauge (part No. C4162 or equivalent) as shown in **Figure 1**.

NOTE: *On dual belt installation, attach gauge to front belt only.*

2. Using ½ in. hinge handle inserted in the ½ in. square hole in the accessory mounting bracket, apply torque to the bracket until the

7

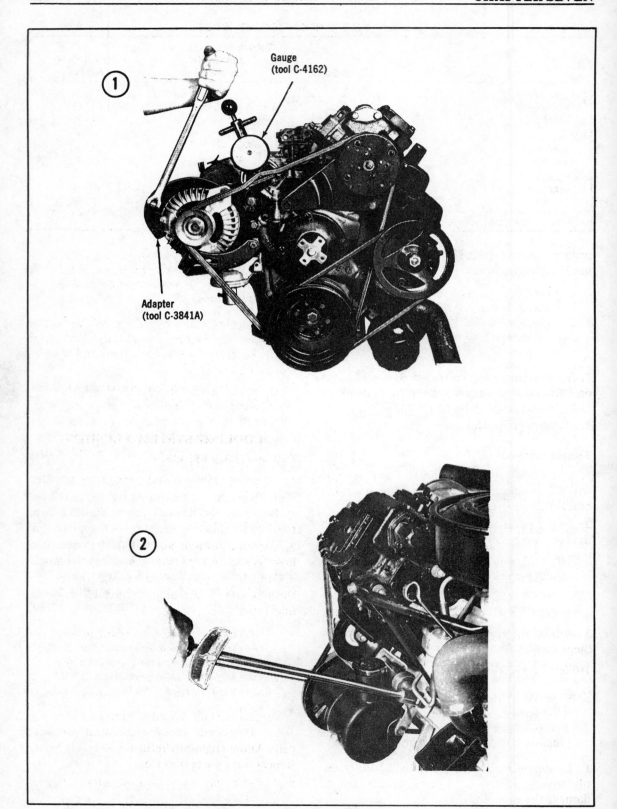

(1) Gauge
(tool C-4162)

Adapter
(tool C-3841A)

(2)

Table 1   BELT TENSION TORQUE VALUES

	225 cid engine	Torque Values (Ft.-Lb.)* 318 and 360 cid engines	383, 400, 440 cid engines
Power steering			
w/air pump	35-20	100-65	100-65
w/o air pump	90-50	50-35	45-30
Alternator			
w/AC	15-10	55-45	120-80
w/o AC	15-10	35-25	70-40
Air pump			
w/AC	35-20	75-50	55-35
w/o AC	40-25	100-65	55-35

*First number is for new belts, second number is for used belts.

proper tension (120 lb. for new belts, 70 lb. for used belts) is obtained.

NOTE: *A special adapter (part No. C3841A) is required for adjusting alternator belt tension. See **Figure 1**. A belt is considered used if it had been in service for more than 30 minutes.*

3. Tighten mounting bolts with gauge installed on belt. Tension should remain the same after bolts are tightened. Readjust if required.

4. Remove gauge and tools.

Torque Method

1. Loosen mounting bolts and install torque wrench in square hole in accessory mounting bracket. See **Figure 2**.

2. Apply specified torque (see **Table 1**), and tighten mounting bolts while holding this torque value.

NOTE: *Use an extension on torque wrench if clearance problems are encountered.*

3. Adjust the tension of all other belts, using Steps 1 and 2.

Deflection Method

NOTE: *This method should be used only when tools are not available to perform either of the procedures given above.*

1. Loosen mounting bolts and use a lever to apply tension to the belt, being careful not to damage the accessory.

NOTE: *If the accessory mounting bracket has a 1/2 in. square hole, a 1/2 in. drive hinge handle may be used to apply tension.*

2. Tighten bolts and check the belt deflection as shown in **Figure 3** (typical). Deflection should be ¼ to ½ in. for new belts and ¼ to ⁵⁄₁₆ in. for old belts.

3. If necessary, repeat the procedure until correct deflection is obtained.

COOLING SYSTEM FLUSHING

Cylinder Block Flushing

1. Drain the radiator and remove the hoses (at radiator).

2. Remove thermostat from housing and reinstall housing.

3. Attach a suitable adapter to the water inlet hose. Attach a drain hose to water outlet hose.

4. Attach a pressurized water source (or flushing gun, if available) to the adapter on the inlet hose.

NOTE: *A flushing gun which utilizes both water and compressed air does the best flushing job. However, a garden hose attached to a pressurized water source may be used.*

5. If flushing gun is used, fill engine block with water, then apply short blasts of air (up to 20 psi). Allow engine to refill between air blasts. Repeat until water runs clear.

6. If water only is used, allow water to run until it turns clear.

7

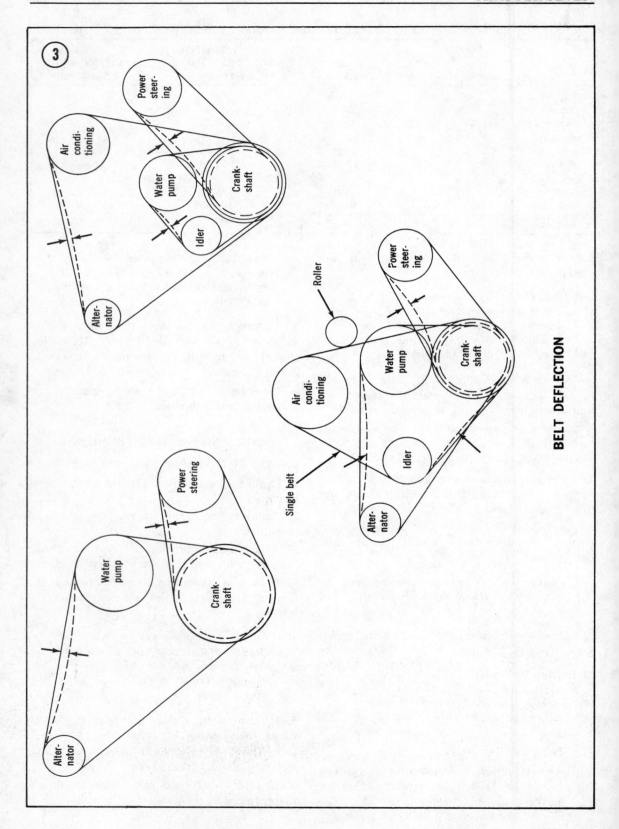

BELT DEFLECTION

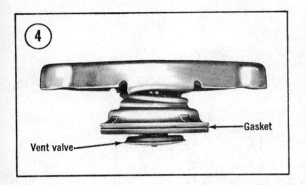

Gasket

Vent valve

7. Install thermostat (a new one is good insurance), using a new housing gasket. Torque bolts to 30 ft.-lb. (4.15 mkg).

8. Flush radiator, using the procedure given below.

9. Remove flushing gun or hose and reinstall radiator hose.

10. Fill cooling system with ethylene glycol antifreeze and water, following the antifreeze manufacturer's instructions for the proper solution for anticipated temperatures.

CAUTION
To avoid rust and corrosion, use at least a 50/50 mixture. Never use plain water.

11. Warm engine to normal operating temperature, and then operate for another 5 minutes.

12. Check for leaks. Also check coolant level. Correct as necessary.

Radiator Flushing

1. With radiator drained and hoses removed, connect a suitable adapter to the lower outlet. Connect a drain hose to upper outlet.

2. Connect a pressurized source of water (or an air/water flushing gun, if available) to the outlet adapter.

CAUTION
If an air/water flushing gun is used, do not allow radiator internal pressure to exceed 20 psi, as radiator damage could result.

3. If flushing gun is used, allow radiator to fill, then apply short bursts of air. Allow radiator to refill between bursts. Repeat until water runs clear.

4. If water only is used, allow water to flush radiator until it runs clear.

5. Remove flushing apparatus and reconnect radiator hoses.

COOLING SYSTEM CLEANING

An alternate method of cooling system cleaning is to use a reliable chemical cleaner in the system. This method does not require the removal of hoses and the thermostat.

1. Drain cooling system and refill, using only clean water.

2. Add cooling system cleaner.

3. Operate engine, following cleaner manufacturer's instructions.

4. Drain cooling system and flush with water until water runs clear.

5. Fill radiator with proper ethylene glycol antifreeze solution for anticipated temperatures. Follow manufacturer's instructions.

PRESSURE CAP

The 16 psi pressure cap (see **Figure 4**) used on all Chrysler-built engines allows the engine to operate at temperatures above the boiling point of water without the loss of coolant. The cap should be checked periodically — at least annually — or whenever a regular loss of coolant is observed. Replace if defective.

RADIATOR HOSES

Check radiator hoses at every oil change and tune-up. Replace hoses that are cracked, hardened, swollen, or restricted. Screw-tightened clamps should be retightened to 15-25 in.-lb. annually. Do not overtighten or hose damage could result.

FANS

Do not attempt to straighten bent fan blades. If a blade becomes damaged, the entire fan should be replaced.

WARNING
Bending fatigues the metal; the blade could break off, causing considerable damage or injury.

7

THERMOSTAT CHECK
AND REPLACEMENT

1. Drain coolant until level is slightly below thermostat housing base.

2. Remove upper radiator hose.

3. Remove thermostat housing bolts and then remove water outlet and gasket from thermostat housing. See **Figure 5**.

4. Remove and inspect thermostat valve for condition.

5. Test thermostat valve as follows:

   a. Place thermostat in a 50% solution of ethylene-glycol antifreeze heated to 20°F above the temperature stamped on the thermostat.

   b. Submerge thermostat and agitate liquid. Valve should open fully.

   c. Remove valve and place in another 50% ethylene-glycol solution heated to 10°F under the temperature stamped on thermostat.

   d. Thermostat should close completely when completely submerged and liquid is agitated.

6. If thermostat fails the above test, it should be replaced. If OK, reinstall in housing, using a new gasket. Tighten bolts securely.

7. Replace radiator hose and refill with coolant.

RADIATOR
REMOVAL/INSTALLATION

Removal

1. Remove the engine cover, drain the cooling system, and remove the upper radiator hose. Disconnect the fusible link in the engine compartment.

2. Remove the attaching nuts and pull the fan shroud rearward. Position it on the engine for maximum clearance. See **Figure 6**.

3. Remove the two top radiator attaching screws. If the vehicle has air conditioning, remove the grille and remove the air conditioner condenser attaching screws.

4. Raise the vehicle. If equipped with automatic transmission, disconnect and cap the

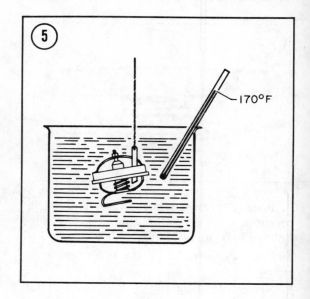

transmission cooler lines from the radiator bottom tank. Remove the lower radiator hose.

5. Support the radiator and remove the two lower mounting screws. Then carefully lower the radiator out of the yoke. See **Figure 7**.

Installation

1. With the vehicle raised, carefully insert the radiator into yoke (**Figure 7**) and install the two lower mounting screws.

2. Install the lower radiator hose and connect the transmission cooler lines to the radiator lower tank outlets. Lower the vehicle.

3. Install the upper radiator attaching screws and then install the air conditioner condenser attaching screws, if so equipped.

4. Position the shroud on the radiator and install the attaching nuts. Connect the fusible link and the upper radiator hose.

> NOTE: *If the radiator hoses are more than a year old, it is good insurance to replace them with new ones.*

5. Fill the cooling system with the proper solution of ethylene glycol antifreeze for anticipated temperatures, following the antifreeze manufacturer's recommendations. Use at least a 50/50 solution to avoid cooling system corrosion.

6. Start the engine and check for leaks, paying particular attention to hose connections. After

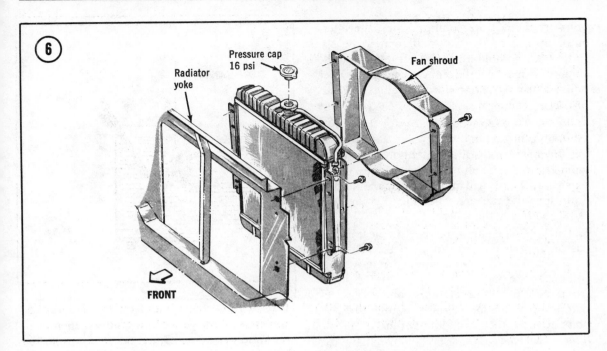

⑥

Radiator
yoke

Pressure cap
16 psi

Fan shroud

FRONT

⑦

the engine warms up, recheck the coolant level and replenish as required. See *Routine Checks*, Chapter Three.

7. If the vehicle is equipped with an automatic transmission, check the transmission fluid level after the transmission has warmed up and replenish if required.

WATER PUMP SERVICE

The water pump is non-repairable. If defective, the entire assembly must be replaced. Special water pumps are used on some air conditioned models. When purchasing a replacement pump, be sure to specify whether or not your vehicle has air conditioning, as the pumps usually are not interchangeable.

Removal (6-Cylinder Engine)

1. Drain the cooling system. If the vehicle has a fan shroud attached to the radiator, remove the attaching screws. Pull the shroud to the rear and position it on the engine out of the way.

2. Loosen all belt-driven accessories (alternator, power steering pump, etc.) and remove the drive belts.

3. Remove the fan blade, spacer, pulley, and bolts as an assembly. Then remove the fan shroud, if so equipped.

4. Disconnect the heater hose and the lower radiator hose from the water pump.

5. Remove the retaining bolts and then remove the water pump from the vehicle. Discard the gasket.

Removal (V8 Engine)

1. Drain the cooling system. If the vehicle has a fan shroud attached to the radiator, remove the attaching screws. Pull the shroud to the rear and position it on the engine out of the way.

2. Loosen all belt-driven accessories (alternator, power steering, etc.) and remove the drive belts.

3. On 318-360 engines without air conditioning, remove the alternator bracket attaching

7

bolts from the water pump. Swing the alternator up out of the way and tighten the adjusting bolt to hold it in this position. On these engines with air conditioning, remove the idler pulley assembly, alternator, and alternator adjusting bracket.

4. Remove the fan blade, spacer (or fluid drive assembly), pulley, and bolts as an assembly. If the fan has a fluid drive assembly (**Figure 8**, typical), do not allow the shaft to point downward as this will allow the silicone fluid to drain into the fan drive bearing. Remove the fan shroud from the vehicle.

5. On 318-360 engines, remove the heater, by-pass and lower radiator hoses. If the vehicle is equipped with air conditioning, remove the compressor clutch assembly, compressor-to-front mounting bracket bolts, and the water pump-to-compressor front mount bracket bolts. Remove the front mount bracket.

6. Remove the retaining bolts and remove the water pump assembly from the vehicle. Discard the gasket.

Installation (All Engines)

1. Check the condition of the by-pass hose and install a new one on the pump if required. Position clamp in center of hose.

2. Install the water pump on the engine, using a new gasket. Tighten retaining bolts to 30 ft.- lb. Check the pump to make sure it rotates freely.

3. On 6-cylinder and 318-360 engines, install the by-pass hose on the engine, using the clamp. Then install the heater hose and lower radiator hose. Use new hoses if old ones are in doubtful condition.

4. On 318-360 engines equipped with air conditioning, install the compressor front bracket. Tighten the compressor-to-bracket bolts to 50 ft.-lb. and the bracket-to-water pump bolts to 30 ft.-lb. Then install the alternator, adjusting bracket, and idler pulley assembly. Install the compressor clutch assembly.

5. On 318-360 engines without air conditioning, install the alternator front bracket.

6. Position the shroud on the engine, out of the way, and install the fan blade, spacer (or fluid drive), pulley and bolts assembly. Install the shroud on the radiator.

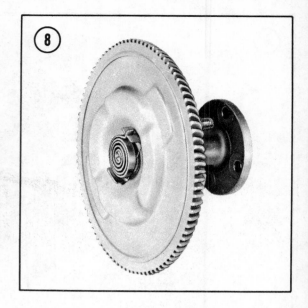

7. Install the drive belts and adjust their tension. See *Accessory Drive Belts,* elsewhere in this chapter. Tighten the attaching and adjusting bolts to 30 ft.-lb.

8. Fill the cooling system with a solution of ethylene glycol antifreeze and water adequate for expected temperatures, following the antifreeze manufacturer's recommendations. Use at least a 50/50 solution to prevent cooling system corrosion.

9. Start the engine and check for leaks. After the engine warms up, recheck the coolant level and replenish as required. See *Routine Checks,* Chapter Three.

AIR CONDITIONING

Major service and repair to air conditioning systems requires specialized training and tools, and the difficulty of the work is compounded in the late heating/air conditioning systems. However, most air conditioning problems do not involve major repair; they are well within the ability of an experienced hobbyist mechanic, armed with an understanding of how the system works.

SYSTEM OPERATION

A typical air conditioning system is shown in **Figure 9**. (Actual component locations may differ, depending on model.)

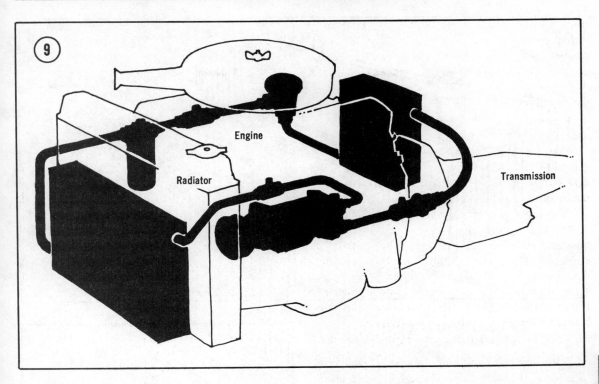

Engine

Radiator

Transmission

The five basic components are common to all air conditioning systems:

1. Compressor
2. Condenser
3. Receiver/drier
4. Expansion valve
5. Evaporator

The components, connected with high-pressure hoses and tubes, form a closed loop. A refrigerant, dichlorodifluoromethane—more commonly referred to as R-12, circulates through the system under high-pressure—as much as 300 psi. As a result, work on the air conditioning system is potentially hazardous if certain precautions are ignored. For safety's sake *read this entire section* before attempting any troubleshooting, checks, or work on the system.

A typical system is shown schematically in **Figure 10**. For practical purposes, the cycle begins at the compressor. The refrigerant, in a warm, low-pressure vapor state, enters the low-pressure side of compressor. It is compressed to a high-pressure hot vapor and pumped out of the high-pressure side to the condenser.

Air flow through the condenser removes heat from the refrigerant and transfers the heat to the outside air. As the heat is removed, the refrigerant condenses to a warm, high-pressure liquid.

The refrigerant then flows to the receiver/drier where moisture is removed and impurities are filtered out. The refrigerant is stored in the receiver/drier until it is needed. Generally, the receiver/drier incorporates a sight glass that permits visual monitoring of the condition of the refrigerant as it flows. This is discussed later.

From the receiver/drier, the refrigerant flows to the expansion valve. The expansion valve is thermostatically controlled and meters refrigerant to the evaporator. As the refrigerant leaves the expansion valve it changes from a warm, high-pressure liquid to a cold, low-pressure liquid.

In the evaporator, the refrigerant removes heat from the cockpit air that is blown across the evaporator's fins and tubes. In the process, the refrigerant changes from a cold, low-pressure liquid to a warm, high-pressure vapor which flows back to the compressor where the refrigeration cycle began.

7

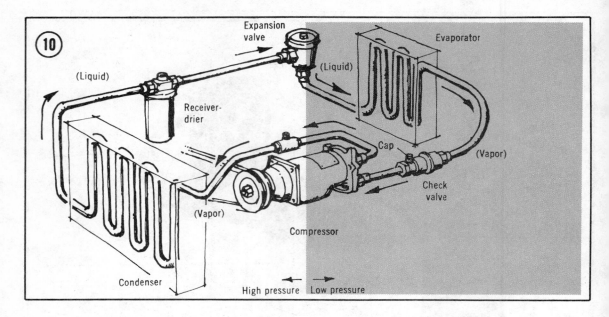

GET TO KNOW YOUR VEHICLE'S SYSTEM

With **Figure 9** as a guide, begin with the compressor and locate each of the following components in turn:

1. Compressor
2. Condenser
3. Receiver/drier
4. Expansion valve
5. Evaporator

Compressor

The compressor is located on the front of the engine, like an alternator, and is driven by one or two drive belts **(Figure 11)**. The large pulley on the front contains an electromagnetic clutch that is activated and operates the compressor when the air conditioning controls are switched on. There are two compressor types — piston-and-crank **(Figure 12)**, and swashplate (axial plate), **Figure 13**.

Condenser

In most cases, the condenser is mounted in front of the radiator **(Figure 14)**. Air passing through the fins and tubes removes heat from the refrigerant in the same manner it removes heat from the engine coolant as it passes through the radiator.

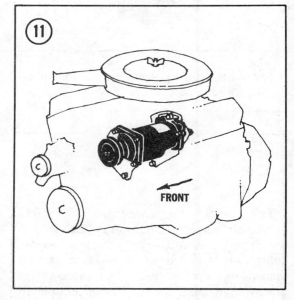

Receiver/Drier

The receiver/drier is a small tank-like unit **(Figure 15)**, usually found mounted to one of the wheel wells. Many receiver/driers incorporate a sight glass through which refrigerant flow can be seen when the system is operating **(Figure 16)**. Some systems have an in-line sight glass **(Figure 17)**. Some early systems do not have a sight glass but it's not essential to system operation — just handy to help diagnose air conditioning troubles.

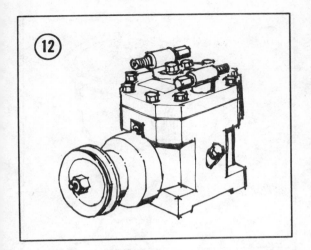

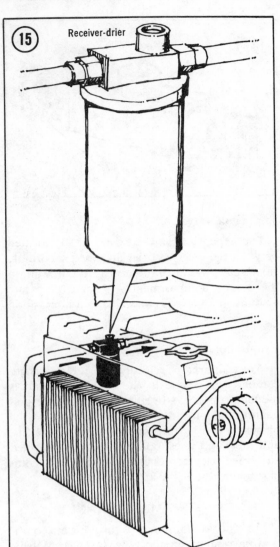

Receiver-drier

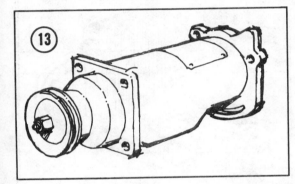

7

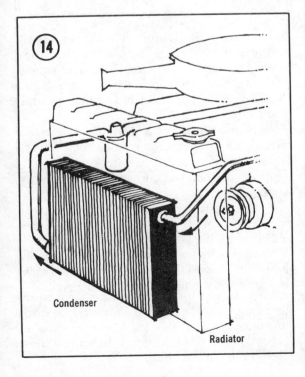

Condenser

Radiator

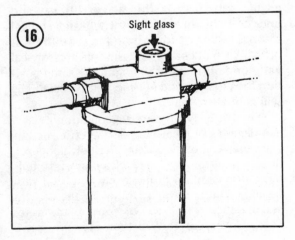

Sight glass

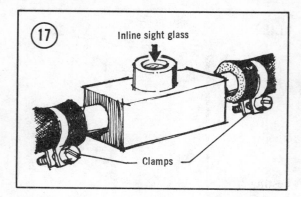

Inline sight glass

Clamps

Expansion Valve

The expansion valve (**Figure 18**) is located between the receiver/drier and the evaporator. It is usually mounted on or near the firewall, in the engine compartment. In some very late systems, the valve is concealed in a housing on the firewall.

Evaporator

The evaporator is located in the passenger compartment, beneath the dashboard, and is hidden from view by the fan shrouding and ducting (**Figure 19**). Warm air from the passenger compartment is blown across the fins and tubes in the evaporator where it is cooled and dried and then ducted back into the compartment through the air outlets.

ROUTINE MAINTENANCE

Preventive maintenance for your air conditioning system couldn't be simpler; at least once a month, even in cold weather, start your engine and turn on the air conditioner and operate it at each of the switch and control settings. Allow it to operate for about 5 minutes. This will ensure that the compressor seal will not deform from sitting in the same position for a long period of time. If this occurs, the seal is likely to leak.

The efficiency of your air conditioning system depends in great part on the efficiency of your engine cooling system. Periodically check the coolant for level and cleanliness. If it is dirty, drain and flush the system and fill it with fresh coolant and water, following the coolant manufacturer's instructions for coolant/water ratio. Have your radiator cap pressure tested

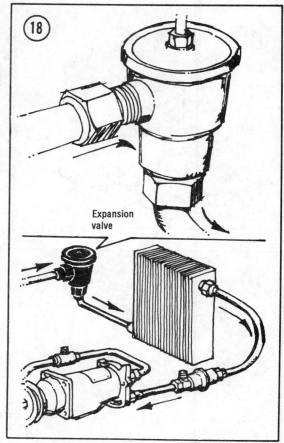

Expansion valve

Expansion valve

and replace it if it will not maintain 13 psi pressure. If the system requires repeated topping up and the radiator cap is in good condition, it is likely that there is a leak in the system. Pressure test it as described earlier in this chapter.

With an air hose and a soft brush, clean the radiator fins and tubes to remove bugs, leaves, and any other imbedded debris.

Check and correct drive belt tension as described earlier.

If the condition of the cooling system thermostat is in doubt, check it as described earlier and replace it if it is faulty.

When you are confident that the engine cooling system is working correctly, you are ready to inspect and test the air conditioning system.

Inspection

1. Clean all lines, fittings, and system components with solvent and a clean rag. Pay par-

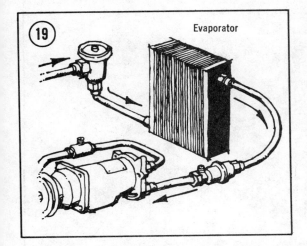

Evaporator

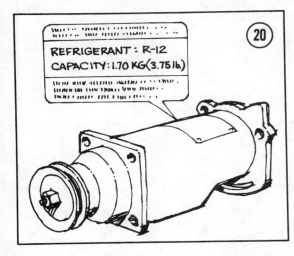

REFRIGERANT: R-12
CAPACITY: 1.70 KG (3.75 lb.)

ticular attention to the fittings; oily dirt around connections almost certainly indicates a leak. Oil from the compressor will migrate through the system to the leak. Carefully tighten the connection, taking care not to overtighten and risk stripping the threads. If the leak persists it will soon be apparent once again as oily dirt accumulates. Clean the sight glass with a clean, dry cloth.

2. Clean the condenser fins and tubes with a soft brush and an air hose, or with a high-pressure stream of water from a garden hose. Remove bugs, leaves and other imbedded debris. Carefully straighten any bent fins with a screwdriver, taking care not to dent or puncture the tubes.

3. Check the condition and tension of the drive belts and replace or correct as necessary.

4. Start the engine and check the operation of the blower motor and the compressor clutch by turning the controls on and off. If either the blower or the clutch fails to operate, shut off the engine and check the condition of the fuses. If they are blown replace them. If not, remove them and clean the fuse holder contacts. Then, recheck to ensure the blower and clutch operate.

Testing

1. With the transmission in PARK (automatic) or NEUTRAL (manual) and the handbrake set, start the engine and run it at a fast idle.

2. Set the temperature control to its coldest setting and turn the blower to high. Allow the system to operate for 10 minutes with the doors and windows open. Then close them and set the blower on its lowest setting.

3. Place a thermometer in a cold-air outlet. Within a few minutes, the temperature should be 35-45°F. If it is not, it's likely that the refrigerant level in the system is low. Check the appearance of the refrigerant flow through the sight glass. If it is bubbly, refrigerant should be added.

Refrigerant

The majority of automotive air conditioning systems use a refrigerant designated R-12. However, a commercial grade, designated R-20, is used in heavy-duty systems. The two are not compatible. Look for an information sticker, usually mounted near the compressor, to determine which refrigerant your system uses (**Figure 20**). Also, check the system capacity indicated on the sticker. Capacity can range from 2 to 5 pounds, depending on the system.

That harmless-looking little can of refrigerant is potentially hazardous. If it is hooked up to the high-pressure side of the compressor, or is hooked up without a gauge set, it becomes a hand grenade.

Charging

WARNING
Do not attempt to add refrigerant to the system without using a gauge set; it's essential that the system pressure during charging not exceed 50 psi.

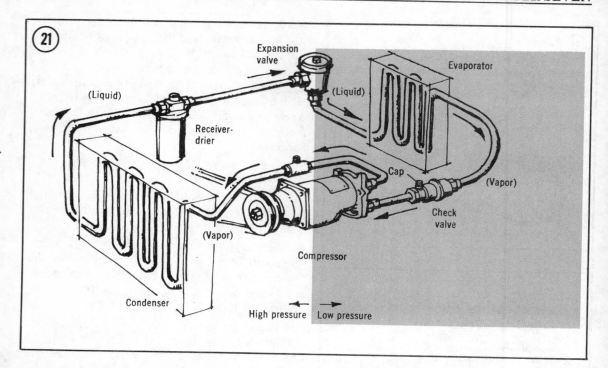

㉑ Expansion valve — (Liquid) — Evaporator — Receiver-drier — (Liquid) — Cap — (Vapor) — Check valve — (Vapor) — Compressor — Condenser — High pressure — Low pressure

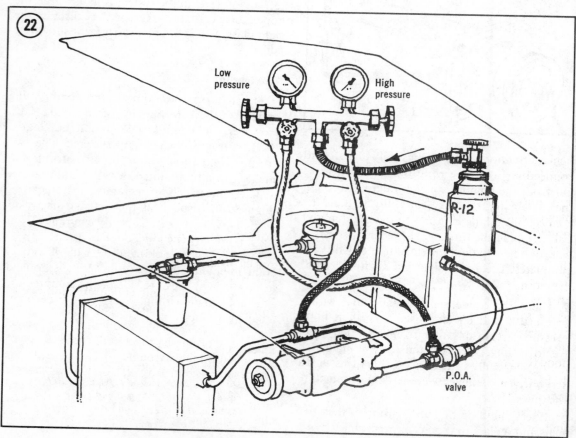

㉒ Low pressure — High pressure — R-12 — P.O.A. valve

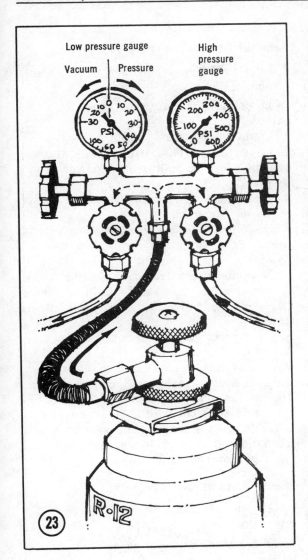

Low pressure gauge

High pressure gauge

Vacuum   Pressure

R·12

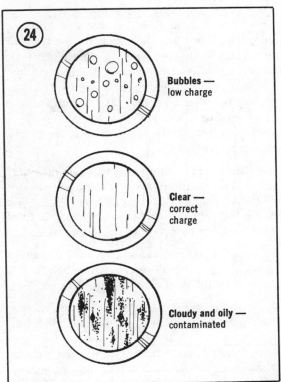

Bubbles — low charge

Clear — correct charge

Cloudy and oily — contaminated

7

6. Slowly open the refrigerant feed valve on the gauge set **(Figure 23)**. Do not allow the refrigerant pressure to exceed 50 psi.

7. Watch the refrigerant as it flows through the sight glass **(Figure 24)**. When it's free of bubbles, the system is charged. Shut off the refrigerant feed valve on the gauge set.

Troubleshooting

Preventative maintenance like that just described will help to ensure that your system is working efficiently. Still, trouble can develop and while most of it will invariably be simple and easy to correct, you must first locate it. The following sequence will help to diagnose system troubles when your air conditioning ceases to cool the passenger compartment.

1. First, stop the vehicle and look at the control settings. One of the most common sources of air conditioning trouble occurs when the temperature control is set for maximum cold and the blower is set on low. This arrangement promotes ice buildup on the fins and tubes of the evaporator, and particularly so in humid

1. Carefully read and understand the gauge manufacturer's instructions before charging the system.

2. Remove the cap from the Schrader valve on the low-pressure side of the compressor **(Figure 21)**. The low-pressure side is labelled SUCTION, SUCT., or SUC.

3. Connect the gauge set to the low-pressure Schrader valve. Connect the refrigerant can to the gauge set and hang the gauge set on the hood **(Figure 22)**.

4. Start the engine and run it at a fast idle (about 1,000 rpm).

5. Set the temperature control at its coldest setting. Set the blower at its lowest setting.

weather. Eventually, the evaporator will ice over completely, and restrict air flow. Turn the blower on high and place a hand over an air outlet. If the blower is running but there is little or no air flowing through the outlet, the evaporator is probably iced up. Leave the blower on high and turn off the temperature control or turn it down to its lowest setting — and wait; it will take 10 or 15 minutes before the ice begins to melt.

2. If the blower is not running, the motor may be burned out, there may be a loose connection, or the fuse may be blown. First check the fuse panel for a blown or incorrectly seated fuse. Then check the wiring for loose connections.

3. Shut off the engine and check the condition and tension of the compressor drive belt. If it is loose or badly worn, tighten or replace it.

4. Start the engine and check the condition of the compressor clutch by turning the air conditioner on and off. If the clutch does not energize, it may be defective, its fuse may be blown, or the evaporator temperature-limiting switches may be defective. If the fuse is defective, replace it. If the clutch still does not energize, refer the problem to an air conditioning specialist.

5. If all components checked so far are OK, start the engine, turn on the air conditioner and watch the refrigerant through the sight glass; remember, if it's filled with bubbles after the system has been operating for a few seconds, the refrigerant level is low. If the sight glass is oily or cloudy, the system is contaminated and should be serviced by an expert as soon as possible. Corrosion and deterioration occur rapidly and if it's not taken care of at once it will result in a very expensive repair job.

6. If the system still appears to be operating satisfactorily but the air flow into the passenger compartment is not cold, check the condenser and cooling system radiator for debris that could block the air flow. Recheck the cooling system as described earlier under *Inspection*.

7. If the above steps do not uncover the difficulty, have the system checked and corrected by a specialist as soon as possible.

HEATER

Removal/Installation (1971-1977)

Refer to **Figures 25A and 25B** for this procedure.

1. Disconnect the negative cable from the battery.
2. Drain the radiator.
3. Cover the alternator with a plastic sheet so coolant won't be spilled on it during heater removal.
4. Disconnect the ground wire and blower motor resistor wires.
5. Disconnect the hoses from the heater core tubes. Plug the hoses so they don't spill coolant.
6. Disconnect the heater control cables.
7. Remove the water valve mounting screws. Lay the water valve aside, together with its hoses.
8. Disconnect the blower motor cooler tube. Take the tube out.
9. Remove the heater housing mounting nuts. Take the heater out through the hood opening.
10. Installation is the reverse of removal. Fill the cooling system with a 50/50 mixture of ethylene glycol-based antifreeze and water. Turn the heater control to maximum hot. Run the engine and check for leaks.

Removal/Installation (1978-on)

Refer to **Figures 26A and 26B** for this procedure.

1. Disconnect the negative cable from the battery.
2. Drain the radiator.
3. Disconnect the hoses from the heater core.
4. Disconnect the temperature control cable from the heater core cover and blend air door crank.
5. Disconnect the blower motor feed and ground wires.
6. Remove 2 screws securing the heater unit to the side cowl. Remove 4 nuts securing the heater unit to the dash panel.
7. Lift the heater unit out.
8. Installation is the reverse of removal. Fill the cooling system with a 50/50 mixture of ethylene glycol-based antifreeze and water. Run the engine and check for coolant leaks.

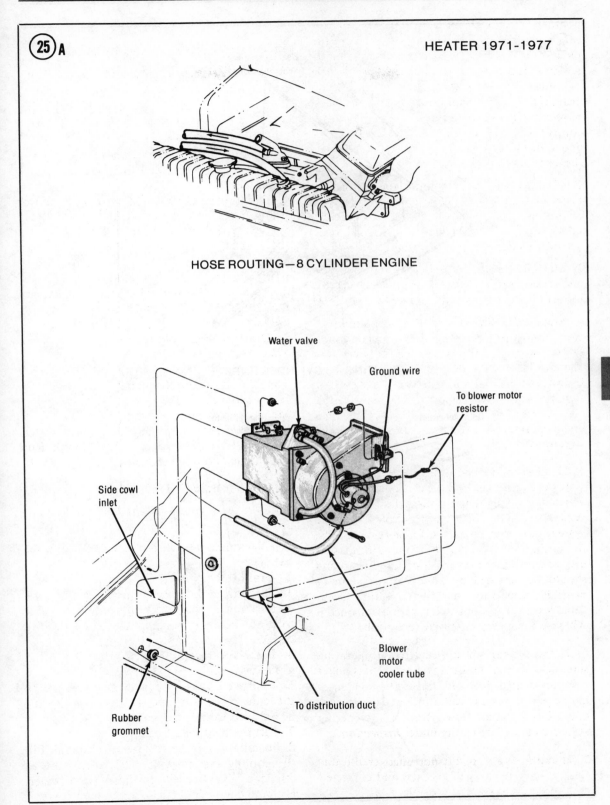

25 A

HEATER 1971-1977

HOSE ROUTING—8 CYLINDER ENGINE

Water valve

Ground wire

To blower motor resistor

Side cowl inlet

7

Blower motor cooler tube

To distribution duct

Rubber grommet

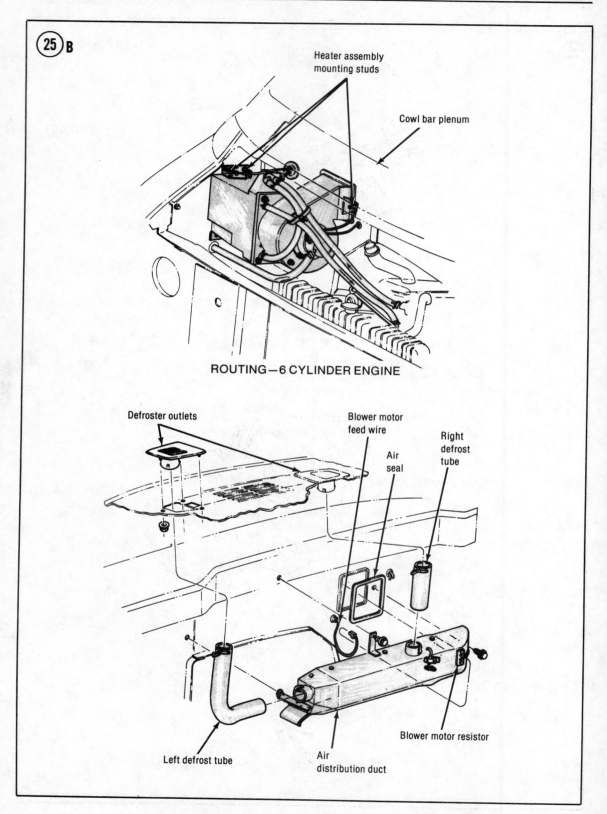

(25) B

Heater assembly
mounting studs

Cowl bar plenum

ROUTING—6 CYLINDER ENGINE

Defroster outlets

Blower motor
feed wire

Air
seal

Right
defrost
tube

Left defrost tube

Air
distribution duct

Blower motor resistor

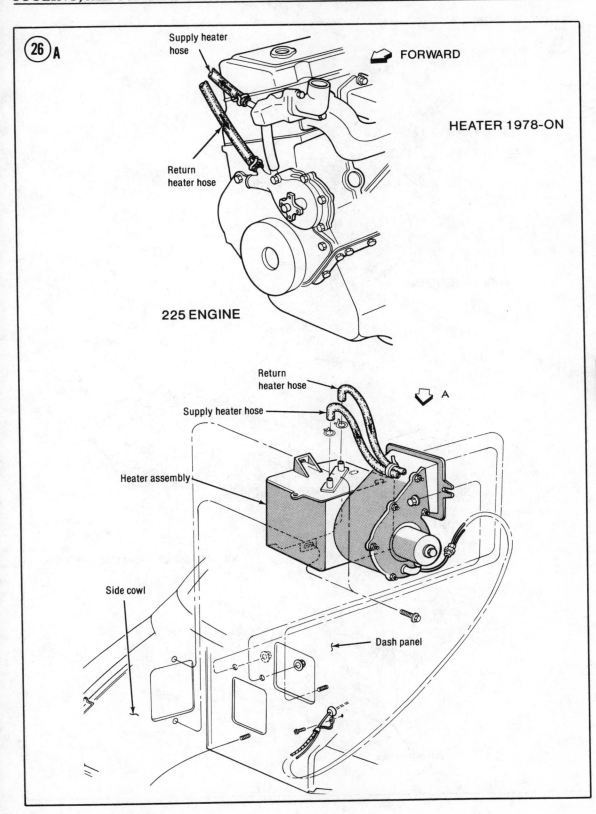

26 A

Supply heater hose

FORWARD

HEATER 1978-ON

Return heater hose

225 ENGINE

7

Return heater hose

A

Supply heater hose

Heater assembly

Side cowl

Dash panel

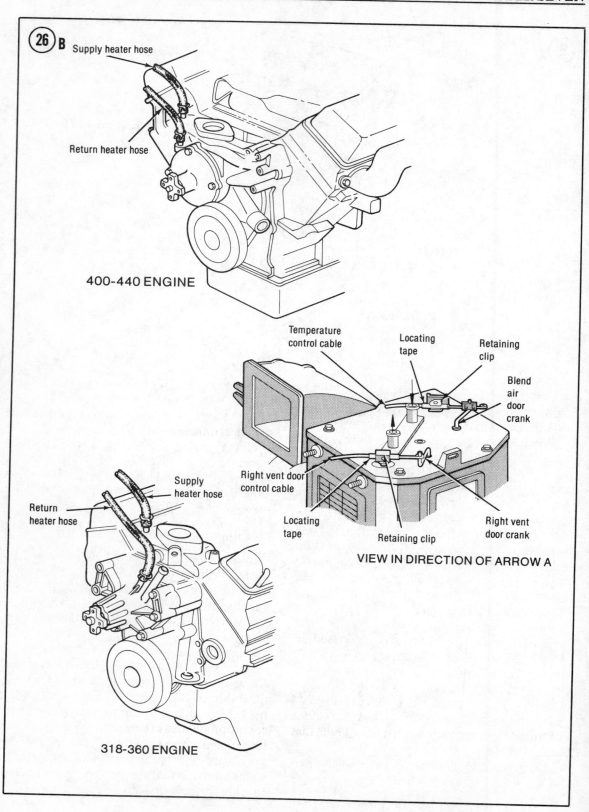

26 B

Supply heater hose

Return heater hose

400-440 ENGINE

Temperature control cable

Locating tape

Retaining clip

Blend air door crank

Right vent door control cable

Supply heater hose

Return heater hose

Locating tape

Retaining clip

Right vent door crank

VIEW IN DIRECTION OF ARROW A

318-360 ENGINE

NOTE: If you own a 1982 or later model, first check the Supplement at the back of the book for any new service information.

CHAPTER EIGHT

ELECTRICAL SYSTEMS

All models are equipped with 12-volt negative-ground electrical systems. Service and checkout procedures for the battery, fuses, starter, charging system, lighting system, and instruments are included in this chapter.

When trouble is experienced in the electrical system, Chapter Two can prove valuable as a guide to isolating problem areas as well as explaining the functions and uses of electrical test equipment. Very often electrical trouble can be traced to a simple cause, such as a blown fuse, a loose or corroded connection, a loose alternator drive belt, or a frayed wire. But, while these problems are easily correctable and of seemingly no major importance, they can quickly lead to serious difficulty if they are allowed to go uncorrected.

If you plan to do much of your own electrical work, a multimeter (described in Chapter Two) combining the functions of an ohmmeter, ammeter, and voltmeter is essential to locating and sorting out problems.

Above all, electrical system repair requires a patient, thorough approach to find true causes of trouble and then correct all of the faults that are involved.

Electrical diagrams are provided at the end of the book. **Tables 1-4** are at the end of the chapter.

BATTERY

The 1971-1978 models use fillable batteries. On 1979 and later models, "Long Life-Low Maintenance" batteries are optional, as are sealed maintenance-free batteries.

Figure 1 shows a typical gasoline engine battery installation. **Figure 2** shows the dual battery installation used with diesel engines. The dual installation is optional with gasoline-engine B300 vans.

Cleaning and Inspection

In addition to checking and correcting the battery electrolyte level at each gas stop (Chapter Three), the battery should be frequently cleaned with a solution of baking soda and water to remove corrosion from the terminals.

Liberally coat the entire top of the battery as well as the terminals with the solution and allow it to stand for several minutes. Carefully flush the residue away with clean water; while the baking soda will neutralize the acids in the corrosion deposits there's no need to risk getting unneutralized acid onto painted surfaces by rinsing the battery with a high-pressure water spray. When the battery has been thoroughly flushed, dry it with an old rag.

8

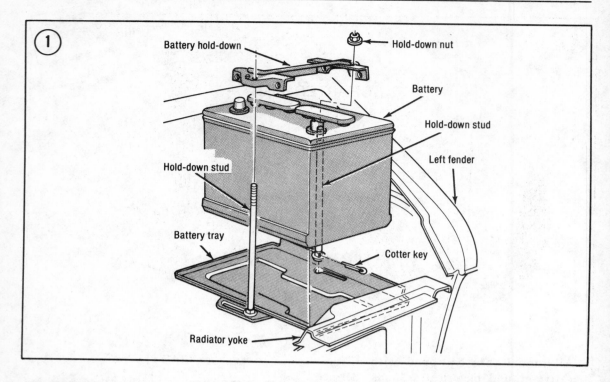

Inspect the battery case for damage, chafing, and cracks. Pay particular attention to moisture on the outside of the case; often this is an indication that the case is damaged to the extent that the battery is leaking electrolyte.

Testing (Standard Battery)

Periodically test the condition of the battery with a hydrometer. If you don't have a hydrometer but would consider buying one (a nominal investment), select one with numbered graduations rather than with just a color-band scale; it's important to know the true condition of the battery—not just good, bad, or so-so.

Draw enough electrolyte from each cell—one at a time—to raise the float in the hydrometer. Read it as shown in **Figure 3**. If the specific gravity is less than that indicated in **Table 1**, taking into account the temperature, and if the difference in specific gravity from one cell to another is greater than 0.050, one or more cells may be sulphated or otherwise poor. In such a case, the battery should be replaced before it causes trouble.

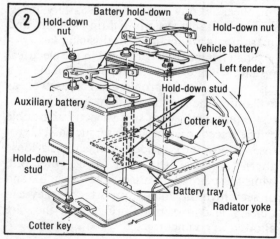

NOTE
When testing the battery with a hydrometer, always return the electrolyte to the cell from which it was removed before testing the next cell.

Testing (Long Life-Low Maintenance Battery)

This type of battery has a built-in test indicator cap on one cell (**Figure 4**). The cap is actually a hydrometer. It encloses a green

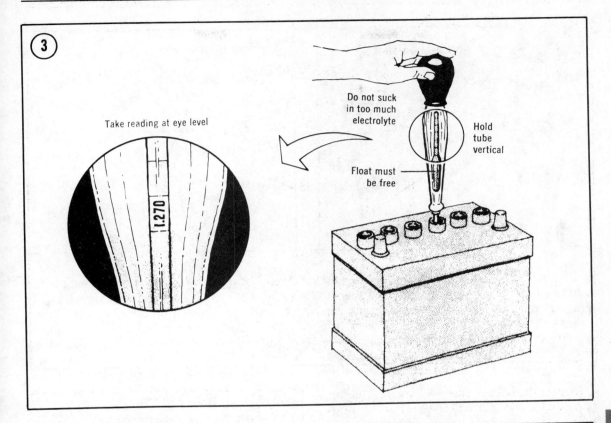

Take reading at eye level

1.270

Do not suck
in too much
electrolyte

Hold
tube
vertical

Float must
be free

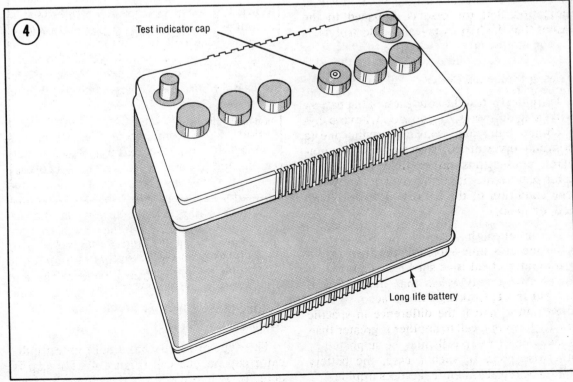

Test indicator cap

Long life battery

8

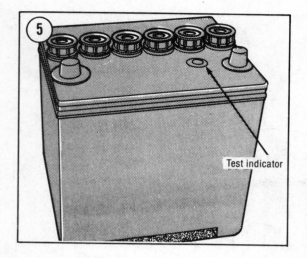

Test indicator

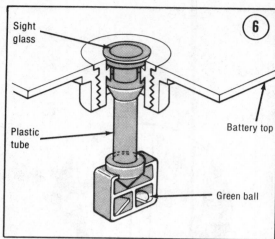

Sight glass

Battery top

Plastic tube

Green ball

plastic ball that floats and is visible through the window in the top of the cap when the specific gravity in that cell is within specifications. The green ball sinks and can't be seen when specific gravity drops below specifications. If the indicator shows a light yellow color, the cell is low on water. The indicator cap should be checked at each fuel stop and the electrolyte level should be checked every 12,000 miles or 12 months, whichever comes first.

Testing (Maintenance-free Battery)

The maintenance-free battery (**Figure 5**) has sealed vent caps and doesn't require the addition of battery water. This battery also has a built-in tester such as the one used on Long Life-Low Maintenance batteries. See **Figure 6**. If the indicator shows green, the battery is adequately charged; if the indicator is dark, the battery should be charged. After charging, have the battery load tested by a dealer or service station.

> *CAUTION*
> *If the indicator turns light yellow, do not attempt to charge, jump start or load test the battery. Damage to the van's charging system could result. Take the battery to your dealer for further testing.*

Charging

There's no need to remove the battery from the vehicle to charge it. Just make certain that the area is well ventilated and that there is no

chance of sparks or an open flame being in the vicinity of the battery; during charging, highly explosive hydrogen is produced by the battery.

Disconnect the ground lead from the battery. Remove the caps from the battery cells and top up each cell with distilled water. Never add electrolyte to a battery that is already in service. The electrolyte level in the cells should be about 1/4 in. above the plates.

Connect the charger to the battery—negative to negative, positive to positive. If the charger output is variable, select a low setting (5-10 amps), set the voltage selector to 12 volts, and plug the charger in. If the battery is severely discharged (below 1.125), allow it to charge for at least 8 hours. Less charge deterioration requires less charging time.

After the battery has charged for a suitable period of time, unplug the charger and disconnect it from the battery. Be extremely careful about sparks. Test the condition of each cell with a hydrometer as described above and compare the results with **Table 1**.

If the specific gravity indicates that the battery is fully charged, and if the readings remain the same after one hour, the battery can be considered to be in good condition and fully charged. Check the electrolyte level and add distilled water if necessary, install the vent caps, and reconnect the ground lead.

Removal/Installation

1. Loosen the bolts in the terminal clamps far enough so the clamps can be spread slightly.

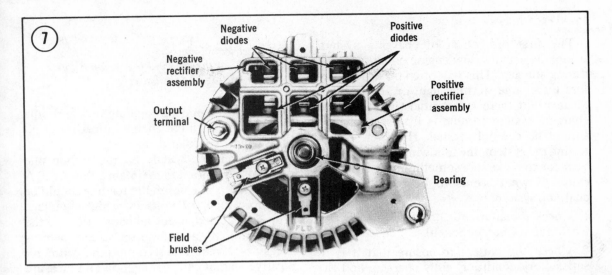

(7)

Negative diodes

Positive diodes

Negative rectifier assembly

Positive rectifier assembly

Output terminal

Bearing

Field brushes

Lift straight up on the clamps (negative first) to remove them from the posts. Twisting or prying on the clamps or posts can result in serious damage to a battery that may otherwise be in good condition.

2. Unscrew the nuts from the hold-down bolts and remove the hold-down frame. Lift the battery out of the engine compartment.

3. Reverse these steps to install the battery. Before setting the battery in place, clean the battery holder with a solution of baking soda and water to neutralize any acids that may have formed.

Allow the solution to stand for several minutes, then carefully flush it away with clean water, and dry it with an old rag. Set the battery into the holder making sure it is squarely seated. Install the hold-down frame and screw on the nuts snugly.

First connect the positive lead to the battery, then the negative. Tighten the clamp bolts securely and check their tightness by trying to rotate them on the posts by hand. Coat the terminals liberally with Vaseline to inhibit corrosion and formation of ash-like acid deposits.

ALTERNATOR

The alternator is a self-rectifying, three-phase current generator consisting of a stationary armature (stator), a rotating field (rotor), and a three-phase rectifying bridge of silicon diodes. The alternator generates alternating current which is converted to direct current by the silicon diodes for use in the vehicle's electrical circuits. The output of the alternator is regulated by a voltage regulator to keep the battery charged. The alternator is mounted on the front of the engine and is driven through a belt by the crankshaft pulley.

When working on the alternator, make sure the connections are not reversed. Current flow in the wrong direction will damage the diodes and render the alternator unserviceable. The alternator output terminal must be connected to battery voltage (**Figure 7**). When charging the battery in the vehicle, disconnect the battery leads before connecting the charger. This is a precaution against incorrect current bias and heat reaching the alternator.

Removal/Installation

1. Disconnect the negative battery cable at the battery. Identify the leads and disconnect them from the rear of the alternator.

2. Loosen the belt tension adjuster at the alternator. Swing the alternator toward the engine and remove the drive belt from the pulley.

3. Unscrew the adjuster bolt and pivot bolt and remove the alternator.

4. Reverse these steps to install the alternator. Make certain the alternator plug has been connected before connecting the negative battery lead. Refer to Chapter Seven and adjust the drive belt tension.

Pre-Test Checks

The first indication of charging system trouble is usually slow engine cranking speed during starting. This will often occur long before the charge warning light or ammeter indicates that there is potential trouble. When charging system trouble is first suspected, it should be carefully tested. However, before testing the system, the following checks should be made to make sure something else is not the cause of what seems to be trouble in the charging system.

1. Check the alternator drive belt for correct tension (see Chapter Seven).

2. Check the battery to ensure that it is in satisfactory condition, fully charged, and the connections are clean and tight (see above).

3. Check all of the connections from the alternator and the voltage regulator to ensure that they are clean and tight.

When the above points have been carefully checked and unsatisfactory conditions corrected, and there are still indications that the charging system is not performing as it should, proceed with system testing.

Resistance Test (In-Car)

1. Disconnect the ground cable from battery.

2. Disconnect the BAT lead at the alternator output terminal and connect a DC ammeter with a 0-100 A scale between the BAT terminal and the disconnected BAT wire. See **Figure 8**.

3. Connect the positive lead of a voltmeter to the disconnected BAT wire and the negative lead to the battery positive terminal. See **Figure 8**.

4. Disconnect the green wire from the field terminal of the alternator and connect a jumper wire between the field terminal and ground. See **Figure 8**.

5. Connect a tachometer to the engine, following the manufacturer's instructions.

6. Reconnect the battery ground cable and connect a variable carbon pile rheostat between the battery terminals. See **Figure 8**.

CAUTION
*To avoid damage to the battery and the electrical circuits, make sure the rheostat is in the **open** or **off** position before connecting it to the battery.*

7. Start the engine and operate it at curb idle speed. Make sure the engine immediately returns to idle speed after starting.

8. Adjust engine speed and the carbon pile rheostat as required to maintain a flow of 20 A in the circuit. The voltmeter reading should be not more than 0.7 volts. If a higher voltage drop is indicated, check all connections in the charging circuit and clean or tighten them as necessary. If required, reconnect the voltmeter positive lead at each connection and measure the voltage drop to determine where the excessive resistance exists.

9. When a voltmeter reading of 0.7 volts or less is obtained, reduce engine speed, turn the rheostat to OPEN or OFF, and turn off the ignition switch.

10. Disconnect the battery ground cable and remove the test equipment. Remove the jumper wire and reconnect the green wire to the alternator field terminal.

11. Reconnect the BAT wire to the alternator BAT terminal and reconnect the battery ground cable.

Current Output
Test (In-vehicle)

1. Disconnect the ground cable from battery.

2. Disconnect the BAT lead at the alternator output terminal and connect a DC ammeter with a 0-100 A range between the output terminal and the disconnected wire. See **Figure 9**.

3. Connect the positive lead of a voltmeter to the output terminal of the alternator and connect a negative lead to ground. See **Figure 9**. Turn the voltmeter to the 0-15 V (minimum) range.

4. Disconnect the green wire from the alternator field terminal and connect a jumper wire between the field terminal and ground. See **Figure 9**.

5. Connect a tachometer to the engine, following the manufacturer's instructions. Reconnect the battery ground cable.

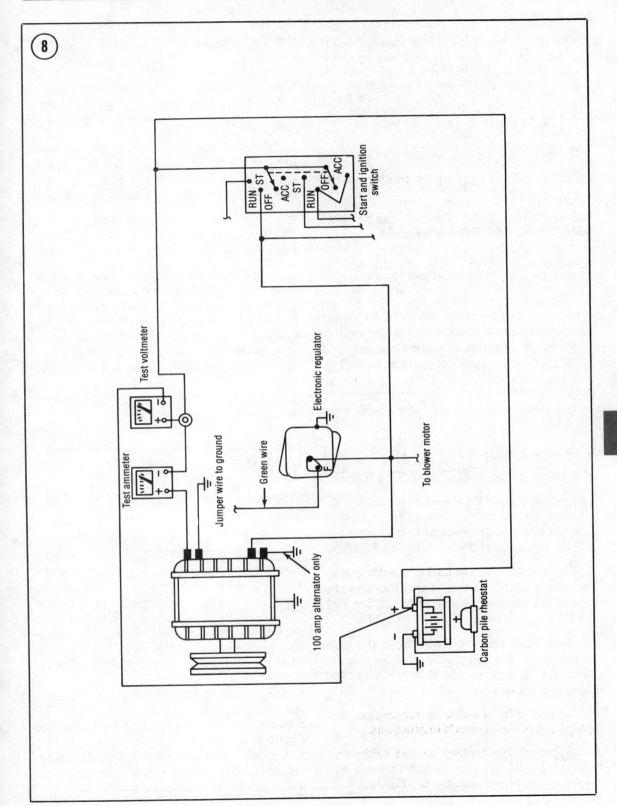

6. Connect a variable carbon pile rheostat between the battery terminals.

CAUTION
*Make sure the rheostat is in the **open** or **off** position before connecting it to the battery to avoid possible damage to the battery and/or the charging circuit.*

7. Start the engine and operate it at curb idle speed.

8. Increase engine speed to 1,250 rpm (900 rpm for 100 A alternator) and slowly adjust the rheostat to obtain a voltmeter reading of 15 volts (13 volts for 100 A alternator).

CAUTION
Do not allow a reading of over 16 volts on the voltmeter. Circuit damage could result.

9. The ammeter reading should be somewhere between the minimum current reading and rated output specifications given in **Table 2** for the size of the alternator being tested. If the reading is less, remove the alternator for bench testing.

10. If the ammeter reading is within the specified limits, reduce the engine speed. Turn off the rheostat and turn off the ignition switch. Disconnect the battery ground cable and remove the test equipment.

11. Remove the jumper wire and reconnect the green wire to the field terminal and the BAT wire to the output terminal of the alternator. Reconnect the battery ground cable.

**Voltage Regulator Test
(In-Vehicle)**

1. Clean the battery terminals and check the battery with a hydrometer (see *Battery Testing,* this chapter) to make sure the battery is fully charged. If not, recharge the battery, as a fully charged battery is required for this test.

2. Connect the positive lead of a voltmeter to the positive terminal of the battery and the

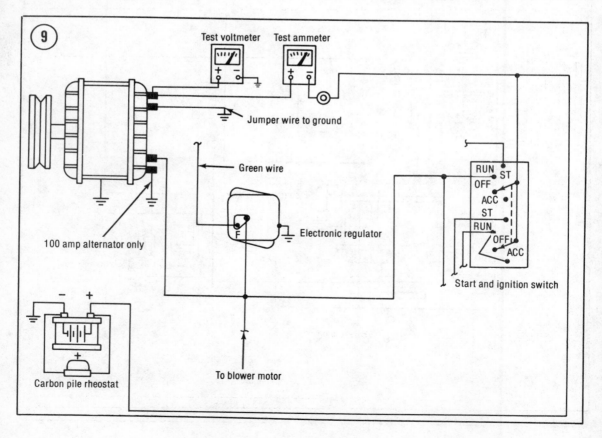

⑨ Test voltmeter   Test ammeter

Jumper wire to ground

Green wire

100 amp alternator only

Electronic regulator

F

RUN   ST
OFF
ACC
ST
RUN
OFF
ACC

Start and ignition switch

To blower motor

Carbon pile rheostat

negative lead to ground. See **Figure 10**. Set voltmeter to 0-15 (minimum) scale.

3. Connect a tachometer to the engine, following the manufacturer's instructions.

4. Start the engine, operate it at 1,250 rpm with all lights and accessories turned off, and read the voltmeter. The reading should be between 13.9 and 14.6 volts at 80° F (slightly higher at colder temperatures or slightly lower at higher temperatures).

5. If the voltage is less than 13.6 volts (except at temperatures above 140° F), check the regulator case-to-vehicle mounting contact for a good ground connection. Clean and scrape contact surfaces and/or tighten mounting screws as required to obtain a good ground connection. Turn off the ignition switch and check the voltage regulator connector and terminal for good clean contact and tight fit. Clean the contacts and tighten the connector terminals as required. Turn on ignition switch, but do not start engine, and make sure battery voltage is present at both wires in the connector. If the voltage is still lower than specified limit, replace the regulator and repeat the test.

6. If the voltage reading is above the specified limits (except in extremely cold temperature, -20° F and below, where the upper limit can be as high as 15.9 volts), turn off the ignition switch and remove the wiring connector from the voltage regulator. Make sure the terminals on the regulator and in the connector are clean and that they fit tightly. Turn on the ignition switch, but do not start the engine, and make sure that battery voltage is present in both wires in the connector. Turn the ignition switch off. If voltage is still above the specified limits, replace the regulator and repeat the test.

Voltage Regulator Replacement

1. Disconnect the negative cable from the battery.

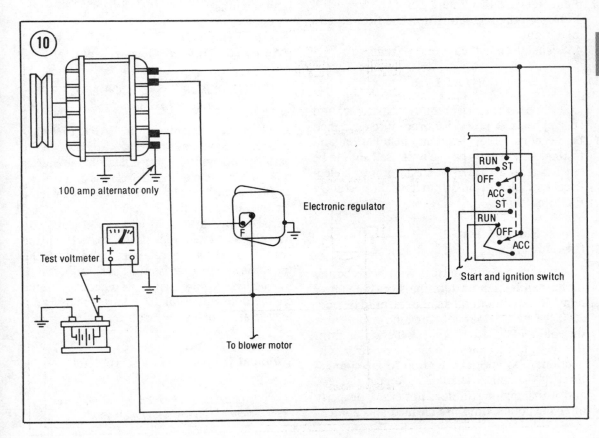

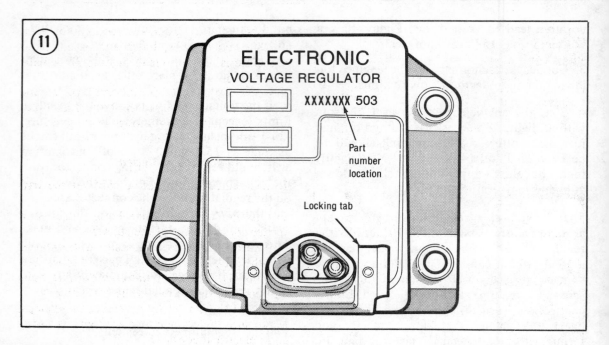

⑪ ELECTRONIC
VOLTAGE REGULATOR

XXXXXXX 503

Part
number
location

Locking tab

2. Disconnect the wiring connector from the regulator, mounted on the engine compartment sidewall. See **Figure 11**.
3. Detach the regulator from the firewall and take it out.
4. Installation is the reverse of removal.

STARTER

Service to the starter requires experience and special tools. The service procedure described below consists of removal, installation and testing. Any repairs on the unit itself should be entrusted to a dealer or an automotive electrical specialist if you do not have the necessary tools and skills.

Starter Solenoid Test
(In-vehicle)

1. Connect a heavy jumper wire between the battery and solenoid terminals on the starter relay. If the engine cranks, the solenoid is good.
2. If the starter does not crank the engine, or if the solenoid "chatters," check the wiring from the relay to the starter for loose or dirty connections. Pay special attention to the connections at the starter terminals. Repeat the test, and if the engine still does not crank properly after the connections are cleaned and tighten-ed, the trouble is in the starter and the starter must be removed from the car for bench testing and repairs.

Starter Relay Test
(Automatic Transmission—In-vehicle)

NOTE
This test should be made after the starter solenoid is tested and found good.

1. Place the transmission in PARK or NEUTRAL and connect a jumper wire between the battery and ignition terminals on the starter relay. If engine cranks, the relay is good.
2. If the engine does not crank, connect a second jumper wire between the ground terminal on the starter relay and a good ground on the engine. Then repeat the test. If engine cranks, the starter relay is good, but the transmission linkage is improperly adjusted or the neutral safety switch is defective. If the engine does not crank, the starter relay is defective and must be replaced.

Starter Relay Test
(Manual Transmission—In-vehicle)

NOTE
This test should be made after the starter solenoid is tested and found good.

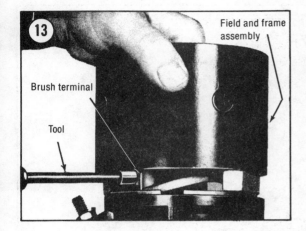

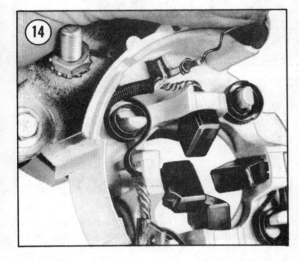

1. While a helper depresses the clutch pedal, connect a jumper wire between the battery and ignition terminals on the starter relay. If the engine cranks, the relay is good.

2. If the engine does not crank, install a second jumper wire between the relay ground terminal and a good ground on the engine. Then repeat the test. If the engine cranks, the starter relay is good, but the neutral start switch is out of adjustment or defective. If the engine does not crank, the starter relay is defective and must be replaced.

Ignition Switch Test (In-vehicle)

NOTE
This test should be made after the starter solenoid and relay have been tested and found to be good.

1. Check all wiring and connections for open and shorted circuits, loose and/or corroded connections. Repair, clean, tighten, or replace as required.

2. If the starter still will not crank the engine with the ignition key, and the starter, solenoid, relay, and battery are known to be good, replace the ignition switch.

Starter Removal/Installation

1. Disconnect the negative cable at the battery.

2. Disconnect the positive battery cable and starter control cable at the starter.

3. Thoroughly clean the outside of the starter and the area at which it is attached to the bell housing. Unscrew the starter mounting bolts and pull the starter out of the bell housing.

4. Install the starter by reversing these steps. Make sure the connections are tight, ensuring good electrical contact.

Brush Replacement

Refer to **Figure 12** for this procedure.

CAUTION
During the next step, tighten the vise just enough to support the starter. Do not clamp the starter with the vise.

1. Place the starter housing in a soft-jawed vise.

2. Remove the through bolts. Take off the starter end head assembly.

3. Carefully pull the armature out of the gear housing and out of the field and frame assembly. Remove the steel and fiber thrust washer.

4. Lift up the field and frame assembly just enough to remove the brush terminal screw. Place 2 small wood blocks under the field and frame assembly. See **Figure 13**.

5. Reach into the field and frame assembly as shown in **Figure 13**. Place a finger behind the brush terminal to support it, then remove the terminal screw as shown.

6. Disconnect the brush wires. Disconnect the shunt field coil wire from the brush terminal.

7. Lift off the field and frame assembly.

8. Unsolder the shunt field coil lead from the starter terminal.

9. Unwind the solenoid lead wire (**Figure 14**).

8

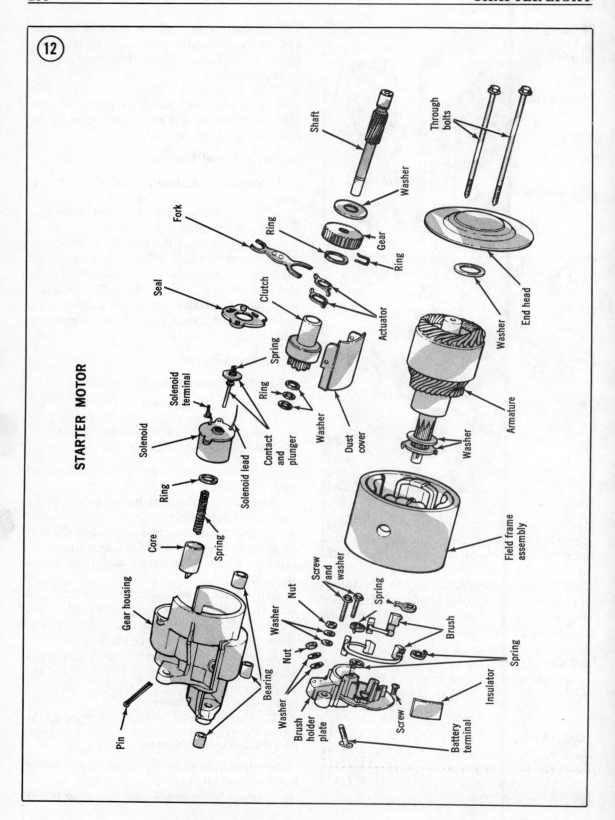

⑫

STARTER MOTOR

Shaft

Through bolts

Washer

Fork

Ring

Gear

Ring

End head

Seal

Clutch

Washer

Actuator

Solenoid terminal

Spring

Armature

Solenoid

Ring

Contact and plunger

Dust cover

Washer

Washer

Solenoid lead

Ring

Core

Spring

Field frame assembly

Gear housing

Screw and washer

Nut

Washer

Spring

Brush

Nut

Spring

Washer

Bearing

Brush holder plate

Insulator

Pin

Screw

Battery terminal

10. Inspect brushes. If brushes are soaked with oil or worn to less than half the length of new brushes, replace them. Unsolder the brush leads and solder new ones in their places. See **Figure 15**. Use a high temperature solder with resin flux. Do not use acid core solder.

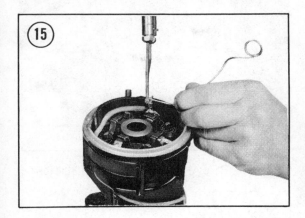

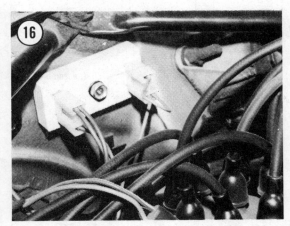

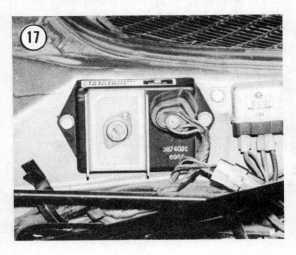

11. Connect a spring scale to the brush springs and pull on it. Brush spring tension should be 32-36 oz. If not, replace the brush and plate assembly.

12. Assemble by reversing Steps 1-9.

FUSES

Whenever a failure occurs in any part of the electrical system, always check the fuse box to see if a fuse has blown. If one has, it will be evident by blackening of the fuse or by a break in the metal link in the fuse.

Usually the trouble can be traced to a short circuit in the wiring connected to the blown fuse. This may be caused by worn-through insulation or by a wire which has worked loose and shorted to ground. Occasionally, the electrical overload which causes the fuse to blow may occur in a switch or a motor.

A blown fuse should be treated as more than a minor annoyance; it should serve also as a warning that something is wrong in the electrical system. Before replacing a fuse, determine what caused it to blow and then correct the trouble. Never replace a fuse with one of higher amperage rating than that of the one originally used.

Never use tinfoil or other metallic material to bridge fuse terminals. Failure to follow these basic rules could result in heat or fire damage to major parts, or loss of the entire vehicle.

The fuse amperage and the circuits protected are shown on the fuse block. To replace or inspect a fuse, carefully pry it out of its holder with the end of a pencil or similar non-metallic probe and snap a new one into place. **Table 3** gives fuse sizes and locations.

IGNITION SYSTEMS

Two types of ignition systems have been used on vehicles covered in this book: the electronic system (1973-on) and the breaker-point system (1971-1972).

Electronic Ignition System

The electronic ignition system consists of the battery, ignition switch, dual ballast resistor (see **Figure 16**), control unit (see **Figure 17**),

8

coil (see **Figure 18**), distributor (see **Figure 19**), spark plugs, and all related wiring, insulators, and connectors. The over-all system is shown in **Figure 20**.

The pick-up coil circuit in the distributor, consisting of the pick-up coil assembly, the reluctor, and the pick-up coil leads, controls a switching transistor in the control assembly to fire the spark plugs at the proper time. The reluctor, rotating with the distributor shaft, causes a voltage pulse in the pick-up coil each time a plug should be fired. This pulse is transmitted via the pick-up coil leads to the control unit, where it causes the switching transistor to interrupt current flow through

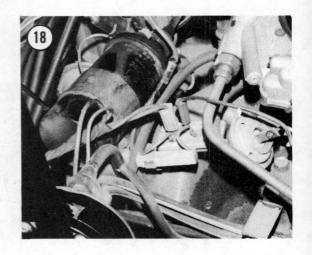

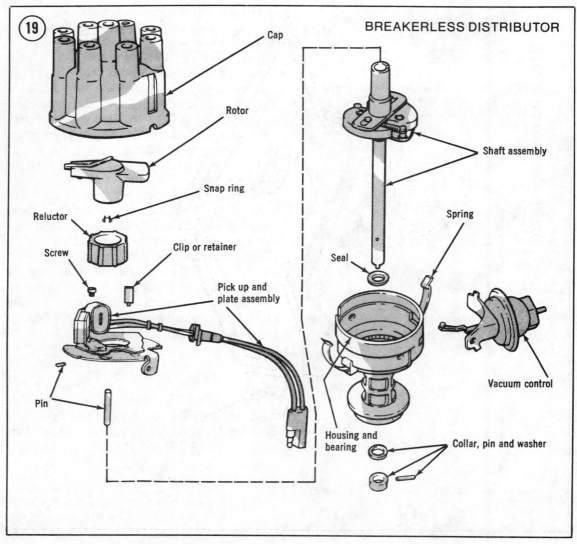

BREAKERLESS DISTRIBUTOR

Cap

Rotor

Snap ring

Reluctor

Screw

Clip or retainer

Pick up and plate assembly

Pin

Shaft assembly

Spring

Seal

Vacuum control

Housing and bearing

Collar, pin and washer

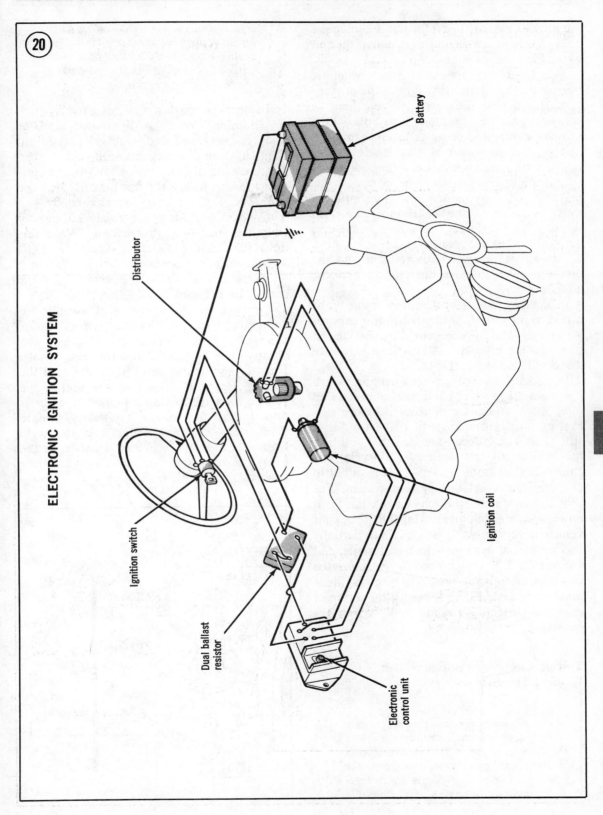

ELECTRONIC IGNITION SYSTEM

Battery

Distributor

Ignition coil

Ignition switch

Dual ballast resistor

Electronic control unit

8

the primary circuit. The interruption induces a high voltage in the secondary circuit of the coil which fires a spark plug.

The length of time that the switching transistor allows current to flow in the primary circuit corresponds to "dwell" in a conventional breaker point distributor. It is not adjustable, and readings taken with dwell meters are meaningless. As dwell affects ignition timing, once basic timing is set to specifications, there should be no reason for periodic checks of timing. Of course, timing must be reset if the distributor has been removed and replaced. For timing procedure, see *Ignition Timing*, Chapter Three.

The air gap between the reluctor and the pick-up coil also does not require periodic adjustment.

In fact, routine maintenance should be limited to inspection of the distributor cap, rotor, wiring, and the changing of spark plugs at the specified intervals. All of these items are discussed in Chapter Three.

If the distributor cap, rotor, wiring and spark plugs are all in good condition, eliminate all other possible causes of trouble before suspecting the ignition system. If the trouble is still present, it is recommended that you take the vehicle to your dealer, as a special test equipment set (tool C-4166-A) is required to properly check out the ignition system. The probability of using this expensive equipment more than once or twice during the life of your vehicle is very slight. It is possible to partially check out the system with a voltmeter and ohmmeter, but this procedure calls for the substitution of parts known to be good. Since most parts dealers do not permit the return of electrical parts, this method could be very expensive.

Testing Electronic Ignition System Without Test Set

NOTE
The electronic ignition system can only be partly checked without Ignition Tester part No. C4503. If the checks given in this procedure do not isolate the cause of ignition problems, the cause is probably in the control unit or ignition

coil. You may want to remove these parts and take them to your dealer for further testing, as it is unlikely that both units have failed simultaneously and replacing both would be expensive.

1. Inspect the spark plug wires and the thick wire running from coil to distributor. Look for poor connections and cracked insulation. Tighten, clean or replace as needed.
2. Check the primary (thin) wires at the ignition coil and ballast resistor for dirty or loose connections. Clean or tighten as needed.
3. Connect a voltmeter between the battery terminals and note the reading. Write this down for later use.
4. Make sure the ignition switch is off.
5. Remove the wiring connector from the control unit (**Figure 17**).
6. Connect the positive lead of a calibrated voltmeter to cavity 1 of the wiring harness connector. See **Figure 21**. Connect the negative lead to ground (nearby bare metal). Turn the ignition switch to ON and read the voltage. It should be within one volt of the voltage recorded in Step 3 with all accessories turned off. If the voltage is different by more than one volt, check the circuit shown in **Figure 21**, paying particular attention to the ballast resistor, ignition switch and wiring connections. See **Figure 22**.

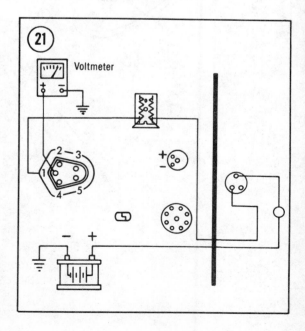

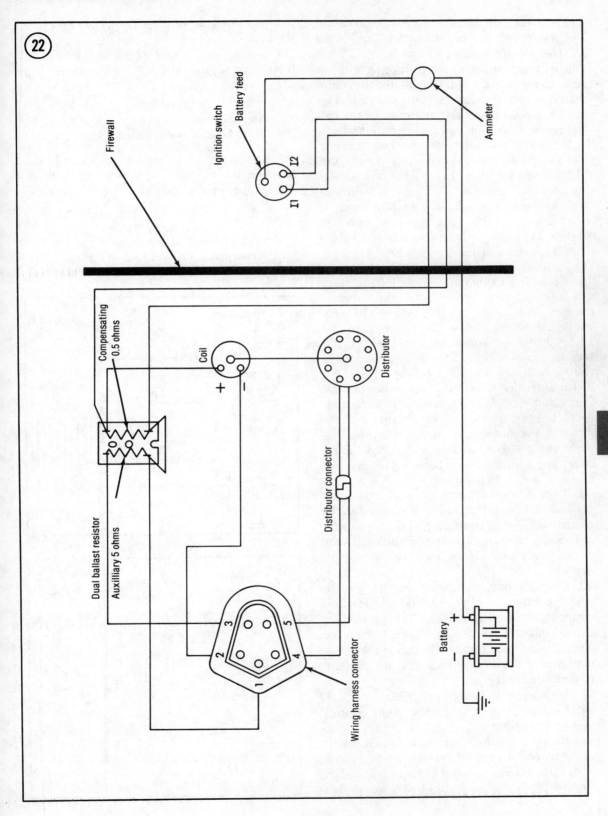

Firewall

Ignition switch

Battery feed

Ammeter

L2

I1

Compensating
0.5 ohms

Coil

Distributor

+   −

Distributor connector

Dual ballast resistor

Auxilliary 5 ohms

3

2   5

1   4

Wiring harness connector

Battery

+

−

22

8

7. Move the voltmeter positive lead to cavity 2 of the wiring harness connector. See **Figure 23**. The voltage reading should be within one volt of the reading made in Step 3 with all accessories turned off. If the difference is more than one volt, check the circuit shown in **Figure 23**, paying particular attention to the ballast resistor, ignition coil and ignition switch.

8. Move the voltmeter positive lead to cavity 3 of the wiring harness connector. See **Figure 24**. The voltage should be within one volt of the reading recorded in Step 3 with all accessories turned off. If the difference is more than one volt, check the circuit shown in **Figure 24**, paying particular attention to the ballast resistor and ignition switch.

9. Turn the ignition switch OFF.

10. Connect a calibrated ohmmeter that uses a 1 1/2-volt battery for operation between cavities 4 and 5 of the wiring harness connector. See **Figure 25**. A reading of 150-900 ohms should be obtained. If the reading is not within these limits, disconnect the 2-lead connector coming from the distributor and check the resistance at the 2-lead connector. See **Figure 26**. If the reading is not 150-900 ohms, the pickup coil assembly in the distributor is faulty and must be replaced. If the reading is within the limits, check the wiring harness between the control unit and the 2-lead connector.

11. Connect one ohmmeter lead to a good ground and the other lead to either lead in the distributor 2-lead connector. If the ohmmeter shows any reading, have the pickup coil in the distributor replaced by a dealer or automotive electrical shop.

12. Connect one ohmmeter lead to ground and the other to pin 5 on the control unit connector. See **Figure 27**. The ohmmeter should indicate continuity. If not, tighten the control unit attaching bolts and recheck for continuity. If continuity is still not present, replace the control unit.

13. Make sure the ignition is OFF.

14. Reconnect the connectors to the control unit and distributor.

15. Remove the distributor cap. Check the air gap between a reluctor tooth and the pickup coil with a non-magnetic feeler gauge. See **Figure 28**. If the gap is not 0.006 in., loosen the pick-up coil hold-down screw, insert a 0.006 in. feeler gauge between the pick-up coil and reluctor tooth and adjust the air gap to 0.006 in. Tighten the hold-down screw and remove the feeler gauge.

CAUTION
Do not use force during the next step or the pick-up coil may be damaged.

16. Attempt to insert a 0.008 in. feeler gauge between the pick-up coil and reluctor tooth. The gauge should not fit. If it does, readjust the air gap.

WARNING
During the next step, hold the wire with a heavily insulated tool such as a plastic-handled screwdriver. Touching the wire

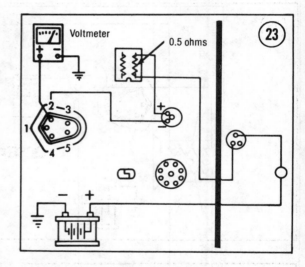

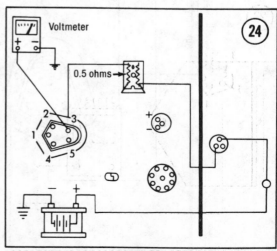

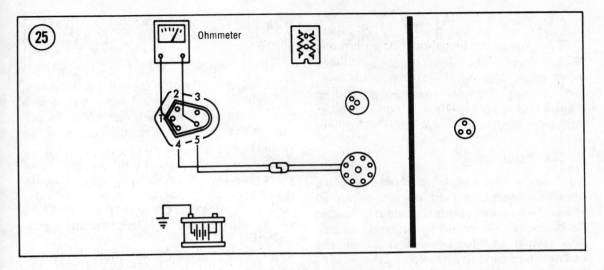

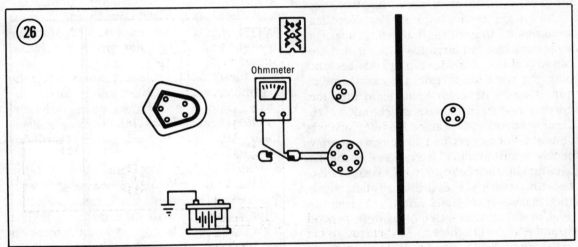

8

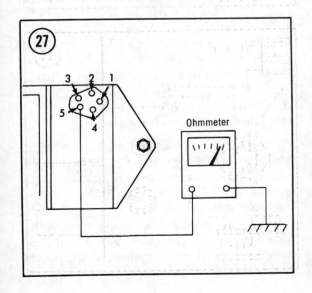

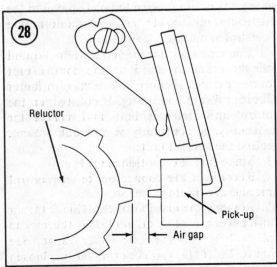

with bare hands may cause a painful shock, even if the insulation is in perfect condition.

17. Disconnect the wire from the center tower of the distributor cap. Hold the wire 3/16 in. from the engine and crank the starter. If sparks do not occur, have the system tested further by a dealer or automotive electrical shop.

Breaker Point Ignition

In the breaker point ignition system, the breaker points function as a mechanical switch. When the points are closed, current flows through the primary circuit of the ignition system and to the ground. When the points are opened (by rotation of the distributor shaft), the primary circuit is interrupted, high voltage is built up in the secondary windings of the coil and flows through the secondary ignition circuit, via the distributor cap and rotor, to a spark plug. At the spark plug, the current arrives at the exact time required to create a spark to ignite the compressed air-fuel mixture in the cylinder. If the current arrives too soon, or too late, misfiring or non-firing occurs and the engine operates poorly or not at all. The terminals in the distributor cap and the rotor, which is attached to and turns with the distributor shaft, act as another switch to make sure that current arrives at the various spark plugs in the proper firing order.

The above is a very simplified explanation of the ignition system, but it should be sufficient to show the need for proper adjustment of the distributor and points to ensure engine performance. These adjustments are described in *Breaker Points* and *Ignition Timing*, both in Chapter Three. Except for spark plug replacement and check-out and replacement of ignition system wiring, also covered in Chapter Three, additional service to the distributor is not recommended because special test equipement is required. The system can be tested as described in Chapter Two.

Distributor Removal/Installation (6-Cylinder)

1. Disconnect the vacuum hose at the distributor and the pick up lead wires at the wiring harness connector (electronic ignition) or primary lead at the coil (breaker point ignition).

2. Remove the distributor cap, leaving the wires attached. Position the cap out of the way, or identify the spark plug wires and detach them from the spark plugs, remove the coil wire from the center tower, and remove the cap from the engine.

3. Rotate the crankshaft until the distributor rotor is facing toward the engine block. Scribe a mark on the block and on the distributor body indicating the position of the rotor. These marks will be used as a reference during installation.

4. Remove the distributor hold-down bolt and carefully lift the distributor from the engine. The shaft will rotate slightly and the rotor will move as the distributor is lifted. Mark the new position of the rotor on the distributor body.

5. If the crankshaft was not moved while the distributor was out of the engine, make sure the O-ring is positioned in the groove on the distributor shank and position the rotor in alignment with the mark made on the distributor body in Step 4.

6. Install the distributor in the engine with the first mark on the distributor body aligned with the mark on the engine block. Engage the distributor drive gear with the camshaft gear. The rotor should now be aligned with the mark on the block and the first mark made on the distributor body. Install the hold-down bolt. Install distributor cap, vacuum hose, and all wires removed in Steps 1 and 2.

7. Start the engine and check and adjust the timing. See *Ignition Timing*, Chapter Three.

Distributor Installation (6-Cylinder Crankshaft Removed)

If the position of the crankshaft was changed while the distributor was out of the engine, the relationship between the distributor shaft and the position of the No. 1 cylinder must be reestablished.

1. Rotate the crankshaft until the mark on the inner edge of the crankshaft pulley is aligned with the 0° (TDC) timing mark on the timing chain cover. See **Figure 29**.

2. Position the rotor so it is pointing slightly ahead of the No. 1 terminal in the distributor cap. See **Figure 30**.

3. Install the distributor in the engine, engaging the drive gear with the camshaft gear. Rotor now should be positioned exactly under the distributor cap No. 1 terminal.

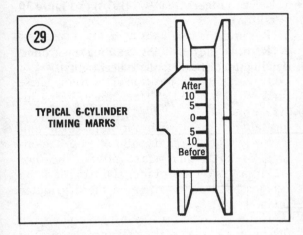

TYPICAL 6-CYLINDER TIMING MARKS

After
10
5
0
5
10
Before

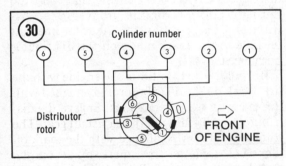

Cylinder number

6   5   4   3   2   1

Distributor rotor

FRONT OF ENGINE

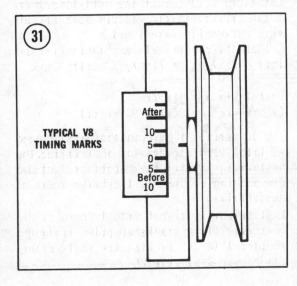

TYPICAL V8 TIMING MARKS

After
10
5
0
5
Before
10

4. Install hold down bolt, distributor cap, vacuum hose, and all wires.

5. Start engine and adjust timing as described in *Ignition Timing*, Chapter Three.

Distributor Removal/Installation (V-8 Engines)

1. Disconnect vacuum hose at distributor and pick-up lead wires at wiring harness connector (electronic ignition) or the primary lead at the coil (breaker point ignition).

2. Remove distributor cap with wires attached and place to one side. If desired, detach wires at spark plugs (after identifying them for replacement), remove coil wire from center tower, and remove distributor cap from engine.

3. Scribe marks on the distributor body and the intake manifold to indicate the position of the distributor rotor. These marks will serve as references during installation.

4. Remove hold-down bolt and clamp and lift distributor from the engine.

5. If crankshaft was not turned while distributor was out of the engine, make sure O-ring is in groove in distributor housing and align rotor with mark previously made on distributor housing.

6. Install distributor in engine with tongue on the end of the shaft engaging with slot in the distributor/oil pump drive shaft. Mark on distributor body, rotor, and mark on intake manifold all should be in alignment.

7. Install hold-down clamp and bolt. Install distributor cap, vacuum hose, and all wires removed in Steps 1 and 2.

8. Start engine and adjust ignition timing. See *Ignition Timing*, Chapter Three.

Distributor Installation (V-8 Engines Crankshaft Removed)

If the position of the crankshaft was changed while the distributor was out of the engine, the relationship between the distributor shaft and the No. 1 piston must be reestablished as follows:

1. Turn crankshaft until the mark on the vibration damper is aligned with the 0° (TDC) mark on the timing chain cover. See **Figure 31**.

8

2. Position the distributor rotor so it is aligned with the No. 1 terminal on the distributor cap. See **Figure 32** (318 and 360 cid engines) or **Figure 33** (400 and 440 cid engines).

3. Install the distributor in the engine so the tongue on the end of the distributor shaft engages the slot in the end of the distributor/oil pump drive shaft. Make sure the rotor is still aligned with the No. 1 terminal in the cap.

4. Install hold-down clamp and bolt. Install the distributor cap, vacuum hose, and all wires removed previously.

5. Start the engine and adjust the timing. See *Ignition Timing*, Chapter Three.

LIGHTS

All lighting elements, with the exception of instrument illumination bulbs, are easily replaced. Individual replacement procedures follow. Bulb types are given in **Table 4**.

Headlight Replacement

Refer to **Figure 34** (1971-1978) or **Figure 35** (1979-on).
1. Remove the headlight trim.
2. Remove the headlight retaining ring (round headlights) or bezel (square headlights).

NOTE
Do not turn the adjusting screws.

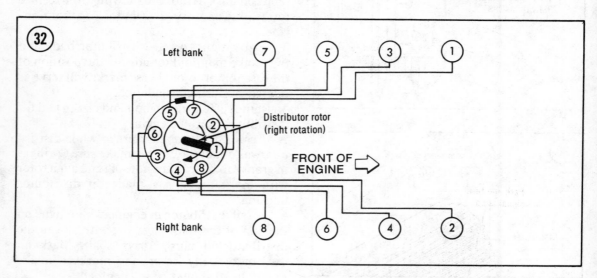

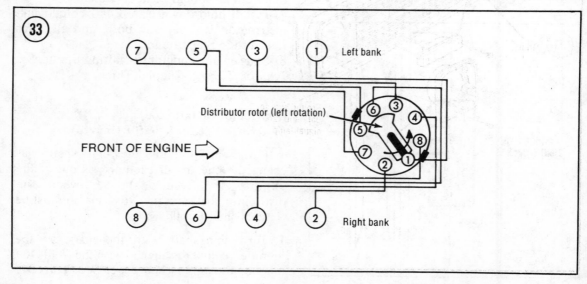

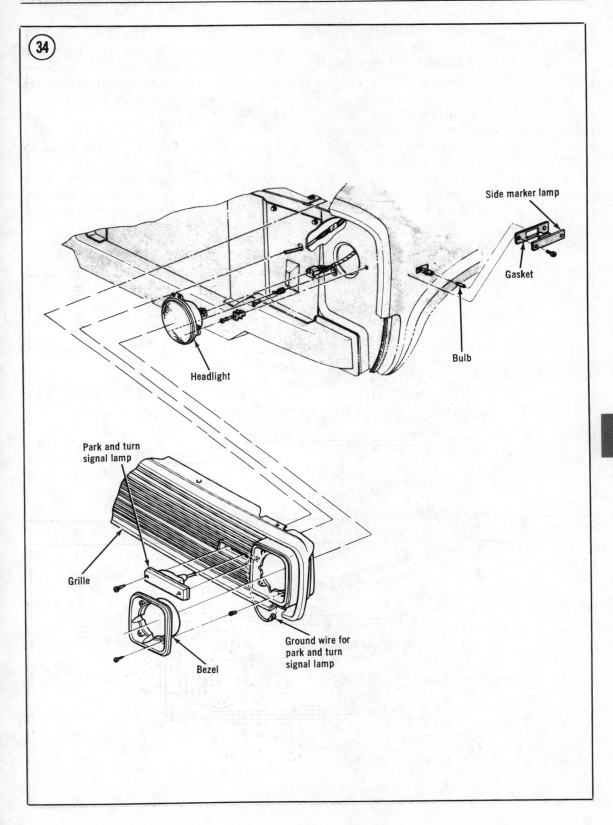

34

Side marker lamp

Gasket

Bulb

Headlight

8

Park and turn
signal lamp

Grille

Ground wire for
park and turn
signal lamp

Bezel

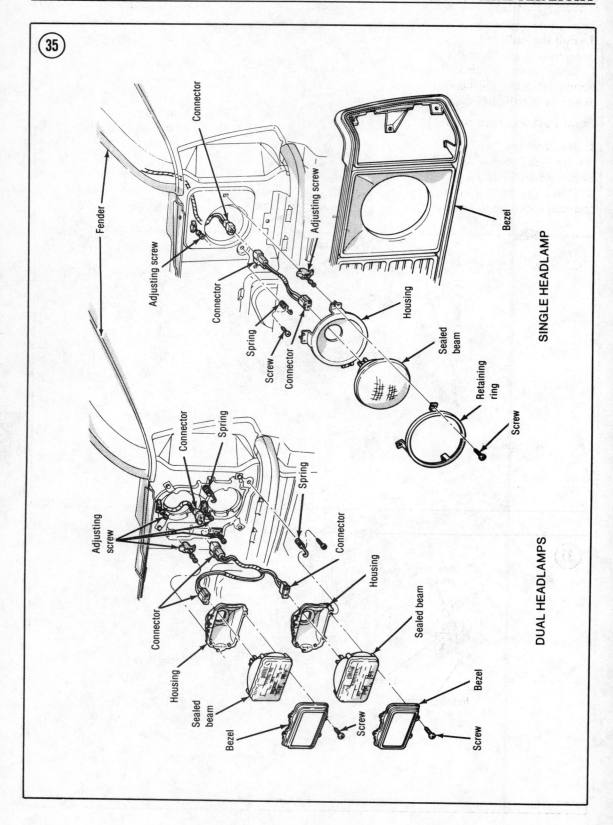

(35)

SINGLE HEADLAMP

Connector

Fender

Adjusting screw

Adjusting screw

Connector

Spring

Screw

Connector

Bezel

Housing

Sealed beam

Retaining ring

Screw

DUAL HEADLAMPS

Connector

Spring

Spring

Connector

Adjusting screw

Connector

Housing

Sealed beam

Housing

Sealed beam

Bezel

Bezel

Screw

Screw

3. Pull the bulb out and disconnect its wiring connector. Take the bulb out.

4. Installation is the reverse of removal. If necessary, have the headlights adjusted by a dealer or certified lamp adjusting station.

Front Parking/Turn Signal Lights

1. Remove the lens securing screws and take off the lens. See **Figure 34** (1971-1978) or **Figure 35** (1979-on).

2. Press the bulb into the socket and turn counterclockwise to remove.

3. Installation is the reverse of removal.

Rear Signal Lights

Rear signal lights include tail, brake, turn signal and backup lights.

1. Remove the lens securing screws and take off the lens. See **Figure 36** (1971-1978) or **Figure 37** (1979-on).

2. Press the bulb into its socket and turn counterclockwise to remove.

3. Installation is the reverse of removal.

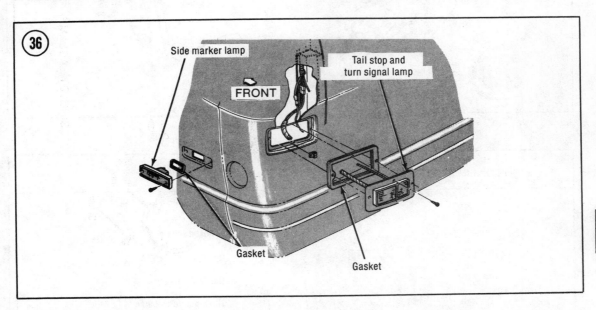

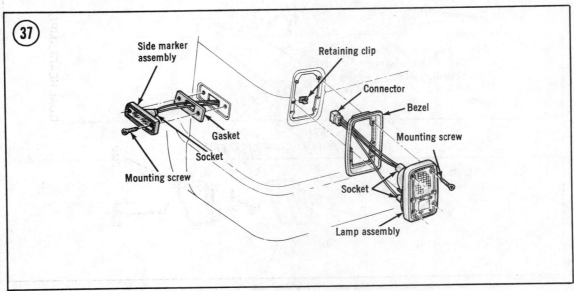

License Plate Lights

Refer to **Figure 38** for this procedure.

1. Remove the lamp assembly mounting screws, then take the assembly out.
2. Remove the lens. Press the bulb into its socket and turn counterclockwise to remove.

3. Installation is the reverse of removal.

Side Marker Lights

1. Remove the lens securing screws and take off the lens.
2. Press the bulb into its socket and turn counterclockwise to remove.

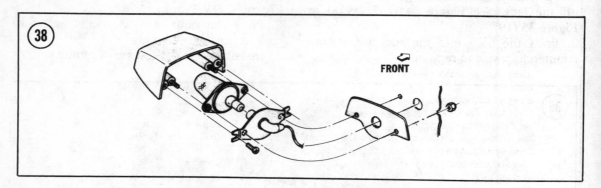

FRONT

Table 1   BATTERY CHARGE (SPECIFIC GRAVITY)

Specific Gravity	State of Charge (at 80 °F)*
1.110-1.130	Discharged
1.140-1.160	Almost discharged
1.170-1.190	One-quarter charged
1.210-1.220	One-half charged
1.230-1.250	Three-quarters charged
1.260-1.280	Fully charged

*For each 10 degrees battery temperature exceeds 80 °F, add 0.004 to the indicated reading; for each 10 degrees battery temperature is less than 80 °F, subtract 0.004 from the indicated reading.

Table 2   ALTERNATOR SPECIFICATIONS

Rated Output (Amperes)	Minimum Current (Amperes)
41	40
50	47
60	57
65	62
100, 117	72

Table 3 FUSES

Components protected	Fuse (amps)
Early models (6-fuse box)	
Radio, backup lights, horn	20
Auxiliary heater, A/C clutch, speed control	20
Heater and A/C blower motors	20
Cigarette lighter, dome light	20
Exterior lights (except headlights)	20
Instrument lights	2
Late models (10-fuse box)	
Instrument panel and control illumination	5
Backup lights, speed control, A/C clutch, turn signals	20
Horns, auxiliary heater and A/C	20
Radio	5
Brake warning light, gauges, oil pressure warning light,	
clock, window lift and heated rear window	
relays (if so equipped)	20
Tail, parking, license plate, side marker, and instrument panel lamps	20
Dome lights, brake lights, courtesy lights, glove box light, cigarette	
lighter, clock feed, ignition time delay light, lighted vanity mirror	
Through 1979	20
1980-on	25
Hazard flashers	20
A/C and heater blowers	20
Heated rear window	25

Table 4 LIGHT BULBS

Application	Trade number
Round headlights	6014
Square headlights	
High beam	4651H
Low beam	4652
Park and turn signal lamps	1157
Backup lights	1156
Separate license plate lamp	168
Bumper license plate lamp	1155
Tail and brake lights	1157
Side marker lights	
1971-1973	1895
1974-on	194

8

CHAPTER NINE

CLUTCH AND TRANSMISSION

CLUTCH

A single, dry disc type clutch is used on all models equipped with the manual transmission. No adjustment is provided for the clutch itself, but the clutch pedal linkage has an adjustable rod which is used to maintain clutch free play within specifications.

Clutch Free Play Adjustment

1. Check the condition of the clutch pedal stop (see **Figure 1**) and install a new bumper if the old one is worn or damaged.

2. Check the rubber insulator at the clutch fork and replace if damaged. See **Figure 2**.

3. Position the insulator so it rests lightly against the clutch fork (see **Figure 2**) and turn self-locking adjusting nut to provide $\frac{3}{32}$ in. of free play at the end of the fork. This will provide about 1 in. of free play at the pedal.

4. If the adjusting nut does not turn freely, make sure the washer is not hanging up on the fork rod threads. Tap washer lightly to free it.

Clutch Removal

1. Remove the transmission. See *Manual Transmission Removal,* this chapter.

2. Remove the clutch housing pan (if so equipped) and remove the return spring from the clutch release fork and clutch housing. See **Figure 2**. It is not necessary to remove clutch housing.

3. Remove the spring washer attaching fork rod to torque shaft (see **Figure 2**) and remove the fork rod together with the adjusting nut, washer, and insulator.

4. Separate and remove the clutch release fork from the clutch release bearing and sleeve and remove the fork and dust seal from the clutch housing.

5. Mark the clutch cover and flywheel with a punch. These marks can be used as references during installation.

6. Loosen the clutch cover attaching bolts and back them off one or two turns at a time, working around the cover. This will help prevent bending of the cover flange. Remove cover.

7. Remove clutch plate and disc from the clutch housing while supporting them. Take care to avoid touching or contaminating the friction surfaces.

Clutch Cleaning and Inspection

1. Clean clutch housing with compressed air. Check for oil leakage around the engine rear

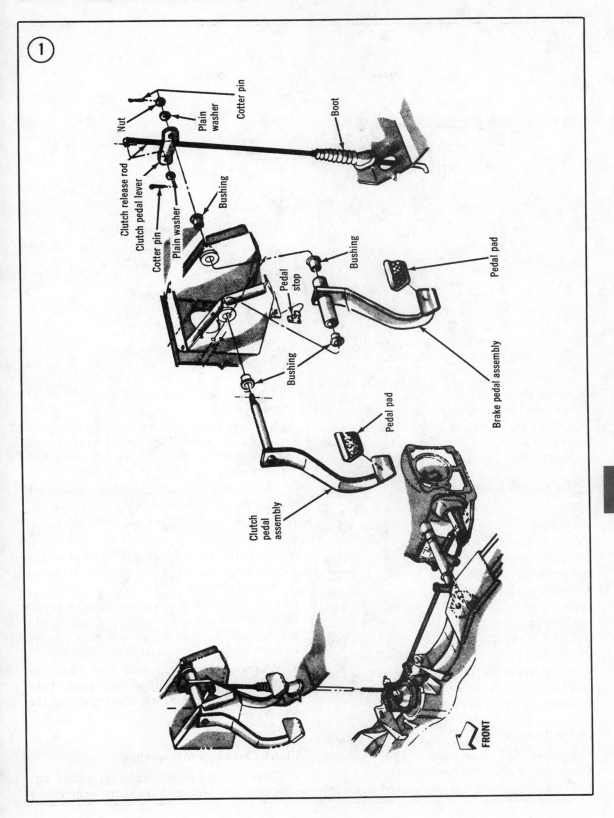

① Cotter pin

Nut

Plain washer

Boot

Clutch release rod

Clutch pedal lever

Cotter pin

Plain washer

Bushing

Bushing

Pedal stop

Bushing

Bushing

Pedal pad

Pedal pad

Brake pedal assembly

Pedal pad

Clutch pedal assembly

FRONT

9

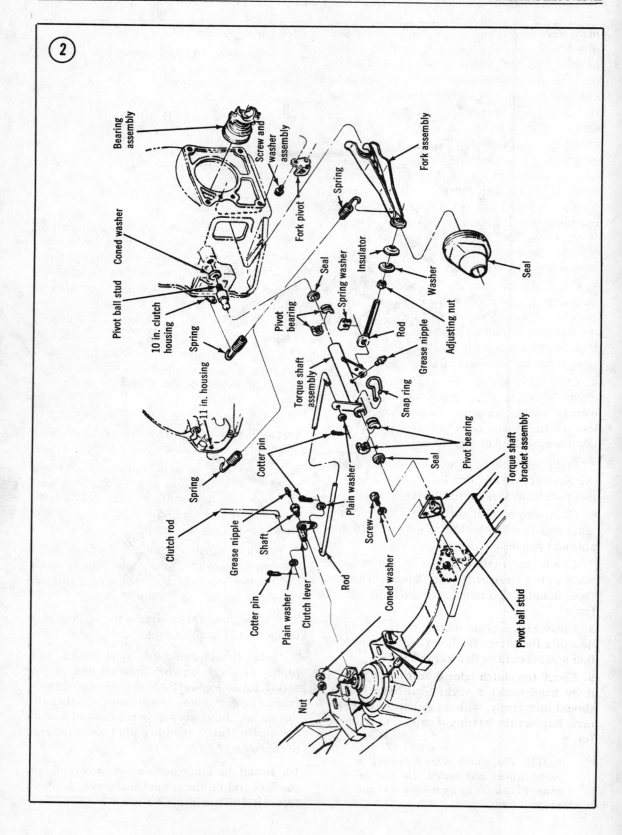

Bearing assembly

Screw and washer assembly

Fork pivot

Spring

Fork assembly

Coned washer

Insulator

Pivot ball stud

Seal

Seal

Washer

10 in. clutch housing

Spring washer

Adjusting nut

Spring

Pivot bearing

Rod

Grease nipple

11 in. housing

Torque shaft assembly

Snap ring

Spring

Cotter pin

Seal

Pivot bearing

Torque shaft bracket assembly

Clutch rod

Grease nipple

Plain washer

Shaft

Screw

Pivot ball stud

Rod

Cotter pin

Plain washer

Clutch lever

Coned washer

Nut

main bearing seal and around the transmission drive shaft seal. If leakage is present, it should be corrected before proceeding. If leakage is detected around the engine seal, see *Rear Main Oil Seal Removal/Installation,* Chapter Four. If transmission leakage is detected, take the transmission to a specialist for seal replacement.

2. Check the friction face of the flywheel for uneven wear. If such wear is present, check flywheel runout with a dial indicator mounted on the clutch housing with the indicator plunger in contact with the outer edge of the wear circle. If runout is more than 0.006 in. throughout a complete rotation of the flywheel, either resurface or replace the flywheel.

3. Check the friction face of the flywheel for excessive heat discoloration, cracks, deep grooves, ridges, or other damage. If present, the flywheel should be resurfaced or replaced. If in doubt, remove the flywheel and take it to your dealer for an expert opinion.

4. Check disc facings for evidence of oil or grease soakage. Also check the facings for wear. If facings are worn to within 0.015 in., or less, of the rivets, or if the facings are contaminated with oil or grease, replace the disc.

5. Make sure all springs are unbroken, and that the metallic parts of the disc show no signs of excessive heat. Make sure all rivets are tight.

6. Clean the friction surfaces of the pressure plate and flywheel with alcohol or other suitable non-petroleum solvent.

7. Check the friction surface of the pressure plate with a straighedge for flatness. The surface should be no more than 0.020 in. out of flat.

8. Check clutch cover mating surface for flatness of a flat plate. The areas around attaching bolt holes should be flat within 0.015 in.

9. Check the clutch release bearing by turning it by hand under a slight load. The bearing should turn freely, with no evidence of roughness. Replace the bearing if condition is doubtful.

> NOTE: *The clutch release bearing is prelubricated and sealed. Do not attempt to clean it by immersing it in solvent.*

Clutch Installation

1. Insert about a half teaspoon of high temperature grease (multi-purpose grease, Chrysler part No. 2932524 or equivalent) in the pilot bushing in the end of the crankshaft. Place grease in the cavity ahead of the bushing and lightly coat the inner surface of the bushing.

2. Make sure the friction surfaces of the flywheel and pressure plate are thoroughly clean. Dress the surfaces lightly with crocus cloth.

3. Position clutch disc, pressure plate, and cover for mounting. Make sure disc springs are facing away from flywheel, and avoid contaminating the facings. Insert a spare transmission drive pinion (or a clutch installation tool of suitable size) through the splined hub of the clutch disc and into the flywheel bushing to properly position the parts.

4. Align the punch marks made on the flywheel and cover during removal and install the cover mounting bolts (don't tighten them at this time).

5. Tighten bolts alternately a few turns at a time until all are snug. Then torque $\frac{5}{16}$ in. bolts to 200 in.-lb. and $\frac{3}{8}$ in. bolts to 30 ft.-lb.

6. Fill cavity of release bearing sleeve with high temperature grease (see Step 1 for grease description) and lightly grease release fork pads on sleeve. Also lubricate release fork fingers and retaining spring contact area.

7. Position release bearing and sleeve in clutch housing and engage release fork fingers under the bearing sleeve springs; then engage fork retaining spring into fork pivot.

8. Engage dust seal groove on the seal opening flange in the clutch housing.

9. Install the adjusting nut, steel washer, and rubber insulator on the threaded end of the fork rod (see **Figure 2**). Make sure curved surface of washer is next to insulator, and that adjusting nut shoulders seat in the tapered hole in the washer. Insert end of rod in hole in the end of the release fork.

10. Install the dampened washer and eye end of the fork rod on the torque shaft lever pin and secure it with the spring washer.

9

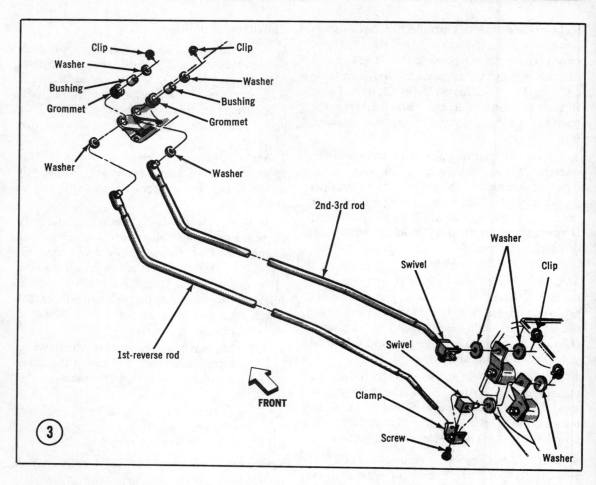

Clip
Washer
Bushing
Grommet
Washer

Clip
Washer
Bushing
Grommet
Washer

2nd-3rd rod

1st-reverse rod

FRONT

Washer
Swivel
Clip
Swivel
Clamp
Screw
Washer

③

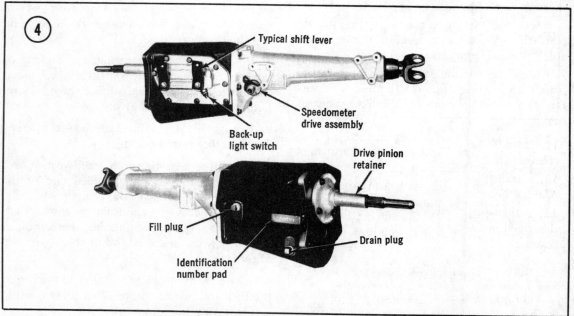

④

Typical shift lever

Speedometer
drive assembly

Back-up
light switch

Drive pinion
retainer

Fill plug

Identification
number pad

Drain plug

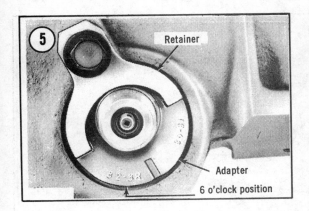

Retainer

Adapter

6 o'clock position

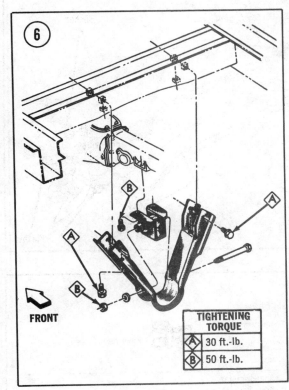

FRONT

TIGHTENING TORQUE	
Ⓐ 30 ft.-lb.	
Ⓑ 50 ft.-lb.	

11. Install the return spring on the clutch release fork and the clutch housing.

12. Install the transmission as described in *Manual Transmission Installation,* this chapter.

13. Adjust the clutch linkage free play as described in *Clutch Free Play Adjustment,* this chapter.

TRANSMISSIONS

Vehicles covered by this book are equipped with a 3- or 4-speed synchronized manual trans-

mission, or a 3-speed automatic Torqueflite transmission. Repairs to any of these transmissions require many expensive special tools and special skills, and therefore are not recommended. However, money can be saved by removing a defective transmission and installing a new or rebuilt unit.

Manual Transmission Removal (3-Speed)

1. Raise the vehicle and remove the shift levers from the left side of the transmission (see **Figure 3**). Leave the shift rods attached to the levers. By doing this you will avoid replacement of the grommets that retain the rods to the levers.

2. Drain transmission fluid into a suitable container.

3. Disconnect the propeller shaft at the rear universal joint. Mark both parts so they can be reassembled to their original relationship. Carefully withdraw the propeller shaft yoke out of the transmission and remove the shaft from the vehicle.

4. Disconnect leads from the back-up switch. See **Figure 4**.

5. Remove the speedometer pinion retaining clamp (see **Figure 5**) and carefully work the adapter and pinion out of the transmission extension housing. Cable should remain attached.

6. Support the engine with a suitable jack or fixture. If possible, weight should be borne by the oil pan flange. Chrysler recommends tool C-3487-A for this operation.

7. Raise the engine slightly with the jack or fixture. Disconnect the transmission rear housing from the removable frame crossmember. See **Figure 6**.

8. Support the transmission with a transmission jack.

9. Remove the bolts attaching the transmission to the clutch housing. Slide the transmission to the rear until the drive pinion shaft clears the clutch disc, then lower the transmission and remove it from the vehicle.

Manual Transmission Installation (3-Speed)

1. Place about ½ teaspoon of high temperature grease (MOPAR 2932524 or equivalent) in the cavity behind the flywheel pinion shaft pilot

9

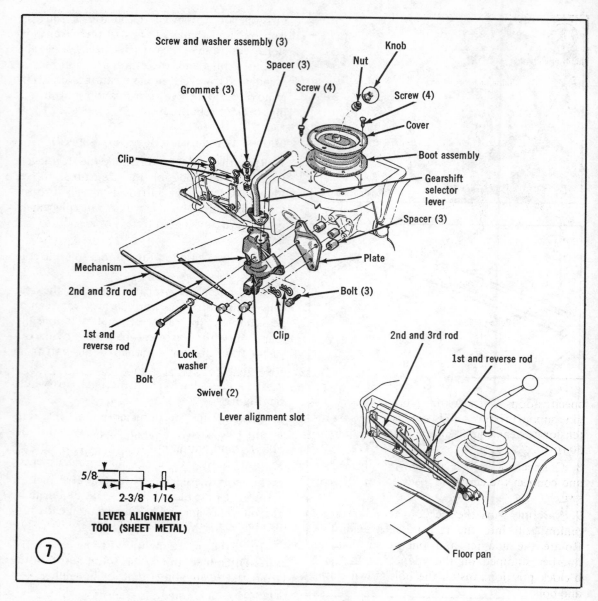

Screw and washer assembly (3)

Spacer (3)

Grommet (3)

Screw (4)

Nut

Knob

Screw (4)

Cover

Clip

Boot assembly

Gearshift selector lever

Spacer (3)

Mechanism

Plate

2nd and 3rd rod

Bolt (3)

1st and reverse rod

Clip

2nd and 3rd rod

1st and reverse rod

Lock washer

Bolt

Swivel (2)

Lever alignment slot

5/8

2-3/8 1/16

LEVER ALIGNMENT TOOL (SHEET METAL)

Floor pan

⑦

bushing. Do not lubricate the end of the transmission pinion shaft, the clutch disc splines, or the clutch release levers.

2. Install transmission on a suitable transmission jack and position it under the vehicle. Raise the transmission until it clears the torsion bar crossmember, then slide it as far to the rear as it will go.

3. Raise transmission until the drive pinion is centered in the clutch housing opening, then move transmission forward until the pinion shaft enters the clutch disc.

4. With transmission in gear, rotate the shaft until the splines mesh with the splines in the clutch disc.

5. Push transmission forward until it is seated against the clutch housing.

6. With the transmission still fully supported by the jack, install the bolts to attach it to the clutch housing. Tighten bolts to 50 ft.-lb. Remove transmission jack.

7. Use a suitable punch or pointed drift to align the bolt holes and install the removable frame crossmember. See **Figure 6**. Tighten bolts to

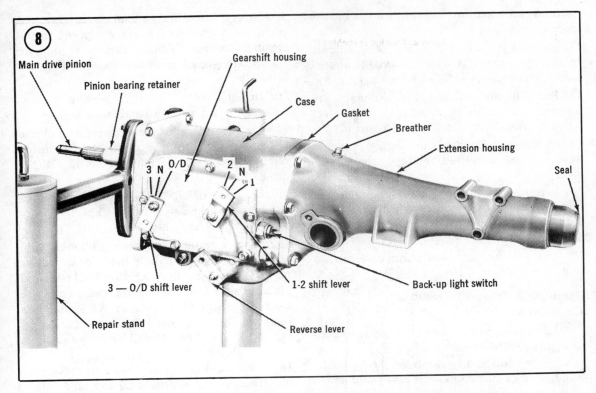

⑧

Main drive pinion
Pinion bearing retainer
Gearshift housing
Case
Gasket
Breather
Extension housing
3 N   O/D   2 N
1
Seal
3 — O/D shift lever
1-2 shift lever
Back-up light switch
Repair stand
Reverse lever

specifications given in the figure. Remove engine support fixture and install transmission extension to rear engine mount. Tighten bolts to 50 ft.-lb.

8. Connect the shift levers to the transmission and connect the electrical leads to the back-up switch.

9. Carefully work the speedometer adapter and pinion gear into the transmission extension. Rotate the adapter and pinion so that the number stamped on the adapter is in the 6 o'clock position. Install the hold-down clamp and bolt.

10. Carefully guide the front universal yoke into the transmission extension housing and onto the mainshaft splines.

11. Align the marks made during removal and connect the propeller shaft to the rear axle pinion yoke. Tighten bolts to 170-200 in.-lb.

12. Fill transmission with automatic transmission fluid. Capacity is approximately 4.25 U.S. pints for A230 transmission; 3.5 U.S. pints for a A390; and 4.5 U.S. pints for A250.

13. Road test vehicle to make sure transmission operates properly.

Manual Transmission Removal (Overdrive 4)

1. Disconnect battery ground cable.

2. Remove retaining screws and slide floor pan boot up and off of shift lever.

3. Remove shift lever.

4. Remove retaining clips and washers and then remove control rods from shift unit levers. See **Figure 7** (typical).

5. Remove retaining bolts and remove shift unit from transmission extension housing.

6. Raise vehicle and drain transmission.

7. Disconnect propeller shaft at the rear universal joint. Make marks on both components to help reassemble components to their original positions.

8. Withdraw propeller shaft yoke from transmission extension housing and remove shaft from vehicle.

9. Disconnect electrical leads from back-up light switch. See **Figure 8**.

10. Remove speedometer pinion retainer bolt and carefully remove adapter and pinion from

9

transmission extension housing with cable attached. See **Figure 5**.

11. Install a suitable fixture or jack to support engine, using the oil pan flanges as a lifting surface. Chrysler tool C-3487-A is recommended.

12. Raise the engine slightly and disconnect the transmission extension housing from the removable frame crossmember. See **Figure 6**.

13. Support the transmision with a suitable transmission jack and remove the crossmember.

14. Remove the attaching bolts and slide the transmission to the rear of the clutch housing until the drive pinion shaft clears the clutch disc.

15. Lower transmission and remove it from the vehicle.

Manual Transmission Installation (Overdrive 4)

1. Insert about ½ teaspoon of high temperature grease (MOPAR multipurpose grease 2932524 or equivalent) behind the pinion shaft pilot bushing in the crankshaft cavity and lightly lubricate the bushing surface.

2. Place transmission on a suitable jack and position it under the vehicle.

3. Raise transmission until drive pinion shaft is centered in opening in clutch housing, then roll transmission forward until shaft enters clutch disc.

4. With transmission in rear, rotate shaft until splines align with those in clutch disc.

5. Push transmission forward until it fully seats against the clutch housing, then install attaching bolts and tighten them to 50 ft.-lb. Remove transmission jack.

6. Use a punch or pointed drift to align bolt holes and install removable frame crossmember and transmission extension to rear engine mount. Tighten attaching bolts to values given in **Figure 6**.

7. Remove the engine support fixture or jack.

8. Attach the shift unit to the transmission extension housing with 2 bolts and lockwashers and tighten to 24 ft.-lb. Install shift rods, washers, and clips. Install boot over shift lever and install and tighten attaching screws. Reconnect battery ground cable.

9. Carefully install speedometer adapter and pinion into transmission extension and install retainer and bolt. Rotate adapter so number stamped thereon is in the 6 o'clock position as it is installed.

10. Install front universal joint yoke into extension housing and onto main shaft splines.

11. Connect propeller shaft to rear axle pinion yoke, making sure the marks made during removal are aligned. Tighten bolts to 170-200 in.-lb.

12. Fill transmission with DEXRON type automatic transmission fluid. Capacity is approximately 7 U.S. pints.

13. Insert a suitable crossover alignment tool as shown in **Figure 9** to hold the floor shift lever in the NEUTRAL position. Remove shift rods and place all shift levers on the transmission in the NEUTRAL position. See **Figure 9**. Rotate the threaded shift rods until they enter the transmission levers, then reinstall washers and clips. Remove alignment tool.

14. Lower and road test vehicle to make sure the transmission works properly and shifts smoothly.

Automatic Transmission Removal

> NOTE: *Transmission and torque converter must be removed as a unit to prevent damage in components. Also, the drive plate should not be subjected to a load during transmission removal.*

1. Remove battery ground cable.

2. If necessary for clearance, detach the exhaust pipe from the exhaust manifold and place it out of the way.

3. Remove engine-to-transmission struts, if so equipped. Remove the transmission oil cooler lines at the transmission. See **Figure 10**.

4. Remove the starter motor. At the same time, remove the oil cooler line bracket.

5. Remove the access cover from the front of the torque converter housing.

6. Drain fluid by loosening transmission oil pan bolts and removing torque converter drain plug. If necessary, tap the pan to break it loose from the transmission. After fluid drains, tighten oil pan bolts and converter drain plug.

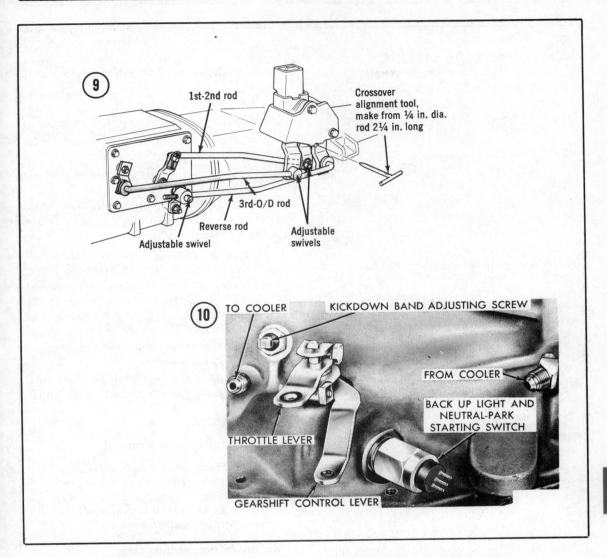

9 1st-2nd rod

Crossover alignment tool, make from ¼ in. dia. rod 2¼ in. long

3rd-O/D rod

Reverse rod

Adjustable swivel

Adjustable swivels

10 TO COOLER KICKDOWN BAND ADJUSTING SCREW

FROM COOLER

BACK UP LIGHT AND NEUTRAL-PARK STARTING SWITCH

THROTTLE LEVER

GEARSHIFT CONTROL LEVER

9

7. Mark the torque converter and the flexible drive plate so they can be realigned during assembly. These parts must be assembled to their original positions to maintain engine/converter balance.

8. Rotate the engine (use a socket wrench on the crankshaft vibration damper) as required for access to the drive plate-to-converter attaching bolts and remove the bolts.

9. Mark parts so they can be reassembled to their original positions and disconnect propeller shaft at the rear universal joint (and the center amount, if so equipped). Carefully pull the propeller shaft out of the transmission extension housing.

10. Disconnect electrical leads from the back-up light and neutral starting switch. See **Figure 10**.

11. Disconnect the gearshift rod and torque shaft assembly from the transmission. See **Figure 11**.

12. Remove throttle rod from lever on left side of transmission. See **Figure 12** (6-cylinder) or **Figure 13** (V-8 engine). If linkage bellcrank is installed on transmission, remove it also.

13. Remove oil filler tube and dipstick. Remove the retaining clamp and remove the speedometer cable adapter and pinion.

14. Install a jack or engine support fixture to support the rear of the engine. Use the oil pan

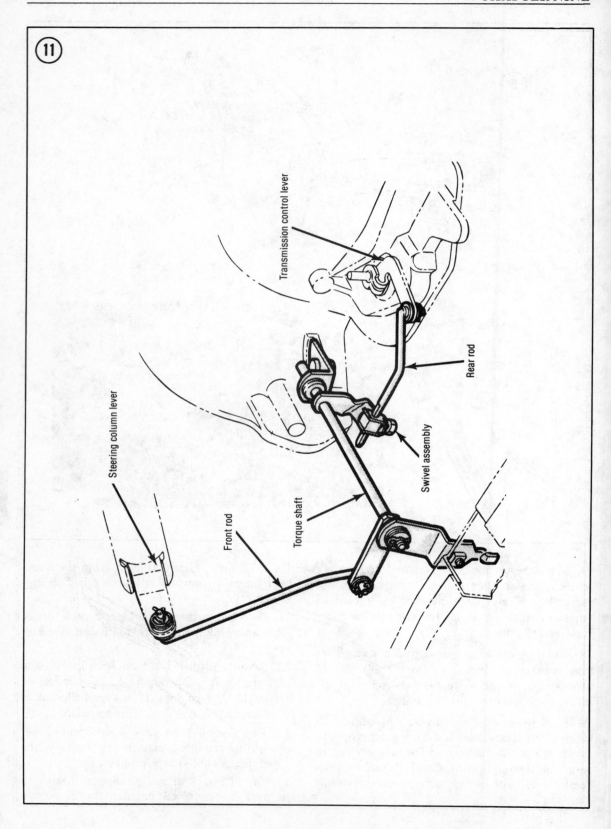

⑪

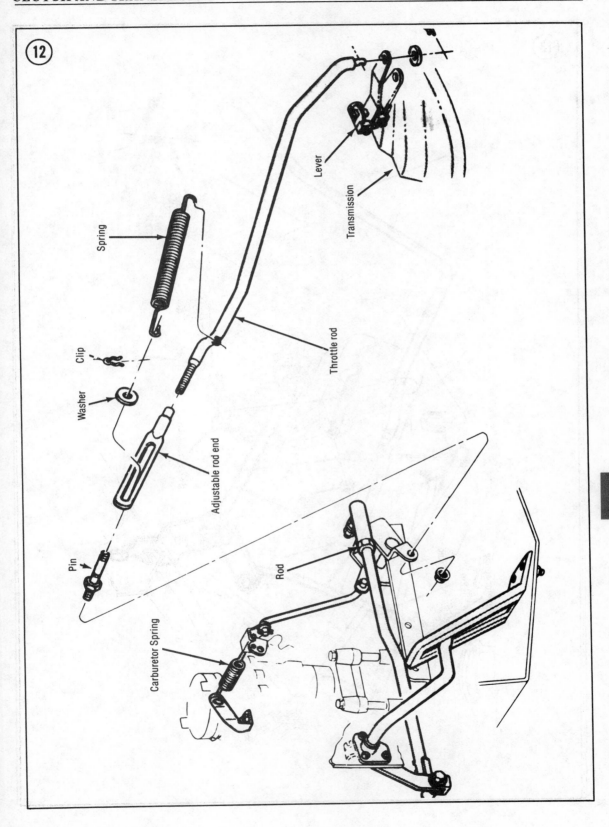

12

Spring

Clip

Washer

Adjustable rod end

Pin

Carburetor Spring

Lever

Transmission

Throttle rod

Rod

9

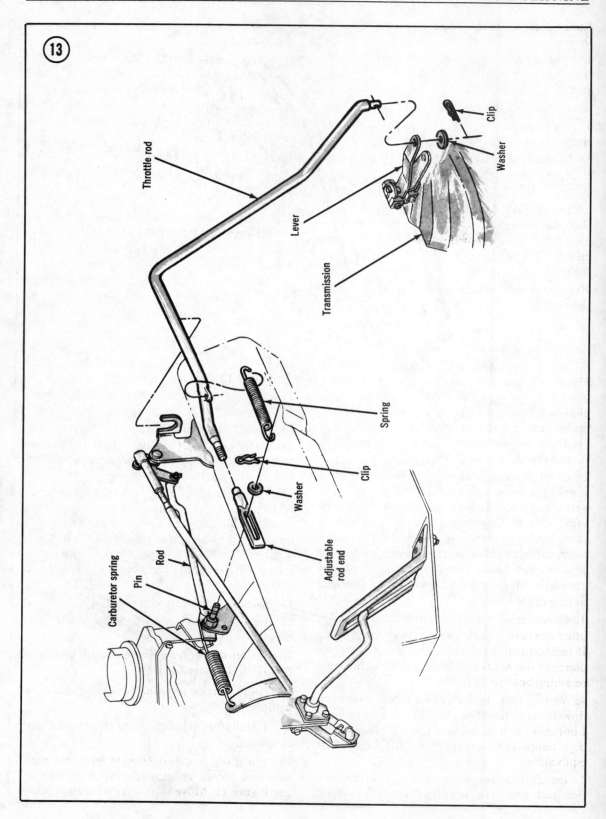

(13)

Throttle rod

Clip

Washer

Lever

Transmission

Spring

Clip

Washer

Adjustable rod end

Carburetor spring

Pin

Rod

flange — not the oil pan itself — as a lifting surface.

15. Support the transmission with a suitable transmission jack.

16. Raise the transmission slightly to take weight from supports.

17. Remove all attaching bolts and remove supporting crossmember from the frame.

18. Remove all bolts attaching the converter housing to the engine.

19. Carefully work the transmission assembly off the aligning dowels of the engine block and slide the assembly to the rear to clear the converter hub from the crankshaft. Attach a C-clamp to the edge of converter housing to retain the converter in place during removal.

20. Lower the transmission and remove it from the vehicle.

Automatic Transmission Installation

1. Install special tool (C-3756) as shown in **Figure 14** and turn pump rotors until the 2 small holes in the end of the tool are vertically aligned. This tool has slots that engage the pump inner rotor lugs, which must be aligned vertically before torque converter is installed. Remove tool.

2. Carefully install torque converter by sliding it over the input and reaction shafts until converter hub slots engage the pump inner rotor lugs. Check for proper installation with a straightedge as shown in **Figure 15**. Converter front lug should be at least ½ in. to rear of straightedge. Install a small C-clamp on edge of converter housing to hold converter in place during installation.

3. Check drive plate for distortion, cracks, or other damage, and replace if damage is present. If replacement is required, install the new drive plate on the crankshaft flange and tighten the retaining bolts to 55 ft.-lb.

4. Verify that both transmission alignment dowels are installed in the engine block. Lubricate the hole in the crankshaft flange with high temperature grease (MOPAR 2932524 or equivalent).

5. Install transmission assembly on a transmission jack and place it under the vehicle. Raise and tilt jack as necessary to align transmission with rear of engine.

6. Rotate the converter so the mark made during removal is aligned with the mark made on the drive plate and carefully work the transmission forward until the proper holes in the housing mate with the engine block alignment dowels and the converter hub enters the opening in the crankshaft flange.

7. Install converter housing attaching bolts and tighten them to 28 ft.-lb. Install frame crossmember and lower transmission so mount on extension can be attached to crossmember. See **Figure 6** and torque bolts to values given in the figure. Remove the engine support fixture or jack installed during the removal procedure.

8. Install the speedometer cable assembly and the oil filler tube.

9. Connect the gearshift rod and torque shaft assembly to the transmission lever and frame. See **Figure 11**.

10. Install throttle rod to transmission lever. See **Figure 12 or 13**.

11. Reconnect electrical leads to back-up light and neutral start switch.

12. Install the propeller shaft in the transmission extension and reconnect shaft to the rear universal, using the marks made during removal for alignment.

13. Connect drive plate to torque converter with the 4 attaching bolts. Rotate the crankshaft as required by using a socket wrench on the vibration damper bolt. Make sure alignment marks made during removal procedure are properly aligned. Tighten attaching bolts to 270 in.-lb.

14. Install converter access cover.

15. Install starter motor and cooler line bracket.

16. Install oil cooler lines to the transmission fittings and tighten securely.

17. Install engine-to-transmission struts, if so equipped.

18. Install the exhaust pipe, if removed for clearance.

19. Place the gearshift lever in P (PARK) position and loosen adjustment swivel lockscrew. See **Figure 11**. Move shift lever on transmission

9

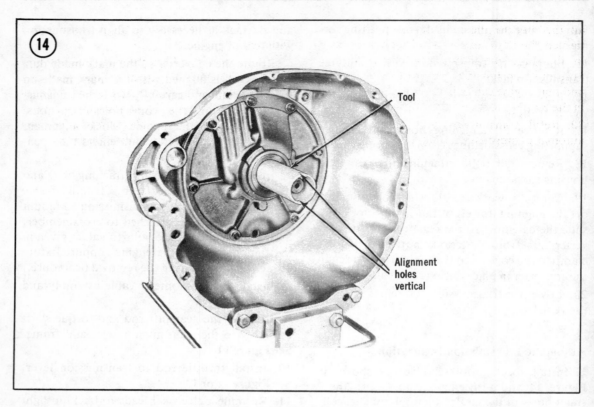

Tool

**Alignment
holes
vertical**

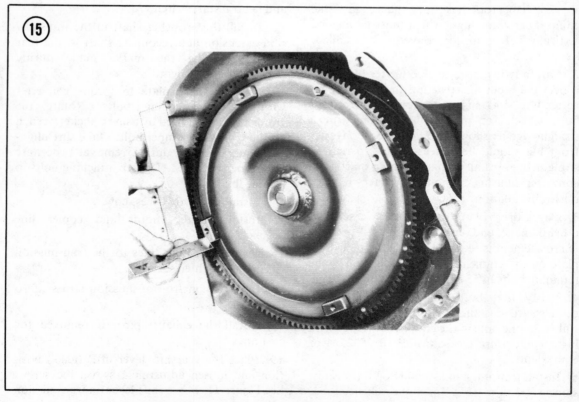

all the way to the rear detent position and tighten the adjustment swivel lockscrew to 90 in.-lb. Make sure that gearshift lever properly positions transmission lever in all other detents, and that engine can only be started with the key in the P or N (NEUTRAL) positions.

20. Refill transmission with DEXRON-type automatic transmission fluid.

21. Road test car to make sure transmission is functioning properly.

22. If necessary, adjust throttle rod. See **Figure 12 or 13**. With engine at normal operating temperature, raise vehicle and loosen adjustable swivel lockscrew. Hold transmission lever firmly against its internal forward stop and tighten the swivel lockscrew to 100 in.-lb.

9

BRAKES AND FRONT WHEEL BEARINGS

On all models, either drum or disc brakes are used in front and drum brakes are used in the rear. Procedures are given for removing and installing all types. Bleeding the hydraulic system also is discussed.

Brakes used on all Chrysler products are self-adjusting and normally do not require adjustment. If brakes have been relined, however, initial adjustment is advisable to assure safe operation. An adjustment procedure is provided later in this chapter.

DRUM BRAKES

Rear Brake Drum Removal (Chrysler)

1. Raise vehicle and remove plug from brake adjusting access hole and use thin screwdriver to hold adjusting lever away from adjusting screw notches.

2. Use brake adjusting tool to engage adjusting screw notches and release brake adjustment by prying down with tool.

3. Remove rear wheel and then remove drum retaining clips from wheel studs. Remove drum to expose lining.

Rear Brake Shoe Removal (Chrysler)

1. With wheel and brake drum removed, remove brake shoe return springs. A special tool (see **Figure 1**) will greatly assist in this operation.

NOTE: *Observe how secondary spring overlaps primary spring (see **Figure 2**).*

2. Remove adjuster cable from anchor and unhook from adjuster lever. Remove cable, overload spring, cable guide, and anchor plate.

3. Remove adjusting lever from spring (slide forward to clear pivot, then work out from under spring). Remove spring from pivot and remove automatic adjuster spring from secondary and primary shoe webs. Remove spring.

4. Remove shoe retainers, springs, and nails. A special tool (see **Figure 3**) will greatly assist in this operation.

5. Spread the anchor ends of the shoes and remove parking brake lever strut and anti-rattle spring (see **Figure 4**).

6. Disengage cable from parking brake lever.

7. Disengage brake shoes from pushrods and remove from support. Remove star wheel assembly.

Rear Brake Shoe Installation (Chrysler)

1. Clean and lubricate shoe tab contact areas (6 places) on support plate. Use crocus cloth to remove rust, etc., if required (see **Figure 5**).

2. Lubricate pivot point and install parking brake lever on inner side of secondary shoe web. Install wave washer and secure with horseshoe clip.

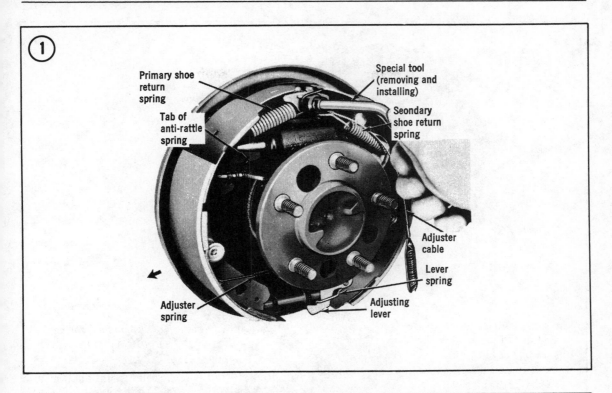

Primary shoe return spring

Tab of anti-rattle spring

Special tool (removing and installing)

Seondary shoe return spring

Adjuster cable

Lever spring

Adjuster spring

Adjusting lever

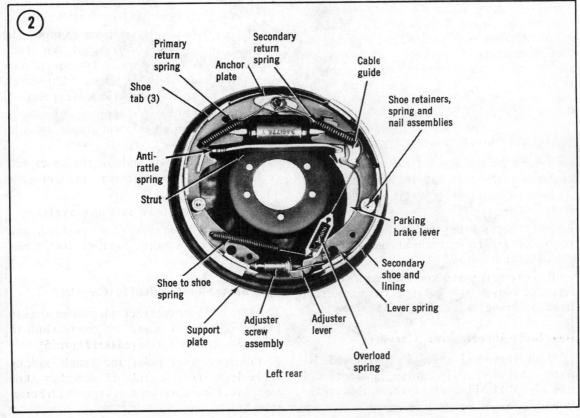

Primary return spring

Secondary return spring

Anchor plate

Cable guide

Shoe tab (3)

Shoe retainers, spring and nail assemblies

Anti-rattle spring

Strut

Parking brake lever

Secondary shoe and lining

Shoe to shoe spring

Lever spring

Support plate

Adjuster screw assembly

Adjuster lever

Overload spring

Left rear

10

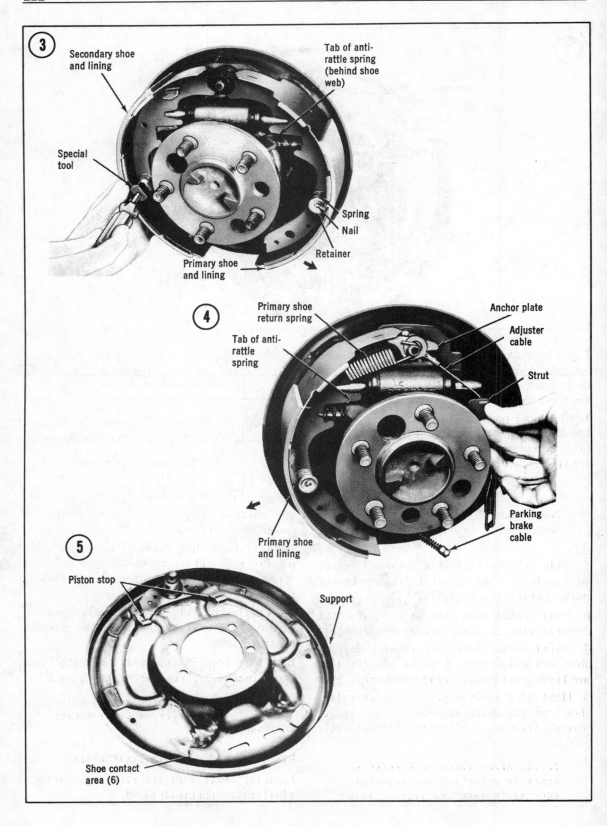

③ Secondary shoe
and lining

Tab of anti-
rattle spring
(behind shoe
web)

Special
tool

Spring

Nail

Retainer

Primary shoe
and lining

④ Primary shoe
return spring

Anchor plate

Adjuster
cable

Tab of anti-
rattle
spring

Strut

Parking
brake
cable

Primary shoe
and lining

⑤ Piston stop

Support

Shoe contact
area (6)

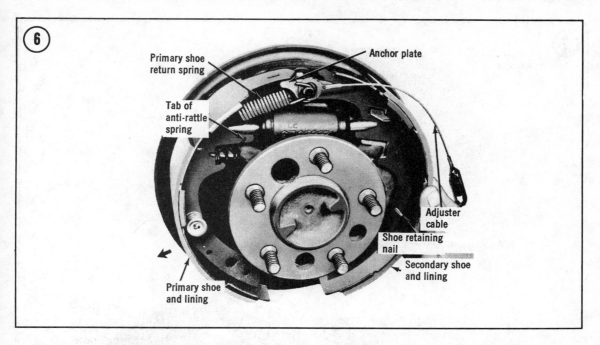

6

Primary shoe
return spring

Anchor plate

Tab of
anti-rattle
spring

Adjuster
cable

Shoe retaining
nail

Secondary shoe
and lining

Primary shoe
and lining

3. Install cable in parking brake lever and slide secondary shoe against support plate. At the same time, engage shoe web with pushrod. Shoe web should rest against anchor.

4. Insert the parking brake strut behind hub and in slot in parking brake lever. Place anti-rattle spring over other end of strut (see **Figure 4**).

> NOTE: *Spring tab must point to rear and up on outside of shoe web on left brake, and to front and down behind web on right brake (see Figure 4).*

5. Slide primary shoe into position. Engage with pushrod, if so equipped, and free end of parking brake strut and spring.

6. Place anchor plate over anchor and install eye of adjuster cable over anchor (see **Figure 6**).

7. Install primary shoe return spring between shoe web and anchor. A special tool (see **Figure 1**) will greatly assist in this operation.

8. Hold cable guide in position on secondary shoe web and install secondary return spring between shoe web and anchor, through cable guide.

> NOTE: *Make certain cable guide remains flat against web and that secondary return spring end loop overlaps primary return spring (see Figure 2). If necessary, squeeze spring end loops with pliers (around anchor) to ensure that they are parallel.*

9. Install adjuster screw assembly, with star wheel adjacent to secondary shoe (see **Figure 2**).

> NOTE: *Left star wheel stud is stamped with "L." Right assembly may or may not be stamped with "R."*

10. Install adjuster spring between primary and secondary shoe webs.

11. Install adjusting lever spring over pivot pin on shoe web and install adjusting lever under spring and over pivot pin. Lock in position by sliding lever slightly to the rear.

12. Install shoe nails, springs, and retainers. A special tool (see **Figure 3**) will greatly assist in this operation.

13. Install adjuster cable over guide and hook end of overload spring in lever (see **Figure 2**).

> NOTE: *Make certain cable eye is pulled tight against anchor and is in a straight line with guide.*

Rear Brake Drum Installation (Chrysler)

1. Install brake drum and retaining clips over wheel studs, then install wheel.

10

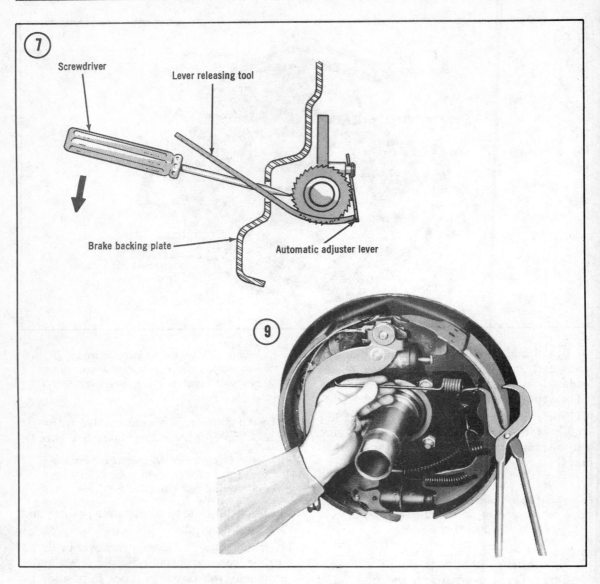

Screwdriver

Lever releasing tool

Brake backing plate

Automatic adjuster lever

2. Adjust brakes, using the procedure given later in this chapter.

Rear Brake Drum Removal (Bendix)

1. Raise vehicle, install jackstands, and remove rear wheel and tire assemblies.

2. Remove the axle shaft nuts, washers, and cones, and remove axle shaft. Rap center of axle shaft smartly to release cones if they stick.

3. Remove the outer hub nut. A special tool, DD-1245, will be very helpful for removing this nut. Straighten and remove lockwasher and inner nut and bearing.

4. Carefully remove brake drum. If there is interference between drum and brake shoes, use a screwdriver and a light piece of metal as shown in **Figure 7** to release the shoes.

Rear Brake Shoe Removal (Bendix)

1. Unhook return spring from adjusting lever. See **Figure 8**. Remove lever and spring from lever pivot pin and unhook lever from adjuster cable assembly.

2. Using brake spring pliers (**Figure 9**), unhook upper shoe-to-shoe spring.

3. Unhook and remove the shoe hold-down springs (**Figure 10**).

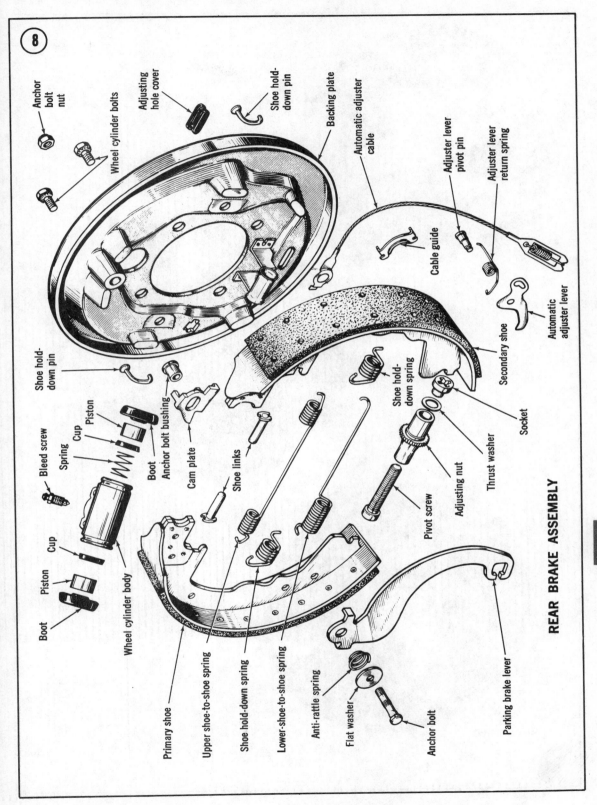

⑧

Anchor bolt nut

Wheel cylinder bolts

Adjusting hole cover

Shoe hold-down pin

Backing plate

Automatic adjuster cable

Adjuster lever pivot pin

Adjuster lever return spring

Cable guide

Automatic adjuster lever

Secondary shoe

Socket

Thrust washer

Shoe hold-down spring

Adjusting nut

Pivot screw

Parking brake lever

Anchor bolt

Flat washer

Anti-rattle spring

Lower-shoe-to-shoe spring

Shoe hold-down spring

Upper shoe-to-shoe spring

Primary shoe

Shoe links

Cam plate

Anchor bolt bushing

Boot

Piston

Cup

Spring

Bleed screw

Shoe hold-down pin

Wheel cylinder body

Piston

Cup

Boot

Piston

Cup

Boot

REAR BRAKE ASSEMBLY

10

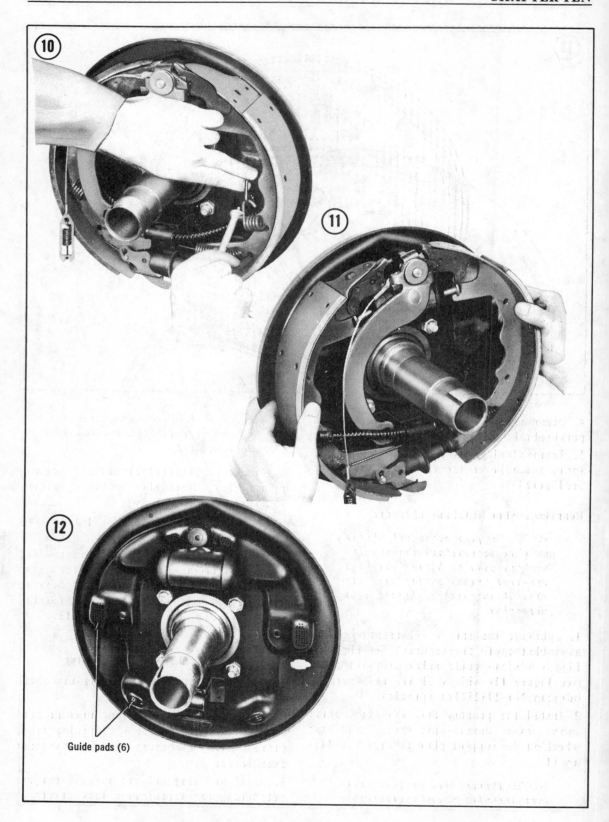

Guide pads (6)

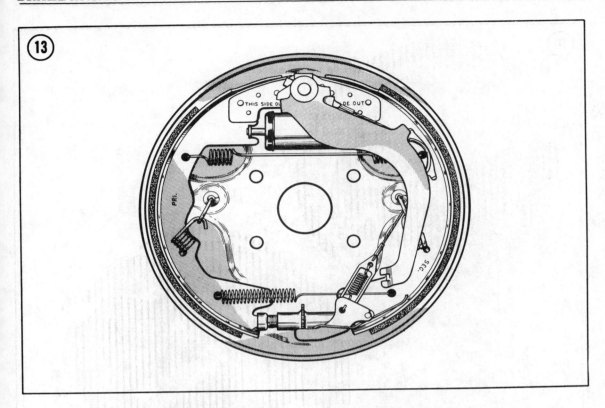

4. Disconnect the parking brake cable from the parking brake lever.

5. Remove both shoes, the lower shoe-to-shoe spring and adjuster star wheel as an assembly. See **Figure 11**.

Rear Brake Shoe Installation (Bendix)

> NOTE: *The pivot screw and adjuster nut of the star wheel assembly have left-hand threads on the left rear wheel and right-hand threads on the right rear wheel. Be sure each is returned to its proper place.*

1. Lubricate the star wheel assemblies and assemble them (if disassembled). See **Figure 8**. Lightly lubricate guide pads on support plates (see **Figure 12**) with MOPAR multi-purpose lubricant No. 2932524 or equivalent.

2. Install the primary and secondary brake shoes, lower shoe-to-shoe spring, and star wheel on the support plate as shown in **Figure 11**.

> NOTE: *Primary shoe (original equipment) is marked* PRI *and secondary shoe*

SEC. *Both shoes are marked* THIS SIDE OUT. *See Figure 13. Make sure shoes are properly placed.*

3. Connect the parking brake cable to the parking brake lever. Install shoe hold-down springs. See **Figure 10**.

4. Replace upper shoe-to-shoe spring, using brake shoe pliers (see **Figure 9**).

5. Install adjuster lever return springs. Red springs go on right, green on left brakes. Install adjuster lever and connect adjuster cable to lever. Route cable over cable guide attached to secondary brake shoe web. See **Figure 13**.

Rear Brake Drum Installation (Bendix)

1. Position drum on axle housing and install bearing and inner nut.

2. Rotate drum while tightening inner nut until a slight bind is felt. Back off adjusting nut ⅙ turn and verify that drum turns freely without excessive end play.

3. Install lock ring and jam nut. Tighten jam nut, making sure adjusting nut does not turn.

10

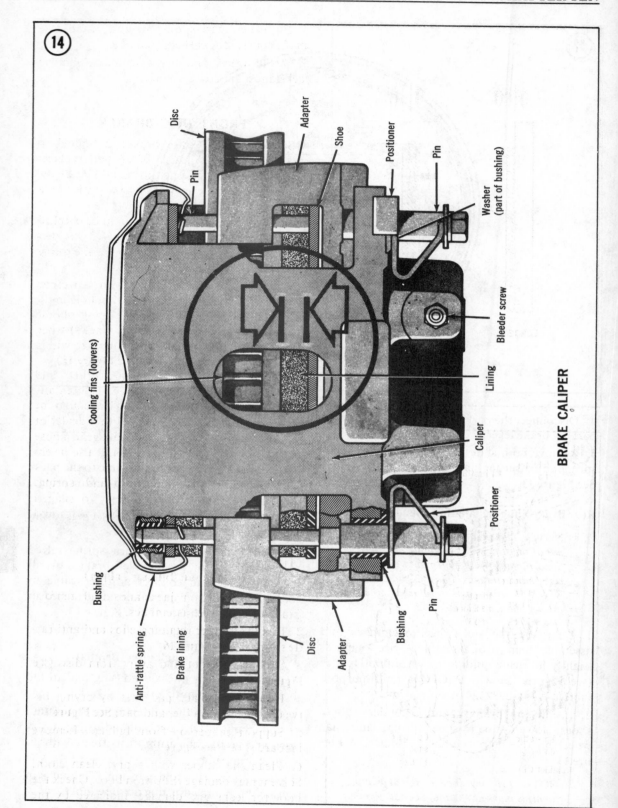

BRAKE CALIPER

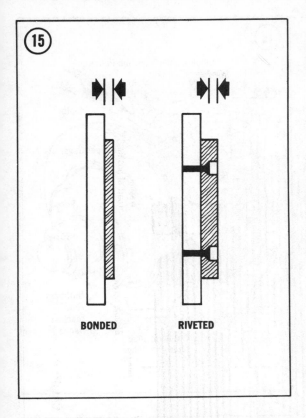

BONDED   **RIVETED**

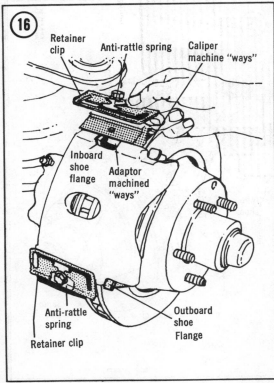

Retainer clip

Anti-rattle spring

Caliper machine "ways"

Inboard shoe flange

Adaptor machined "ways"

Anti-rattle spring

Retainer clip

Outboard shoe Flange

4. Place new gasket on hub and install axle shaft, cones, lockwashers, and nuts.

5. Install wheel and tire assemblies, remove jackstands, and lower vehicle.

FRONT DISC BRAKES

Service to front disc brakes is limited to cleaning, inspection, and brake pad replacement. Major service, such as rebuilding of the calipers, should be entrusted to a dealer or a brake specialist.

The brake lining thickness should be checked routinely each time lubrication service is performed. In addition, the condition of the rotors (discs) and lines should be checked.

Measure the brake lining with a vernier caliper, through the large inspection hole in the brake caliper (see **Figure 14**). The linings should be replaced as a set (both front wheels) when the lining on any one pad wears down to within 0.030 in. of the shoe or rivets (see **Figure 15**).

Inspect all of the brake lines and fittings, and the calipers, for signs of leakage. Tighten any fitting that evidences leakage and if it cannot be corrected, it should be entrusted to a dealer or brake specialist. Likewise, any leakage in a hose or line, or around the caliper should also be entrusted to a dealer or specialist.

Inspect the rotors for grooves and scoring. Any groove that is deep enough to snag a fingernail is reason for having both discs and sets of pads reconditioned.

Disc Brake Pad
Removal/Installation (Sliding Caliper)

1. Raise vehicle on jackstands and remove front wheel and tire assemblies.

2. Remove caliper retaining clips and anti-rattle springs. See **Figure 16**.

3. Slide caliper out and away from disc (see **Figure 17**).

4. Remove outboard pad first by prying between fingers on caliper and pad. See **Figure 18**.

5. Support caliper on front linkage. Remove inboard shoe (see **Figure 19**).

6. Clean the caliper with a dry, clean cloth. Solvent may damage the piston boot. Check the boot for leaks and damage, indicated by the

10

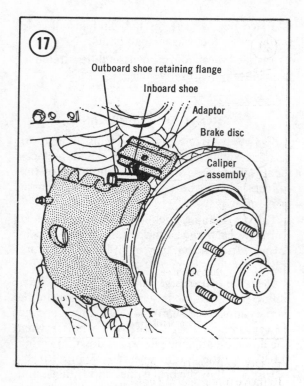

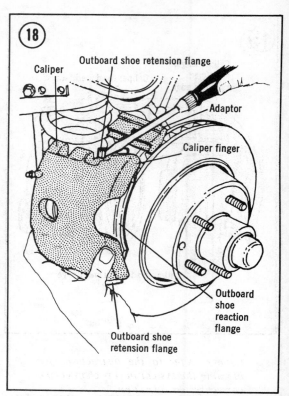

presence of brake fluid around the boot. If boot is torn, cracked, or deteriorated, or if brake fluid is present, dirt and water may have entered the caliper, in which case it should be referred to a dealer or brake specialist for rebuilding.

7. Install a new outboard shoe in the caliper, making sure there is no clearance between the shoe and the caliper (**Figure 20**). If necessary, bend the flanges to create a slight interference fit (**Figure 21**).

8. Install the anti-rattle springs and retaining clips, with the inboard shoe anti-rattle spring on top of the retainer spring plate (**Figure 16**).

9. Service the opposite caliper in the manner just described. After installing the wheels and lowering the vehicle, check the fluid level in the master cylinder and correct if necessary. Apply the brakes several times or until there is a firm pedal pressure. Again, check the fluid level in the master cylinder.

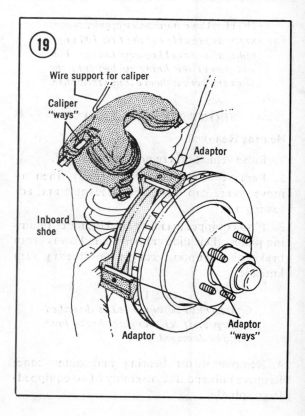

WARNING
Do not drive the vehicle until pedal pressure and travel are correct. If pressure cannot be obtained by pumping the brake pedal with the vehicle sta-

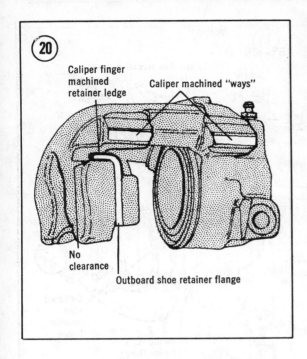

Caliper finger machined retainer ledge

Caliper machined "ways"

No clearance

Outboard shoe retainer flange

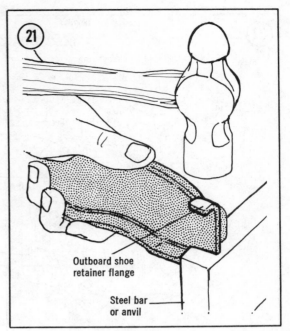

Outboard shoe retainer flange

Steel bar or anvil

tionary, refer to the instructions for bleeding the system in this chapter and correct system operation.

NOTE: *Avoid hard brake application as much as possible for the first 100 or so miles after installing new linings. This will permit the lining to bed into the discs and permit them a long service life.*

FRONT WHEEL BEARING

Bearing Removal

1. Raise vehicle and remove wheel cover.
2. Remove wheel and tire assembly, then remove grease cap, cotter pin, locknut, and adjusting nut.
3. If so equipped, remove brake caliper retaining plates, then slide caliper up and away from brake disc. Support caliper on steering arm knuckle.

CAUTION
Caliper must be supported as described in Step 3. If left hanging, brake hose could be damaged.

4. Remove thrust bearing and outer cone. Remove hub and disc assembly (if so equipped) from spindle.

5. Use soft drift to drive out inner oil seal. Remove inner bearing cone.

Cleaning and Inspection

1. Use kerosene, mineral spirits, or similar cleaning fluid to clean hub, drum, spindle, and bearings.

CAUTION
Do not dry bearings by spinning with compressed air, as damage could result.

2. Check bearing cups for imperfections. If cups are damaged, remove them from hub with a soft drift.
3. Check cup seating areas in hub for damage which could prevent seating of cups.
4. Check bearing cones and rollers for smoothness and evidence of scoring or overheating. Replace bearings of doubtful quality. Ends of rollers and both cone flanges must be smooth and free of chipping and other damage.

Bearing Installation

1. If bearing cups were removed, install new cups by starting them evenly and tapping them flush with hub using a soft steel block and a

10

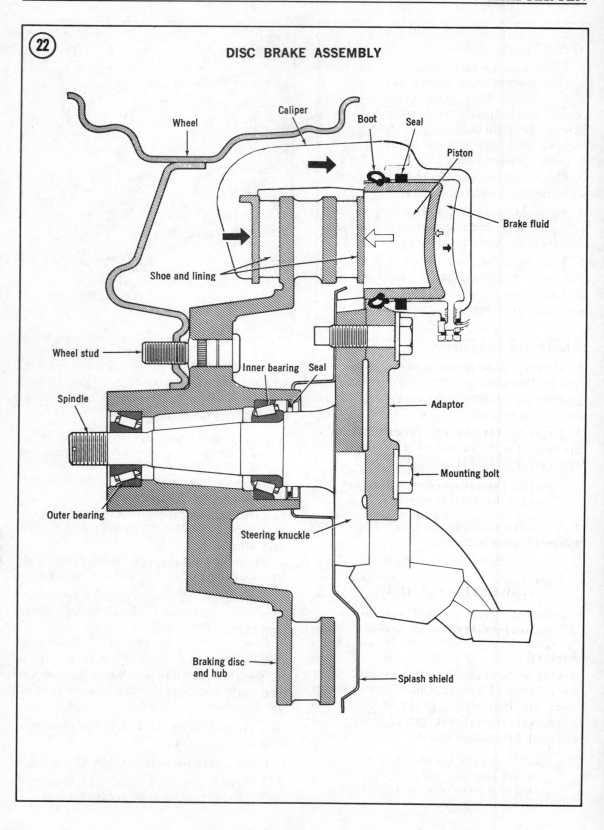

DISC BRAKE ASSEMBLY

hammer. Seat the cups, using a soft drift, against shoulders in hubs.

2. Fill hub grease cavity (see **Figure 22**) with a small amount of wheel bearing lubricant.

3. Lubricate bearing cones forcing grease between rollers. Install inner bearing cone and new seal (with lip facing out) in hub. Seal must be positioned flush with end of hub. Take care to avoid damage to seal.

4. Clean spindle and lubricate lightly with wheel bearing lubricant.

5. Install hub and disc assembly (if so equipped) on spindle and install outer bearing cone, thrust washer, and adjusting nut.

6. If so equipped, lower caliper into position, and install retaining plates.

7. Install tire and adjust and secure using the procedure given below.

Wheel Bearing Adjustment

1. Tighten adjusting nut to 30-40 ft.-lbs. while rotating the wheel.

2. Back off adjusting nut to completely release the bearing preload.

3. Finger-tighten adjusting nut and then install the locknut with one pair of slots aligned with cotter pin hole. Install cotter pin.

NOTE: *This adjustment should result in no more than 0.003 in. of end play.*

4. Clean and install grease cap, wheel and tire assembly, and wheel cover.

WHEEL CYLINDERS

NOTE: *Wheel cylinders must be removed from the vehicle for service.*

Removal

With brake drums removed, inspect cylinders for evidence of leakage. Check boots for cuts, tears, and heat cracks. If any of these conditions exist, the cylinder should be rebuilt or replaced. Proceed as follows.

NOTE: *A slight amount of oil on the cylinder boot may not be a leak, but could be a preservative oil used during assembly.*

1. Remove the brake shoes as previously described.

2. Disconnect brake hose.

3. Remove attaching bolts and slide cylinder assembly out of support.

Disassembly

1. Remove boots from cylinder and remove pushrods. See **Figure 23**.

2. Force out pistons, cups, and springs by pressing in on one piston.

3. Clean parts thoroughly in solvent and dry, preferably with compressed air. Inspect cylinder bore and pistons for pits and scores.

CAUTION
Do not use a rag for cleaning, as lint could adhere to surfaces and eventually result in brake failure.

4. Replace cylinders having badly pitted or scored bores. Light scratches and corrosion usually can be removed with crocus cloth used with a circular motion. Black stains on cylinder walls are caused by the piston cups and are harmless.

Assembly

1. Dip pistons and new cups in brake fluid.

2. Wash cylinder with alcohol and blow dry, then coat bore with brake fluid.

3. Install spring, then install piston cups in each end of cylinder. Open ends of cups face each other.

4. Install pistons with recessed ends facing out of cylinder.

5. Install new boots on cylinders by pressing over ends until boots are seated on cylinder shoulders.

Installation

1. Slide cylinders into position on support plate and install attaching bolts and torque to 95 in.-lb.

2. Connect brake hoses and tighten securely.

BRAKE ADJUSTMENT

NOTE: *All Chrysler brakes are self-adjusting. The following should be used as*

10

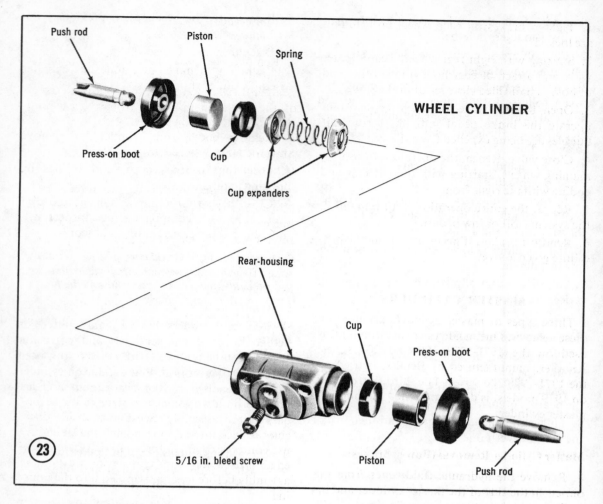

WHEEL CYLINDER

Push rod

Piston

Spring

Press-on boot

Cup

Cup expanders

Rear-housing

Cup

Press-on boot

5/16 in. bleed screw

Piston

Push rod

(23)

the initial adjustment after brakes have been relined.

1. Raise vehicle so all wheels can be freely turned and verify that parking brake lever is fully released and parking brake cable is slack.

2. Remove adjusting hole covers and insert adjusting tool to engage star wheel.

3. Move handle of adjusting tool upward until a slight drag is felt when wheel is rotated.

4. Use a thin screwdriver to push adjusting lever out of contact with star wheel. Take care not to bend lever or distort lever spring.

5. While holding adjusting lever out of the way, back off star wheel just enough to ensure free wheel rotation with no brake shoe drag.

6. Repeat the procedure for all wheels, making sure adjustment is equal for all wheels. Rein-

stall adjustment hole covers. With parking brake released, take up parking brake cable slack until a slight drag is felt on both rear wheels, then loosen until wheels rotate freely. Back off adjustment nut 2 additional turns. Apply brake several times, then verify that wheels still rotate freely.

HYDRAULIC SYSTEM BLEEDING

NOTE: *Chrysler Corporation recommends against the manual bleeding of the brake system. Instead, it recommends the use of a one-man bleeder tank which keeps the master cylinder full at all times. If care is taken to make sure master cylinder is filled with recommended fluid (see Chapter Three), the following procedure can be used in an emergency.*

1. Tighten brakes on each wheel until brakes are locked.

2. Starting with right rear wheel, clean bleeder valve and attach bleeder hose. Insert other end of hose in half filled clear jar of brake fluid.

3. Open bleeder valve and have an assistant operate the brake pedal until no further air bubbles are being expelled from the system.

4. Close valve. Repeat the operation for the remaining wheels, starting with the left rear and ending with the right front.

5. Repeat the entire operation if air remains in the system (soft or low pedal).

6. Readjust brakes, if necessary, using the procedure given above.

MASTER CYLINDERS

Three types of master cylinders are used on these vehicles. One, a Chrysler cast iron unit, is used on the 1971-1978 100 and 200 series. Another, manufactured by Bendix, is used on the 1971-1978 300 series. The third, introduced on 1979 models, is designated the "aluminum" master cylinder.

Master Cylinder Removal (Power Brakes)

1. Remove the hydraulic fluid tubes from the outlets in the side of the master cylinder and install plugs in the outlets.

2. Remove the nuts that attach the master cylinder to the power brake booster.

3. Pull the master cylinder straight forward to remove it from the booster.

Master Cylinder Removal (Manual Brakes)

1. Remove the hydraulic fluid tubes from the outlets in the side of the master cylinder and install plugs in the outlets.

2. Disconnect the stop switch mounting bracket (under the instrument panel) and allow it to hang out of the way.

3. Pull the brake pedal backward, using about 50 pounds of pressure, to disengage the pushrod from the master cylinder piston.

NOTE: *The pushrod retention grommet will be destroyed when the pushrod is disengaged. Install a new one when the master cylinder is reinstalled.*

4. Remove the nuts that attach the master cylinder to the fire wall and pull the assembly straight forward to remove it. Remove all traces of the retention grommet from the pushrod groove and the piston socket.

Master Cylinder Disassembly (Chrysler Cast Iron)

Refer to **Figure 24** for this procedure.

1. Discard the brake fluid in the master cylinder reservoir and clean the outside of the reservoir and the master cylinder.

2. Remove the secondary piston retaining screw from inside the master cylinder housing. See **Figure 25**.

3. Remove the snap ring from the master cylinder bore. Use snap ring pliers as shown in **Figure 26**.

4. Remove the primary (front) piston assembly from the housing. See **Figure 27**.

5. Tap the open end of the master cylinder housing on a workbench to remove the secondary piston assembly. See **Figure 28**. If difficulty is encountered in removing the assembly, use compressed air to force it out. If compressed air is used, new cups must be installed on the assembly before it is reassembled into the housing.

6. Remove all cups, except the primary cup of the primary piston, from the pistons. Be sure to note the position of the cup lips so they can be reassembled correctly.

7. If the brass tube seats in the master cylinder outlets are to be replaced, remove the old ones by threading an Easy-Out tool firmly into the seat and then tapping out the tool and seat. See **Figure 29**.

Cleaning and Inspection

1. Clean the master cylinder bore thoroughly with clean brake fluid and inspect the bore for scratches, pitting, or scoring. Replace the master cylinder if any of these conditions are present.

2. If the pistons appear to be worn or scored, discard them and install new ones.

10

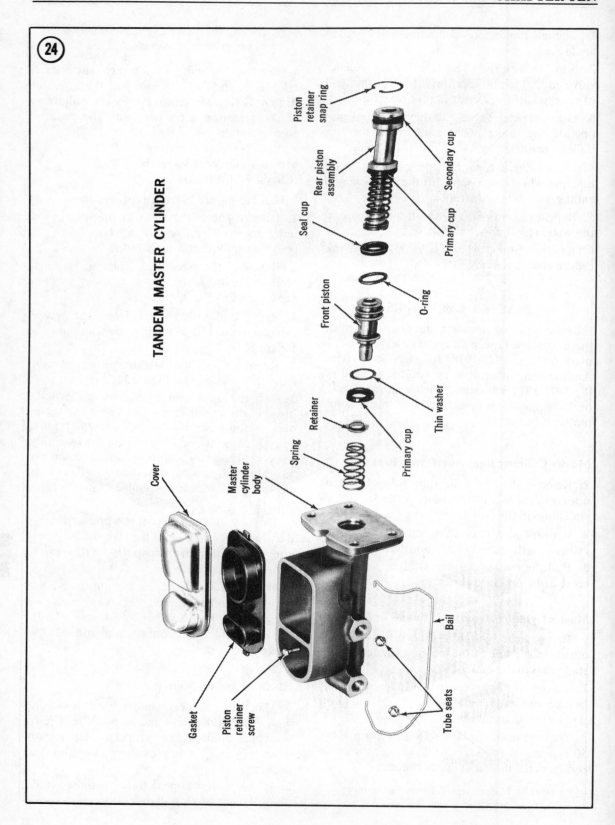

㉔

TANDEM MASTER CYLINDER

Piston retainer snap ring

Secondary cup

Rear piston assembly

Primary cup

Seal cup

O-ring

Front piston

Thin washer

Retainer

Primary cup

Spring

Cover

Master cylinder body

Gasket

Piston retainer screw

Bail

Tube seats

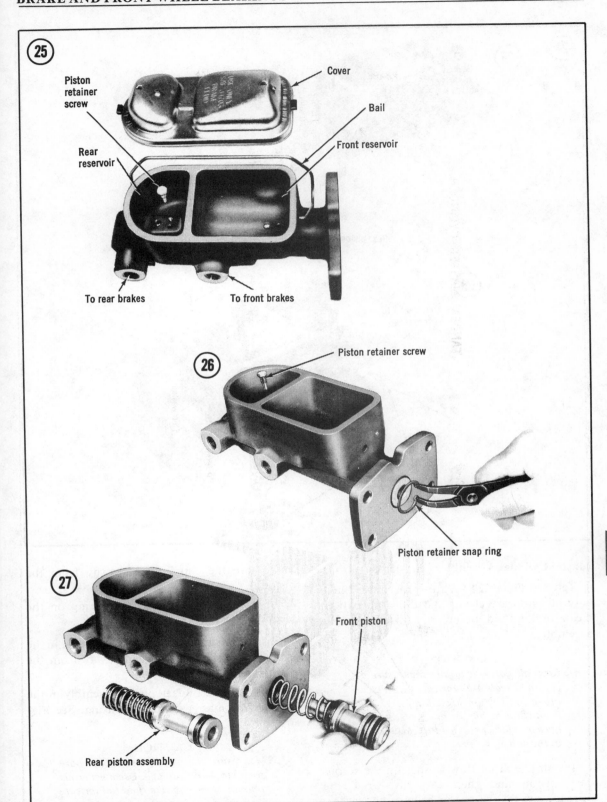

(25)

Piston retainer screw

Cover

Bail

Rear reservoir

Front reservoir

To rear brakes

To front brakes

(26)

Piston retainer screw

Piston retainer snap ring

(27)

Front piston

Rear piston assembly

10

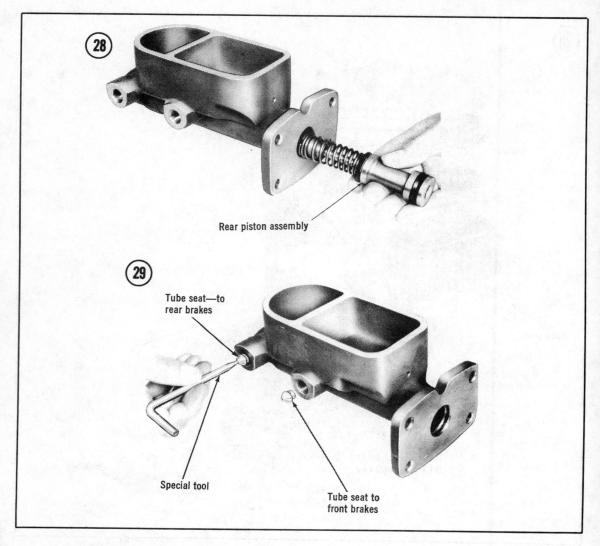

Rear piston assembly

Tube seat—to
rear brakes

Special tool

Tube seat to
front brakes

Master Cylinder Assembly (Chrysler Cast Iron)

Refer to **Figure 24** for this procedure. Make sure all parts are clean, and dip each part in clean brake fluid before installing it in the assembly.

> CAUTION
> *Keep all parts clean and make sure all cups and seals are lubricated with clean brake fluid before installation. The introduction of dirt or dry seals into the master cylinder can lead to early failure of the unit.*

1. Install the check flow washer on the secondary piston and then carefully work the primary cup on the piston behind the washer.

Make sure the cup lip faces away from the piston.

2. Install the cup retainer and spring on the secondary piston.

3. Install the secondary cup in the groove in the piston, with the cup lip facing away from the piston.

4. Install the secondary piston assembly in the bore of the master cylinder housing. See **Figure 28**.

> CAUTION
> *Make sure the cup lips enter the bore evenly to avoid damage. Use a generous amount of clean brake fluid to lubricate the cups.*

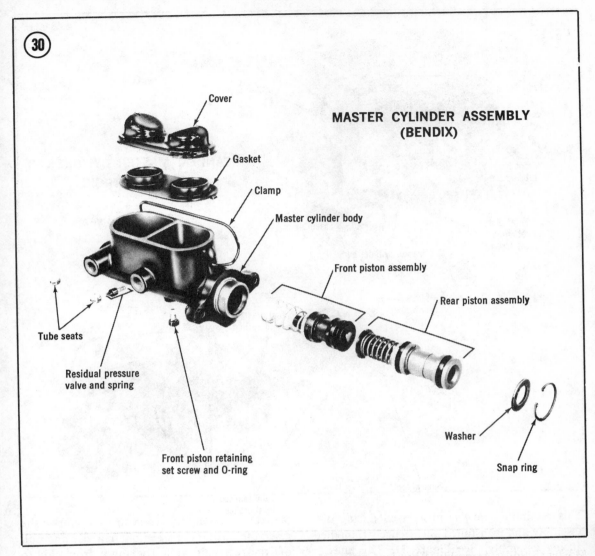

Cover

Gasket

Clamp

Master cylinder body

Front piston assembly

Rear piston assembly

Tube seats

Residual pressure
valve and spring

Washer

Front piston retaining
set screw and O-ring

Snap ring

**MASTER CYLINDER ASSEMBLY
(BENDIX)**

10

5. Install the secondary cup over the rear end of the primary piston, with the larger lip toward the piston. See **Figure 27**.

6. Center the primary piston spring retainer on the secondary piston and install the primary piston assembly in the master cylinder bore up to the primary piston cup. Carefully work the cup into the bore, using a generous amount of clean brake fluid as lubricant. Then push the assembly in up to the secondary seal. Carefully work the lip into the bore and then push the piston in until seated.

7. Depress the piston assembly with a wood or brass rod and install the retaining snap ring. See **Figure 26**.

8. Install the secondary piston retaining screw in the housing and turn it until it fully seats. See **Figure 25**.

9. If the tube seats were removed, install new ones by firmly pressing them into the master cylinder side outlets.

Master Cylinder Disassembly/Assembly (Bendix)

Refer to **Figure 30**. The disassembly and assembly procedures for the Bendix master cylinder are similar in all respects to those for the Chrysler cast iron master cylinder, except that a front piston retaining screw is used instead of a secondary piston retaining screw.

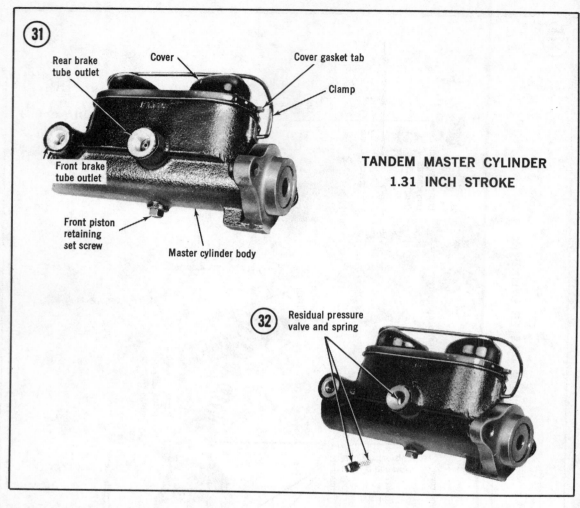

31

Rear brake tube outlet

Cover

Cover gasket tab

Clamp

Front brake tube outlet

TANDEM MASTER CYLINDER 1.31 INCH STROKE

Front piston retaining set screw

Master cylinder body

32 Residual pressure valve and spring

This retaining screw is unscrewed during disassembly and is installed and securely tightened during assembly. See **Figure 31**. This master cylinder also has a residual pressure valve and spring, located in the rear brake tube outlet. See **Figure 32**.

Master Cylinder Disassembly/Assembly (Aluminum)

Refer to **Figure 33**. The disassembly and assembly procedures for the aluminum master cylinder are similar in all respects to those for the Chrysler cast iron master cylinder, except that a secondary piston retaining pin is used instead of a retaining screw. This pin is removed and installed with a pair of needle nose pliers. Also, the aluminum master cylinder has a de-

tachable black nylon reservoir. To remove the reservoir, install the assembly in a vise and pull off the reservoir while rocking it from side to side. See **Figure 34**. Then remove the grommets. See **Figure 35**.

Master Cylinder Bleeding (All)

NOTE: *The master cylinder must be bled following overhaul before installation in the vehicle.*

1. Mount the master cylinder in a vise and install bleeding tubes. See **Figure 36**, typical.
2. Fill both reservoirs with DOT-3 type brake fluid and use a wood or brass rod to depress the primary cylinder slowly. Allow the pistons to return under spring pressure. Repeat this step until all air bubbles are expelled.

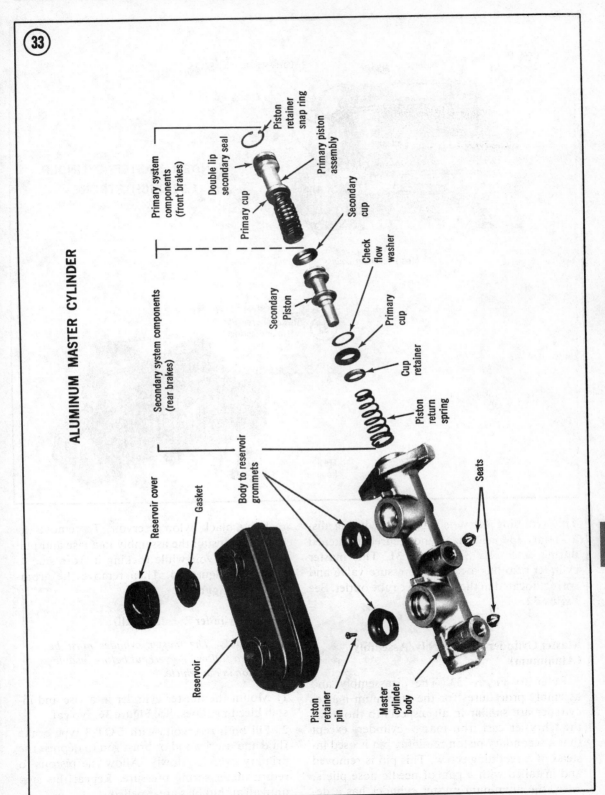

33

ALUMINUM MASTER CYLINDER

Primary system components (front brakes)

Piston retainer snap ring

Double lip secondary seal

Primary piston assembly

Primary cup

Secondary cup

Check flow washer

Secondary Piston

Primary cup

Cup retainer

Secondary system components (rear brakes)

Piston return spring

Body to reservoir grommets

Reservoir cover

Gasket

Seats

Reservoir

Piston retainer pin

Master cylinder body

10

(34) Reservoir

Grommet

Master
cylinder
housing

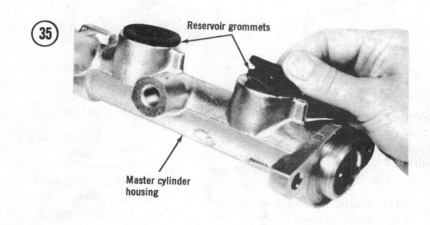

(35) Reservoir grommets

Master cylinder
housing

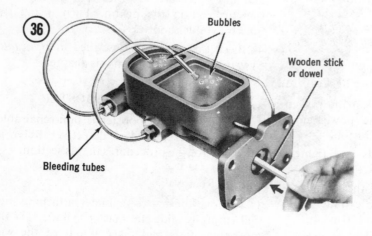

(36) Bubbles

Wooden stick
or dowel

Bleeding tubes

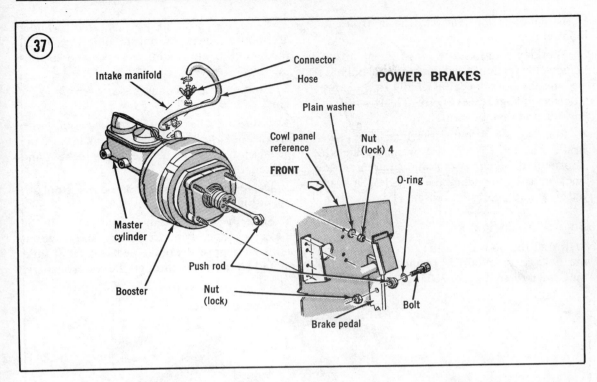

3. Remove the bleeding tubes from the master cylinder and plug the outlets to prevent further spillage. Install the reservoir cap and install the assembly.

> NOTE: *The bleeding tubes recommended by Chrysler are tool set C-4029. One tube in this set is equipped with a residual valve to prevent spillage. The other tube can be equipped with a residual valve by adding valve SP-5195. If this tool set is not available, and a substitute set is used, take care when removing the tubes.*

Master Cylinder Installation (Power Brakes)

1. Position the master cylinder on the power brake unit studs and align the power unit pushrod with the master cylinder piston.

2. Install the nuts on the studs and tighten them to 170-230 in.-lb.

3. Remove the plugs and install the front and rear brake tubes to the master cylinder side outlets. Tighten the connectors to 150 in.-lb.

4. Bleed the brakes as described in *Hydraulic System Bleeding*, earlier in this chapter.

Master Cylinder Installation (Manual Brakes)

1. Install a new pushrod grommet on the pushrod.

2. Place the master cylinder in position on the fire wall and install the attaching nuts. Tighten the nuts to 170-230 in.-lb.

3. Working under the instrument panel, moisten the pushrod grommet with water, align the pushrod with the master cylinder piston, and apply pressure with the brake pedal to seat the pushrod in the piston. Then install the master cylinder boot.

4. Bleed the brakes as described in *Hydraulic System Bleeding*, earlier in this chapter.

POWER BRAKE BOOSTER

The power brake booster is non-repairable, and must be replaced if defective. Refer to **Figure 37** for the procedures in this section.

Booster Removal

1. Remove the master cylinder attaching nuts and carefully slide the master cylinder off the mounting studs and place it out of the way against the fender well.

10

2. Disconnect the vacuum hose from the booster unit.

3. Working under the instrument panel, remove the retaining locknut from the bolt connecting the brake pedal assembly to the power booster linkage. See **Figure 37**. Discard the locknut and remove the pin.

4. Remove the 4 nuts attaching the power brake booster to the fire wall. Rotate the booster and linkage as required and remove the booster assembly from the vehicle. Save the bushings and sleeves for reuse.

Booster Installation

1. Install the booster on the fire wall, rotating the linkage as required. Install the attaching nuts and tighten them to 200 in.-lb.

2. Carefully position the master cylinder assembly on the power booster unit, then install the mounting nuts and tighten them to 200 in.-lb.

3. Connect the vacuum hose to the booster unit.

4. Lubricate the pedal attaching bolt with grease and install it through the linkage and the pedal shaft. Install a new retaining locknut and tighten to 30 ft.-lb.

5. Depress the brake pedal and check stoplight operation.

6. Start the engine, remove the cover of the master cylinder front reservoir, and have an assistant depress the brake pedal. A jet of fluid should be forced up through the reservoir front chamber.

CHAPTER ELEVEN

SUSPENSION AND STEERING

Major work on suspension and steering frequently requires the use of special tools that are available only to dealers. In addition, a great deal of specialized experience is required that places such work beyond the abilities of a hobbyist mechanic.

Work should be confined to the procedures described below. All other work should be entrusted to a dealer or a qualified specialist.

SHOCK ABSORBERS

The shock absorbers can be routinely checked while installed on the vehicle. However, this is only a general indication of their condition; if there is any doubt about their serviceability, they should be removed as described later and checked more accurately.

To check their general condition, bounce first the front, then the rear of the vehicle up and down several times and release. The vehicle should not continue to bounce more than twice. Excessive bouncing is an indication of worn shock absorbers. Keep in mind, however, that this test is not conclusive; the spring stiffness of a truck makes it difficult to detect shock absorbers in marginal condition. If there is doubt about the condition of the units, remove them and have them tested.

Removal/Installation (Front and Rear)

1. Jack up the front of the vehicle and support it on frame stands. Remove the wheels. See **Figure 1** for front and **Figure 2** for rear shock absorber (typical).

2. Unscrew the nut(s) and bolt(s) from the lower mount.

3. Unscrew the nut from the upper mount, remove the washer and bushings. Remove shock absorber from vehicle.

4. Install the new shock absorbers with new rubber bushings. Install the upper bracket first, but do not tighten the nuts until the bottom has been installed. Then tighten all nuts and bolts (front top to 25 ft.-lb. bottom to 200 in.-lb.; rear to 75 ft.-lb.).

Inspection

1. Check the piston rod for bending, galling, and abrasion. Any one of these conditions is reason for replacement.

2. Check for fluid leakage. A light film on the rod is normal, but severe leakage is reason for replacement.

3. With the shock absorber in the installed position, completely extend the rod, then invert the shock absorber and completely compress the rod. Do this several times to expel trapped

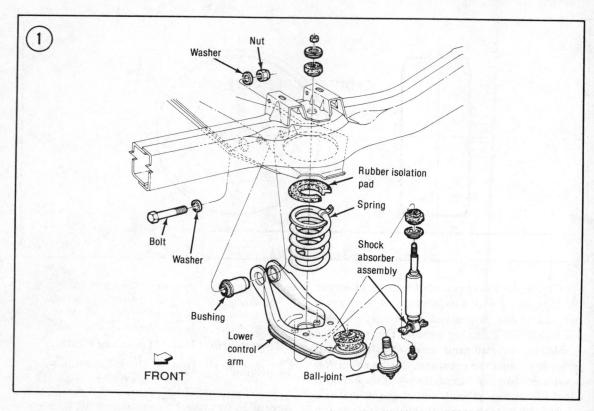

Washer
Nut
Rubber isolation pad
Spring
Bolt
Washer
Shock absorber assembly
Bushing
Lower control arm
Ball-joint
FRONT

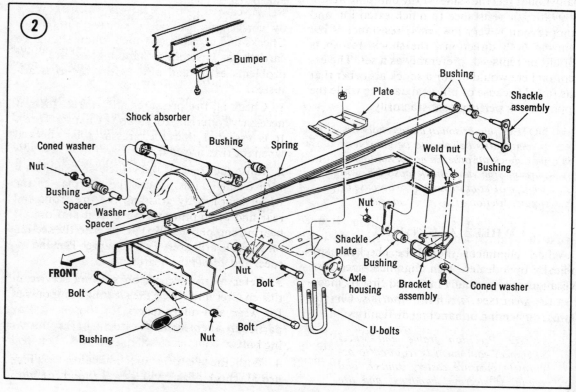

Bumper
Plate
Bushing
Shackle assembly
Shock absorber
Bushing
Spring
Coned washer
Weld nut
Nut
Bushing
Bushing
Spacer
Washer
Spacer
Nut
Shackle plate
FRONT
Nut
Bolt
Bushing
Axle housing
Bolt
Bracket assembly
Coned washer
Bolt
Bushing
Nut
Bolt
U-bolts

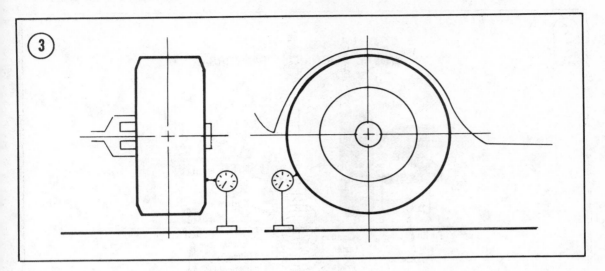

air. Clamp the lower end of the shock absorber in a vise fitted with jaw protectors. Compress and extend the piston rod as fast as possible and check the damping action. The resistance should be smooth and uniform throughout each stroke, and the resistance during extension should be greater than during compression. Also, the action of both shock absorbers in a pair should feel the same. If the damping action is erratic, or resistance to quick extension and compression is very low, or if resistance is the same in both directions, the shock absorbers should be replaced, preferably as a set. The exception here would be for a shock absorber that has failed because of physical damage while the opposite unit performs satisfactorily.

> NOTE: *Comparison of a used shock absorber that is believed to be good to a new shock absorber is not a valid comparison; the new shock absorber will seem to offer more resistance because of greater friction of the new rod seal.*

WHEEL ALIGNMENT

Wheel alignment should be checked periodically by a dealer or an alignment specialist. Misalignment is usually indicated first by incorrect tire wear (see *Tire Wear Analysis*, Chapter Two), or steering or handling difficulties.

> NOTE: *Precision frame and wheel alignment equipment is required to accurately measure caster, camber, and toe-in. If steering, handling, and tire*

wear difficulties cannot be corrected by the checks and corrections presented below, the vehicle should be entrusted to a dealer or an automotive alignment specialist.

Inspection

Steering and handling problems which may appear to be caused by misalignment may very well be caused by other factors which are readily correctable without expensive equipment. Checks and inspections which follow should be carried out if steering, handling, or tire wear problems exist, and also before toe-in is adjusted.

1. Check all tire pressures and correct them if necessary, referring to **Table 1**, Chapter Three. It is essential that the pressures be checked when the tires are cold.

2. Raise the front of the vehicle and support it with frame stands. Check the end play of the wheel bearings by grasping the tire front and rear and attempting to move it in and out. If bearing end play can be felt, refer to the section on wheel bearing service in Chapter Ten and inspect and adjust the bearings.

3. Refer to the section on steering service in this chapter and check the steering components for wear and all fasteners for looseness. Pay particular attention to the steering gear mounting bolts.

4. With the aid of a dial indicator (see **Figure 3**), check radial and lateral runout of both

11

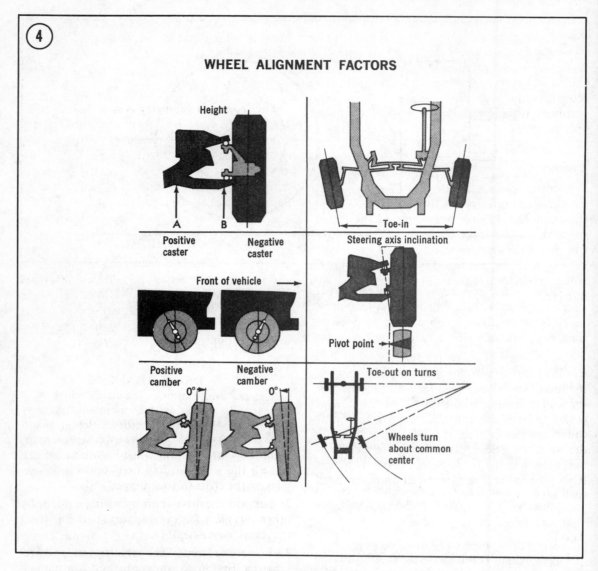

④

WHEEL ALIGNMENT FACTORS

Height

A   B

Positive   Negative
caster   caster

Front of vehicle →

Positive   Negative
camber   camber
        0°   0°

Toe-in

Steering axis inclination

Pivot point

Toe-out on turns

Wheels turn
about common
center

---

front tires. Place the indicator against the tread first and slowly rotate the wheel. Then place the indicator against the outer sidewall of the tire and again rotate the wheel slowly. If either the radial or lateral runout is greater than 0.080 in., the tire should be deflated and rotated 90 degrees on the wheel.

> NOTE: *It will probably be necessary to soap the wheel rim before the tire can be turned.*

Reinflate the tire to the correct pressure shown in Chapter Three (**Table 1**), and recheck

the runout. If necessary, the tire should be rotated again if the runout is still excessive.

5. Examine the plates and U-bolts for signs of damage that may have bent them.

If steering, handling, and tire wear problems cannot be corrected by carrying out the above inspections and adjustments, the vehicle should be referred to a dealer or alignment specialist for a precision inspection and for corrective work.

Front Suspension Height

The specified height of the front suspension provides the reference from which some other measurements are made in front end alignment. As vehicles grow older, they tend to settle. This is especially true when the vehicle is new. In view of this, height should be measured from the floor to the lowest point of the lower control arm inner pivot bushing. See **Figure 4**. Adjustment is required if not within ⅛ in. of specifications.

Camber

Camber is the angle the top of the wheel is tilted inward or outward from the true vertical position. See **Figure 4**. Inward tilt is called negative camber and outward tilt is positive camber. Excessive negative camber causes excessive wear on the inside of the tire tread, while positive camber causes wear on the outside.

Caster

Caster is the angle of tilt (forward or backward) of the spindle support arm, measured at the top of the wheel. See **Figure 4**. If the top of the arm is inclined to the rear of the car, caster is said to be positive. Inclination to the front is called negative. Caster is the factor that causes the wheel to return to the straight ahead position after a turn. It also helps prevent the car from wandering due to wind and uneven road surfaces.

Toe-In

Toe is the relationship between the leading and trailing edges of the front tires. See **Figure 4**. If the leading edges of the tires are closer together than the trailing edges, toe-in exists. If the trailing edges are closer, toe-out exists. Camber and road resistance tend to force the front wheels outward at the leading edges. To compensate for this tendency, the wheels are aligned so they have a small amount of toe-in when the car is at rest.

Steering Axis Inclination

Steering axis inclination is the angle between the spindle support center line and true vertical. See **Figure 4**. This angle is fixed and does not change unless components are damaged or bent, in which case the damaged components must be replaced.

Toe-Out on Turns

The front end geometry is such that in turns one front wheel turns more sharply than the other. The amount is measured in degrees and is called toe-out in turns. See **Figure 4**. This angle cannot be adjusted, and if it deviates from specifications, check for bent or damaged parts. Replace all damaged parts.

STEERING

Service to the steering gear is limited to checking and correcting the lubricant level (see Chapter Three), checking and correcting play in the steering wheel and column (see Chapter Three), and checking and tightening the steering gear mounting bolts (see **Figure 5**).

DRIVE SHAFT

Removal

Refer to **Figure 6** for this procedure.

1. Raise the vehicle and remove both clamps from the rear hub yoke. See **Figure 6**. Do not disturb the strap used to hold bushing assemblies on the cross (if so equipped).

2. Support the drive shaft by wiring it up, or by other means, to prevent damage to the front universal joint assembly.

3. Lower the front of the vehicle slightly to prevent the loss of transmission fluid (on manual transmission) and pull the drive shaft and sliding front yoke assembly to the rear to separate it from the transmission output shaft. Remove the shaft and yoke assembly from the car.

4. Check the sliding yoke seal in the transmission extension for signs of wear or damage, and replace it if necessary. See the appropriate procedure for your transmission in Chapter Nine. Also check the machined surface of the yoke for damage. Dress minor nicks and burrs with crocus cloth or a fine file, taking care not to damage the surface. If the surface is heavily damaged, replace the yoke.

11

Installation

Refer to **Figure 6** for this procedure.

1. Make sure the mating surfaces of the front sliding yoke are free of damage and clean, then engage the yoke splines with the splines on the end of the transmission output shaft. Take care not to damage the splines.

2. Install the rear universal joint cross and bushings in the hub yoke seats and install the clamps and attaching screws. Tighten the screws to 170 in.-lb.

UNIVERSAL JOINTS

Disassembly

Refer to **Figure 6** for this procedure.

1. Remove the drive shaft as previously described in this chapter.

2. Make matching marks on the sliding yoke and the drive shaft so they can be returned to their original relationship. Remove the snap rings from the bushings and then apply penetrating oil to the bushings.

3. Support one of the yokes and use a $1\frac{1}{8}$ in. socket as a tool to remove the bushings. See **Figure 7**. Striking the socket with a hammer will cause the yoke to move down and the bushing to move up and into the socket.

4. Repeat Step 3 until all bushings have been removed, then remove the cross.

Assembly

Refer to **Figure 6** for this procedure.

1. Align the marks made in Step 2 of *Disassembly*, position the cross in the yoke ears and hold it with one hand, and tap in a bushing with a soft-faced hammer. See **Figure 8**. Install the snap ring retainer on the bushing.

2. Install the opposite bushing and snap ring in the same manner.

3. On the front universal joint, repeat Steps 1 and 2 for the sliding yoke.

4. On the rear universal joint, install the bushings and snap rings on the cross and use tape to hold them in place until the drive shaft is installed in the vehicle.

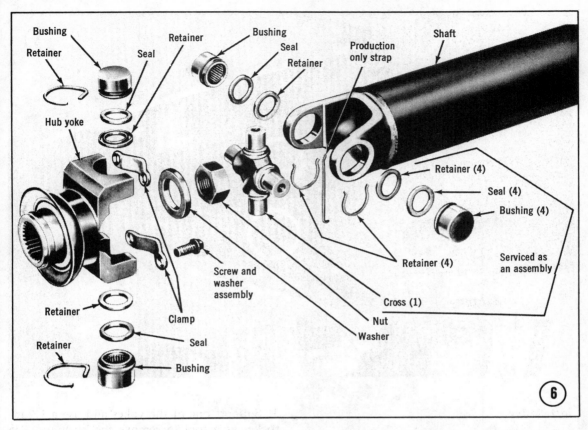

Bushing
Retainer
Seal
Retainer
Bushing
Seal
Retainer
Production only strap
Shaft
Hub yoke
Retainer (4)
Seal (4)
Bushing (4)
Screw and washer assembly
Retainer (4)
Serviced as an assembly
Retainer
Clamp
Cross (1)
Retainer
Seal
Nut
Bushing
Washer

6

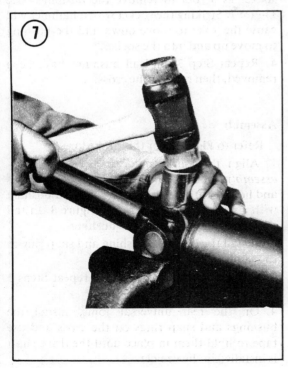

7

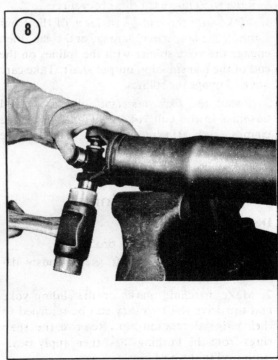

8

11

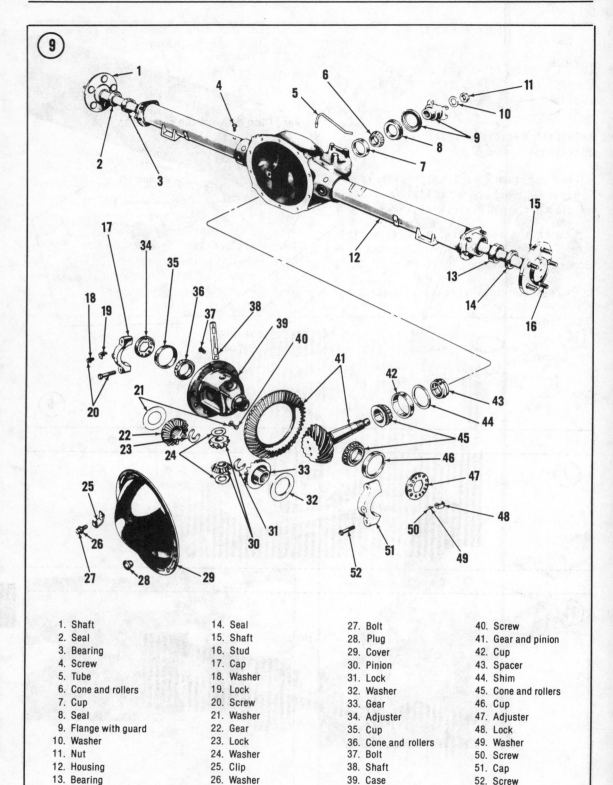

1. Shaft
2. Seal
3. Bearing
4. Screw
5. Tube
6. Cone and rollers
7. Cup
8. Seal
9. Flange with guard
10. Washer
11. Nut
12. Housing
13. Bearing

14. Seal
15. Shaft
16. Stud
17. Cap
18. Washer
19. Lock
20. Screw
21. Washer
22. Gear
23. Lock
24. Washer
25. Clip
26. Washer

27. Bolt
28. Plug
29. Cover
30. Pinion
31. Lock
32. Washer
33. Gear
34. Adjuster
35. Cup
36. Cone and rollers
37. Bolt
38. Shaft
39. Case

40. Screw
41. Gear and pinion
42. Cup
43. Spacer
44. Shim
45. Cone and rollers
46. Cup
47. Adjuster
48. Lock
49. Washer
50. Screw
51. Cap
52. Screw

REAR AXLE

Dodge and Plymouth vans may be equipped with Chrysler or Spicer rear axles. Axle models are identified by a tag on the axle assembly.

Axle Shaft Removal/ Installation (Chrysler)

Refer to **Figure 9** for this procedure.

1. Securely block both front wheels so the vehicle will not roll in either direction.

2. Loosen the rear wheel nuts. Jack up the rear of the van, place it on jackstands and remove the rear wheels.

3. Place a pan beneath the center of the axle.

4. Clean the area around the differential cover, then remove the cover from the back of the axle.

5. Turn the differential case so the C-washer lock is accessible. See **Figure 10**.

6. Push the axle shaft toward the center of the van, then remove the C-washer lock.

7. Pull the axle shaft from the housing. If necessary, use a slide hammer and adapter. These are available from rental dealers.

8. Check the rear wheel bearing for looseness. Rotate it and check for rough or noisy movement. If these conditions are found, remove the bearing and seal with a slide hammer and adapter. See **Figure 11**.

9. Installation is the reverse of removal. The old bearing can be reinstalled if in good condition. Always use a new seal.

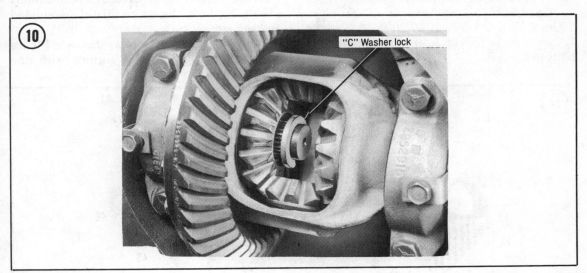

⑩ "C" Washer lock

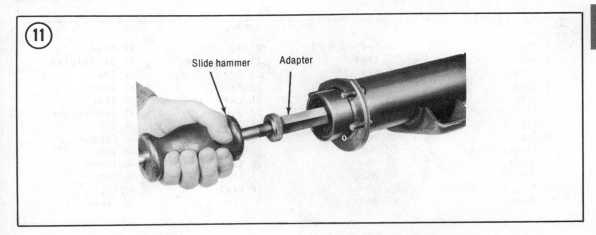

⑪ Slide hammer   Adapter

11

Axle Shaft Removal/ Installation (Spicer)

Refer to **Figure 12** for this procedure.

1. Securely block both front wheels so the van will not roll in either direction.
2. Loosen the rear wheel nuts. Jack up the rear of the van, place it on jackstands and remove the rear wheels.
3. Remove the axle shaft flange nuts and lockwashers (or Durlock bolts).
4. Give the axle shaft a firm tap in the center of the flange. This frees the dowels.
5. Pull the axle shaft out.
6. Spin the brake drum. Check for rough or noisy movement. If this is found, remove the bearing as described under *Rear Brake Drum Removal (Bendix)*, Chapter Ten.
6. Installation is the reverse of removal. Tighten 7/16x20 nuts to 40-70 ft.-lb. Tighten 1/2x20 nuts to 65-105 ft.-lb. Tighten Durlock bolts to 60 ft.-lb.

Differential Inspection (All Models)

The following procedure will tell you if differential repairs are necessary. Repairs require a large number of special tools, as well as special training. If problems are found, take the rear axle to a dealer or properly equipped mechanic for repairs.

1. Place a pan beneath the center of the rear axle.
2. Clean the area around the inspection cover, then remove it from the back of the rear axle.
3. Check the ring gear teeth for obvious damage such as chipping. If damage is found, have the differential overhauled.
4. Set up a dial indicator as shown in **Figure 13**. Turn the ring gear one full turn and measure runout. If it exceeds specifications (**Table 1**), have the differential disassembled and adjusted.
5. Set up the dial indicator as shown in **Figure 14**. Hold the pinion from turning with one

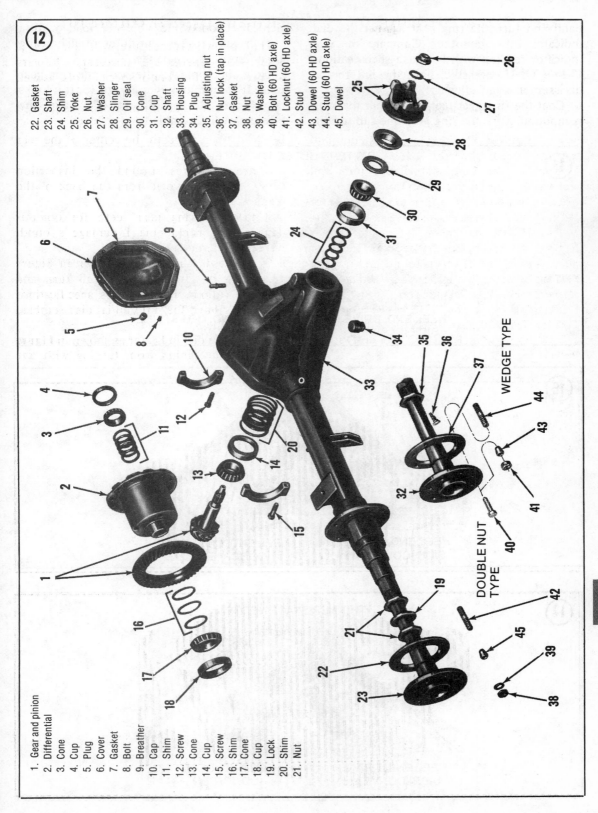

(12)

1. Gear and pinion
2. Differential
3. Cone
4. Cup
5. Plug
6. Cover
7. Gasket
8. Bolt
9. Breather
10. Cap
11. Shim
12. Screw
13. Cone
14. Cup
15. Screw
16. Shim
17. Cone
18. Cup
19. Lock
20. Shim
21. Nut

22. Gasket
23. Shaft
24. Shim
25. Yoke
26. Nut
27. Washer
28. Slinger
29. Oil seal
30. Cone
31. Cup
32. Shaft
33. Housing
34. Plug
35. Adjusting nut
36. Nut lock (tap in place)
37. Gasket
38. Nut
39. Washer
40. Bolt (60 HD axle)
41. Locknut (60 HD axle)
42. Stud
43. Dowel (60 HD axle)
44. Stud (60 HD axle)
45. Dowel

WEDGE TYPE

DOUBLE NUT TYPE

11

hand and turn the ring gear against the dial indicator with the other. Compare the dial indicator reading with backlash specifications (**Table 1**). If excessive, have the differential disassembled and adjusted.

6. Coat the ring gear teeth with gear marking compound. Turn the ring gear one full turn in each direction while applying load with a screwdriver between the differential housing and differential case flange.

7. Note the contact pattern on the ring gear teeth. It should look like **Figure 15**. If it looks like **Figure 16** or **Figure 17**, have the differential disassembled and adjusted.

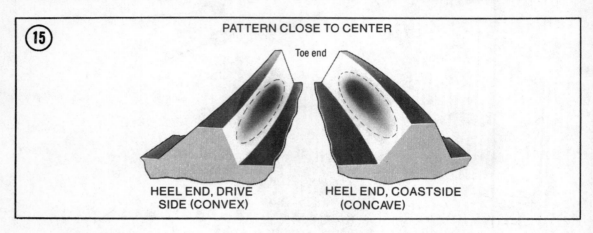

(15) PATTERN CLOSE TO CENTER

Toe end

HEEL END, DRIVE
SIDE (CONVEX)

HEEL END, COASTSIDE
(CONCAVE)

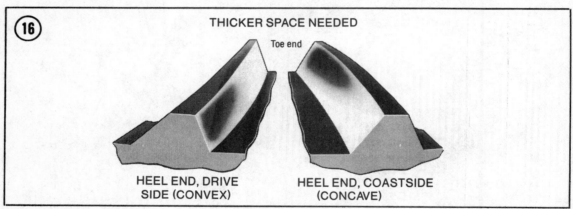

(16) THICKER SPACE NEEDED

Toe end

HEEL END, DRIVE
SIDE (CONVEX)

HEEL END, COASTSIDE
(CONCAVE)

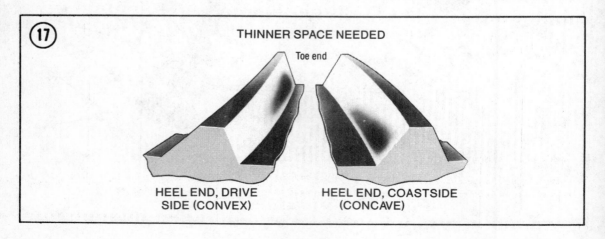

(17) THINNER SPACE NEEDED

Toe end

HEEL END, DRIVE
SIDE (CONVEX)

HEEL END, COASTSIDE
(CONCAVE)

8. After inspection, install the inspection cover. Clean all old gasket material from the cover. Apply a 1/16-3/32 in. wide bead of silicone sealer around the cover gasket flange. See **Figure 18**. Clean the cover mating surface on the axle housing with solvent, then let it dry completely. This allows time for the sealer to cure. Install the cover and tighten its bolts evenly.

Axle Assembly
Removal/Installation

1. Securely block both front wheels so the van will not roll in either direction.
2. Support the brake pedal in the "up" position with a wooden block.
3. Loosen the rear wheel nuts. Jack up the rear of the van, place it on jackstands and remove the rear wheels.
4. On Spicer axles, remove the rear brake drums, hubs and wheel bearings. See *Rear Brake Drum Removal (Bendix)*, Chapter Ten.

5. Disconnect and cap the rear wheel brake lines. Plastic vacuum caps, available from auto parts stores, work well for this.
6. Disconnect the parking brake cables.
7. Make match marks on the drive shaft and differential flanges so they can be reassembled in the same relative positions.
8. Place a jack beneath the axle to support it.
9. Detach the shock absorbers from the spring plate studs.
10. Remove the spring U-bolts. See **Figure 19** (100, 200, 150 and 250 models) or **Figure 20** (300 and 350 models).
11. Lift the axle assembly off the springs, then take it out.
12. Installation is the reverse of removal. Tighten U-bolt nuts to the following specifications:
   a. 1971-1973: 65 ft.-lb.
   b. 1974-on 100, 20, 150 and 250 models: 45 ft.-lb.
   c. 1974-on 300 models: 110 ft.-lb.

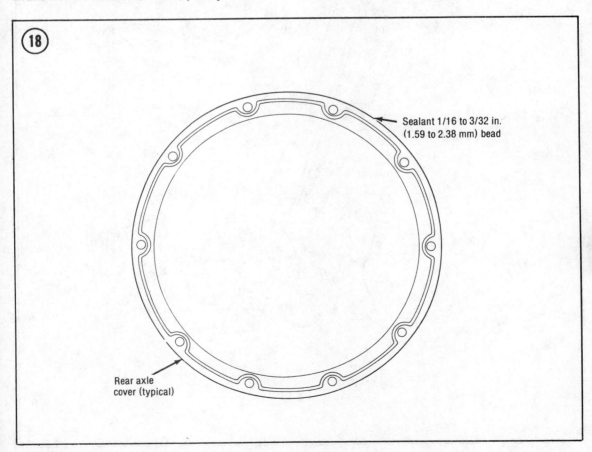

(18)

Sealant 1/16 to 3/32 in.
(1.59 to 2.38 mm) bead

Rear axle
cover (typical)

11

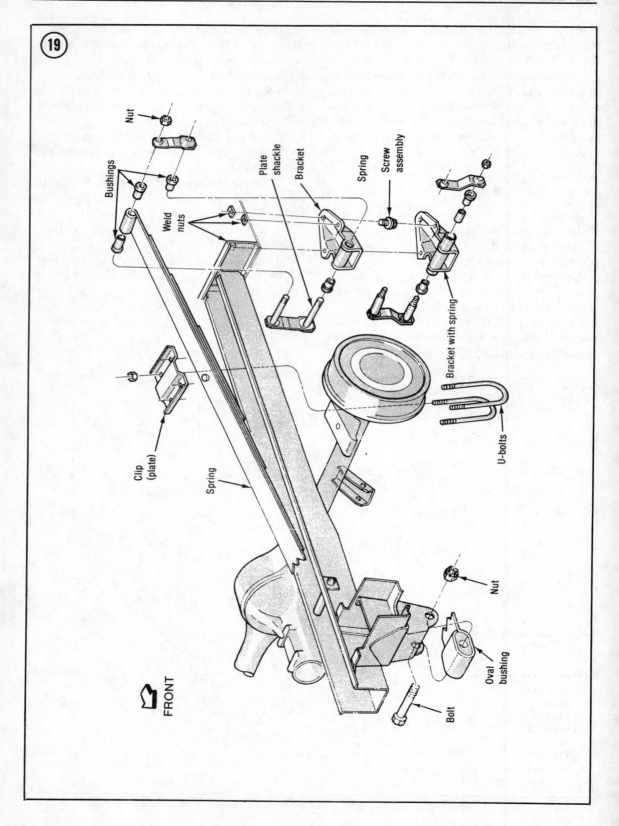

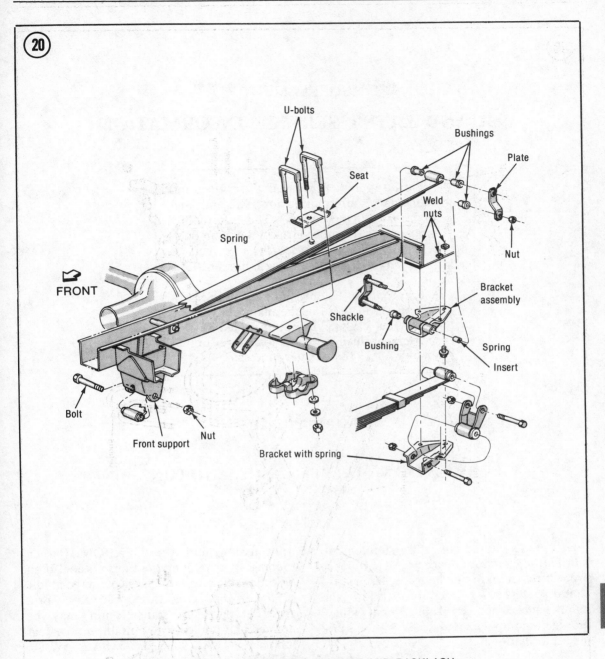

20

U-bolts

Bushings

Plate

Seat

Weld nuts

Spring

FRONT

Shackle

Bracket assembly

Bushing

Spring

Insert

Bolt

Nut

Front support

Bracket with spring

Nut

11

Table 1. RING GEAR RUNOUT AND BACKLASH

Chrysler axles	
Runout	0.005 in. (0.13mm) or less
Backlash	0.006-0.008 in. (0.15-0.20mm)
Spicer axles	
Runout	0.006 in. (0.15mm) or less
Backlash	0.004-0.009 in. (0.10-0.23mm)*

*No more than 0.002 in. (0.5mm) variation between points checked.

1982 AND LATER SERVICE INFORMATION

This supplement contains service and maintenance information for 1982 and later Dodge and Plymouth vans. This information supplements the procedures in the main body of the book. In some cases, the specifications and tolerances are the same as for pre-1982 models.

The chapter headings in this supplement correspond to those in the main body of the book. If a chapter is not included in this supplement, then there are no changes in that chapter for 1982 and later models.

CHAPTER THREE

LUBRICATION, MAINTENANCE, AND TUNE-UP

Except as noted in this supplement, lubrication, maintenance and tune-up procedures remain unchanged. **Tables 1-4** contain 1982 and later lubrication and maintenance schedules. **Table 5** and **Table 6** provide tune-up data and **Table 7** gives spark plug information.

LUBRICATION

Engine Oil

API service SF oil is recommended for 1982 and later models.

Manual Transmission Lubricant

The Overdrive-4 manual transmission is factory-filled with DEXRON II automatic transmission fluid. Use DEXRON II when topping up or refilling the transmission. If an objectionable gear rattle is encountered at idle or under load conditions, Chrysler Corp. specifies that the transmission may be drained and refilled with a multipurpose gear lubricant of SAE 90, SAE 75, SAE 75W-80, SAE 80W-90 or SAE 85W-90 viscosity.

IGNITION TUNE-UP

Cylinder head bolt torque has been changed on both the 318 cid and the 360 cid V8 engines. The new specification for both engines is 105 ft.-lb.

Table 1 SCHEDULED MAINTENANCE
(1982 LIGHT DUTY: UNDER 8,500 LB. GVWR)(1)

Every 7,500 miles	• All schedules: • Change engine oil • Replace engine oil filter @ initial oil change and every second change thereafter • Schedule B only: • Apply solvent to carburetor choke shaft • Apply solvent to fast idle cam and pivot pin
Every 15,000 miles	• All schedules: • Check and adjust drive belts • Schedule A only: • Replace spark plugs (without catalytic converter) • Check and replace ignition cables (without catalytic converter) as necessary • Schedule B only: • Check and adjust idle speed • Check PCV valve operation
Every 22,500 miles	• All schedules: • Lubricate front suspension ball-joints • Lubricate propeller shaft U-joint and slip spline • Lubricate wheel stop (2) • Inspect brake linings • Inspect front wheel bearings • Lubricate steering linkage • Lubricate clutch linkage bellcrank
Every 30,000 miles	• All schedules: • Apply solvent to carburetor choke shaft • Apply solvent to fast idle cam and pivot pin • Replace spark plugs (with catalytic converter) • Drain, flush cooling system (after initial service) and refill • Schedules A and B: • Replace air cleaner element • Schedule B only: • Clean crankcase inlet air cleaner • Replace fuel filter • Check and replace ignition cables (with catalytic converter) as necessary • Apply solvent to manifold heat control valve • Replace PCV valve • Inspect and replace fuel system and emission hoses as necessary
Every 37,500 miles	• All schedules: • Drain and refill manual transmission (3) • Drain and refill automatic transmission (4)
Every 48,000 miles	• All schedules: • Clean and lubricate rear wheel bearings (full-floating axle)
Every 52,500 miles	• All schedules: • Initial drain, cooling system flush and refill

(1) Three maintenance schedules are used: A, B and C. Check the Vehicle Emission Control Information (VECI) label in the engine compartment to determine which schedule applies to the vehicle being serviced.
(2) Daily, if used in water.
(3) Every 18,000 miles for severe service.
(4) Every 12,000 miles for severe service.

12

**Table 2 SCHEDULED MAINTENANCE (1982
HEAVY DUTY: MORE THAN 8,500 LB. GVWR)**

Every 6,000 miles	• Change engine oil • Replace engine oil filter @ initial oil change and every second change thereafter • Check and replace brake hoses as necessary
Every 12,000 miles	• Apply solvent to carburetor choke shaft • Clean air cleaner • Clean crankcase inlet air cleaner • Apply solvent to fast idle cam and pivot pin • Check PCV valve • Lubricate brake booster bellcrank pivot • Check operation of EGR system
Every 12 months	• Inspect cooling system
Every 18,000 miles	• Check and adjust automatic choke • Check drive belts • Replace fuel filter • Check and adjust ignition timing as necessary • Check and replace ignition cables, distributor cap and rotor as necessary • Check and adjust idle speed as necessary • Apply solvent to manifold heat control valve • Replace spark plugs • Check and replace fuel and emission hoses as required
Every 24,000 miles	• Replace air cleaner element • Replace PCV valve • Lubricate front suspension ball-joints • Lubricate propeller shaft slip splines (1) • Lubricate wheel stop • Lubricate clutch bellcrank pivot • Inspect front wheel bearings • Drain and refill automatic transmission (2) • Check brake linings
Every 30,000 miles	• Drain, flush and refill cooling system (after initial service)
Every 36,000 miles	• Drain and refill manual transmission (3)
Every 48,000 miles	• Drain, flush and refill cooling system (initial service) • Clean and lubricate rear wheel bearings (full floating axle)

(1) Every 3,000 miles for severe service; daily if used in water.

(2) Every 12,000 miles for severe service.

(3) Every 18,000 miles for severe service.

Table 3 SCHEDULED MAINTENANCE
(1983 LIGHT DUTY: UNDER 8,500 LB. GVWR)

Every 7,500 miles	• Change engine oil[1] • Check brake system and hoses
Every 15,000 miles	• Change oil filter • Check drive belt tension and condition • Replace spark plugs (without catalytic converter) • Lubricate transmission linkage pivot pin area
Every 12 months	• Check coolant condition and cooling system operation
Every 22,500 miles	• Lubricate drive shaft U-joint and slip splines[1] • Lubricate wheel stops[2] • Inspect front wheel bearings
Every 22,500 miles or 12 months	• Lubricate clutch linkage bellcrank • Lubricate steering linkage • Lubricate front suspension ball-joints[3] • Lubricate manual transmission gearshift control
Every 30,000 miles	• Apply solvent to carburetor choke shaft • Replace carburetor air filter (6-cylinder only) • Replace spark plugs (with catalytic converter)
Every 30,000 miles or 12 months	• Apply solvent to fast idle cam and pivot pin
Every 37,500 miles	• Drain and refill automatic transmission fluid[4]
Every 37,500 miles or 2 years	• Drain and refill manual transmission[5]
At first 3 years or 48,000 miles,then every 2 years or 30,000 miles	• Drain, flush and refill cooling system

1. Every 3 months or 3,000 miles for severe service.
2. Lubricate daily if vehicle is used in water.
3. Regrease @ every oil change if used for off-road operation.
4. Every 12,000 miles for severe service.
5. Every 18,000 miles for severe service.

Table 4 SCHEDULED MAINTENANCE
(1983 HEAVY DUTY: MORE THAN 8,500 GVWR)

Every 6,000 miles	• Change engine oil[1] • Check brake system and hoses
Every 12,000 miles	• Change engine oil filter • Clean air cleaner • Check EGR operation • Check PCV valve operation • Lubricate transmission linkage pivot pin areas
Every 12,000 miles or 12 months	• Apply solvent to carburetor choke shaft • Clean crankcase inlet air cleaner • Apply solvent to fast idle cam and pivot pin • Lubricate brake booster bellcrank pivot
Every 12 months	• Check cooling system operation and coolant condition

(continued)

12

Table 4 SCHEDULED MAINTENANCE
(1983 HEAVY DUTY: MORE THAN 8,500 GVWR) (continued)

Every 18,000 miles	• Check and adjust choke
	• Check drive belt condition and tension
	• Replace fuel filter
	• Check and adjust carburetor and ignition timing
	• Check ignition cables
	• Apply solvent to manifold heat control valve
	• Replace spark plugs
	• Inspect emission hoses
Every 24,000 miles	• Replace air cleaner element
	• Replace PCV valve
	• Drain and refill automatic transmission[2]
	• Lubricate wheel stops[3]
	• Inspect front wheel bearings
Every 24,000 miles or 2 years	• Lubricate steering linkage
	• Lubricate drive shaft slip spline[1]
	• Lubricate front suspension ball-joints[4]
	• Drain and refill manual transmission[5]
Every 36,000 miles	• Drain and refill manual transmission
Every 48,000 miles	• Lubricate rear wheel bearings (full floating axle)
At first 3 years or 48,000 miles, then every 2 years or 30,000 miles	• Drain, flush and refill cooling system

1. Every 3 months or 3,000 miles for severe service.
2. Every 19,000 miles for severe service.
3. Lubricate daily if used in water.
4. Regrease @ every oil change if used for off-road operation.
5. Every 18,000 miles for severe service.

Table 5 TUNE-UP SPECIFICATIONS (1982 MODELS)

Engine Cyl./Carb.	CID/Duty/ Usage (1)	Trans- mission (2)	Basic Timing (° BTDC) (3)	Curb Idle Speed (rpm)	Propane Enriched Idle Speed (rpm)
6/1 bbl	225/LD/Fed	M	12	600	675
6/1 bbl	225/LD/Cal	M	12	800	900
6/1 bbl	225/LD/Can	M	12	725	825
6/1 bbl	225/LD/Fed	A	16	600	675
6/1 bbl	225/LD/Cal	A	16	800	900
6/1 bbl	225/LD/Can	A	16	750	850
6/1 bbl	225/HD/Can	M	12	725	825
6/1 bbl	225/HD/Can	A	16	750	850
8/2 bbl	318/LD/Fed	M-A	12	750	850
8/2 bbl	318/LD/Can	M-A	12	750	850

(continued)

Table 5 TUNE-UP SPECIFICATIONS (1982 MODELS) (continued)

Engine Cyl./Carb.	CID/Duty/ Usage (1)	Trans- mission (2)	Basic Timing (° BTDC) (3)	Curb Idle Speed (rpm)	Propane Enriched Idle Speed (rpm)
8/2 bbl	318/HD/Can	A	2 ATDC	750	820
8/4 bbl	318/LD/Cal	M	12	750	840
8/4 bbl	318/LD/Fed	A	16	750	840
8/4 bbl	318/LD/Cal	A	16	750	840
8/4 bbl	318/HD/Fed	M-A	8	750	810
8/4 bbl	318/HD/Cal	M-A	8	750	810
8/2 bbl	360/HD/Can	A	4	750	810
8/4 bbl	360/HD/Fed	A	4	700	800
8/4 bbl	360/HD/Can	A	4	700	800
8/4 bbl	360/HD/Cal	A	10	750	800

1. LD=Light duty; HD=Heavy duty.
2. M=Manual; A=Automatic.
3. Basic ignition timing ±2°.

Table 6 TUNE-UP SPECIFICATIONS (1983)

Engine Cyl/Carb.	CID/Duty/ Usage[1]	Trans- mission[2]	Propane Basic Timing (°BTDC)[3]	Curb Idle Speed (rpm)	Enriched Idle Speed (rpm)
With Electronic Spark Advance					
6/1 bbl.	225/LD/Fed	M	12	600	675
6/1 bbl.	225/LD/Cal	M	12	750	850
6/1 bbl.	225/LD/Can	M	12	725	825
6/1 bbl.	225/LD/Fed	A	16	650	725
6/1 bbl.	225/LD/Cal	A	16	750	850
6/1 bbl.	225/LD/Can	A	16	750	850
6/1 bbl.	225/HD/Can	M	12	725	825
6/1 bbl.	225/HD/Can	A	16	750	850
8/2 bbl.	318/LD/Fed	M, A	16	700	800
8/2 bbl.	318/LD/Cal	M	16	700	825
8/2 bbl.	318/LD/Cal	A	16	700	760
With Electronic Control Unit					
8/2 bbl.	318/LD/Fed	M, A	12	750	850
8/2 bbl.	318/LD/Can	M, A	12	750	850
8/2 bbl.	318/HD/Can	A	2 ATDC	750	820
8/4 bbl.	318/LD/Fed	A	12	750	840
8/4 bbl.	318/LD/Cal	M	12	750	840
8/4 bbl.	318/HD/Fed	M, A	8	750	810
8/4 bbl.	318/HD/Cal	M, A	8	750	810
8/2 bbl.	360/HD/Can	M	4	750	790
8/2 bbl.	360/HD/Can	A	4	750	810
8/4 bbl.	360/HD/Fed	A	4	700	800
8/4 bbl.	360/HD/Can	A	4	700	800
8/4 bbl.	360/HD/Cal	A	10	750	800

1. LD = light duty; HD = heavy duty.
2. M = manual; A = automatic.
3. Basic ignition timing ±2°.

12

Table 7 SPARK PLUGS

Engine	Spark Plug*	Size	Reach	Gap	Gasket	Torque
225-1	560 PR	14 mm	0.460 in.	0.035 in.	No	10 ft.-lb.
318-1	64 PR	14 mm	3/4 in.	0.035 in.	Yes	30 ft.-lb.
360-1	65 PR	14 mm	3/4 in.	0.035 in.	Yes	30 ft.-lb.

* Mopar or equivalent.

CHAPTER FOUR

ENGINE

Engine availability remains the same as for earlier models: however, some specifications and tightening torques have been changed. These are provided in **Table 8** and **Table 9**.

Table 8 ENGINE SPECIFICATIONS

225 CID 6	
Crankshaft main bearing clearance	
Desired	0.0010-0.0025 in.
Connecting rod bearing clearance	
Desired	0.0010-0.0022 in.
Piston ring side clearance	
Compression rings	0.0015-0.0040 in.
Valve face angle	44.5-45°
318 CID V-8	
Piston pins	
Clearance in piston	0.0000-0.0005 in.
Piston ring side clearance	
Compression rings	0.0015-0.0040 in.
Oil rings	0.0002-0.005 in.
360 CID V8	
Piston ring side clearance	
Compression rings	0.0015-0.0040 in.
Oil rings	0.0002-0.005 in.

Table 9 TIGHTENING TORQUES

225 CID 6	
Connecting rod nut	50 ft.-lb.
Crankshaft rear bearing seal retainer	45 ft.-lb.
Cylinder head cover (with load spread washers)	80 in.-lb.
Engine front mount insulator to frame/engine nut	75 ft.-lb.
Oil pump cover bolt	130 in.-lb.
318/360 CID V8	
Cylinder head bolt	105 ft.-lb.
Cylinder head cover (with load spread washers)	80 in.-lb.
Engine front mount insulator to frame/engine nut	75 ft.-lb.

CHAPTER FIVE

FUEL AND EXHAUST SYSTEMS

CARBURETORS

A Holley 6145 feedback carburetor is used with 1983 225 cid 6-cylinder engines first sold in California. The Model 6145 is similar to the Model 1945, but contains a fuel regulator solenoid which varies the air-fuel ratio according to directions from the Electronic Fuel Control Computer.

The idle mixture screw on Model 6145 carburetors is covered by a sealed plug in accordance with Federal regulations. Tampering with the plug/mixture screw is a violation of Federal law. If an idle mixture problem seems apparent, return the vehicle to your dealer.

The idle speed can be checked, but idle speed may vary from the set speed due to the electronic control of the air-fuel mixture. It is best to have idle speed adjustments made by a dealer, who has the specialized equipment and trained technicians to determine if the feedback system is operating properly.

FUEL PUMP CHECKS

Fuel pump pressure specifications are changed for 1982 and later models. The reading should be 3-4.5 psi for 6-cylinder engines or 4.75-6.25 psi for V8 engines.

12

CHAPTER SIX

EMISSION CONTROL SYSTEMS

A vacuum actuator has been added to the manifold heat control valve to provide more precise control over the flow of hot exhaust gases to the mini-converter. To test the valve's operation, disconnect the vacuum line at the actuator diaphragm and connect a hand vacuum pump. Apply 6 in. Hg vacuum to the valve. If the valve is not fully closed, replace it.

Dual aspirator valves are used on some 1982 and later 318 cid V8 engines.

CHAPTER EIGHT

ELECTRICAL SYSTEM

A sealed maintenance-free battery is standard with all 1983 models.

A heavy duty 1.8 HP starter motor is used with all 1983 engines. Service procedures remain unchanged from those provided in Chapter Eight of the main book.

INDEX

13

13

1971
PART I

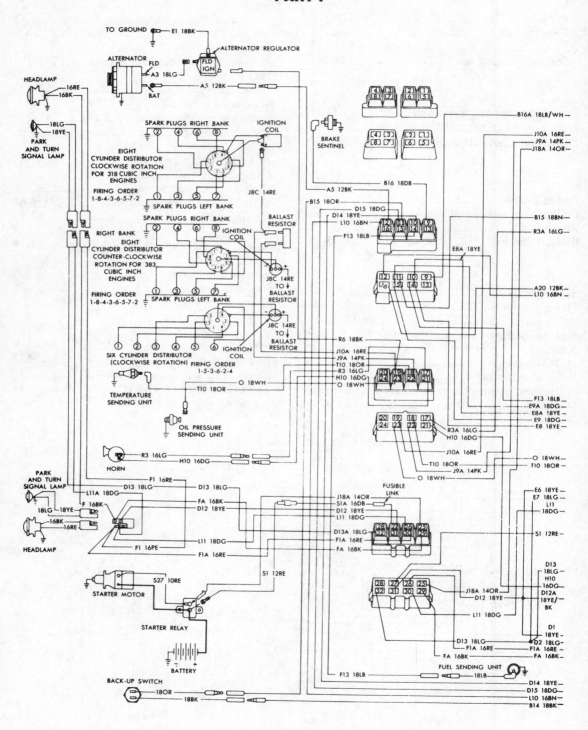

1971
PART II

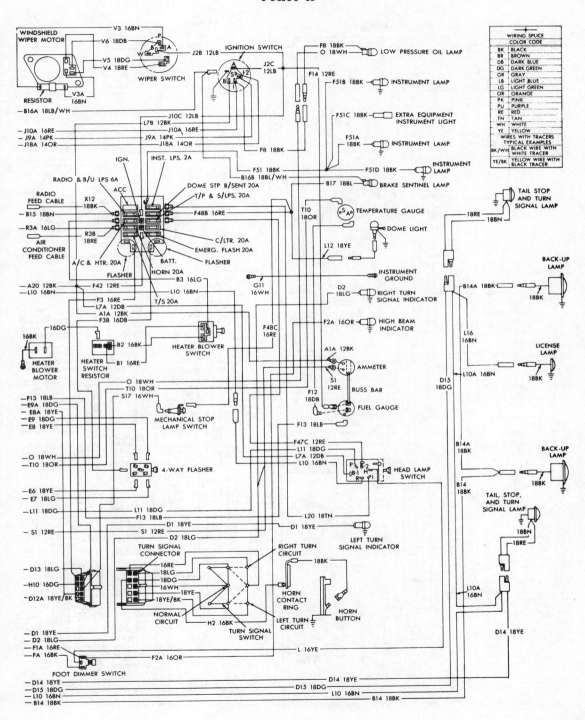

1972
PART I

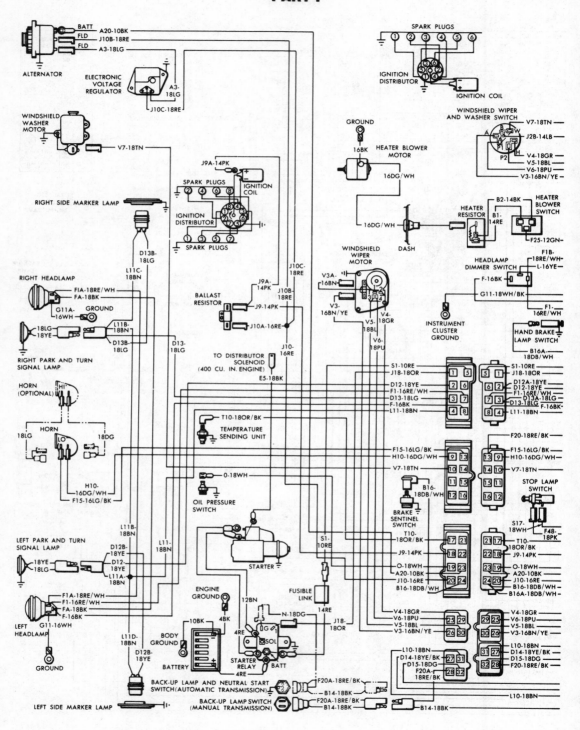

1972
PART II

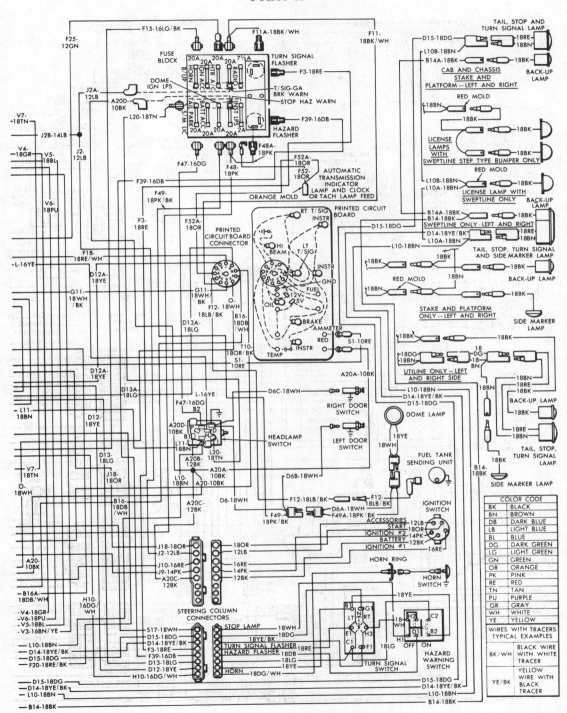

1973
PART I

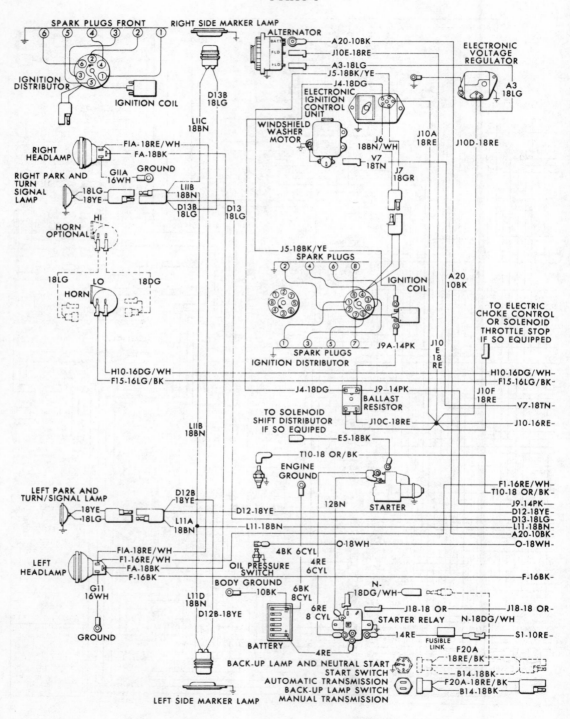

1973
PART II

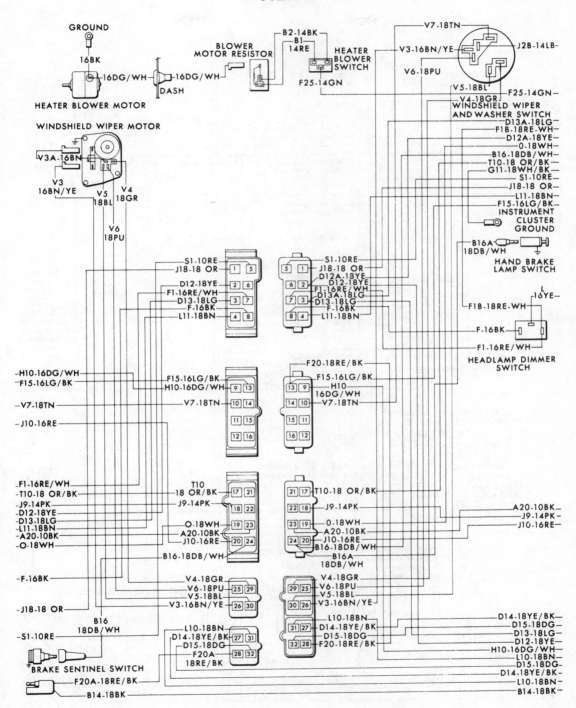

1973
PART III

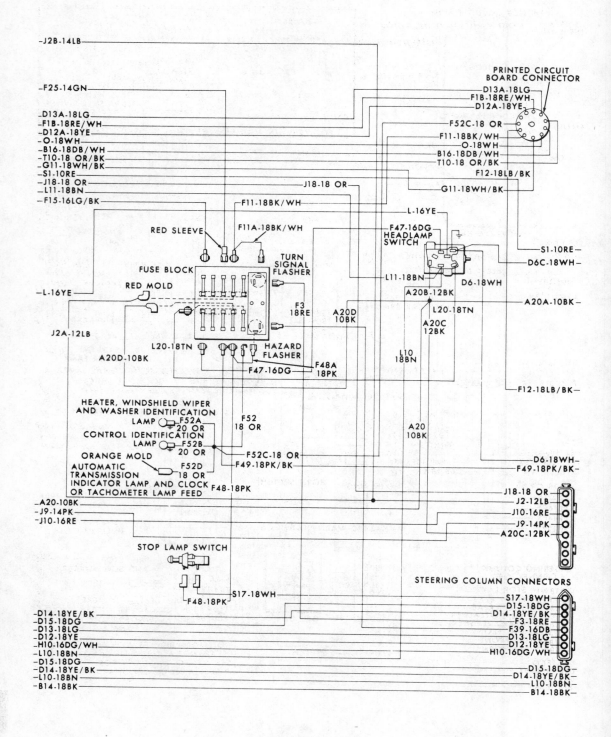

1973
PART IV

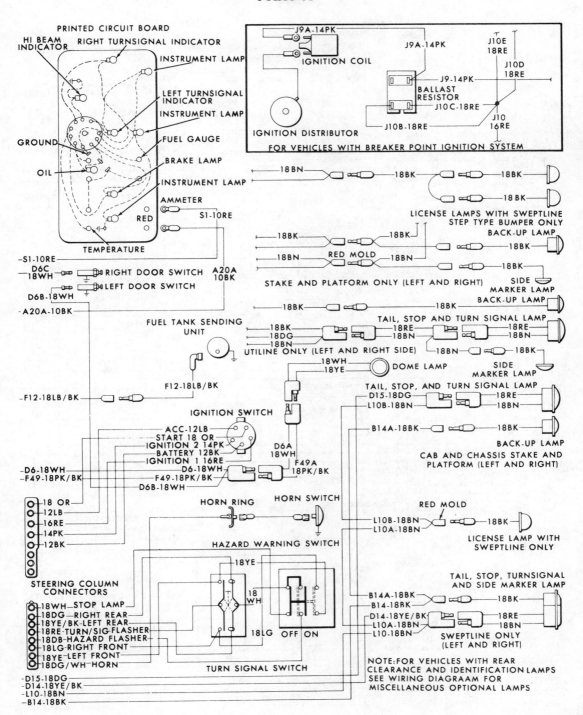

PRINTED CIRCUIT BOARD

HI BEAM INDICATOR
RIGHT TURNSIGNAL INDICATOR
INSTRUMENT LAMP
LEFT TURNSIGNAL INDICATOR
INSTRUMENT LAMP
GROUND
FUEL GAUGE
OIL
BRAKE LAMP
INSTRUMENT LAMP
AMMETER
RED
S1-10RE
TEMPERATURE

IGNITION COIL
J9A-14PK
J9A-14PK
J10E 18RE
J10D 18RE
J9-14PK
BALLAST RESISTOR
J10C-18RE
J10B-18RE
J10 16RE
IGNITION DISTRIBUTOR
FOR VEHICLES WITH BREAKER POINT IGNITION SYSTEM

-S1-10RE
D6C 18WH — RIGHT DOOR SWITCH — A20A 10BK
D6B-18WH — LEFT DOOR SWITCH
-A20A-10BK

FUEL TANK SENDING UNIT

-F12-18LB/BK

IGNITION SWITCH
ACC-12LB
START 18 OR
IGNITION 2 14PK
BATTERY 12BK
IGNITION 1 16RE
D6-18WH
-D6-18WH
-F49-18PK/BK
F49-18PK/BK
-D6B-18WH
D6A 18WH
F49A 18PK/BK

18 OR
12LB
16RE
14PK
12BK

STEERING COLUMN CONNECTORS

HORN RING
HORN SWITCH

HAZARD WARNING SWITCH

-18WH—STOP LAMP
-18DG—RIGHT REAR
-18YE/BK—LEFT REAR
-18RE—TURN/SIG FLASHER
-18DB—HAZARD FLASHER
-18LG—RIGHT FRONT
-18YE—LEFT FRONT
-18DG/WH—HORN
-D15-18DG
-D14-18YE/BK
-L10-18BN
-B14-18BK

18YE
18
WH
18LG
OFF ON

TURN SIGNAL SWITCH

18BN
18BK
18BK
18BK
18BK
LICENSE LAMPS WITH SWEPTLINE STEP TYPE BUMPER ONLY
BACK-UP LAMP

18BK
18BK
18BN
RED MOLD
18BN
18BK
STAKE AND PLATFORM ONLY (LEFT AND RIGHT)
SIDE MARKER LAMP
BACK-UP LAMP

18BK
18BK
TAIL, STOP AND TURN SIGNAL LAMP
18BK
18RE
18RE
18DG
18BN
18BN
18BN
18BN
18BK
UTILINE ONLY (LEFT AND RIGHT SIDE)
SIDE MARKER LAMP

18WH
18YE
DOME LAMP

TAIL, STOP, AND TURN SIGNAL LAMP
D15-18DG
18RE
L10B-18BN
18BN
B14A-18BK
18BK
BACK-UP LAMP
CAB AND CHASSIS STAKE AND PLATFORM (LEFT AND RIGHT)

RED MOLD
L10B-18BN
L10A-18BN
18BK
LICENSE LAMP WITH SWEPTLINE ONLY

TAIL, STOP, TURNSIGNAL AND SIDE MARKER LAMP
B14A-18BK
18BK
B14-18BK
D14-18YE/BK
18RE
L10A-18BN
18BN
L10-18BN
SWEPTLINE ONLY (LEFT AND RIGHT)

NOTE: FOR VEHICLES WITH REAR CLEARANCE AND IDENTIFICATION LAMPS SEE WIRING DIAGRAAM FOR MISCELLANEOUS OPTIONAL LAMPS

14

1974
PART I

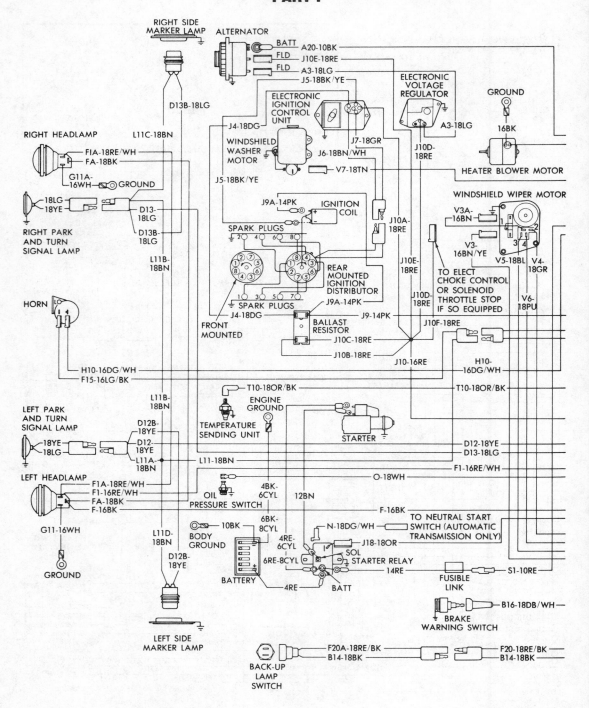

1974
PART II

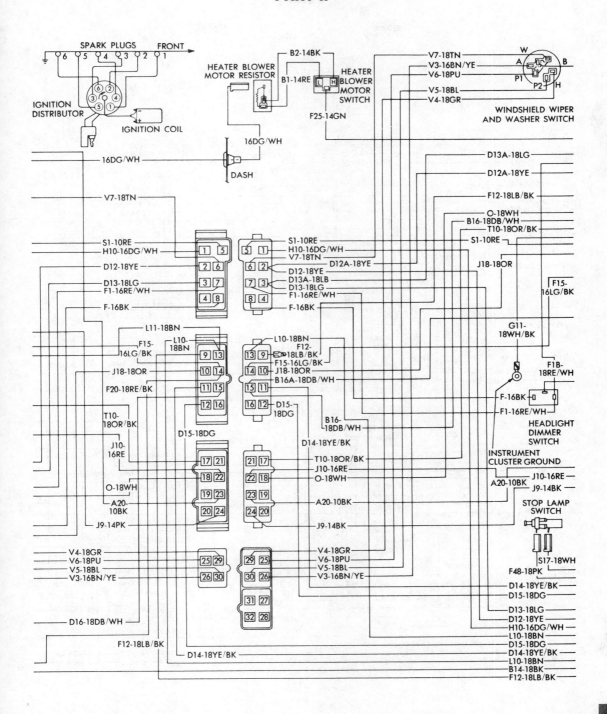

1974
PART III

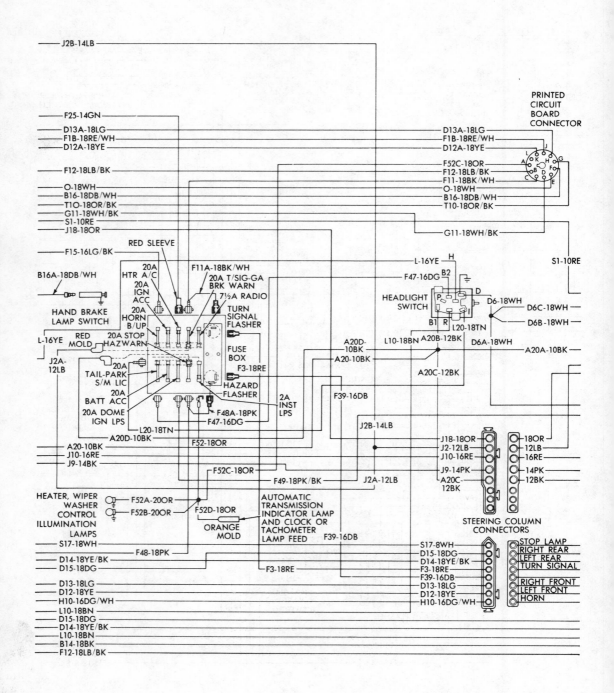

1974
PART IV

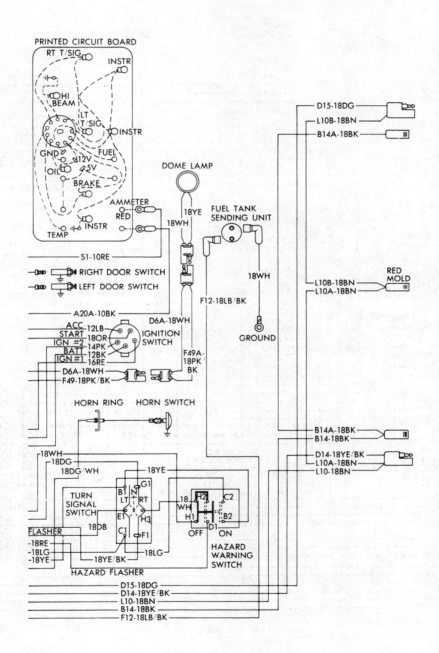

1974 AUXILIARY EQUIPMENT
PART I

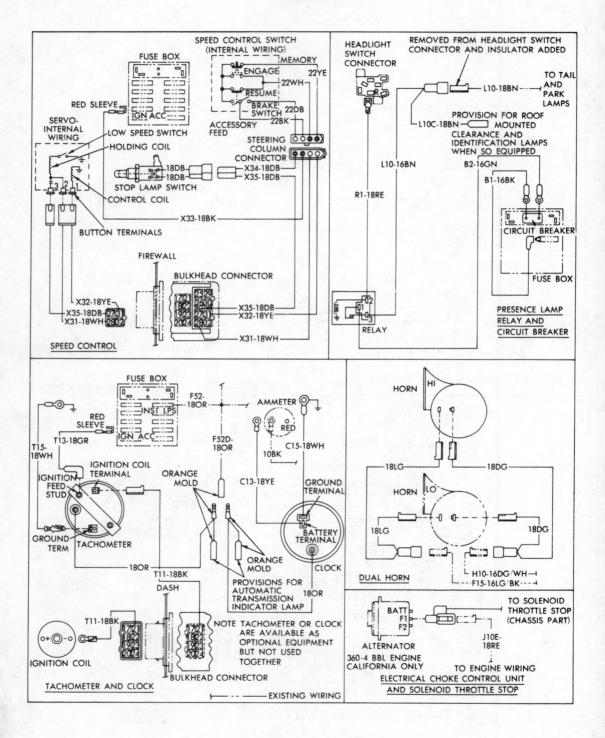

1974 AUXILIARY EQUIPMENT
PART II

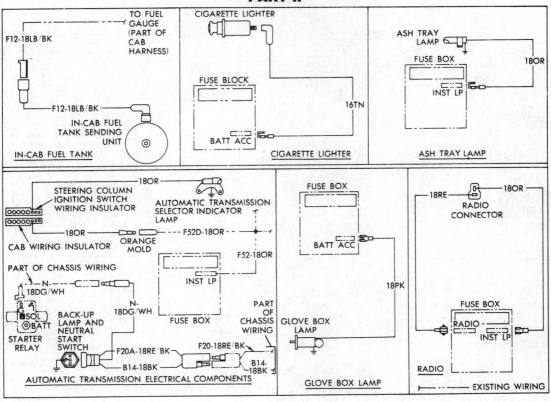

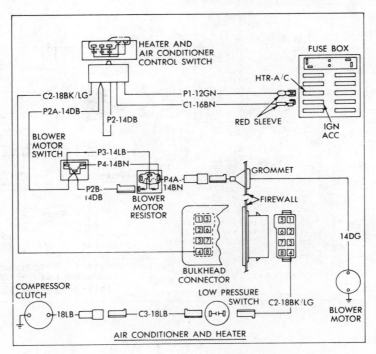

14

1975
PART I

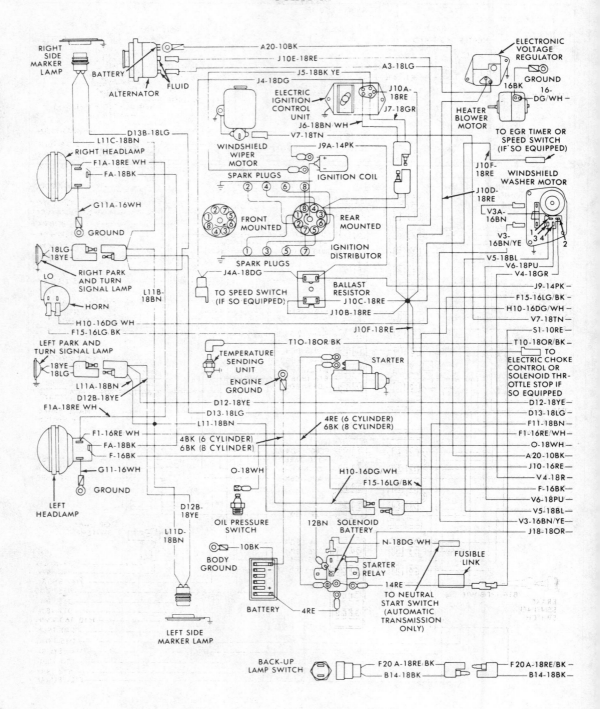

**1975
PART II**

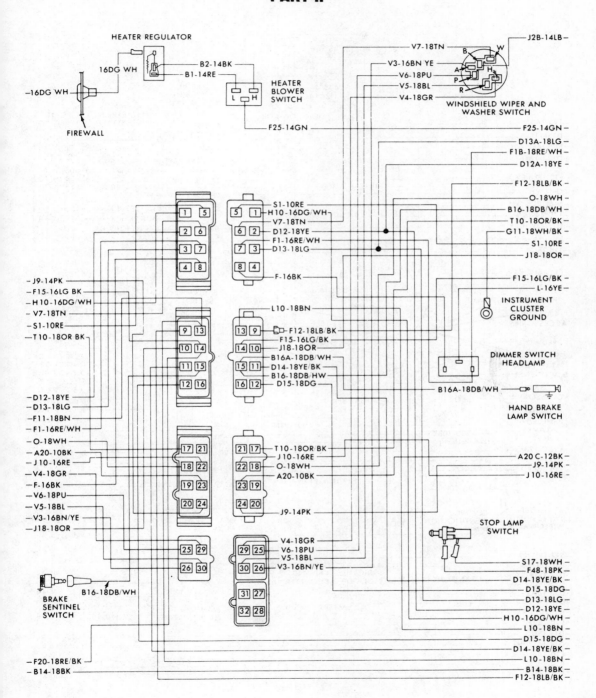

HEATER REGULATOR

16DG WH

B2-14BK
B1-14RE

—16DG WH

FIREWALL

HEATER
BLOWER
SWITCH

F25-14GN

V7-18TN
V3-16BN YE
V6-18PU
V5-18BL
V4-18GR

J2B-14LB —

WINDSHIELD WIPER AND
WASHER SWITCH

F25-14GN —
D13A-18LG —
F1B-18RE/WH —
D12A-18YE —
F12-18LB/BK —
O-18WH —
B16-18DB/WH —
T10-18OR/BK —
G11-18WH/BK —
S1-10RE —
J18-18OR —

S1-10RE
H10-16DG/WH
V7-18TN
D12-18YE
F1-16RE/WH
D13-18LG

F-16BK

F15-16LG/BK —
L-16YE —

INSTRUMENT
CLUSTER
GROUND

—J9-14PK
—F15-16LG BK
—H10-16DG/WH
—V7-18TN
—S1-10RE
—T10-18OR BK

L10-18BN

F12-18LB/BK
F15-16LG/BK
J18-18OR
B16A-18DB/WH
D14-18YE/BK
B16-18DB/HW
D15-18DG

DIMMER SWITCH
HEADLAMP

B16A-18DB/WH —

HAND BRAKE
LAMP SWITCH

—D12-18YE
—D13-18LG
—F11-18BN
—F1-16RE/WH
—O-18WH
—A20-10BK
—J10-16RE
—V4-18GR
—F-16BK
—V6-18PU
—V5-18BL
—V3-16BN/YE
—J18-18OR

T10-18OR/BK
J10-16RE
O-18WH
A20-10BK

J9-14PK

A20 C-12BK —
J9-14PK —
J10-16RE —

STOP LAMP
SWITCH

V4-18GR
V6-18PU
V5-18BL
V3-16BN/YE

S17-18WH —
F48-18PK —
D14-18YE/BK —
D15-18DG —
D13-18LG —
D12-18YE —
H10-16DG/WH —
L10-18BN —
D15-18DG —
D14-18YE/BK —
L10-18BN —
B14-18BK —
F12-18LB/BK —

BRAKE
SENTINEL
SWITCH

B16-18DB/WH

—F20-18RE/BK
—B14-18BK

14

1975
PART III

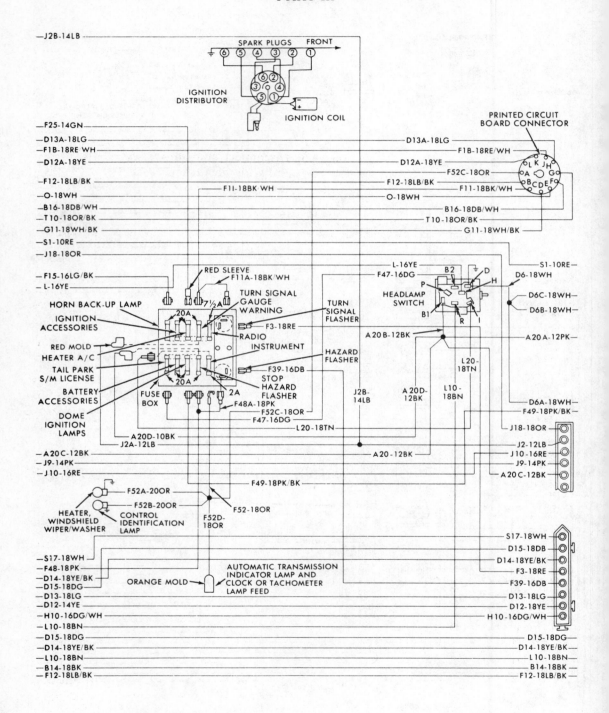

1975
PART IV

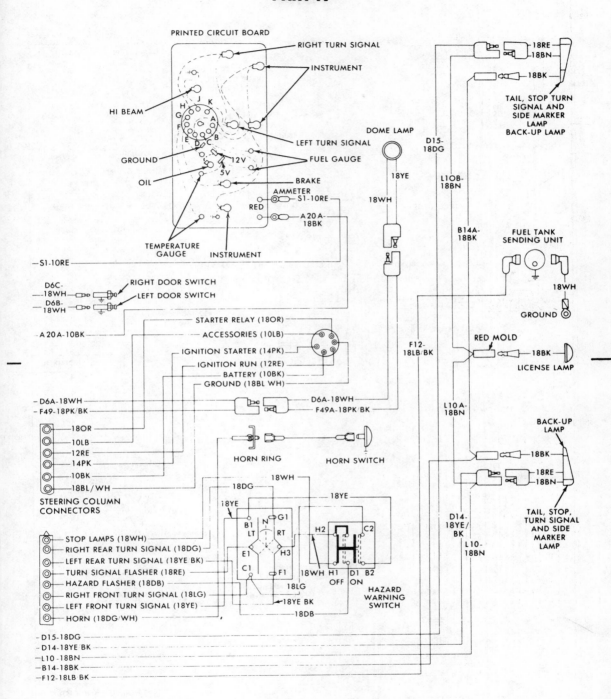

1975 AUXILIARY EQUIPMENT
PART I

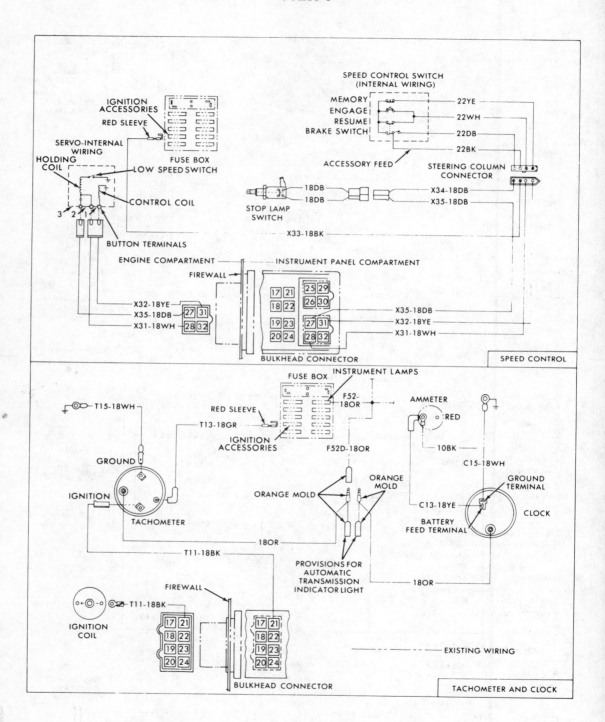

SPEED CONTROL SWITCH
(INTERNAL WIRING)

MEMORY — 22YE
ENGAGE — 22WH
RESUME — 22DB
BRAKE SWITCH — 22BK

ACCESSORY FEED

STEERING COLUMN
CONNECTOR

IGNITION
ACCESSORIES

RED SLEEVE

FUSE BOX

SERVO-INTERNAL
WIRING

HOLDING
COIL

LOW SPEED SWITCH

CONTROL COIL

3 2 1

BUTTON TERMINALS

STOP LAMP
SWITCH

18DB
18DB

X34-18DB
X35-18DB

X33-18BK

ENGINE COMPARTMENT — INSTRUMENT PANEL COMPARTMENT

FIREWALL

X32-18YE
X35-18DB
X31-18WH

17 21   25 29
18 22   26 30
27 31
19 23   27 31
28 32   28 32

X35-18DB
X32-18YE
X31-18WH

BULKHEAD CONNECTOR

SPEED CONTROL

FUSE BOX

INSTRUMENT LAMPS

F52-18OR

T15-18WH

RED SLEEVE

T13-18GR

IGNITION
ACCESSORIES

AMMETER

RED

10BK

GROUND

IGNITION

TACHOMETER

F52D-18OR

ORANGE MOLD

ORANGE
MOLD

C15-18WH

GROUND
TERMINAL

CLOCK

C13-18YE

BATTERY
FEED TERMINAL

18OR

T11-18BK

PROVISIONS FOR
AUTOMATIC
TRANSMISSION
INDICATOR LIGHT

18OR

FIREWALL

T11-18BK

IGNITION
COIL

17 21   17 21
18 22   18 22
19 23   19 23
20 24   20 24

EXISTING WIRING

BULKHEAD CONNECTOR

TACHOMETER AND CLOCK

1975 AUXILIARY EQUIPMENT
PART II

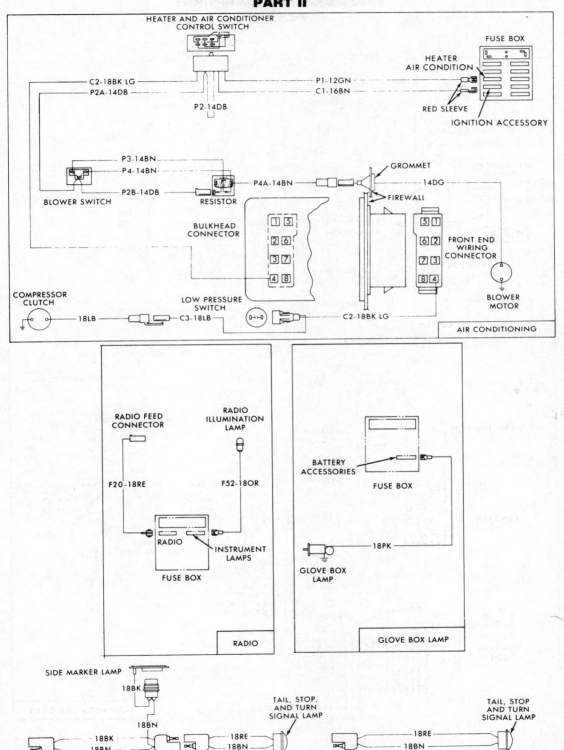

1975 AUXILIARY EQUIPMENT
PART III

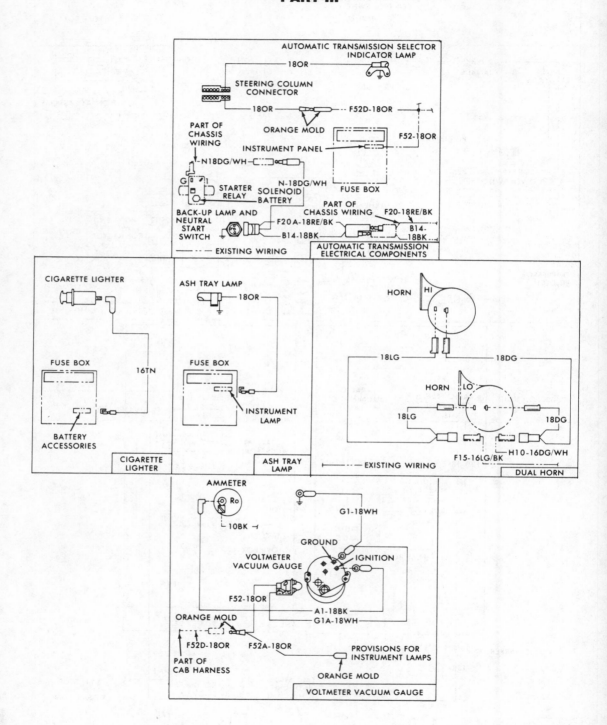

1975 AUXILIARY EQUIPMENT
PART IV

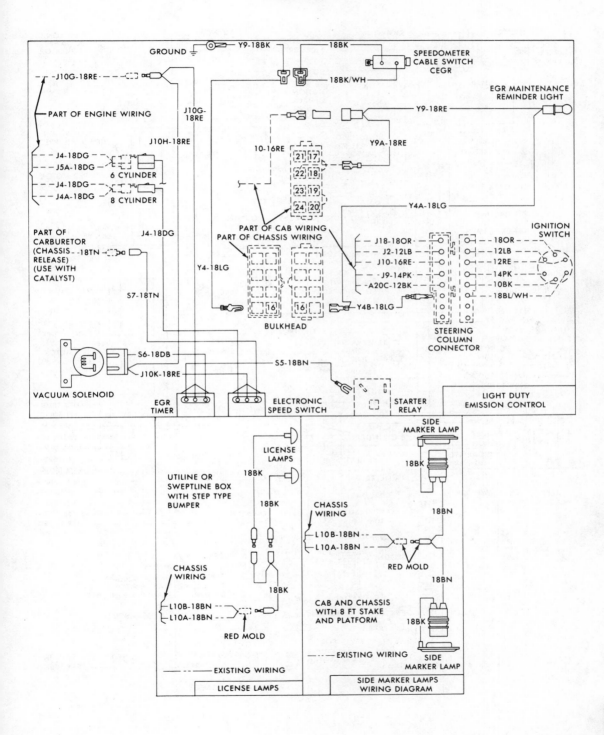

1976-1977, WITHOUT 100 AMP ALTERNATOR
PART I

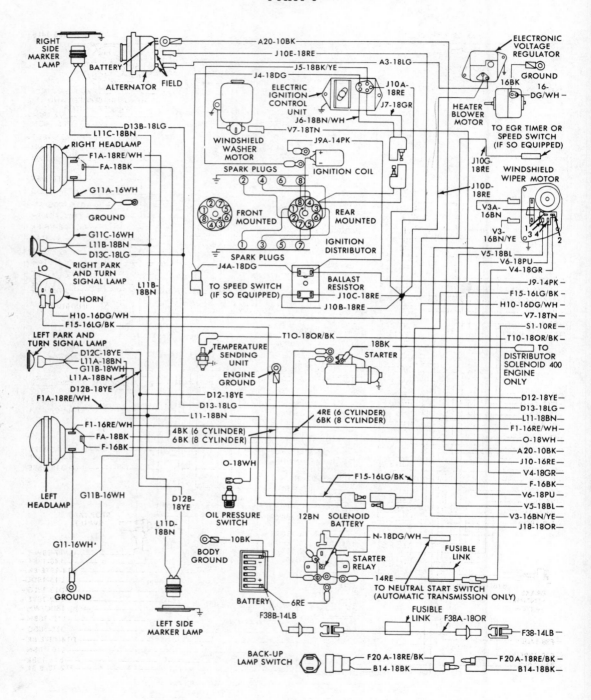

1976-1977, WITHOUT 100 AMP ALTERNATOR
PART II

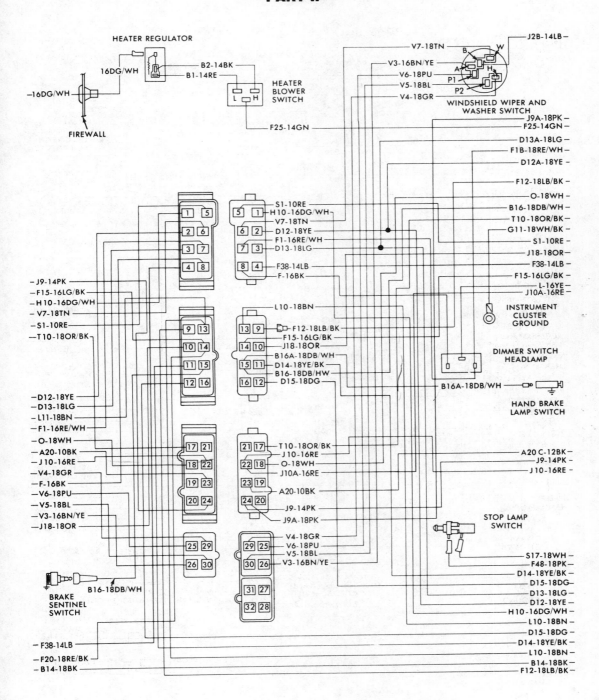

1976-1977, WITHOUT 100 AMP ALTERNATOR
PART III

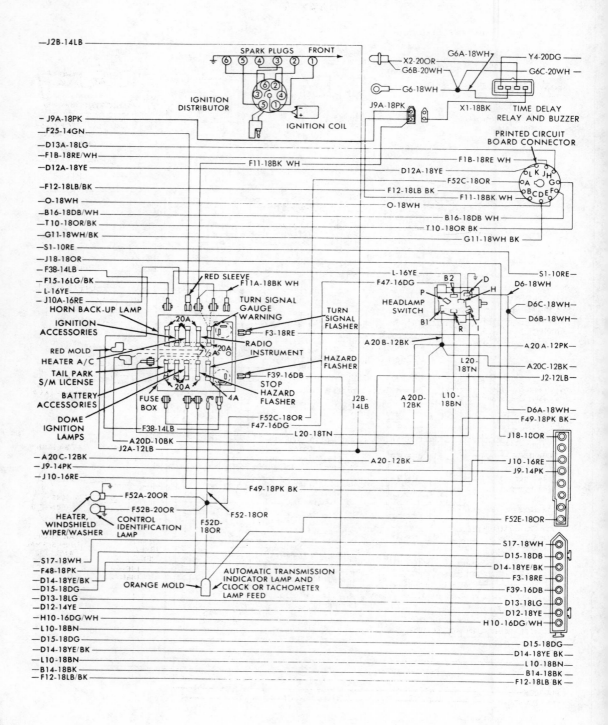

1976-1977, WITHOUT 100 AMP ALTERNATOR
PART IV

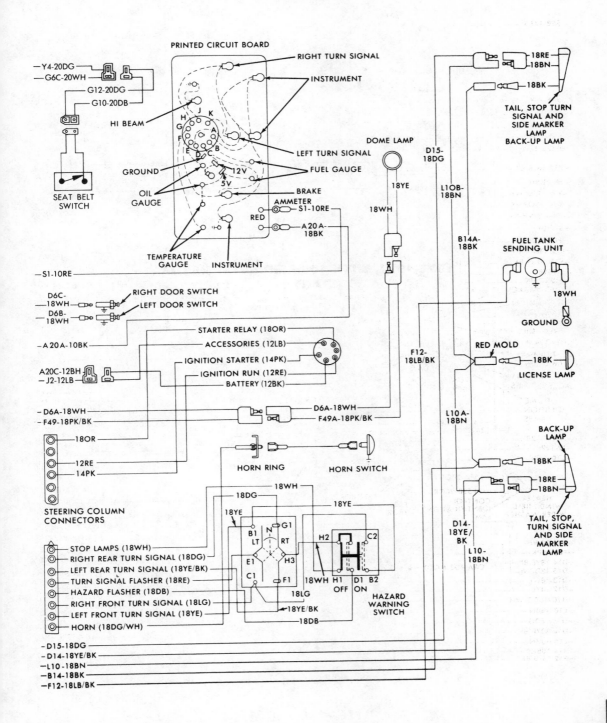

PRINTED CIRCUIT BOARD

RIGHT TURN SIGNAL

INSTRUMENT

Y4-20DG
G6C-20WH

G12-20DG

G10-20DB

HI BEAM

HI BEAM

LEFT TURN SIGNAL

GROUND

12V

5V

FUEL GAUGE

OIL GAUGE

BRAKE

SEAT BELT SWITCH

AMMETER
S1-10RE
A 20 A-18BK

RED

TEMPERATURE GAUGE

INSTRUMENT

S1-10RE

D6C-18WH
D6B-18WH

RIGHT DOOR SWITCH
LEFT DOOR SWITCH

A 20 A-10BK

STARTER RELAY (18OR)

ACCESSORIES (12LB)

A20C-12BH
J2-12LB

IGNITION STARTER (14PK)
IGNITION RUN (12RE)
BATTERY (12BK)

D6A-18WH
F49-18PK/BK

D6A-18WH
F49A-18PK/BK

18OR
12RE
14PK

HORN RING

HORN SWITCH

STEERING COLUMN CONNECTORS

STOP LAMPS (18WH)
RIGHT REAR TURN SIGNAL (18DG)
LEFT REAR TURN SIGNAL (18YE/BK)
TURN SIGNAL FLASHER (18RE)
HAZARD FLASHER (18DB)
RIGHT FRONT TURN SIGNAL (18LG)
LEFT FRONT TURN SIGNAL (18YE)
HORN (18DG/WH)

18WH
18DG
18YE

18YE

18WH

18YE

B1 N G1
LT   RT
E1   H3
C1   F1

H2   C2

H1   D1 B2
18WH   OFF ON

18LG
18YE/BK
18DB

HAZARD WARNING SWITCH

D15-18DG
D14-18YE/BK
L10-18BN
B14-18BK
F12-18LB/BK

DOME LAMP

18YE

18WH

D15-18DG

L10B-18BN

B14A-18BK

F12-18LB/BK

18RE
18BN

18BK

TAIL, STOP TURN SIGNAL AND SIDE MARKER LAMP
BACK-UP LAMP

FUEL TANK SENDING UNIT

18WH

GROUND

RED MOLD

18BK

LICENSE LAMP

L10A-18BN

BACK-UP LAMP

18BK

18RE
18BN

D14-18YE/BK

L10-18BN

TAIL, STOP, TURN SIGNAL AND SIDE MARKER LAMP

1976-1977, WITHOUT 100 AMP ALTERNATOR
PART V

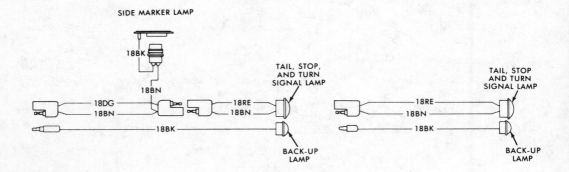

1976-1977, WITH 100 AMP ALTERNATOR
PART I

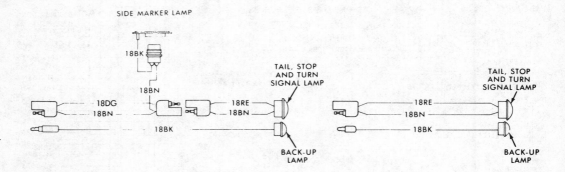

1976-1977, WITH 100 AMP ALTERNATOR
PART II

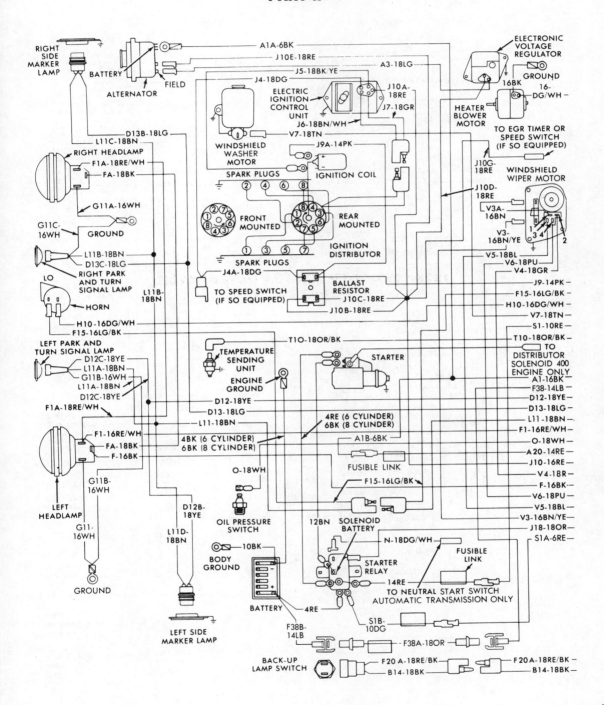

1976-1977, WITH 100 AMP ALTERNATOR
PART III

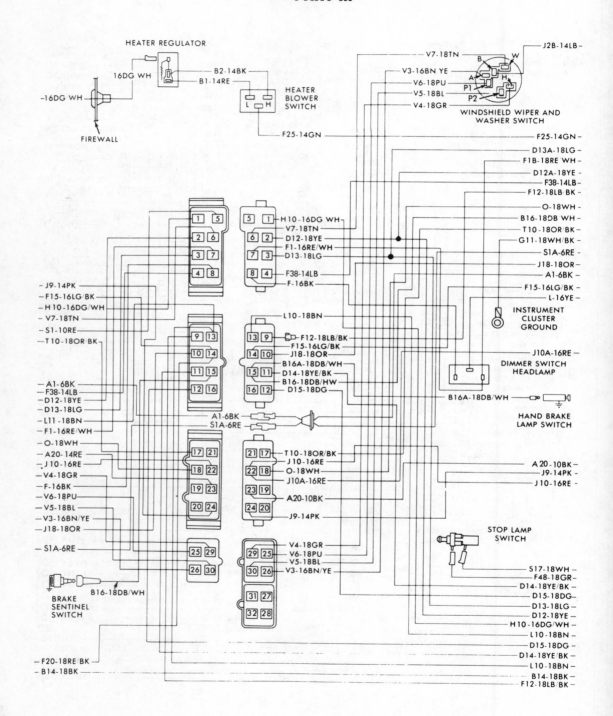

1976-1977, WITH 100 AMP ALTERNATOR
PART IV

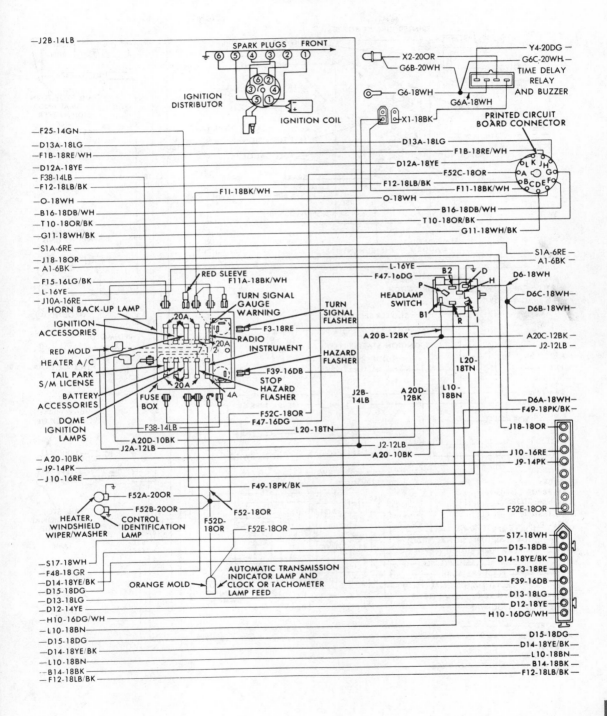

1976-1977, WITH 100 AMP ALTERNATOR
PART V

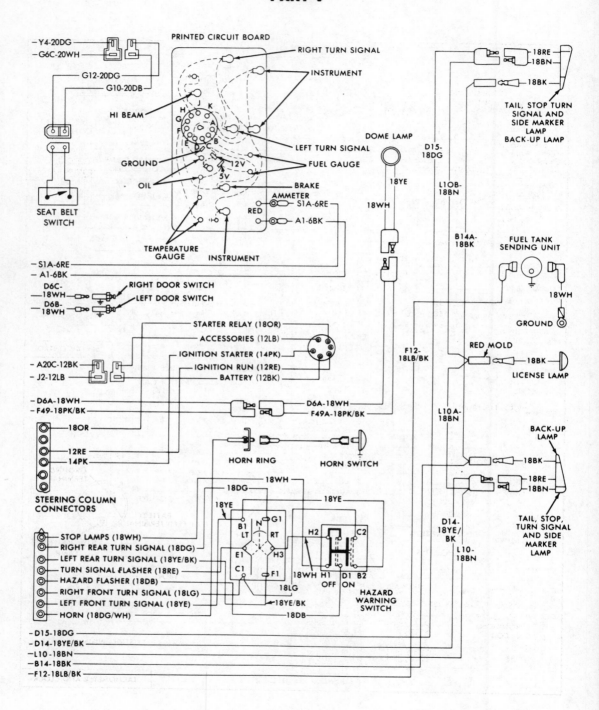

1976-1977 AUXILIARY EQUIPMENT
PART I

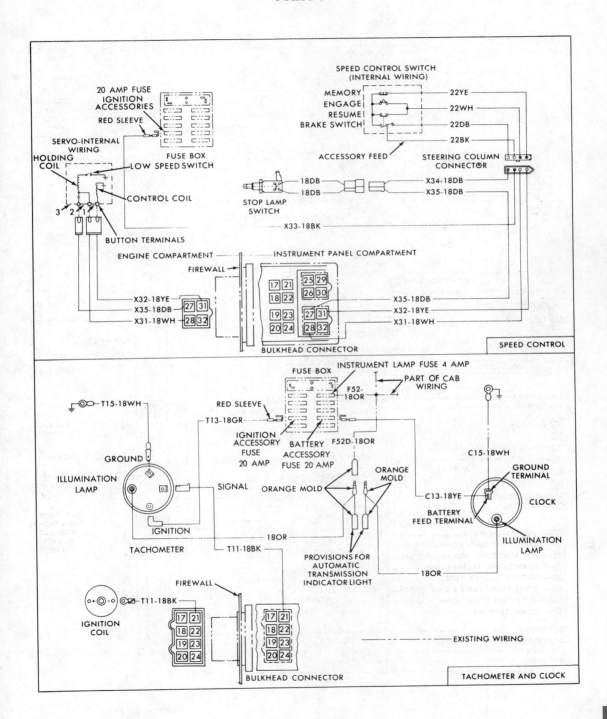

1976-1977 AUXILIARY EQUIPMENT
PART II

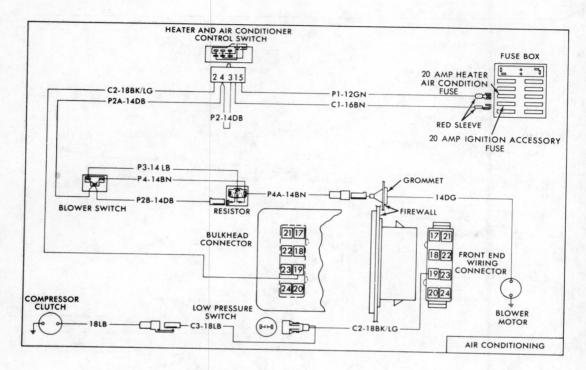

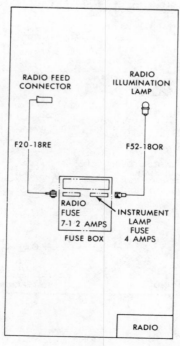

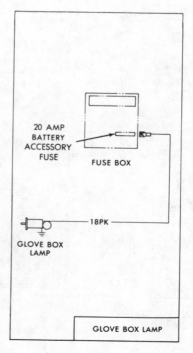

1976-1977 AUXILIARY EQUIPMENT
PART III

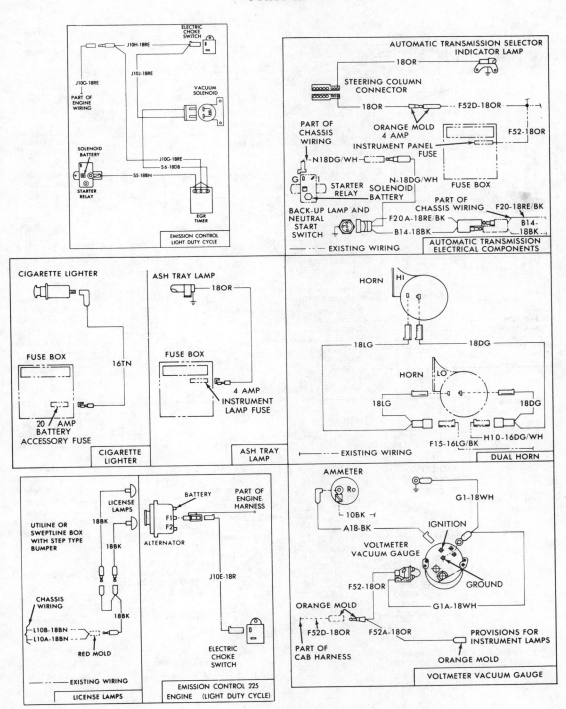

1978, WITHOUT 100 AMP ALTERNATOR
PART I

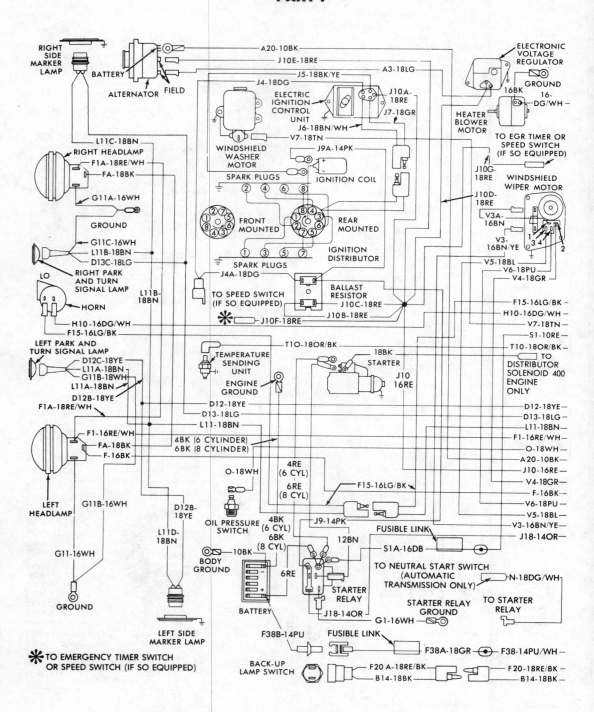

1978, WITHOUT 100 AMP ALTERNATOR
PART II

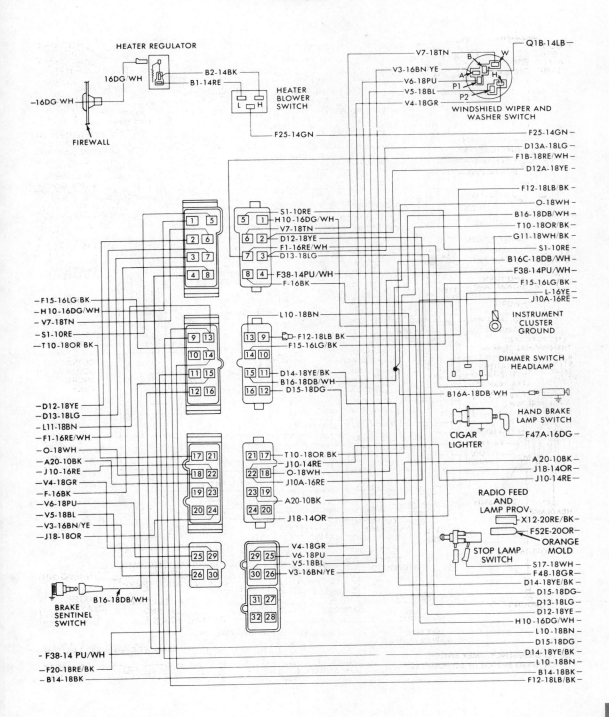

1978, WITHOUT 100 AMP ALTERNATOR
PART III

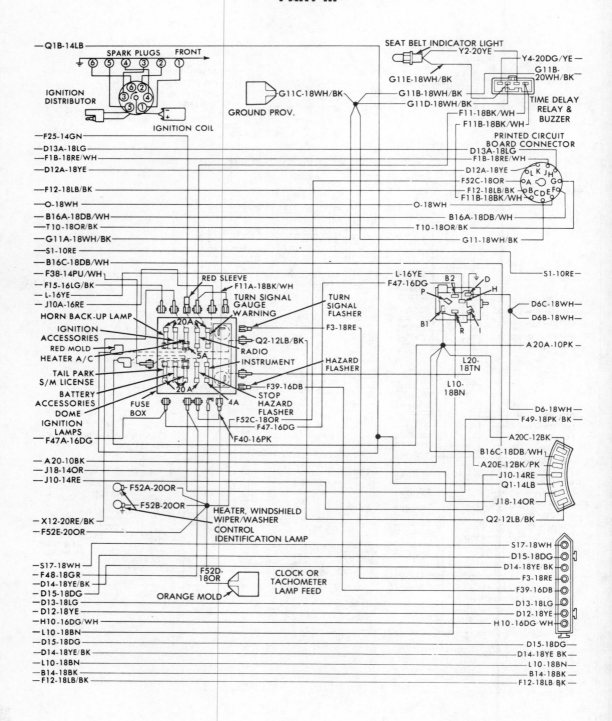

1978, WITHOUT 100 AMP ALTERNATOR
PART IV

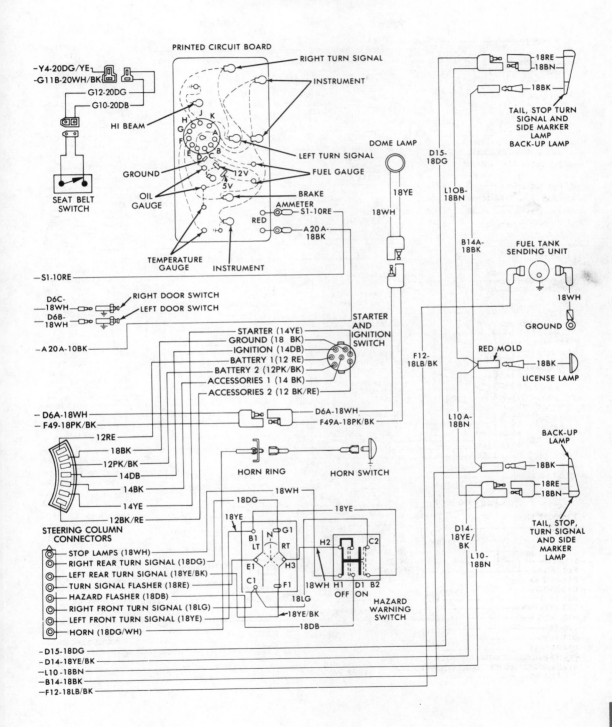

PRINTED CIRCUIT BOARD

RIGHT TURN SIGNAL

INSTRUMENT

–Y4-20DG/YE
-G11B-20WH/BK
G12-20DG
G10-20DB
HI BEAM

HI J K
G
F
E D C B
A

GROUND
OIL GAUGE
12V
5V

SEAT BELT SWITCH

TEMPERATURE GAUGE
INSTRUMENT

LEFT TURN SIGNAL
FUEL GAUGE

BRAKE
AMMETER
–S1-10RE
RED
A20A-18BK

–S1-10RE

DOME LAMP
18YE
18WH

TAIL, STOP TURN SIGNAL AND SIDE MARKER LAMP BACK-UP LAMP

18RE
18BN
18BK

D15-18DG

L10B-18BN

B14A-18BK

FUEL TANK SENDING UNIT

18WH

GROUND

D6C-18WH
D6B-18WH

RIGHT DOOR SWITCH
LEFT DOOR SWITCH

–A20A-10BK

STARTER (14YE)
GROUND (18 BK)
IGNITION (14DB)
BATTERY 1 (12 RE)
BATTERY 2 (12PK/BK)
ACCESSORIES 1 (14 BK)
ACCESSORIES 2 (12 BK/RE)

STARTER AND IGNITION SWITCH

F12-18LB/BK

RED MOLD

18BK

LICENSE LAMP

–D6A-18WH
–F49-18PK/BK

D6A-18WH
F49-18PK/BK

–12RE
–18BK
–12PK/BK
–14DB
–14BK
–14YE
–12BK/RE

STEERING COLUMN CONNECTORS

HORN RING
HORN SWITCH

18WH
18DG
18YE
18YE

L10A-18BN

BACK-UP LAMP

18BK

18RE
18BN

–Stop Lamps (18WH)
–Right Rear Turn Signal (18DG)
–Left Rear Turn Signal (18YE/BK)
–Turn Signal Flasher (18RE)
–Hazard Flasher (18DB)
–Right Front Turn Signal (18LG)
–Left Front Turn Signal (18YE)
–Horn (18DG/WH)

B1 N G1
LT RT
E1 H3
C1 F1

H2 C2

18WH H1 D1 B2
OFF ON

18LG
18YE/BK
18DB

HAZARD WARNING SWITCH

D14-18YE/BK
L10-18BN

TAIL, STOP, TURN SIGNAL AND SIDE MARKER LAMP

–D15-18DG
–D14-18YE/BK
–L10-18BN
–B14-18BK
–F12-18LB/BK

14

1978, WITH 100 AMP ALTERNATOR
PART I

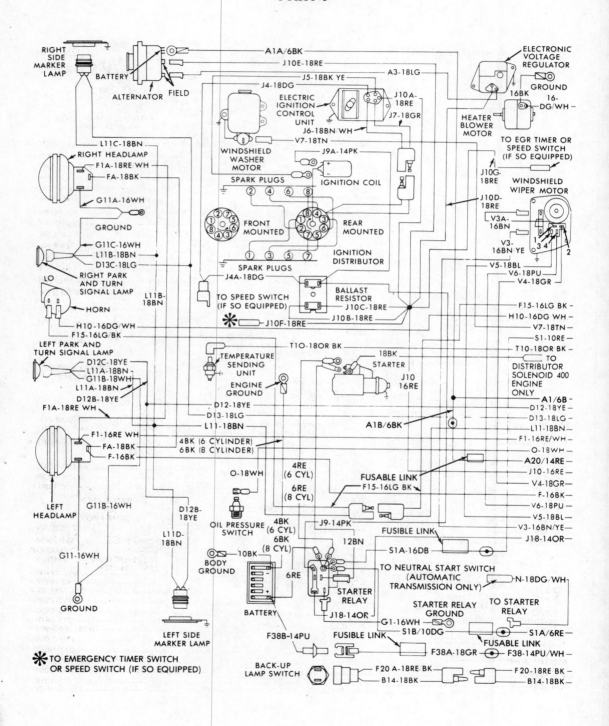

1978, WITH 100 AMP ALTERNATOR
PART II

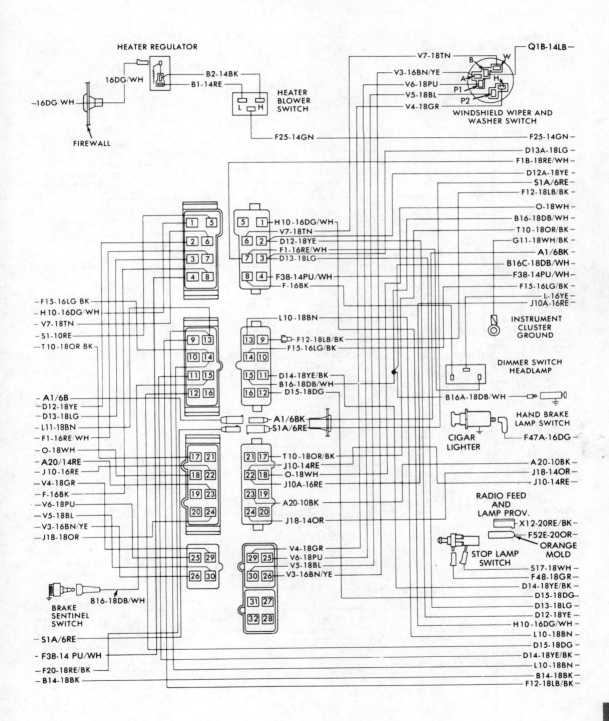

14

1978, WITH 100 AMP ALTERNATOR
PART III

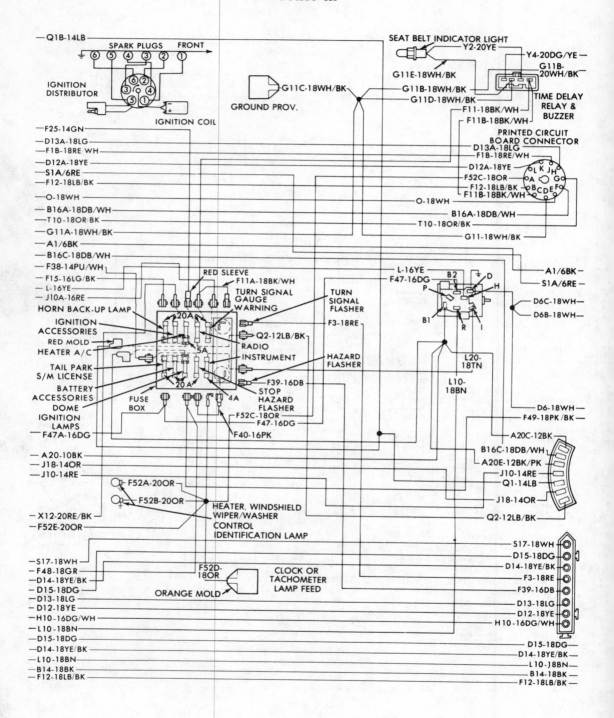

1978, WITH 100 AMP ALTERNATOR
PART IV

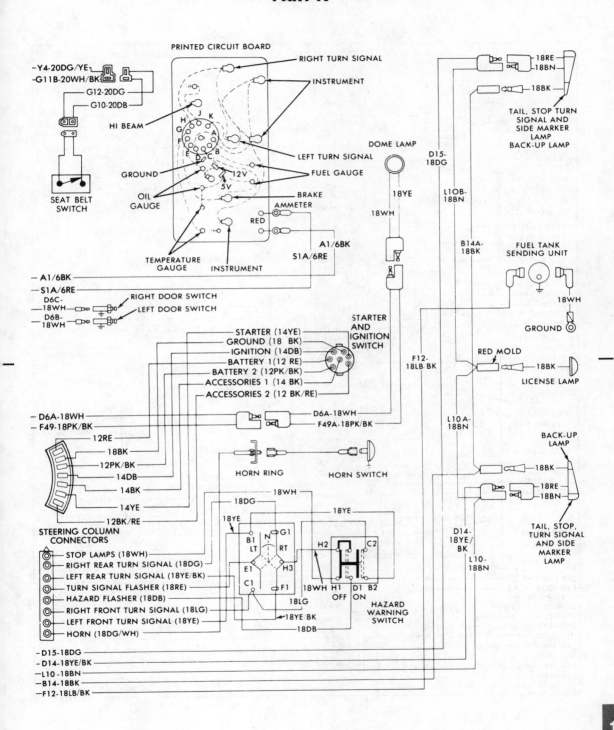

1978 AUXILIARY EQUIPMENT
PART I

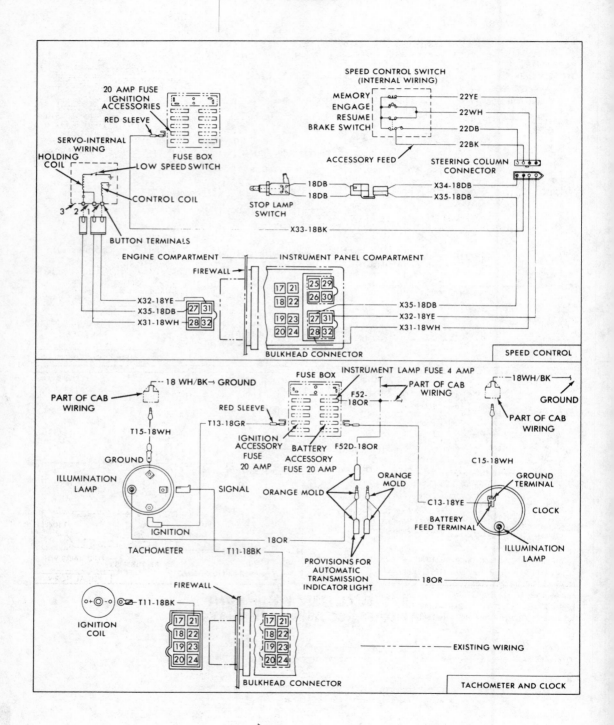

1978 AUXILIARY EQUIPMENT
PART II

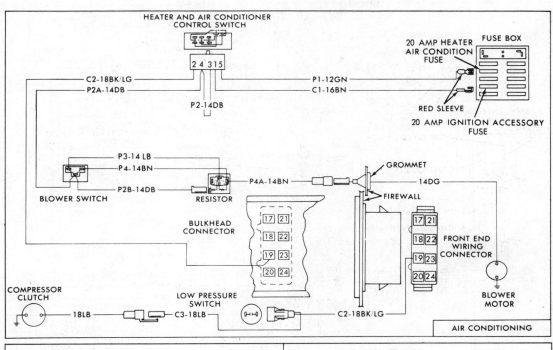

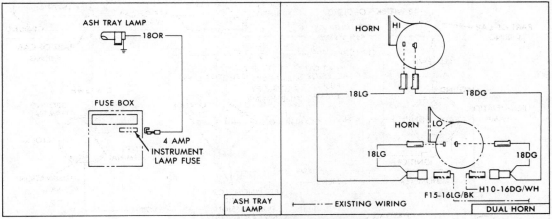

1978 AUXILIARY EQUIPMENT
WITHOUT 100 AMP ALTERNATOR

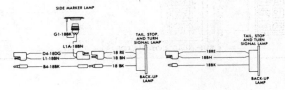

14

1978 AUXILIARY EQUIPMENT
PART III

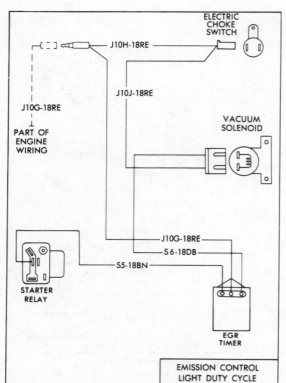

ELECTRIC CHOKE SWITCH

J10H-18RE

J10J-18RE

VACUUM SOLENOID

J10G-18RE

PART OF ENGINE WIRING

J10G-18RE
S6-18DB
S5-18BN

STARTER RELAY

EGR TIMER

EMISSION CONTROL LIGHT DUTY CYCLE

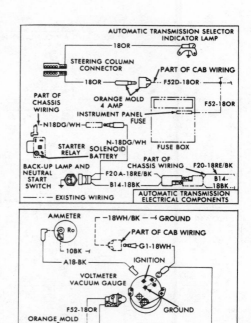

AUTOMATIC TRANSMISSION SELECTOR INDICATOR LAMP

18OR

STEERING COLUMN CONNECTOR

18OR

PART OF CAB WIRING
F52D-18OR

ORANGE MOLD 4 AMP
INSTRUMENT PANEL FUSE

F52-18OR

PART OF CHASSIS WIRING

N18DG/WH

N-18DG/WH

FUSE BOX

STARTER RELAY
SOLENOID
BATTERY

PART OF CHASSIS WIRING
F20-18RE/BK

BACK-UP LAMP AND NEUTRAL START SWITCH

F20A-18RE/BK
B14-18BK

B14-18BK

— · · · — EXISTING WIRING

AUTOMATIC TRANSMISSION ELECTRICAL COMPONENTS

AMMETER

Ro

18WH/BK — GROUND

PART OF CAB WIRING
G1-18WH

10BK

A18-BK

IGNITION

VOLTMETER VACUUM GAUGE

F52-18OR

GROUND

ORANGE MOLD

G1A-18WH

F52D-18OR
F52A-18OR

PROVISIONS FOR INSTRUMENT LAMPS

PART OF CAB HARNESS

ORANGE MOLD

VOLTMETER VACUUM GAUGE

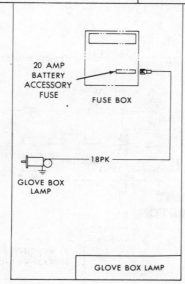

20 AMP BATTERY ACCESSORY FUSE

FUSE BOX

18PK

GLOVE BOX LAMP

GLOVE BOX LAMP

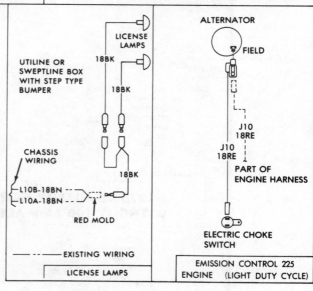

LICENSE LAMPS

UTILINE OR SWEPTLINE BOX WITH STEP TYPE BUMPER

18BK

18BK

18BK

CHASSIS WIRING

L10B-18BN
L10A-18BN

RED MOLD

— · · · — EXISTING WIRING

LICENSE LAMPS

ALTERNATOR

FIELD

J10 18RE

J10 18RE

PART OF ENGINE HARNESS

ELECTRIC CHOKE SWITCH

EMISSION CONTROL 225 ENGINE (LIGHT DUTY CYCLE)

1978 AUXILIARY EQUIPMENT
PART IV

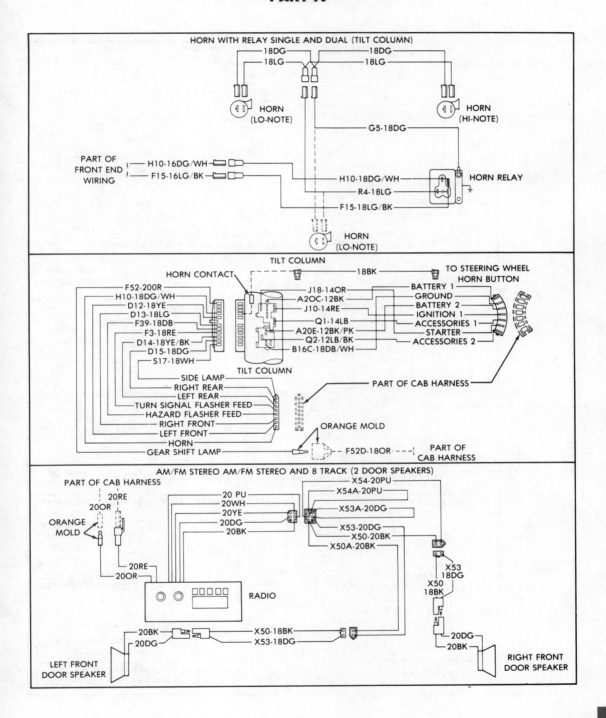

1978 AUXILIARY EQUIPMENT
PART V

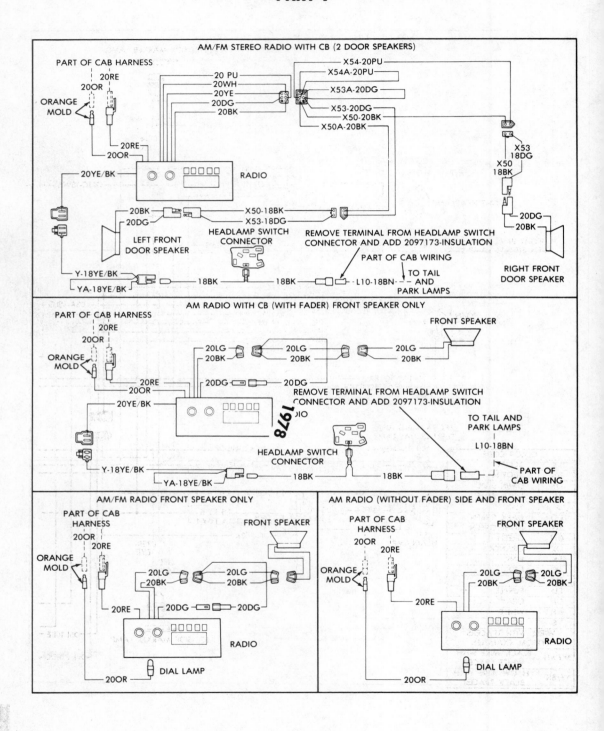

1979 GASOLINE, WITHOUT 117 AMP ALTERNATOR
PART I

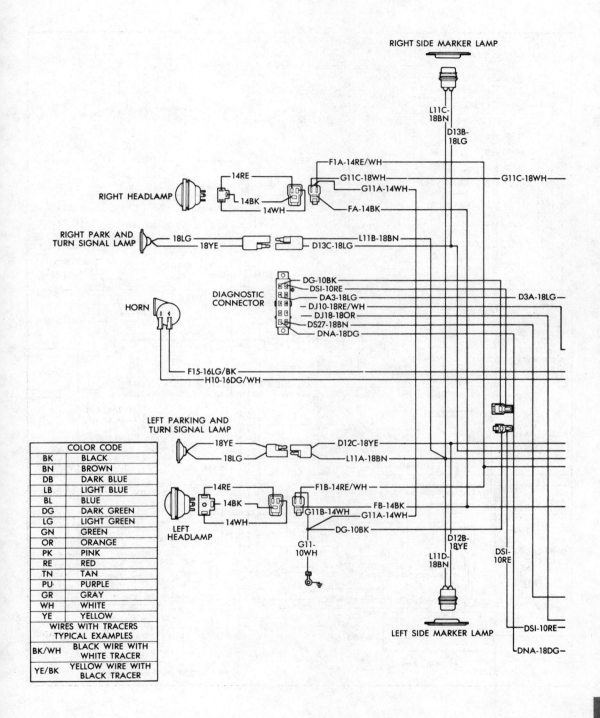

RIGHT SIDE MARKER LAMP

L11C-18BN

D13B-18LG

RIGHT HEADLAMP

F1A-14RE/WH
G11C-18WH
G11A-14WH
FA-14BK
14RE
14BK
14WH

G11C-18WH

RIGHT PARK AND
TURN SIGNAL LAMP

18LG
18YE
D13C-18LG
L11B-18BN

DIAGNOSTIC
CONNECTOR

DG-10BK
DSI-10RE
DA3-18LG
DJ10-18RE/WH
DJ18-18OR
DS27-18BN
DNA-18DG

D3A-18LG

HORN

F15-16LG/BK
H10-16DG/WH

LEFT PARKING AND
TURN SIGNAL LAMP

18YE
18LG
D12C-18YE
L11A-18BN

	COLOR CODE
BK	BLACK
BN	BROWN
DB	DARK BLUE
LB	LIGHT BLUE
BL	BLUE
DG	DARK GREEN
LG	LIGHT GREEN
GN	GREEN
OR	ORANGE
PK	PINK
RE	RED
TN	TAN
PU	PURPLE
GR	GRAY
WH	WHITE
YE	YELLOW

WIRES WITH TRACERS TYPICAL EXAMPLES	
BK/WH	BLACK WIRE WITH WHITE TRACER
YE/BK	YELLOW WIRE WITH BLACK TRACER

LEFT
HEADLAMP

14RE
14BK
14WH

F1B-14RE/WH
FB-14BK
G11B-14WH
G11A-14WH
DG-10BK

G11-
10WH

D12B-
18YE

L11D-
18BN

DSI-
10RE

LEFT SIDE MARKER LAMP

DSI-10RE

DNA-18DG

14

1979 GASOLINE, WITHOUT 117 AMP ALTERNATOR
PART II

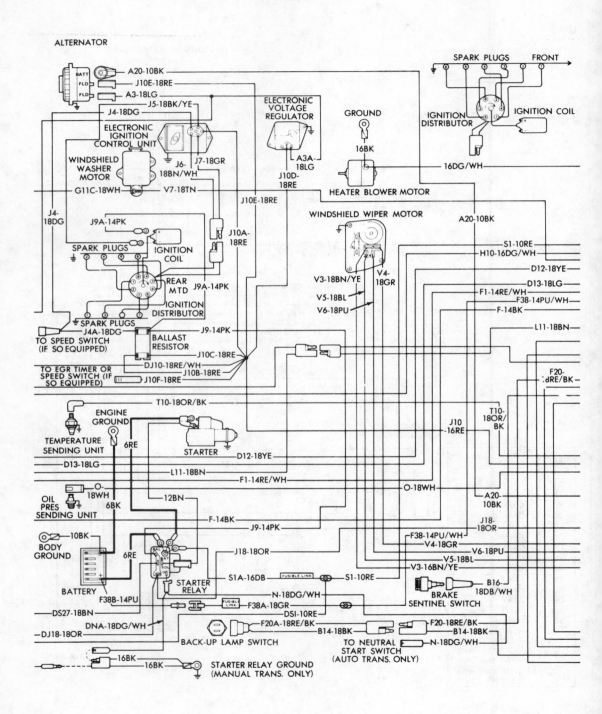

1979 GASOLINE, WITHOUT 117 AMP ALTERNATOR
PART III

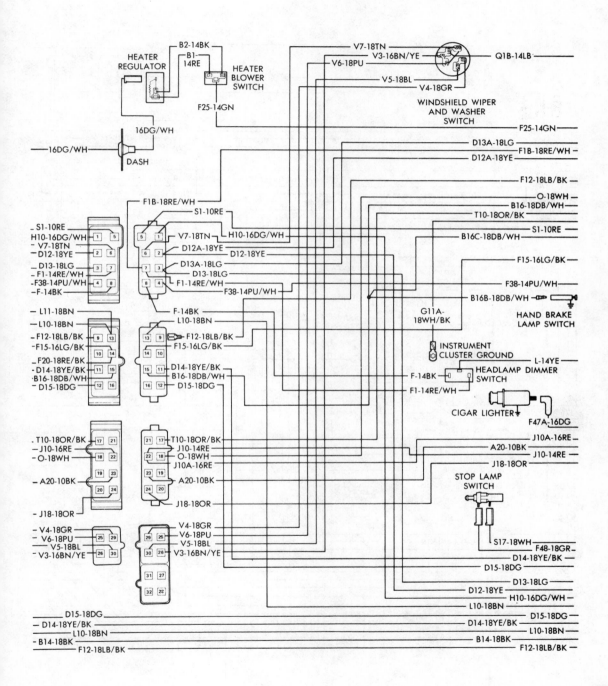

1979 GASOLINE, WITHOUT 117 AMP ALTERNATOR
PART IV

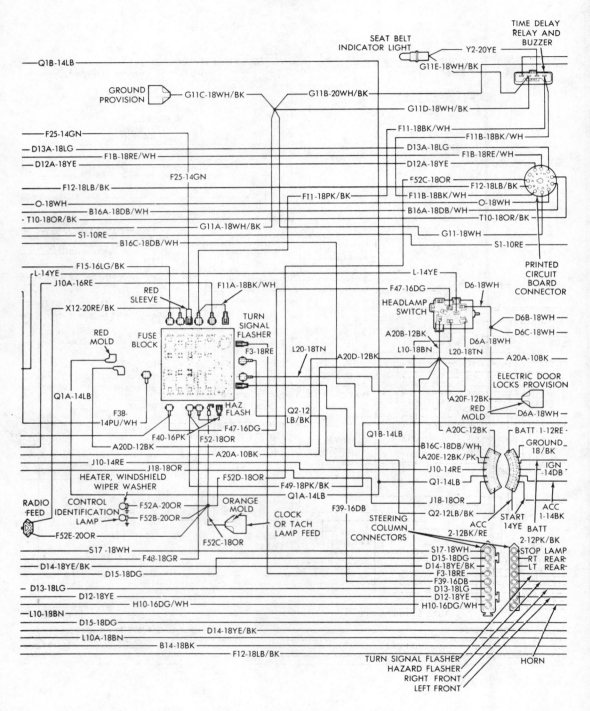

1979 GASOLINE, WITHOUT 117 AMP ALTERNATOR
PART V

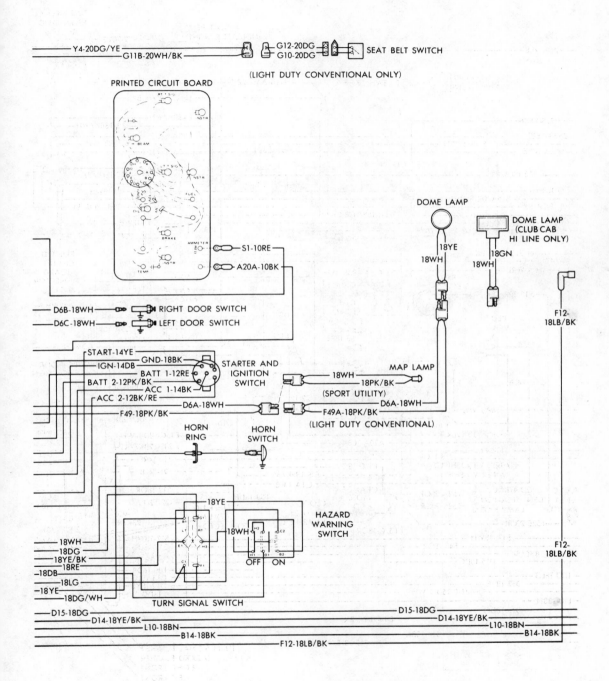

1979 GASOLINE, WITH 117 AMP ALTERNATOR
PART I

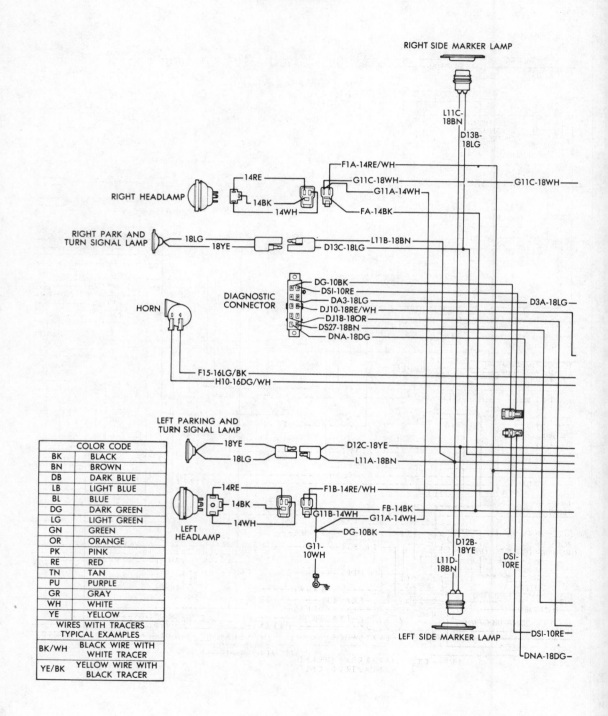

1979 GASOLINE, WITH 117 AMP ALTERNATOR
PART II

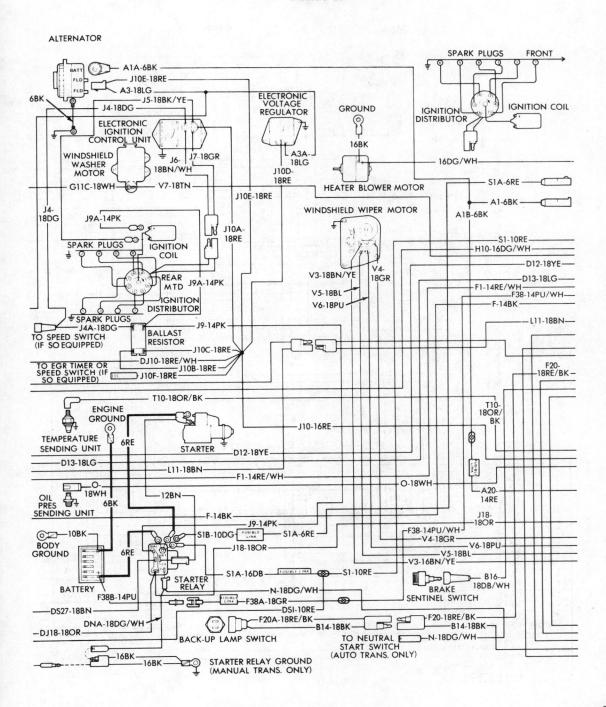

1979 GASOLINE, WITH 117 AMP ALTERNATOR
PART III

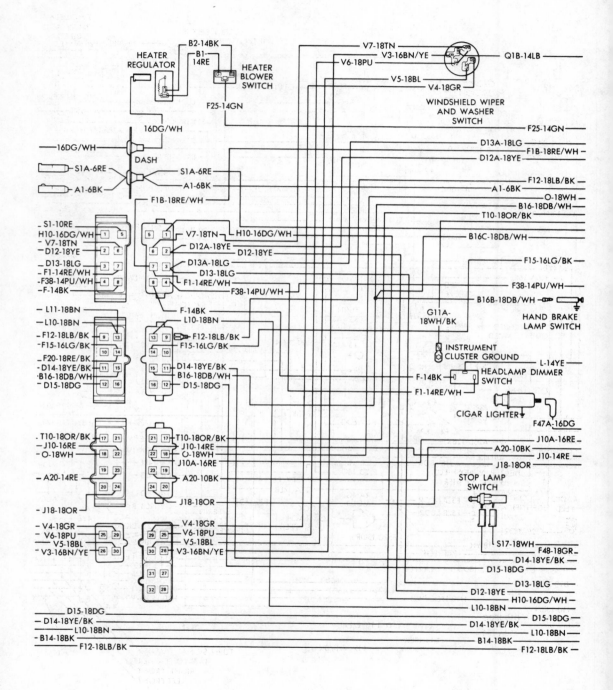

1979 GASOLINE, WITH 117 AMP ALTERNATOR
PART IV

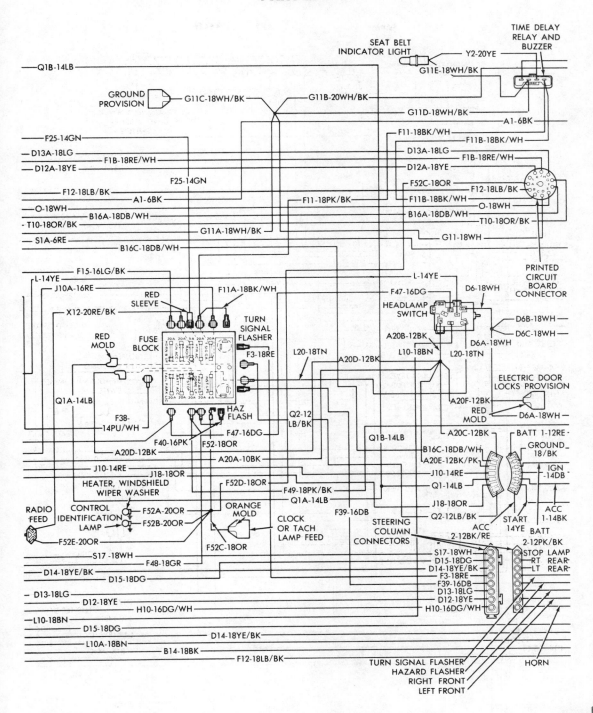

1979 GASOLINE, WITH 117 AMP ALTERNATOR
PART V

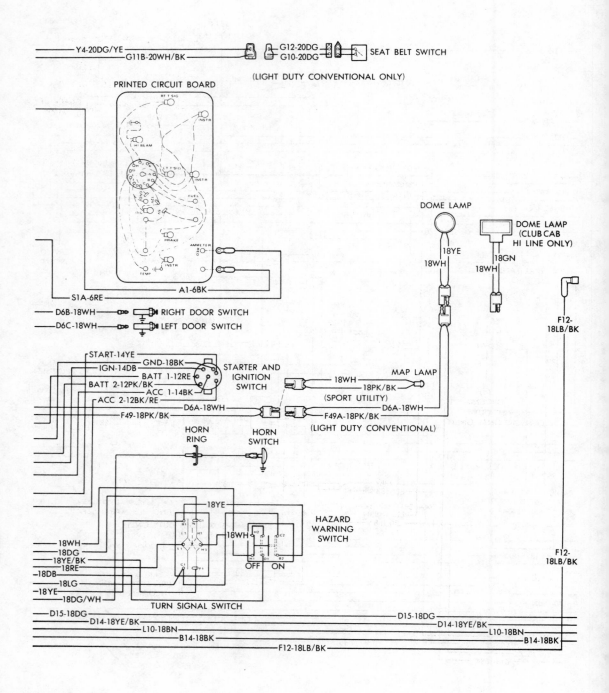

1979 GASOLINE, WITH 117 AMP ALTERNATOR
PART VI

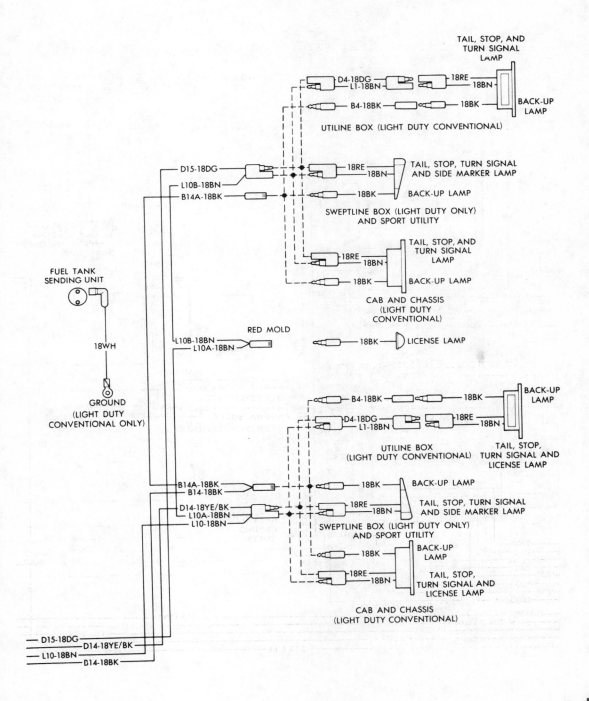

1979 DIESEL, WITH 60 AMP ALTERNATOR
PART I

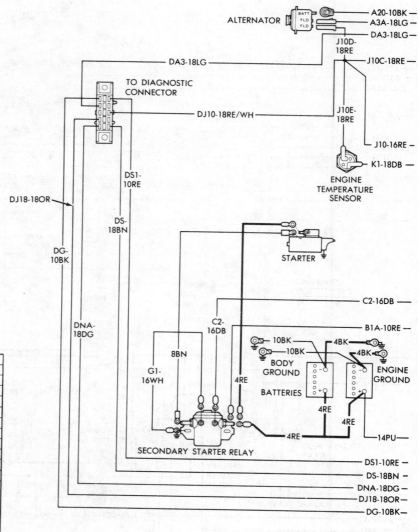

COLOR CODE	
BK	BLACK
BN	BROWN
DB	DARK BLUE
LB	LIGHT BLUE
BL	BLUE
DG	DARK GREEN
LG	LIGHT GREEN
GN	GREEN
OR	ORANGE
PK	PINK
RE	RED
TN	TAN
PU	PURPLE
GR	GRAY
WH	WHITE
YE	YELLOW
WIRES WITH TRACERS TYPICAL EXAMPLES	
BK/WH	BLACK WIRE WITH WHITE TRACER
YE/BK	YELLOW WIRE WITH BLACK TRACER

1979 DIESEL, WITH 60 AMP ALTERNATOR
PART II

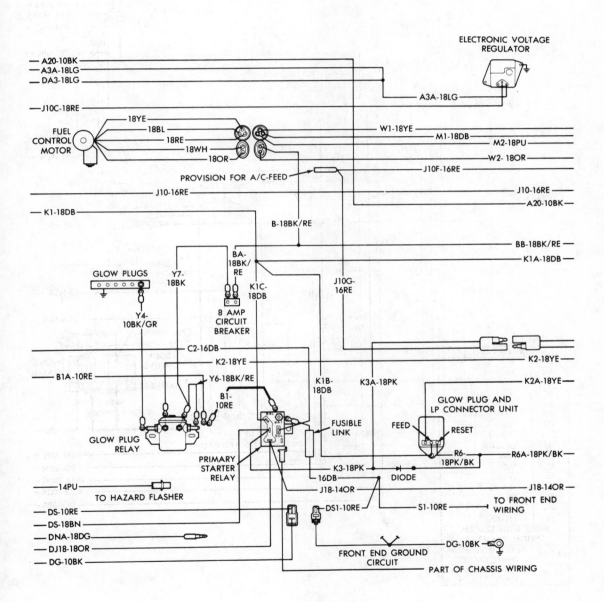

1979 DIESEL, WITH 60 AMP ALTERNATOR
PART III

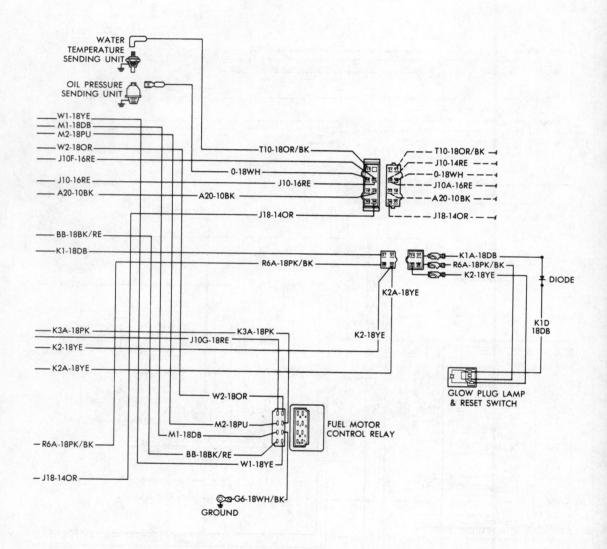

1979 DIESEL, WITH 117 AMP ALTERNATOR
PART I

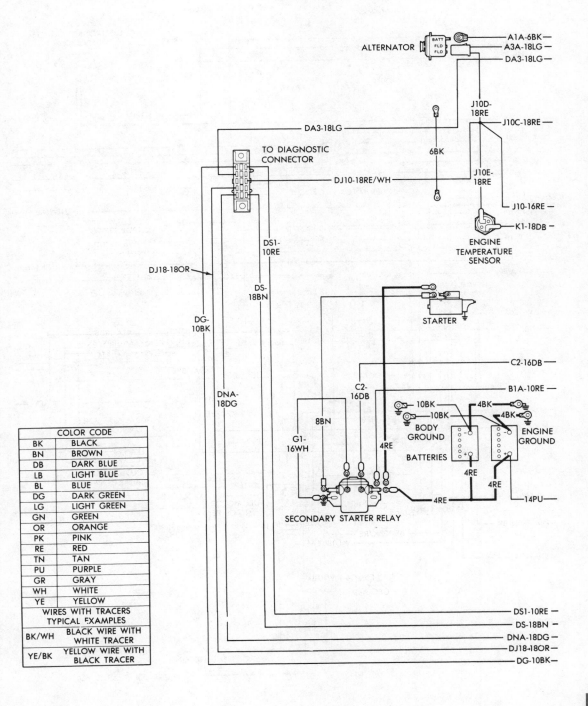

COLOR CODE	
BK	BLACK
BN	BROWN
DB	DARK BLUE
LB	LIGHT BLUE
BL	BLUE
DG	DARK GREEN
LG	LIGHT GREEN
GN	GREEN
OR	ORANGE
PK	PINK
RE	RED
TN	TAN
PU	PURPLE
GR	GRAY
WH	WHITE
YE	YELLOW
WIRES WITH TRACERS TYPICAL EXAMPLES	
BK/WH	BLACK WIRE WITH WHITE TRACER
YE/BK	YELLOW WIRE WITH BLACK TRACER

1979 DIESEL, WITH 117 AMP ALTERNATOR
PART II

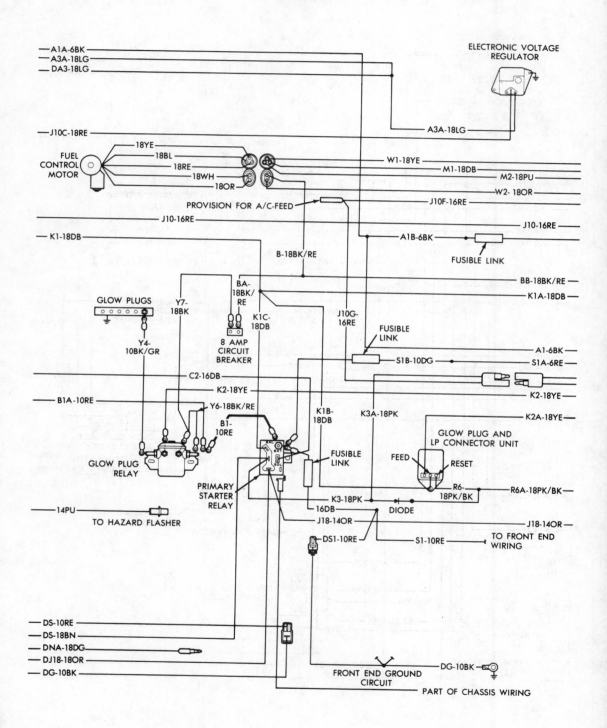

1979 DIESEL, WITH 117 AMP ALTERNATOR
PART III

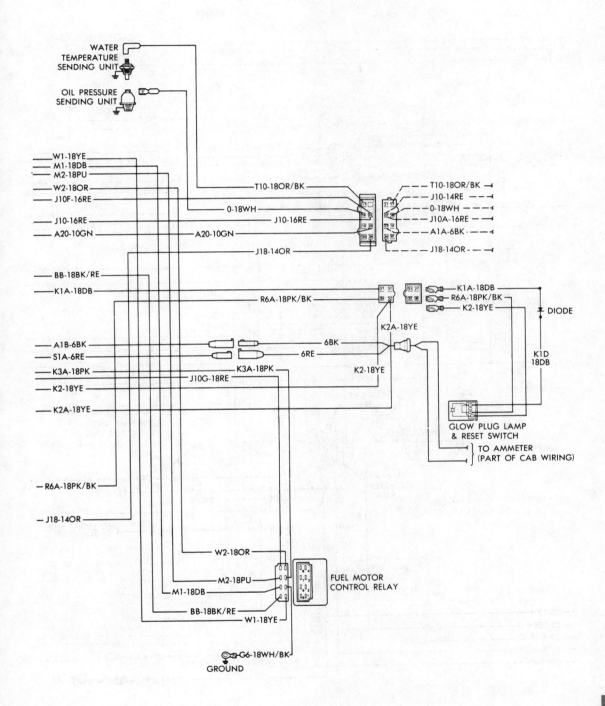

WATER TEMPERATURE SENDING UNIT

OIL PRESSURE SENDING UNIT

W1-18YE
M1-18DB
M2-18PU
W2-18OR
J10F-16RE

J10-16RE
A20-10GN

BB-18BK/RE
K1A-18DB

A1B-6BK
S1A-6RE
K3A-18PK
K2-18YE
K2A-18YE

R6A-18PK/BK

J18-14OR

T10-18OR/BK
0-18WH
J10-16RE
A20-10GN
J18-14OR

R6A-18PK/BK

K2A-18YE

6BK
6RE

K3A-18PK
J10G-18RE

K2-18YE

T10-18OR/BK
J10-14RE
0-18WH
J10A-16RE
A1A-6BK
J18-14OR

K1A-18DB
R6A-18PK/BK
K2-18YE

DIODE

K1D
18DB

GLOW PLUG LAMP
& RESET SWITCH

TO AMMETER
(PART OF CAB WIRING)

W2-18OR
M2-18PU
M1-18DB
BB-18BK/RE
W1-18YE

FUEL MOTOR
CONTROL RELAY

G6-18WH/BK
GROUND

14

1980 COMPLETE VEHICLE
PART I

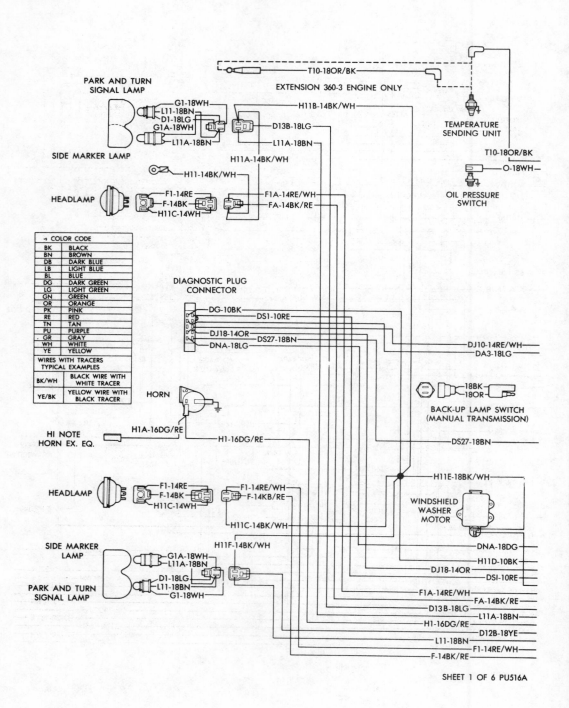

SHEET 1 OF 6 PU516A

1980 COMPLETE VEHICLE
PART II

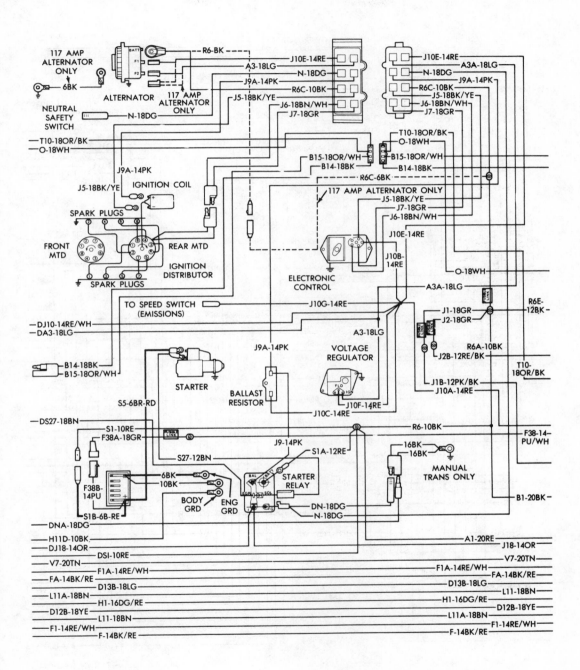

1980 COMPLETE VEHICLE
PART III

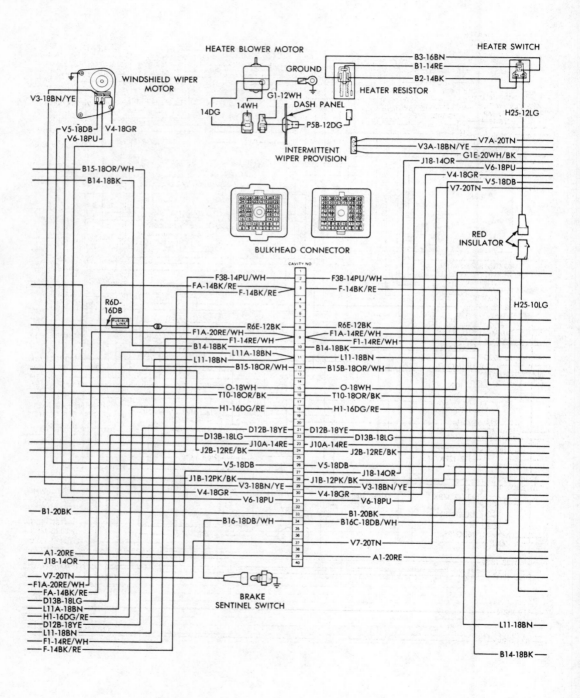

1980 COMPLETE VEHICLE
PART IV

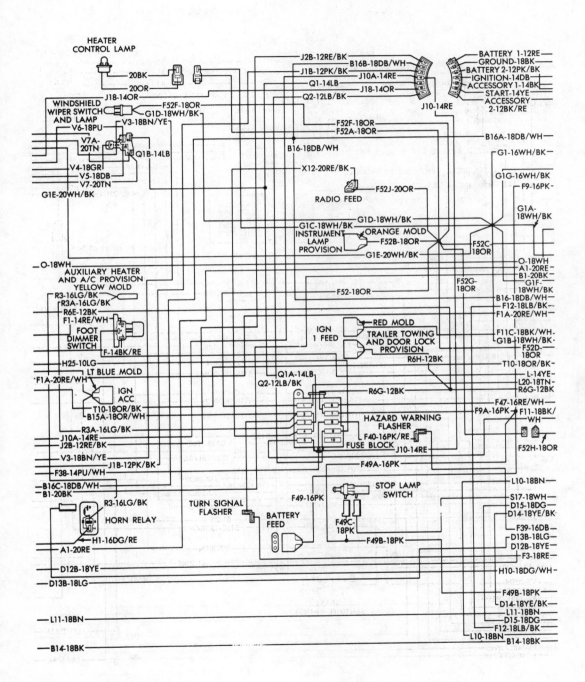

1980 COMPLETE VEHICLE
PART V

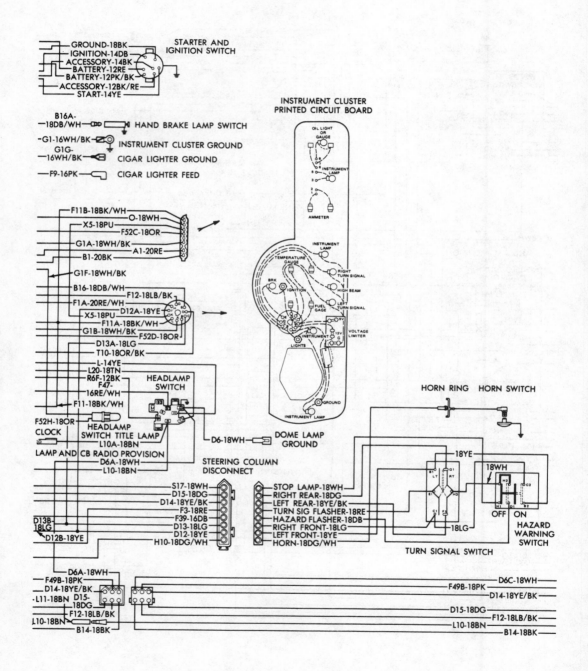

1980 COMPLETE VEHICLE
PART VI

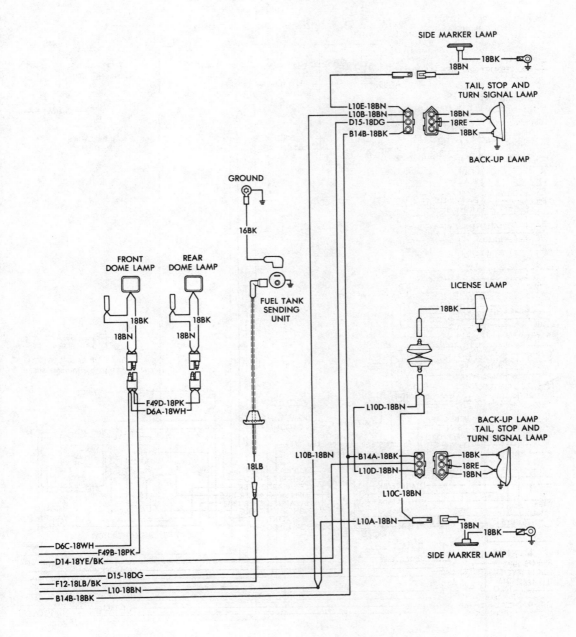

SIDE MARKER LAMP

18BK

18BN

TAIL, STOP AND
TURN SIGNAL LAMP

L10E-18BN   18BN
L10B-18BN   18RE
D15-18DG   18BK
B14B-18BK

BACK-UP LAMP

GROUND

16BK

FRONT   REAR
DOME LAMP   DOME LAMP

FUEL TANK
SENDING
UNIT

LICENSE LAMP

18BK

18BK   18BK

18BN   18BN

F49D-18PK
D6A-18WH

L10D-18BN

BACK-UP LAMP
TAIL, STOP AND
TURN SIGNAL LAMP

L10B-18BN   B14A-18BK   18BK
              L10D-18BN   18RE
18LB   18BN

L10C-18BN

L10A-18BN

D6C-18WH   SIDE MARKER LAMP
F49B-18PK   18BN   18BK
D14-18YE/BK
D15-18DG
F12-18LB/BK
L10-18BN
B14B-18BK

14

1981 8-CYLINDER ECU IGNITION
PART I

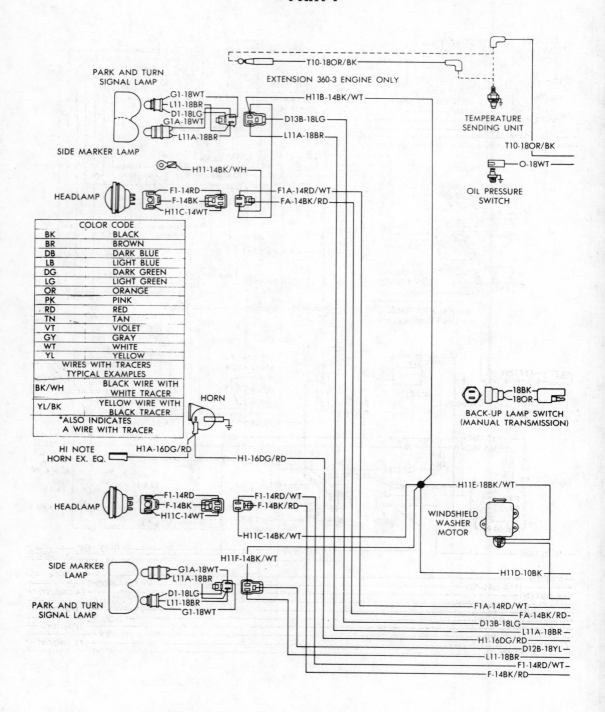

1981 8-CYLINDER ECU IGNITION
PART II

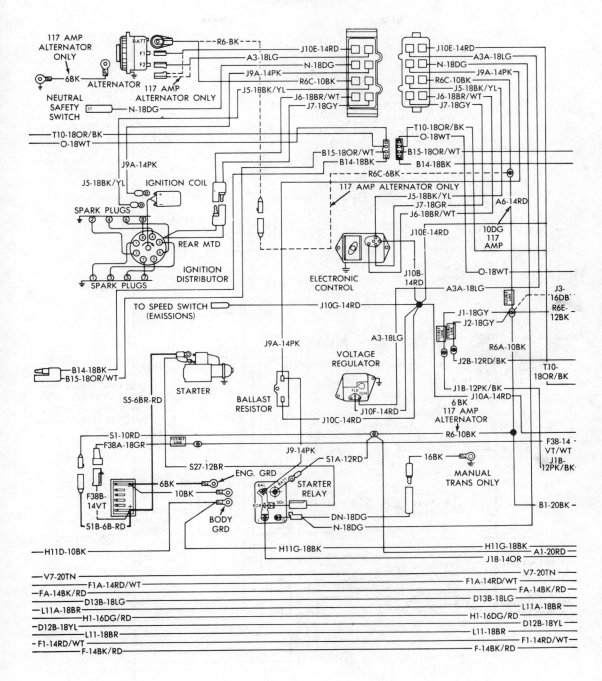

1981 8-CYLINDER ECU IGNITION
PART III

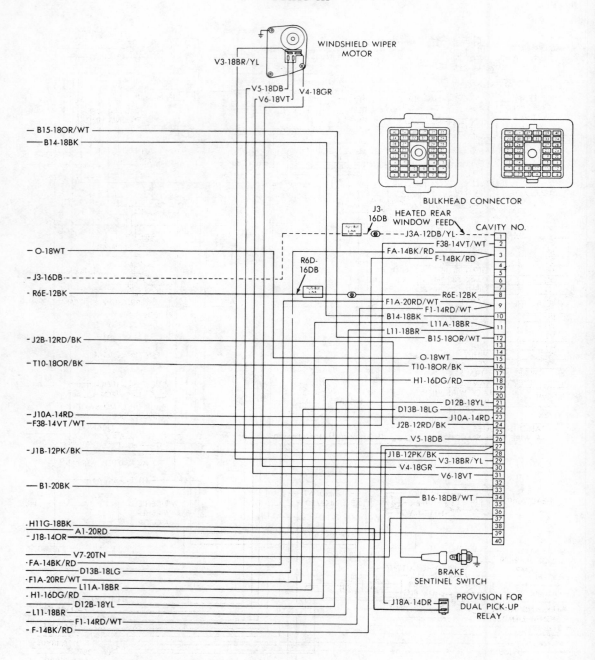

1981 6-CYLINDER ELECTRONIC SPARK ADVANCE
PART I

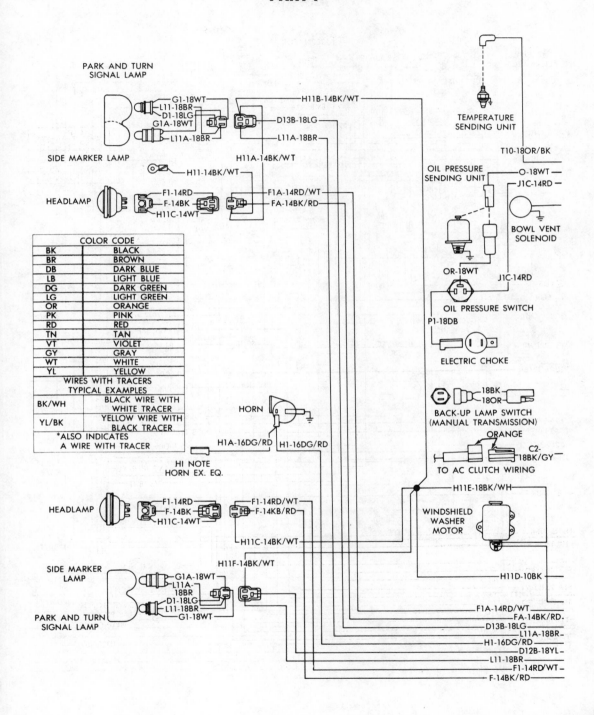

COLOR CODE	
BK	BLACK
BR	BROWN
DB	DARK BLUE
LB	LIGHT BLUE
DG	DARK GREEN
LG	LIGHT GREEN
OR	ORANGE
PK	PINK
RD	RED
TN	TAN
VT	VIOLET
GY	GRAY
WT	WHITE
YL	YELLOW
WIRES WITH TRACERS TYPICAL EXAMPLES	
BK/WH	BLACK WIRE WITH WHITE TRACER
YL/BK	YELLOW WIRE WITH BLACK TRACER
*ALSO INDICATES A WIRE WITH TRACER	

1981 6-CYLINDER ELECTRONIC SPARK ADVANCE
PART II

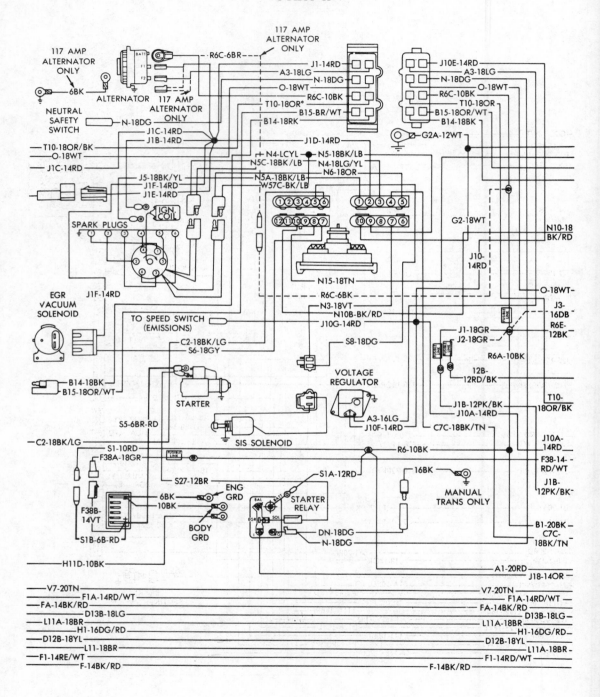

1981 6-CYLINDER ELECTRONIC SPARK ADVANCE
PART III

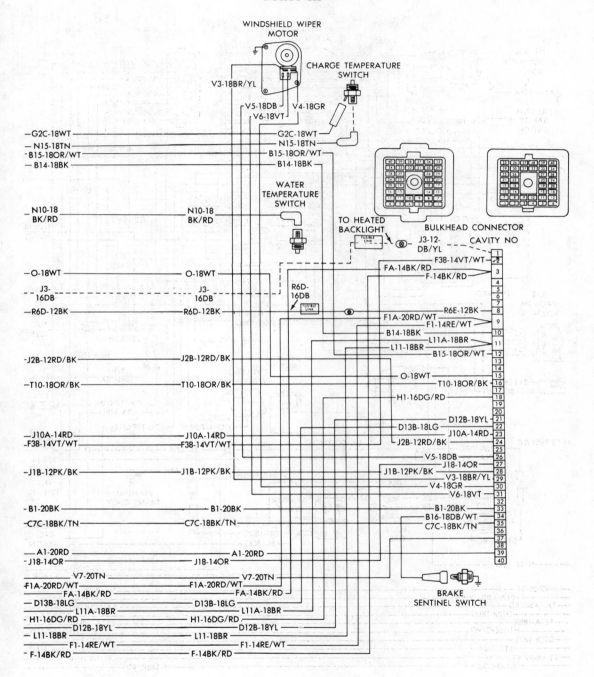

1981 COMPLETE BODY, ALL VEHICLES PART I

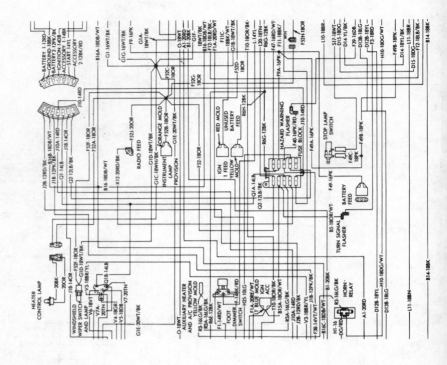

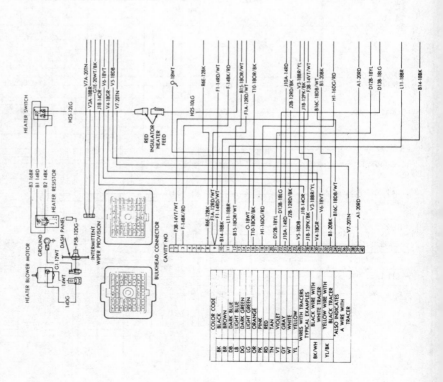

1981 COMPLETE BODY, ALL VEHICLES PART II

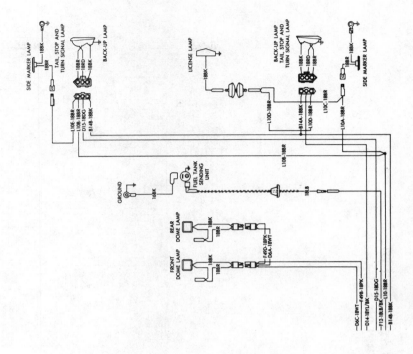

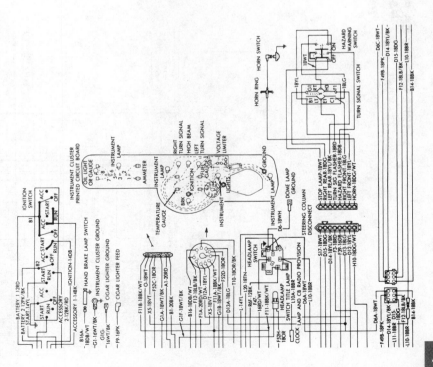

**1982 ENGINE COMPARTMENT WIRING
8-CYLINDER ELECTRONIC SPARK ADVANCE
PART 1**

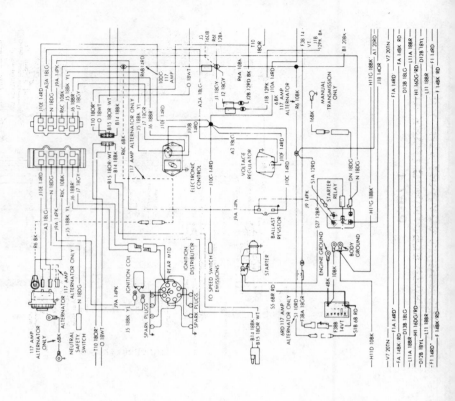

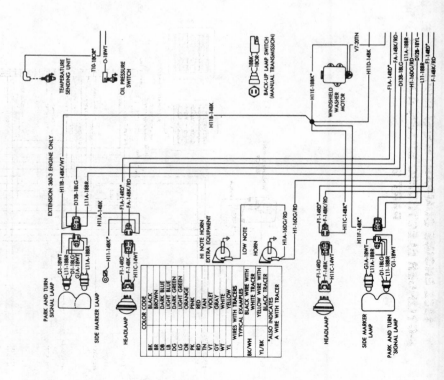

1982 ENGINE COMPARTMENT WIRING 6-CYLINDER ELECTRONIC SPARK ADVANCE PART 1

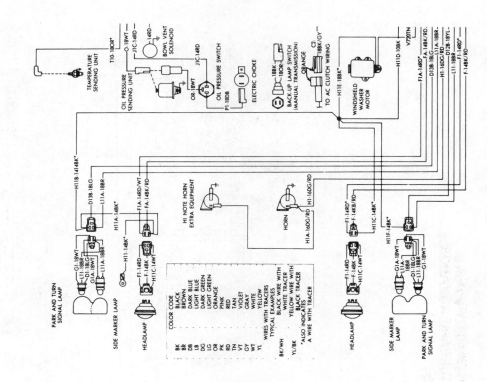

1982 ENGINE COMPARTMENT WIRING 8-CYLINDER ELECTRONIC SPARK ADVANCE PART 2

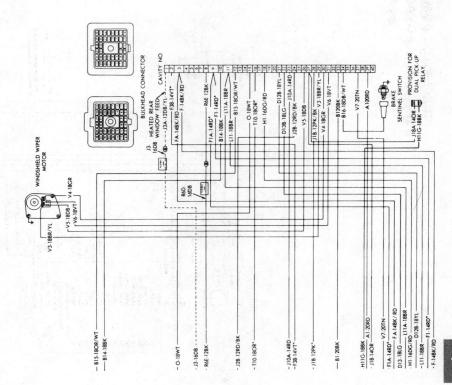

14

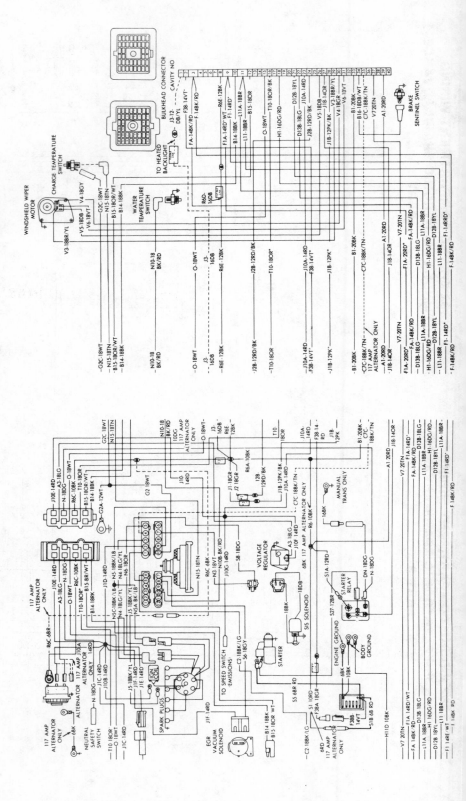

1982 ENGINE COMPARTMENT WIRING
6-CYLINDER ELECTRONIC SPARK ADVANCE
PART 2

1982 COMPLETE BODY WIRING DIAGRAM
ALL VEHICLES
PART 1

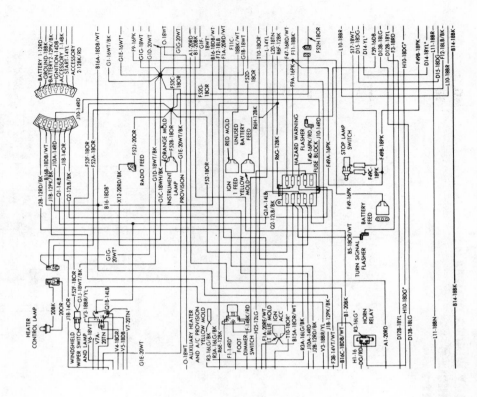

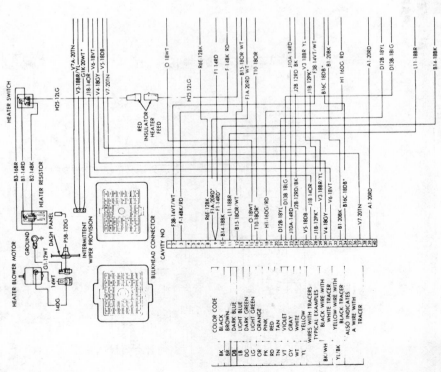

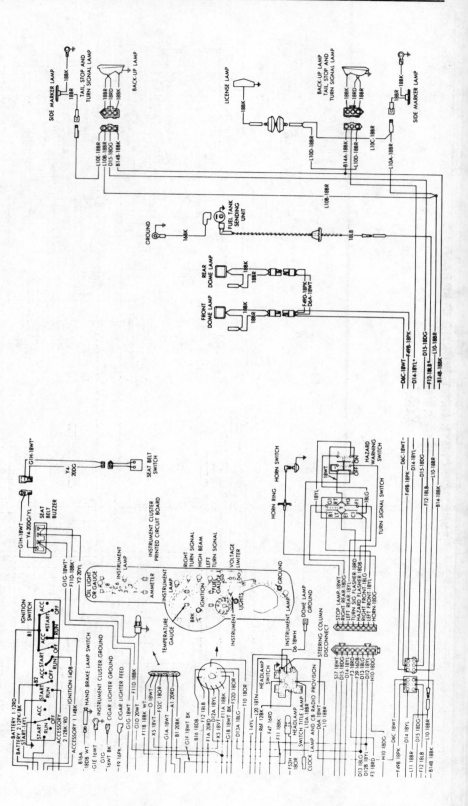

**1982 COMPLETE BODY WIRING DIAGRAM
ALL VEHICLES
PART 2**

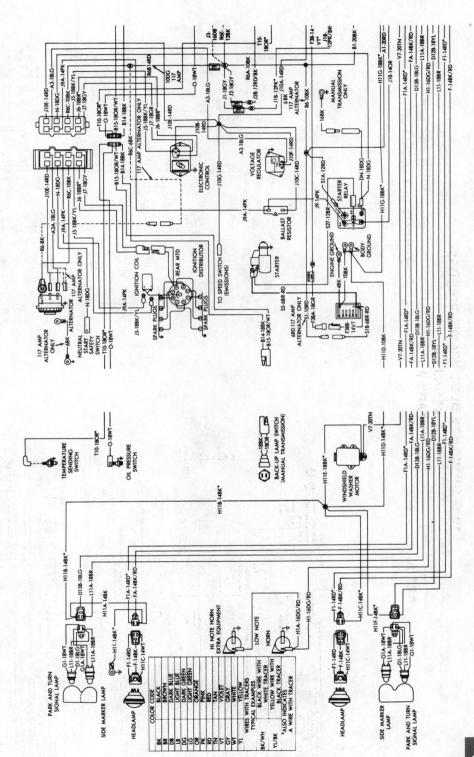

1983 ENGINE COMPARTMENT WIRING
8-CYLINDER ECU IGNITION
PART 1

1983 ENGINE COMPARTMENT WIRING ELECTRONIC SPARK ADVANCE WITHOUT O₂ FEEDBACK PART 1

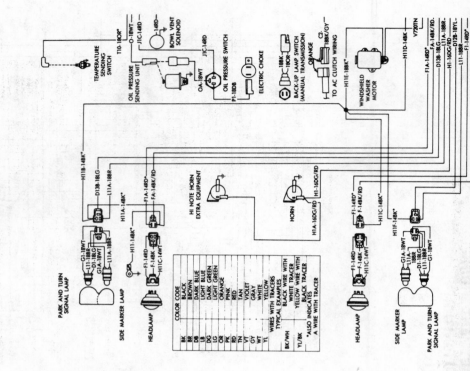

1983 ENGINE COMPARTMENT WIRING 8-CYLINDER ECU IGNITION PART 2

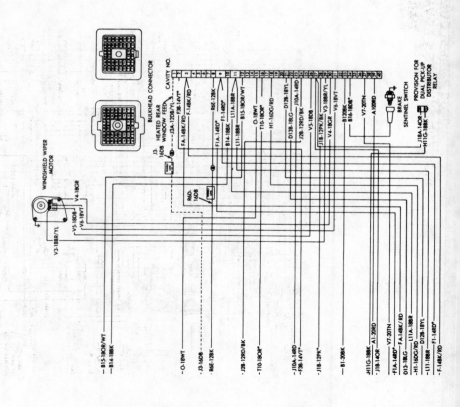

1983 ENGINE COMPARTMENT WIRING
ELECTRONIC SPARK ADVANCE WITHOUT O₂ FEEDBACK
PART 2

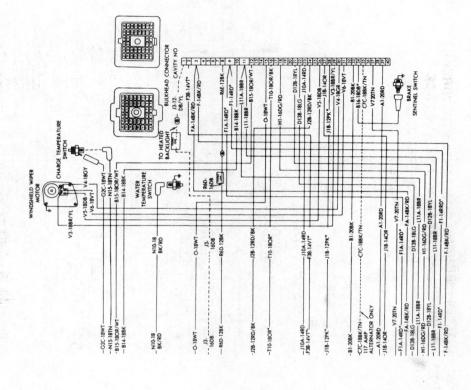

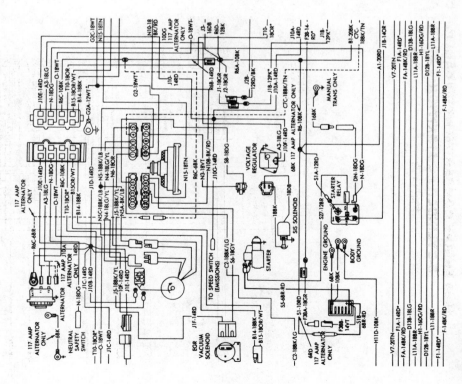

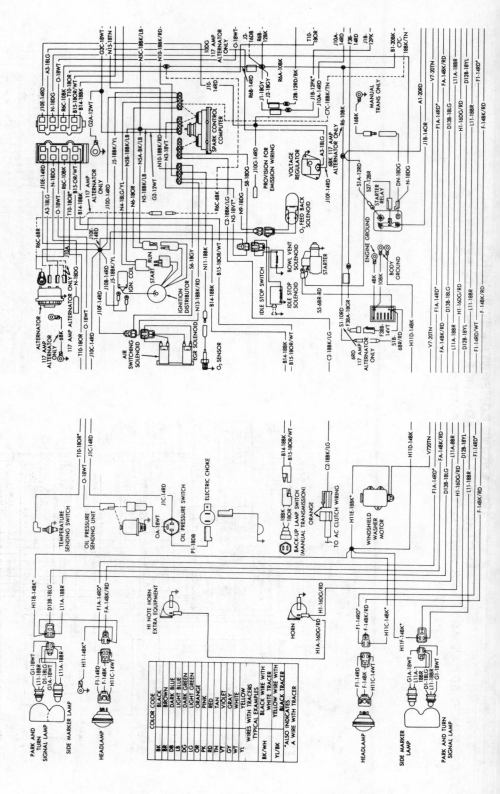

1983 ENGINE COMPARTMENT WIRING
ELECTRONIC SPARK ADVANCE WITH O_2 FEEDBACK

COLOR CODE	
BK	BLACK
BR	BROWN
DB	DARK BLUE
LB	LIGHT BLUE
DG	DARK GREEN
LG	LIGHT GREEN
OR	ORANGE
PK	PINK
RD	RED
TN	TAN
VT	VIOLET
GY	GRAY
WT	WHITE
YL	YELLOW

WIRES WITH TRACERS TYPICAL EXAMPLES	
BK/WH	BLACK WIRE WITH WHITE TRACER
YL/BK	YELLOW WIRE WITH BLACK TRACER

*ALSO INDICATES A WIRE WITH TRACER

**1983 COMPLETE BODY WIRING DIAGRAMS
ALL VEHICLES
PART 1**

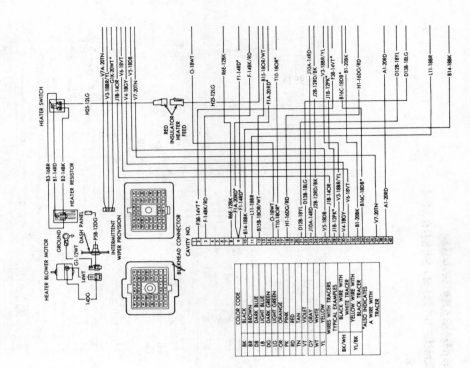

**1983 ENGINE COMPARTMENT WIRING
ELECTRONIC SPARK ADVANCE WITH O₂ FEEDBACK
PART 2**

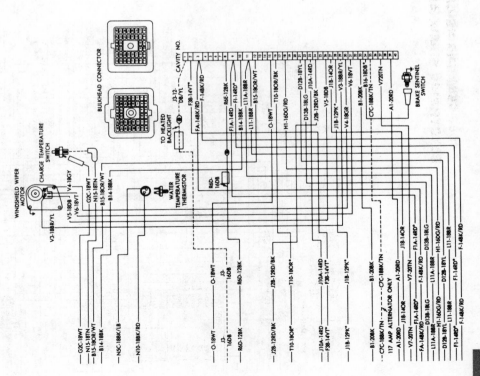

14

1983 COMPLETE BODY WIRING DIAGRAMS ALL VEHICLES PART 2

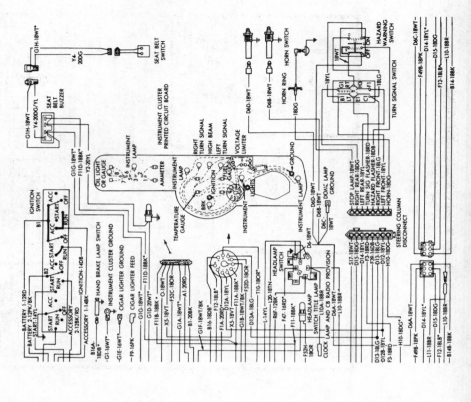

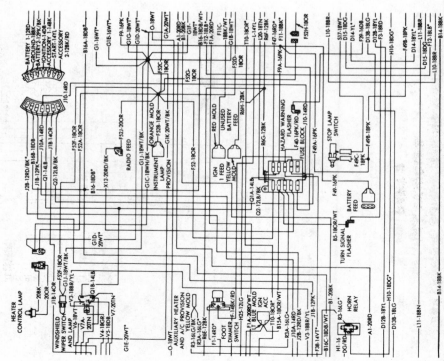

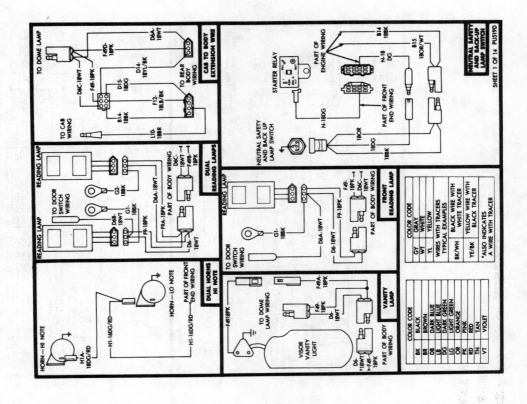

AUXILIARY WIRING DIAGRAMS
1 of 14

1983 COMPLETE BODY WIRING DIAGRAMS
ALL VEHICLES
PART 3

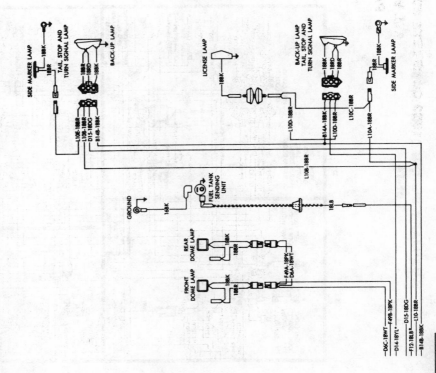

14

AUXILIARY WIRING DIAGRAMS
3 of 14

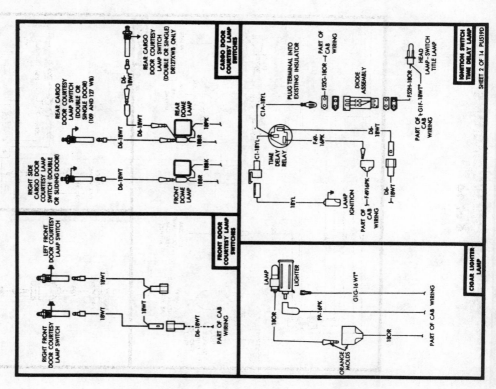

AUXILIARY WIRING DIAGRAMS
2 of 14

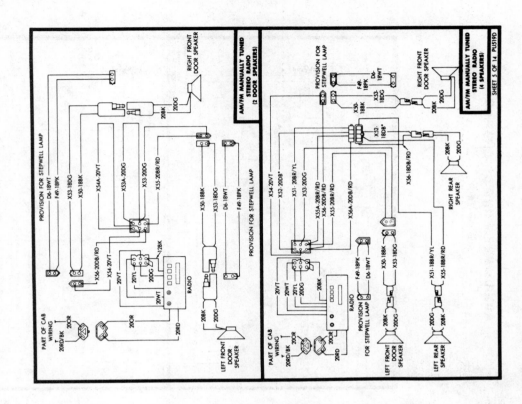

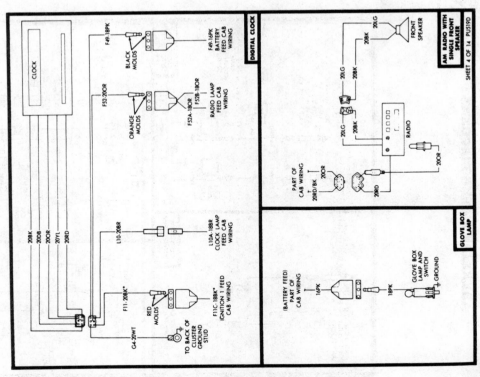

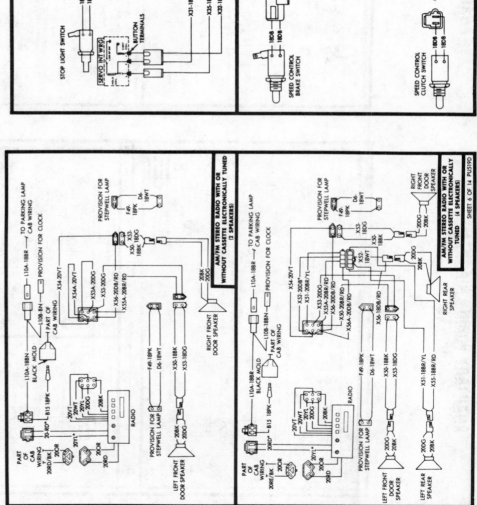

AUXILIARY WIRING DIAGRAMS
7 of 14

AUTOMATIC SPEED CONTROL

SPEED CONTROL WITH MANUAL TRANSMISSION

SHEET 7 OF 14 PU519D

AUXILIARY WIRING DIAGRAMS
6 of 14

AM/FM STEREO RADIO WITH OR WITHOUT CASSETTE ELECTRONICALLY TUNED (2 SPEAKERS)

AM/FM STEREO RADIO WITH OR WITHOUT CASSETTE ELECTRONICALLY TUNED (4 SPEAKERS)

SHEET 6 OF 14 PU519D

AUXILIARY WIRING DIAGRAMS
9 of 14

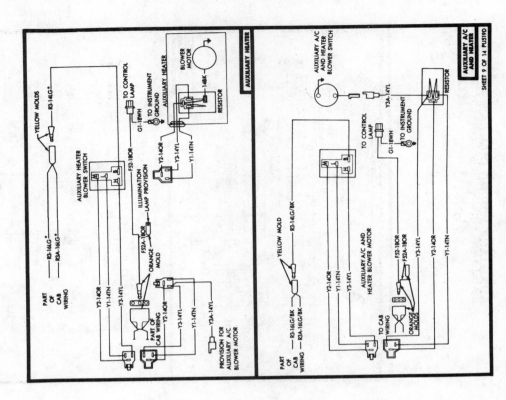

AUXILIARY WIRING DIAGRAMS
8 of 14

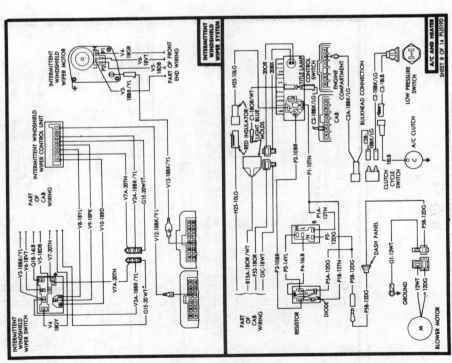

AUXILIARY WIRING DIAGRAMS
11 of 14

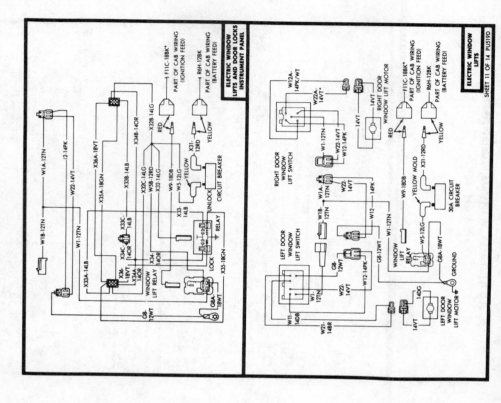

AUXILIARY WIRING DIAGRAMS
10 of 14

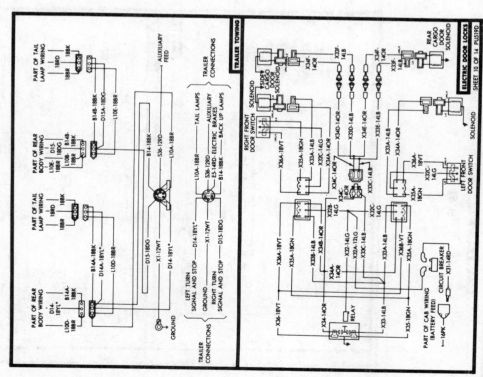

AUXILIARY WIRING DIAGRAMS
13 of 14

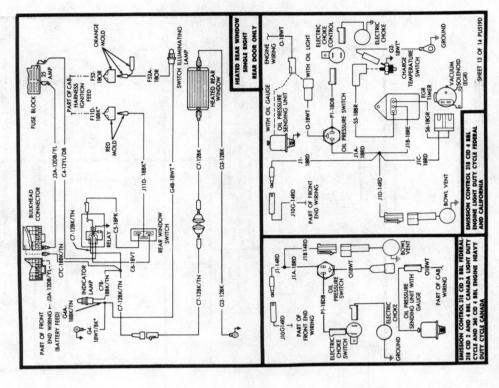

AUXILIARY WIRING DIAGRAMS
12 of 14

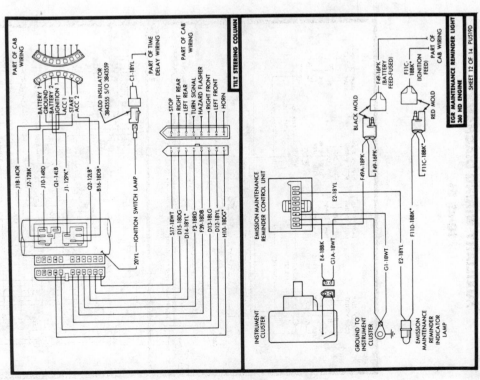

WIRING DIAGRAMS

AUXILIARY WIRING DIAGRAMS
1 of 16

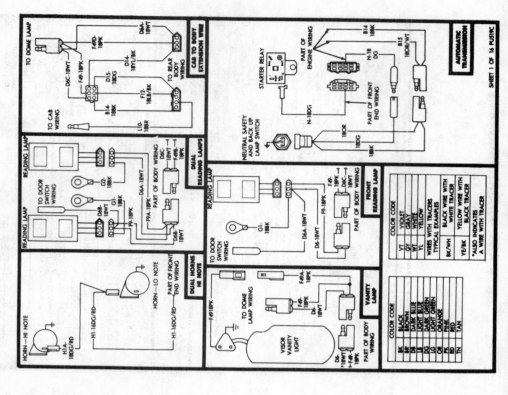

AUXILIARY WIRING DIAGRAMS
14 of 14

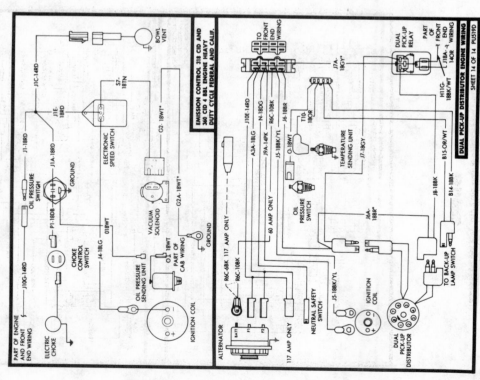

AUXILIARY WIRING DIAGRAMS 3 of 16

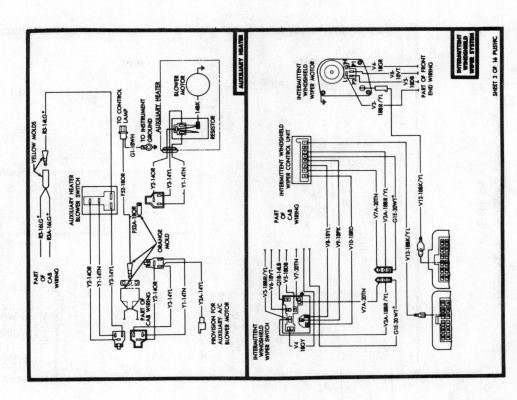

AUXILIARY WIRING DIAGRAMS 2 of 16

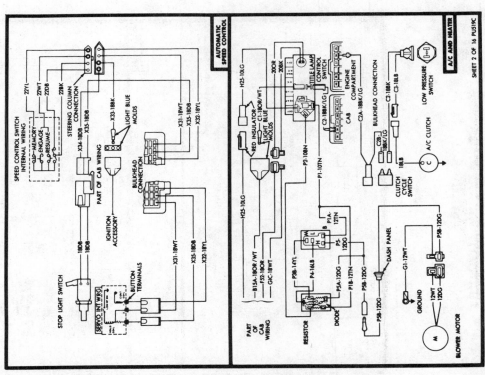

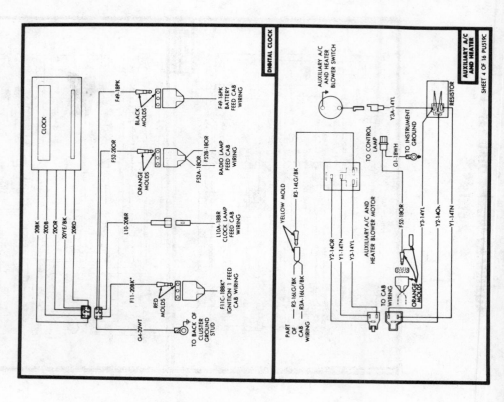

AUXILIARY WIRING DIAGRAMS
5 of 16

TRAILER TOWING RELAY AND CIRCUIT BREAKER

RELAY

L10-18BR

L1-16BN*

R8A-12BK — BATTERY FEED

20A CIRCUIT BREAKER

R6A-12BK

C2-16YL

YELLOW MOLD

PART OF BODY EXTERIOR WIRING — L10-18BR

PART OF CAB WIRING — L11-18BR / L10-18BR

GLOVE BOX LAMP

(BATTERY FEED) PART OF CAB WIRING

16PK

18PK

GLOVE BOX LAMP AND SWITCH

GROUND

AM/FM RADIO WITHOUT TAPE SINGLE FRONT SPEAKER ONLY

SHEET 5 OF 16 PU519C

20LG

20K

20BK

FRONT SPEAKER

20LG

20BK

RADIO

20OR

PART OF CAB WIRING

20OR/BK

20RD/BK

20E

AM RADIO WITH SINGLE FRONT SPEAKER

20RD/BK

20OR

PART OF CAB WIRING

20RD

20LG

20BK

20K

20LG

FRONT SPEAKER

RADIO

20OR

GROUND

AUXILIARY WIRING DIAGRAMS
4 of 16

DIGITAL CLOCK

CLOCK

F49-18PK

BLACK MOLDS

F49-16PK BATTERY FEED CAB WIRING

F52-20OR

ORANGE MOLDS

F52A-18OR

F52B-18OR

RADIO LAMP FEED CAB WIRING

L10-18R

L10A-18BR CLOCK LAMP FEED CAB WIRING

20BK
20DB
20OR
20YE/BK
20RD

F11-20BK*

RED MOLDS

F11C-18BK* IGNITION 1 FEED CAB WIRING

G4-20WT

TO BACK OF CLUSTER GROUND STUD

AUXILIARY A/C AND HEATER

AUXILIARY A/C AND HEATER BLOWER SWITCH

Y3A-14YL

RESISTOR

TO CONTROL LAMP

G1-18WH

TO INSTRUMENT GROUND

YELLOW MOLD

R3-14LG/BK

AUXILIARY A/C AND HEATER BLOWER MOTOR

F52-18OR

Y3-14YL
Y2-14OR
Y1-14TN

Y2-14OR
Y1-14TN
Y3-14YL

PART OF CAB WIRING

R3-16LG/BK

R3A-16LG/BK

ORANGE MOLDS

TO CAB WIRING

SHEET 4 OF 16 PU519C

AUXILIARY WIRING DIAGRAMS
7 of 16

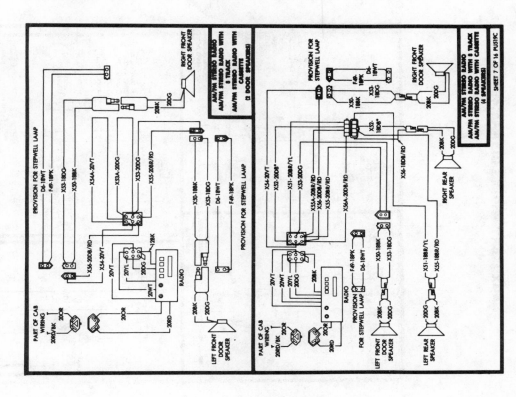

AUXILIARY WIRING DIAGRAMS
6 of 16

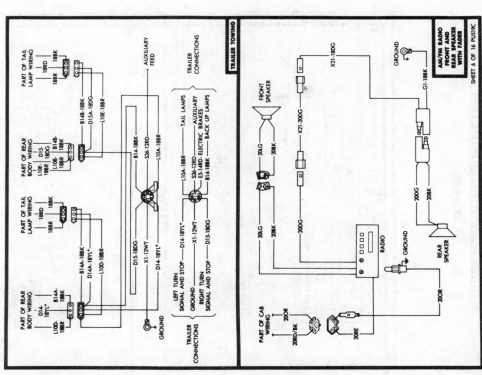

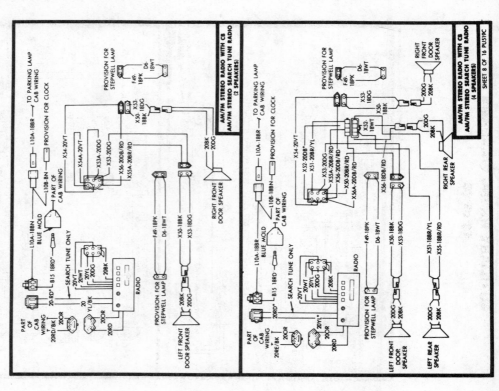

AUXILIARY WIRING DIAGRAMS
9 of 16

AUXILIARY WIRING DIAGRAMS
8 of 16

AUXILIARY WIRING DIAGRAMS
11 of 16

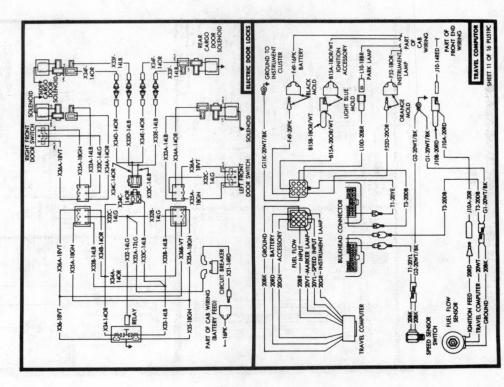

AUXILIARY WIRING DIAGRAMS
10 of 16

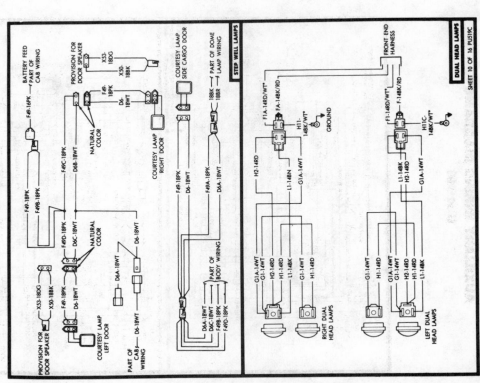

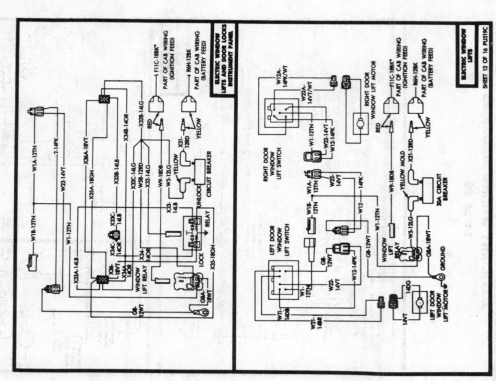

AUXILIARY WIRING DIAGRAMS
13 of 16

AUXILIARY WIRING DIAGRAMS
12 of 16

AUXILIARY WIRING DIAGRAMS
15 of 16

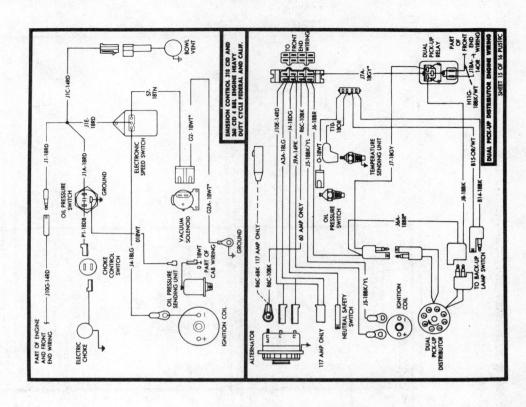

AUXILIARY WIRING DIAGRAMS
14 of 16

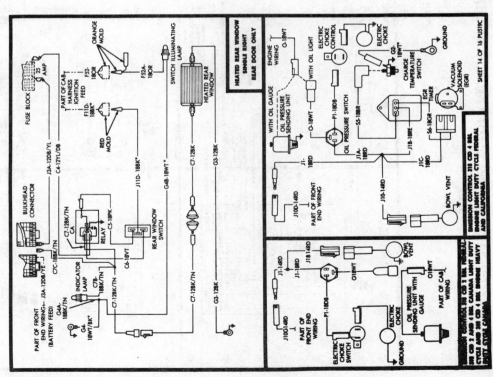

14

AUXILIARY WIRING DIAGRAMS
16 of 16

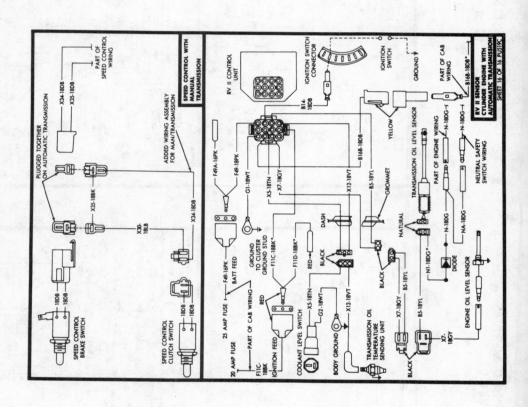